# SPEAKING OF OUR PAST

## A Narrative History
## of
## Owings Mills, Maryland
## 1640 - 1988

D1600368

# By Marie Forbes

Copyright 1988 By
Marie Forbes

Published 1988 By

HERITAGE BOOKS, INC.
1540E Pointer Ridge Place, Bowie, Maryland 20716
(301)-390-7709

ISBN 1-55613-142-9


A Complete Catalog Listing Hundreds Of Titles On
History, Genealogy, And Americana
Available Free Upon Request

*The debate about what is history and what is not really isn't that important. What is important is the role of history in our lives. If oral history infuses in us an interest in the past, that's good, and if it can fill in the gaps left by traditional historians who neglected blacks, women, native Americans and working class people in this country, then it will help give future generations a better picture of what life was like for us today.* -John Morrow, from "Options in Education" series broadcast by member stations of National Public Radio

*Remembrances are the seeds of the past, always ready to spring anywhere into instant and beneficial bloom.* -Author Unknown

# CONTENTS

v

Hog Jowls and "Ponhaus" - High Button Shoes and Feed
Bag Dresses - Needles and Pins - Hard Soap and Soft
Soap - Washday Every Monday - Ironing Every Tuesday

# LIST OF ILLUSTRATIONS

E. B. Bowen

E. Bennett Bowen has inspired several generations of young people and adults to explore and appreciate the history of the Owings Mills community. At 93 years of age, he continues his active research into the past while taking a lively interest in both present and future events. Photo courtesy of the author.

## ACKNOWLEDGEMENTS

If this book can be said to have a guiding spirit, surely it is the scholarly and ever-gracious E. Bennett Bowen who provides its essence. As a teacher in Baltimore County schools until well into his eighth decade, Mr. Bowen has inspired several generations of Baltimore County youngsters with his ability to make learning come alive. Ever fascinated with his community and its past, he has generously shared with me thousands of pages of his notes and comments and endless hours of his time. It is with deepest gratitude that this book is dedicated to the man who - more than any other - has earned the title of "Owings Mills's Historian".

A very special thanks to all those who consented to be interviewed and to those who shared their remembrances and expertise at meetings of the Owings Mills History Council. (See Appendix I for list of narrators). I feel honored and blessed to have known each and every one of you.

Many of those who contributed their reminisences are no longer with us. I freely admit that it was hard to maintain my objectivity when listening to the narrations of such dear departed friends as Joseph Brown, Grace Bowen Pape, Nancy Offutt, Henry Hipsley, Frank Parker, William Hull and others whose voices are now still. It is my sincerest wish that this book should serve in some small way as a memorial to them and to the times in which they lived.

My heartfelt thanks to Genvieve Berryman Kelley who undertook the task of indexing thousands of pages of tape transcripts, thereby making the job of locating needed material infinitely simpler. Along the way, she graciously supplied the correct spelling of names and appended notes to clarify the text.

Without the members of the Owings Mills History Council who have offered support and encouragement this book simply would not exist. While it is hardly fair - or possible - to single out any one person from this vital group, the late Wilson Herera deserves particular mention for the boundless enthusiasm he brought to the task of providing programs for History Council meetings and for his generous sharing of information on the history of Methodism and on the Soldiers Delight region.

Thanks also to Joyce Layman who contributed generously from her research into the Cradock family, to George Ward who contributed his delightful history of the origins of the Owings Mills Volunteer Fire Company, and to the Rev. Edward Schell of the Methodist Museum for his assistance in researching the history of Methodism. Doris Victor has managed the financial affairs of the Council and William D. Groff, Jr., Jean Reese Worthley, Frank Burkholder, and Mrs. Helen Bowers have been among faithful participants whose recollections of the past have proved invaluable. Thanks to Frances Zepp Keeney and Jean Reese Worthley for their work in conducting oral history interviews. John McGrain's continued interest in this project and the clippings and photos he has contributed for our History Council files have made him a valuable addition to our group. Alan Layman, Richard Parsons, George Horvath, and others gave valuable assistance with photos and illustrations.

Gratitude for financial assistance goes to the Maryland Cup Company and to the Baltimore County Commission for the Arts and Sciences and its chairperson, Lois Kahl Baldwin. Thanks also to the Rouse Company and the Owings Mills Mall for their interest and cooperation.

I would be particularly remiss if I failed to thank my parents, Carl and Bessie von Gunten, for the many times I called upon them to confirm facts or to point my research in the proper direction. The story of Owings Mills in the past century is one they both lived and their insights were of infinite value to me in writing this book.

Throughout the years of research and writing my husband has been an unwavering source of support and encouragement. If this book is my accomplishment, it is equally Jim's, and I offer it to him with all my love and gratitude.

My final thanks are reserved for Owings Mills itself. To have shared in the life of this community as it changed from a tiny rural enclave to a booming metropolis has been, and continues to be, a rewarding and enriching experience, one that makes me ever more aware of the links that bind past to present and present to future.

Marie Forbes
May, 1988

# PREFACE

## The Savaging and Salvaging of a Town's Past

When, in the mid-1970s, my home community of Owings Mills was selected as one of two new "town center" sites for Baltimore County, the announcement generated strong and - in many cases - conflicting feelings.

While some regarded the proposed development as a golden opportunity, others viewed it as a distinct threat. In particular, many long-time residents were reluctant to contemplate their quiet, rural community being catapulted overnight into the throes of major expansion, and they were apprehensive that each succeeding step in the development process would pose an even larger threat to the quality of life they had long enjoyed. Already they had seen many of the community's 18th-century landmarks carelessly bulldozed into rubble in the name of "progress"; they had witnessed the destruction of neighborhood ties as family land holdings were broken up and as older residents fled from the chaos brought about by massive change; now they feared the ultimate effect of further development would be to destroy the last vestiges of the community as they had known it.

In 1980, believing it vitally important that some accounting of the past which had shaped our community be preserved for future generations, a group of concerned citizens formed the Owings Mills History Council, an organization whose purpose would be to collect, preserve and disseminate information about the town's history.

One of the Owings Mills History Council's first and major projects was to tap the remembrances of the town's older residents by means of an oral history project. Over seventy such interviews were conducted; they provided a wealth of information on a wide variety of topics and directed attention to areas that required further research. At History Council meetings, speakers from specialized fields of interest such as archeology, architecture, geneology, transportation and numerous other subjects broadened and deepened the group's understanding of the forces that have affected our community's history.

As a free-lance writer and as an active participant in the History Council from its inception, I felt a particular interest in publishing the wealth of information accumulated in the Council's files. Although I was able to publicize some of this material through newspaper and magazine articles, I soon realized that a book would be the most effective means by which it might be made accessible to large numbers of people.

I was reluctant, however, to create simply another "history text", another dull compendium of dry fact and soon-forgotten dates. Instead, I was determined to find an approach which would combine historical accuracy with a narrative form that would grip the reader's imagination and emotions. In short, I wanted to tell the story of Owings Mills's past in such an exciting way that readers would feel that they were staring for a moment or two through the window of time, that they were observing real people as they lived and worked and played.

Perhaps because a large part of the research for this book consisted of oral history interviews, I kept returning to the idea of having the story told in the exact words of those who had created the community's history. While this was an appealing concept, it presented one very large obstacle: the remembrances of our oral history narrators extended back only to the latter part of the 1800s, while the community's history began some two hundred years earlier.

At first, it seemed as if this "time barrier" would force the book I envisioned either to take place entirely within the 20th century or to be exactly the sort of de-humanized listing of events, times and places that I wished to avoid.

But upon reviewing the copious research notes I had collected about those earlier periods, it occurred to me that whatever events took place in the 18th and 19th centuries also involved living, breathing people - people whose dress and modes of transportation may have varied considerably from those of the present day, but whose feelings and aspirations were not all that different from our own. Even in the year 1700 there were people who fell in love...people who were greedy for fame and riches...people who chose to serve God and their fellow humans...people who laughed and grieved and dreamed and despaired much as we do today.

Gradually - just as the oral history interviewees' voices emerged from the tapes on which they were collected - certain voices began to emerge from my notes...a country doctor...the child of one of the community's founders...a farm woman...an itinerant preacher...an inn-keeper. Each character had a unique story to tell, and when all those stories were combined they began to form a very compelling montage of life in the Owings Mills community over the past four centuries.

Part I of this book - "Voices Past" - introduces readers to the history of Owings Mills through stories told by these characters from the community's past. In Part II, "Voices Present," we continue the tale, this time through the actual words narrated by persons whose lives have been deeply rooted in the community. Through their comments we learn how the narrators' personal experiences have shaped and been shaped by the unique place in which they have lived, played, worked and worshipped throughout their lives.

These recollections are sometimes touching, sometimes humorous, sometimes sad. It is hoped that readers who share these moments from the past will share too in the emotions they arouse and that they will view Owings Mills with a fresh appreciation of its history and of the people who formed its past.

PART I. VOICES PAST

Introduction to Part I

This early history of the Owings Mills community opens with a story told by a Susquehanna Indian in the year 1660 and concludes with excerpts from the actual diary of our town's physician from the year 1891. While chronological order was chosen primarily as providing the most logical framework, it carries an unexpected bonus: one begins to see the strong connections that bind us as a community down through the centuries: family names are repeated; an Indian trail becomes a wagon track which, in turn, becomes a paved road and then a superhighway; an economy goes from tobacco culture to the raising of grain to industrialization; events have their own echoes down through the years.

But I also recognize this method's limitations: While the facts upon which these narrations are based were carefully researched, documentation of that research was sacrificed so that the narrative might flow without interruption. For those wishing to explore the history of Owings Mills in greater depth, the references listed in the Bibliography at the end of this text will prove helpful.

1

# CHAPTER 1

## 1640: A Whisper of Mocassins on the Trail

*For nearly 10,000 years, the area we know today as Owings Mills was inhabited only by native American Indians. In the centuries preceding the coming of the European settlers, the Susquehannock tribe made frequent use of the Owings Mills area as a summer hunting ground. Since no written records remain of the Indians' occupation of the land, we depend upon a fictional narrator to relate events of a particular summer during that latter period.*

-/-/-/-

I am Grey Hawk, son of Bear Claw, *Werowance,* or Chief, of the tribe of the Susquehannock. This morning, as I pass along the ancient trail that leads to my tribe's summer hunting grounds, I feel a weight upon my shoulders, as heavy as the carcass of a slain deer. For the first time, Father has entrusted me to lead those of the tribe who go to The Place of Two Streams Meeting.

At the last campfire before our departure, Father rose and passed to me his pipe-bowl. "You are now a man of fifteen summers, my son," he said. "I trust you to guard the women and the younger warriors from all dangers."

"I hear you well, O Father," I replied. "You may sleep without fear, for I promise that should the treacherous Piscataway tribe or the Nanticokes threaten to invade our hunting grounds I will fight bravely and well to uphold the honor of our tribe." Then I drew deeply into myself the fumes from Father's pipe-bowl, willing myself not to choke as the smoke from the tobac weed entered my body.

Grandfather - who is called the Old Chief - also spoke to me, his words causing my heart to swell with pride: "You have been given a great honor, Grey Hawk. For more seasons than there are hairs upon my head, the tribe has traveled to The Place of Two Streams Meeting and always they have returned with the pots and baskets overflowing with nuts and berries and smoked venison. Those of us who remain here upon the Great Smooth-Flowing River will be depending upon you to see that much food and many hides are gathered against the coming of the snows."

Ai-yee! It is a great responsibility!

Our journey began with the rising of yesterday's sun and before that same sun sank below the edge of the earth, we had left behind the

3

flatlands that border the mighty Susquehannock River. The second sun to light our journey has scarcely glided midway across the sky and already we have reached the wooded hills that border our hunting grounds. The trail is easy to follow here, and I am reminded once again of Grandfather's words as I see how our pathway has been worn smooth by the many feet that have traveled this way.

Behind me on the trail I hear the whisper of the women's mocassins. If I were to turn I would see my mother carrying in her arms the huge soapstone bowl that is her prized possession. And perhaps I would catch a glimpse of Laughing Rain, that impertinent young female who dared to smile yesterday when I failed to strike the rabbit I aimed at with my throwing stick.

Indian Artifacts From Owings Mills Area

Claockwise: soapstone bowl discovered on Oliver Disney farm, arrowheads from Red Run stream valley, polished stone axe-head discovered in field near Gwynns Falls. Photo courtesy of the author.

Of course a warrior of the Susquehannock tribe of the Iroquois nation does not turn to stare at women.

4

Already the scent of water fills my nostrils as we draw near to the larger of the two streams that waters our hunting grounds. We will follow that stream until it reaches the broad meadow where the smaller stream - which runs red in the season of rains - joins it. There, among the willows and sweet grasses that line the stream banks, we will set up camp. By nightfall, the shelters will have been built and the sleeping benches covered with reeds and mats. Before the sun sinks, the air will be filled with the smoke of the cooking fires, and my mother and the other women will have rabbits simmering upon the glowing coals...or perhaps a dozen or so tasty quail if my arrows fly true.

Tomorrow our work will begin. We must use the long days well. From now until the short days return, the women will gather and dry the blueberries and wild cherries and grapes and mulberries that grow in such abundance in the woodlands and meadows. Mixed with ground maize and bear grease, the berries will provide the pemmican our braves carry with them for nourishment on long treks.

If we are lucky, perhaps a young lad of the tribe will spot a bee heading homeward to the tree of his hive, and we will return home with a good supply of honey for the pleasure of all. Near the end of our stay, when the crowns of the mighty chestnuts turn golden, the women and children will go into the forest to gather the falling nuts that will be spread upon the coals to roast as we gather by the campfires in the Time of the Snows. Aiee-yee!...my nose twitches at the memory of that scent!

We men will be kept busy, too. Our task will be to hunt birds and small game and deer. "Ah," Grandfather sighed as we left, "how I do wish I could travel with you so that I might hunt once more in the Place of Small Trees. Many is the time I have seen the pigeons come to roost there in clouds so thick they covered the very sky. And, in the first light of morning, I have seen more deer than I can number come down to the streams to drink. Any brave who returns empty-handed irom the Place of the Small Trees has poor aim with his throwing stick, indeed!"

In the last Season of Long Days, I was with my uncle, Great Storm Cloud, in the Place Of Small Trees when he brought down a huge bear...I can only hope for such fortune again this season. We would see then if Laughing Rain would smile!

But if the Place Of Small Trees is our best hunting ground, it is also a place of mystery. Not even Grandfather in all his wisdom can explain why it differs so from the land that surrounds it, or what it is that makes the trees so stunted, and why there is rock instead of soil. And Mother - who knows the name of every plant that grows - even she cannot give names to many of the strange flowers and weeds that flourish there.

Once - as many seasons ago as there are fingers on one hand - something even more amazing than a bear appeared in The Place Of Small Trees. It was here that one of our tribe's warriors lay hidden and watched in amazement as a party of strange men with pale skin and clothes that gleamed in the sun passed by. "Stumbling about like infant mice deserted by their mother..." the warrior reported, "cursing in a strange tongue at the brambles which tore at their clothing as they tried to find their way out of that wilderness."

At first we laughed, thinking how frightened these pale, little men must have been. But later, when the tribe returned home and the tale was repeated around the campfire, Father looked grave. "It was told to me by a warrior we captured - if one may believe the lying words of an Algonquin - that these pale men come in huge canoes with wings from across the Big Water That Roars. It is said that already there are small tribes of them dwelling near the mouth of the Great Shellfish Bay."

Grandfather, too, seems to feel there is some mysterious danger in the coming of the pale men. The night before my departure he stared into the flames and said, "I have had a dream that troubles me greatly. In my dream I see the pale men descending upon our lands...more of them than the grains of the sands along the Great Shellfish Bay. I see our people fleeing...driven from their beloved Susquehannock...driven from the hunting grounds...."

At that my Father slapped his thigh and exclaimed, "Come now, Father...surely warriors such as these -" he gestured toward my brothers and me - "surely they will never permit these pale mice of men to defeat us!"

We all laughed at that and my youngest brother raised his hunting axe to show how he would wield it should the pale men dare to attack. But I don't know. Grandfather has the wisdom of many winters and as he spoke I felt a cold breeze upon my shoulders.

But that is foolishness. The Place Of Small Trees holds nothing more dangerous than the bear. When the women go to pick the blueberries and blackberries that grow there in such abundance, perhaps Laughing Rain will be stooping to gather berries, and suddenly there will be a roar and a bear will come charging from behind the trees. I will throw myself between Laughing Rain and the huge beast and with my spear I will run him through, like so - Aiii-eee!

Then - when Laughing Rain has ceased her trembling and shaking - she will look upon me with eyes that glisten as they did last harvest time when the red ear of corn was her lot. A handsome husband, they say the red corn means. I do not think I was mistaken when I felt Laughing Rain's eyes glance for a brief moment into my own.

When my cousin travels this season to the mountains to trade for arrowheads I will ask him if he will offer some of my best shells in exchange for some pretty soapstone beads. And I plan to offer Laughing Rain the furs of the finest red foxes I capture for her winter robe. Perhaps then....

Ah...the forest thins and I see in the distance the broad meadow and the two streams glistening in the sunlight as they flow together. I signal for those behind to move faster...it is the Season of Long Days and there is no time to waste.

6

## CHAPTER 2

### 1741: No More Muddy Sundays

*By the early 1700s, a few settlers had arrived to claim land and build homes in the Owings Mills area. Samuel Owings, son of Richard Owings (or Owens), a Welsh immigrant to the Maryland colony, settled on the north side of the Patapsco River and soon became one of the area's leading landholders. We encounter him as he returns to his home in the Greenspring Valley from Baltimore Towne where he has attended a meeting of the Vestry of Saint Paul's Church.*

*-/-/-/-*

Would that I had refused that last glass of brandy! These wretched roads alone are enough to set my mind to reeling! Steady there, fellow!...don't stumble. Had not the vestry meeting dragged on so long you would be in your stable by now, and I should be enjoying my supper.

I fear Urath will be greatly concerned for the lateness of my return. Entirely the fault of those vestry members who live in Baltimore Towne...they have little concern for those of us who must travel great distances to reach our homes.

Ah, well...if all our discussion today was not for naught, we shall soon solve that problem. Surely Governor Bladen will grant our petition once he understands what a blessing a chapel of worship could provide for those of Saint Paul's parishioners who reside far from the city...how was it that one Baltimore vestryman kept referring to us?...as "the forest inhabitants"?

Of course, those who have established homes or who own land in the area north of the Patapsco strongly support the idea of a new church. As Christopher Gist so aptly remarked: "Sarah declares that if she must continue to make the arduous journey down to Saint Paul's to worship, she may just decide to become a heathen!"

Christopher Randall agreed. "Aye! -" he said, slapping his knee, "and that's mild compared to what my Catherine had to say when her new gown was ruined by mud after the horses mired down last Sabbath! In fact, Friend Gist, it was you she blamed for her dilemma - seeing as you've been made overseer of the Old Indian Road down past the Garrison."

7

It was not to my liking, however, when Gist pointed to me, "Aye! - but it's Samuel Owings here who was appointed to attend to that trail even before me! I daresay no more improvement was made in his time than in mine!"

One of the vestrymen who makes his residence in Baltimore Towne shook his head at that. "It still amazes me that you people have the fortitude to reside in a wilderness so far removed from the amenities of civilization. My Elizabeth says that she'd never consider living in a place where she must pass each moment in fear of Indian attack and then slog her way through mud roads to get to church besides!"

Gist challenged him immediately: "Don't forget, my friend, we have the Garrison Fort for protection. Besides, our rich loam makes the sandy soil around Baltimore Towne and in Southern Maryland look like desert by comparison! Small wonder tobacco's the only crop you gentlemen can grow while we've got fields of corn and rye and wheat and barley as well."

"'S true, by Jove!" Christopher Randall joined in. "We already keep a miller busy, and unless I miss my wager, one of these days the area around the Gwynns Falls will echo to the sound of mill-wheels turning night and day."

"Gentlemen, gentlemen!" the Reverend Bourdillon interposed, "We must not digress! Now it is my feeling that we must put it to Governor Bladen that not only do such landowners as yourself require a more convenient place to worship, but also that the soldiers quartered out there at the Garrison fort are sadly in need of religious sustenance."

"A good point, indeed, Reverend," I agreed. "And surely the Governor must take into account that without a church, we have no place to conduct our business or to settle our disputes. Why just last week Christopher Choate - the fellow who has that land called "Choate's Contrivance" up on the west side of the Gwynns Falls - he was forced to turn loose a thief he caught with one of his mares because it was too much trouble to bring the scroundrel all the way into the court at Joppatowne for a hearing. Had we a chapel of our own, the Vestry could decide such minor matters, not to mention collecting taxes and taking care of other official functions."

"Not to mention that Vestry meetings can provide a likely occasion for hearty eating and drinking and perhaps a bit of horse-racing and cock-fighting thrown in!" Nicholas Haile jested.

The Reverend Bourdillon had his hands full, indeed, keeping the discussion upon its proper path. There were those who wished to discuss at length the injustice of a system whereby the King's Governor has the power to say yea or nay to the founding of an Anglican house of worship while the people of the parish are allowed no voice in the matter.

"Gentlemen! Gentlemen!" the Reverend interposed at one point, "let us not forget that it is the tolerant policies of our founder, Cecilius Calvert, that make it possible for all religions to find acceptance in the Maryland Colony. Besides, what difference that the power of appointment rests in government hands so long as the Church of England is still the colony's official ecclesiastical establishment?"

Just before adjourning, we did accomplish one other piece of business - the name "Saint Thomas" was chosen for the new church. A goodly name, I do think...already in my mind's eye I can see its spire and its mullioned windows...and a lych gate, perhaps. And - best of all - we shall have no more muddy Sundays to ruin our ladies' gowns!

I've got a piece of land already in mind that will make a perfect location for the chapel. That high ridge on Christopher Gist's property...the one that borders the old Indian Trail they now call the Garrison Road. A chapel there would be convenient to both the Greenspring and Caves Valleys as well as to the new settlers who take up land along the Gwynns Falls and the Red Run.

Just about home and a good thing it is for I am saddle-weary indeed. Easy, fellow... we've topped the last ridge now. We'll take a moment here for you and me to rest.

Ah! - this view! Each time I look upon these rich, green valleys stretching to the east...the forested ridges rising grandly above the barrens to the West...streams flowing gently through it all - I give thanks to God that He has brought Urath and the children and me to such a likely place.

If all goes well at Green Spring Punch plantation this year I will buy that tract over yonder where the Red Run flows into the Gwynns Falls. Provided, that is, the land dealer Harrison is willing to part with it for a reasonable price. Good and level it lies and well timbered at that. Indeed! - there's a likely name for the plot..."Timbered Level".

Wilderness, indeed! One of these days we shall show that dandyish Baltimore Town fop and his delicate Elizabeth who enjoys the "amenities of civilization"! My sons and grandsons and their sons will see to it that someday there are homes and farms and, yes, even thriving businesses all along that valley. And the chapel of Saint Thomas rising above it all like God's own benediction.

Hup! now fellow...it's time we were getting home.

9

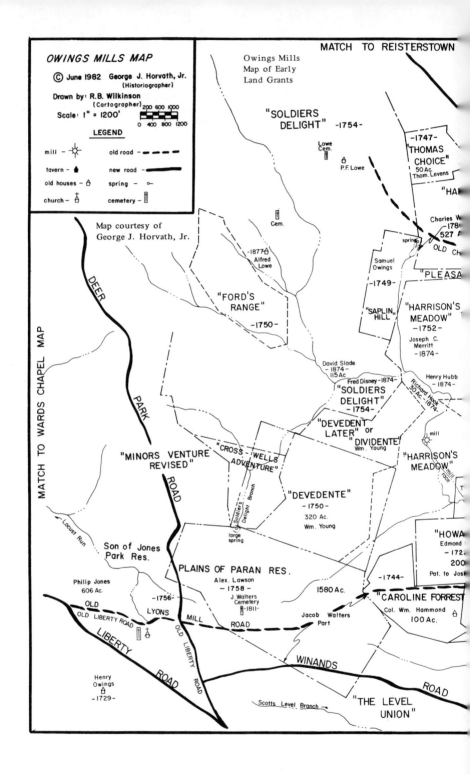

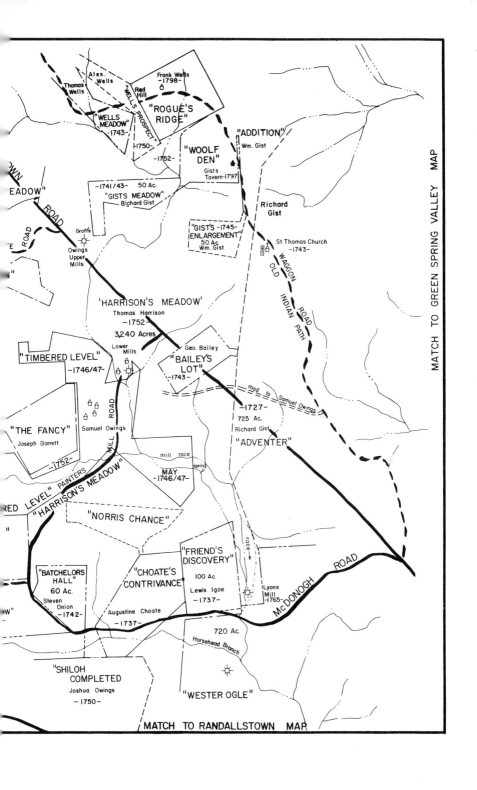

Thomas Wells

Alex. Wells

Frank Wells
-1798-

Red Hill

"ROGUE'S RIDGE"

"WELLS MEADOW" -1743-

"WELLS PROSPECT"

-1750-

-1752-

"ADDITION"

Wm. Gist

"WOOLF DEN"

Gists Tavern-1797

-1741/43- 50 Ac.
"GISTS MEADOW"
Richard Gist

Richard Gist

"GIST'S -1745- ENLARGEMENT" 50 Ac.
Wm. Gist

St. Thomas Church -1743-

OLD WAGGON ROAD INDIAN PATH

Groff's

Owings Upper Mills

"TOWN MEADOW"

ROAD

'HARRISON'S MEADOW'
Thomas Harrison
-1752-
3,240 Acres

Lower Mills

Geo. Bailey

"BAILEY'S LOT"
-1743-

road to Samuel Owings

-1727-
725 Ac.
Richard Gist

"TIMBERED LEVEL"
-1746/47-

"THE FANCY"
Joseph Barrett
-1752-

Samuel Owings

MILL ROAD

PAINTERS

"RED LEVEL"

"HARRISON'S MEADOW"

mill race

spring

MAY
-1746/47-

"ADVENTER"

"NORRIS CHANCE"

race

"FRIEND'S DISCOVERY"
100 Ac.
Lewis Igoe
-1737-

Lyons Mill
-1765-

McDONOGH ROAD

"BATCHELORS HALL"
60 Ac.
Steven Onion
-1742-

"CHOATE'S CONTRIVANCE"

Augustine Choate
-1737-

720 Ac.

Horsehead Branch

"SHILOH COMPLETED
Joshua Owings
-1750-

"WESTER OGLE"

# CHAPTER 3

## 1745: God's Voice in the Wilderness

*The plans of Saint Paul's vestry for the erection of a church to serve the settlers of the valleys and forests surrounding the Garrison Fort were implemented. In the year 1745, the poetic and scholarly Reverend Thomas Cradock departed from England, bound for the Maryland Colony where he would serve as the church's first rector. We encounter the Reverend Cradock on board the ship that will carry him to his new post.*

*-/-/-/-*

### 1. The Winds of Chance

The captain says we shall sail as soon as the wind shifts. How fitting that my last moments upon English soil should depend upon the vagaries of a fickle breeze...the winds of chance!

Has not my entire life been like that! Were it not disloyal to the God I have vowed to serve, I would truly believe my destiny has been decided not by the Reason or by the Logic I struggle to instill into the minds of my parishioners and my students, but by blind, unreasoning Fate.

Of course, were I a believer in the Greek mythology I love so well, I would lay all my troubles at fickle Aphrodite's door. For who but that capricious Goddess would arrange that I, a lowly cleric, should fall swooningly in love with the one woman in the world I may not have?...with my own noble patron's sister-in-law?

How right my brother was to warn me that I had best apply myself to my sermons, my students and my poetry! "Far better that you concentrate upon your duties, Thomas," John advised me in his sober fashion. "Your success as master of the Free School at Trentham has earned you high praise from your superiors in the church, and now that you have received your appointment as Curate of the church at Blurton and Assistant to the Rector of Kingsbury your career is well launched. I beg you not to jeopardize all you have achieved."

But did I heed John's words? Nay! I insisted. I was in love...all would be well! The mere thought that the Lady Frances returned my affections set my mind reeling with ecstacy. How could I keep my mind on my ecclesiastical duties when all I could think of was her gentle smile...her tender looks...the celestial music of her sweet voice....

Did I truly believe that because the Duke of Bedford had educated John and me out of gratitude for our Mother's having raised his own son he would look favorably on me as a suitor for his wife's sister? What insanity!

I see now that the Lady Frances is as far above me as yon moon that drifts serenely above the masttops. The Duke convinced me of that the day he confronted me in the Bishop's study. "Should you choose, Thomas, to continue your courtship of one so...so far above your station...you may seriously jeopardize your career. And - painful as it is for me to put it so bluntly - you would also be demonstrating a marked lack of gratitude for the benefits you have enjoyed because of my personal patronage."

Then the Bishop entered into it, impressing upon me that my "prospects" as a member of the clergy are hardly in keeping with the style of living required by a "lady of the nobility". It will be better, they both said, if I "absent myself for a period of time from the lady's presence" in order to allow our "youthful infatuation" to cool.

The words were genteel and courteously phrased, but I understood all too well the consequences should I fail to take heed. With the greatest reluctance, I accepted the Bishop's "offer" of a pastorate in the Maryland colony.

So now, on this bleak February day in the year of our Lord 1744, I must say farewell to both my native country and the woman I love, knowing I am unlikely ever to lay eyes on either of them again. My heart within my chest is as bleak and icy as the wintery Atlantic that stretches before me. How shall I survive a life without my beloved at my side? And what possible service can I render to the Church, stranded in a savage wilderness such as this Maryland colony?...a colony founded by the Papist, Cecilius Calvert.

On that last point, at least, I have some small consolation - the Duke has assured me he will speak to his friend, Lord Baltimore, and ask him to secure for me a good parish. In fact, in parting he was most gracious and held out a hope that was, perhaps, more than I deserved: "My son, a brilliant future may still be yours within the Church. Already there are Churchmen in our country who see a strong necessity for the colonies to have their own Bishops."

I know his words to be true - the lack of a resident Bishop in the colonies imposes many hardships. It is only by making the long and perilous voyage to England that any American can be ordained to the ministry. And - while the colonial governor has the power to appoint a clergyman to a specific parish - there his authority ends. He cannot remove him for any reason or exert any control whatsoever over his actions as a Bishop might.

Ah!...the captain has given the order to set the mainsail. Already the shoreline is slipping away behind us, our wake tracing its sad signature upon the dark waters. Farewell, my beloved England...farewell, my beloved....

## 2. The Wilderness Church

It seems an American Bishophry is not to be my lot. How shall I describe the despair that has gripped my soul since learning that I have been assigned to a newly-formed parish - St. Thomas - a wilderness church miles from any civilized town or community...that I will be compelled to deliver my sermons from a pulpit whose only protection from heathen savages is a handful of men quartered in a garrison fort some mile or so distant?

The journey from Baltimore Towne to St. Thomas was a formidable undertaking. The road leading from Baltimore northward toward Pennsylvania is called Mr. Digges's Wagon Road...a most appropriate name, since one often has to literally "dig" one's way out of its mire-filled ruts. As we headed north, the horses floundered through snow drifts up to their withers and in crossing a small stream my mount's hooves broke through the ice and I was thrown from the saddle, much to my pain and embarrassment.

I must confess, too, that although my companions on the journey repeatedly assured me that any danger of attack by savages was remote, each thicket we traversed seemed to me to be full of lurking red men brandishing stone axes with which to split our skulls.

But if the ride was a cold one, I must say that upon my arrival I received a warm and cordial welcome from each of St. Thomas's newly-appointed Vestrymen. "You have no idea how eagerly we settlers here have awaited your coming, good Reverend!" Joshua Owings informed me. "And what a blessing that we will no longer have to travel those fifteen arduous miles to attend services at St. Paul's."

Reflecting upon my own journey, 1 could well appreciate his comment.

But - as the poet, Horace, said - "They change their clime, but not their disposition, Who run across the sea." In spite of the congenial welcome, these past six months I have felt myself an exile not only from my native land and all I loved there, but also an exile within the Maryland Colony. How to describe the remoteness and isolaton of my post?...the sparcity of the habitations and the distances between them? As for the roads, the less said the better.

And, I must say, that though Saint Thomas's communicants are, on the whole, men of substance - at least compared to the odd mixture of penniless adventurers and former schoolmasters and butchers and dry-goods merchants and indentured servants who constitute the bulk of land-holders in other parts of the Maryland colony - I find them lacking the veneer of the polite English society from which they came. Often their rough-hewn actions and blunt speech make them seem as strange to me as if we had not been raised under the same crown.

Still, I remind myself, they are King George's subjects and I am both his and God's representative...God's voice in the wilderness, so to speak.

Dreams of her whom I left behind still torture my nights. Fortunately, my duties occupy most of my waking hours. By the time I arrived, the chapel itself had already been constructed with funds raised by a subscription collected among the membership of St. Paul's. As is usual here in the Maryland Colony, many of the pledges were made in tobacco and the Reverend Benedict Bourdillon, Rector of St. Paul's, himself very generously pledged 2,000 pounds of tobacco. Unfortunately, I shall not have the privilege of meeting this clergyman at whose instigation the St. Thomas Church was founded. Two weeks before my arrival the Reverend Mr. Bourdillon died. Upon his passing, St. Thomas was forever separated from its parent church, St. Paul's, and a new parish created for it, extending from the Patapsco Falls northward to the Pennsylvania line and westwardly as far as Anne Arundel and Frederick counties and thence east to the streams known as Piney Run and Western Run.

In all, the church is admirably well constructed, considering the primitive nature of its surroundings and the difficulties encountered in transporting building materials to the site. It is situated in a most pleasant location adjacent to the rough trail that connects at its southerly end with the road leading to the county courts at Joppatowne. Construction is now nearly complete on the chapel's exterior although the bricks shipped from England fell somewhat short of the required number, making it necessary to leave the gable ends some four or five feet lower than originally planned. The interior is spacious, being some 56 feet long by 36 feet in breadth. However, the floor is still only packed earth and the congregation must sit upon crude log benches for want of proper pews.

Have I mentioned my salary? It is to be paid for by a tax of forty pounds of tobacco imposed on every white male and every servant over sixteen years of age residing within the parish. Since there are now in the entire wilderness area that comprises my parish no more than 675 taxables I shall receive 27,000 pounds of tobacco or the equivalent of a little over 60 pounds sterling, a sum which reminds me rather forcefully of how foolish I have been to aspire to the hand of a lady accustomed only to the finest of gowns and the most handsome of carriages.

If it seems odd that I should receive my salary in tobacco rather than coin, let me hasten to add that practically all commerce within the Maryland colony is carried on in this medium. Five thousand pounds of tobacco will buy a 200-acre plantation while one hundred pounds is sufficient to pay for a well-made coffin.

The Vestry has recently contracted with Colonel William Hammond to level the church floor and lay it with brick. Therefore, on days when the weather permits, I mount my horse and visit my parishioners in hopes of persuading them to donate generously to the project.

One of my first calls was upon "Green Spring Punch" plantation, the home of Samuel and Urath Owings, Samuel being the brother of our Vestryman, Joshua Owings. Accompanied by the slave who serves as his farm overseer, Samuel proudly showed me about his impressive acreage and spoke of his plans to put under cultivation another tract he had recently acquired. I remarked that he must already be one of the largest landholders in the parish. He nodded - "I intend, Reverend, to insure that my children have land."

Seeing that there were six young ones running about the place already and that Urath was obviously expecting another shortly, I jested, "In that case, Samuel, you had better be prepared to acquire a lot of acres!"

Exterior St. Thomas Church, 1869

Exterior of St. Thomas Church as it appeared before it was restored to the original design in 1869 by the addition of gable ends to the hip roof. Photo from *The Garrison Church* by the Rev. Ethan Allen, edited by Rev. Hobart Smith.

He took my jest in good spirit, "Aye, Reverend! -" he replied, "we Owingses are planning to populate this entire area before we're through!"

Another fine day, I rode west from the chapel. After stopping for a short visit at "Harmony Hall", the home of Joshua Owings, I rode on, intending to visit William Baseman - or "Beasman" as he is sometimes called. Baseman's estate lies along the north branch of the Patapsco and to reach it, I must needs traverse a strange and barren area of stunted trees. Before long, however, I found myself hopelessly lost, each trail that promised to lead out of the thickets and groves taking me only deeper into that wilderness. You can imagine my relief when finally I spotted a dwelling...a primitive, backwoods cabin, to be sure, but a place of human habitation none the less.

I stopped to inquire my way and was greeted with courtesy but also with great reserve and an apparent degree of suspicion by a man who identified himself as Ephraim Baker. As we spoke, a bare-footed woman with an infant in her arms and several equally bare-footed youngsters clutching at her skirts peered at me from the doorway. Behind the house, I could see a crude log stable although there was no evidence of any livestock except for a litter of pigs that rooted about a wooden trough.

Invited to enter Baker's cabin, I did so and found myself in a home that contrasted strongly with the plantation houses of the Valley which, simple as they may be, always boast of a good English-made sideboard or a display of family silver. Here was no seating more elegant than a couple of three-legged stools and a backless bench while the family's table was simply a log slab with crude legs. Wooden pins inserted between the chinks of the logs held the family's few scant articles of clothing and the entire place reeked of the bear grease and hog fat from which were made the crude candles that apparently supplied the only illumination.

I later learned that - the soil of the barrens being completely unfit for the growing of crops - these backwoods folk must depend upon wild game and berries to fill their stomachs. Considering the number of deer and smaller game I encountered on my way, I felt they probably did not fare so badly at that.

Another amenity these backwoods dwellers do enjoy is plenty of good fresh water. The stream known as the Red Run has its beginnings here and there are a number of excellent springs throughout the area.

However, it would be hard to describe the isolation the people living on these meager holdings must endure - the womenfolk in particular. Often, it is said, they see no neighbors from the first heavy snowfall until the summer heat has dried up the spring ruts from the trails.

And so with clerical duties and attending to the needs of my parishioners, my first summer as rector of Saint Thomas Church is slowly passing. Although I await the coming of each packet boat from England with great expectation, hoping to hear even the merest word from her whom I still adore, such solace, it appears, is not to be mine. My broken heart refuses to mend.

## 3. Heart's Ease

How shall I explain the incredible turn of events my Fate has now decreed for me? Perhaps it is the distance that now separates me from the one I loved so passionately. Or perhaps it is something in the air of this new colony that breathes fresh purpose into my battered soul. Whatever the cause, not many months after assuming the ministry of St. Thomas, the grief and pain that so recently tormented my every waking hour have been replaced by other, more pleasurable - if no less turbulent - emotions.

Her name is Catherine. Catherine Risteau. At first, I attempted to deny that my feelings for the young woman who sat so demurely in one of St. Thomas's front pews were anything other than that which a cleric might properly feel for a member of a prominent family within his parish.

After all, her father, Captain John Risteau, had donated a full 500 pounds of tobacco for the building of the sanctuary. I have learned from listening to parish gossip that Risteau was among the Huguenots who fled from France to Maryland after the Catholic king, Louis XIV, repealed the Edict of Nantes, a document which had guaranteed the Protestant Huguenots their religious freedom. I learned, too, that Risteau is a man of prominence in the colony who has served as one of the gentleman justices of the Baltimore County Circuit Court and that he has recently been appointed high sheriff of the entire county.

It all began one fine August morning when parish business took me to the Risteau plantation which lies southward from Saint Thomas along the Garrison road. Dismounting, I was greeted by Captain Risteau who made me welcome and insisted upon showing me about his acres.

I was much interested to discover that the garrison is located upon Captain Risteau's estate, particularly since I number the Rangers quartered there among my parishioners. "Only a couple of Rangers are assigned here at the present time," Risteau informed me, "and they are out on patrol just now, Reverend. Come, let me show you about our little fortress."

Just at that moment, however, one of his slaves arrived to announce there was difficulty with a mare that was foaling in the barn. "Perhaps Catherine would serve as a guide in my place, Reverend," Captain Risteau said as he prepared to depart. "She knows as much about the garrison house as I do."

And so it was that the Captain's daughter and I strolled together across the short distance that separates the Risteau home irom the stone fortress. As we walked she explained to me something of the history of the garrison. "The Maryland Council ordered this garrison and three others built after the Indian alarms in 1692," she said. "Of course, at that time, there were hardly any settlers living here...just a few hunters and fur trappers. Some folks still refer to the fortress as Oulton's Garrison after one of the early commanders who served here. At that time a full complement of seven Baltimore County Rangers and their commander was garrisoned here.

The Garrison Fort

The building presumed to be the original colonial garrison or fort built in 1693 has survived through the centuries in its location just east of Stevenson Road even though the area around has been developed with modern residences. It is believed to be the oldest permanent fort in Maryland. Photo from *The Garrison Church* by the Rev. Ethan Allen, edited by the Rev. Hobart Smith

When we reached the building, I remarked that I found it strange that the only entrances should both be located on the same side and that their doorsills should be placed well above ground level. Catherine explained that the entrances were deliberately designed in this fashion to prevent hostile Indians from easily forcing an entry. I found myself feeling somewhat grateful to those savages who had dictated this arrangement, as it made necessary my assisting Catherine to enter. Oddly enough, when I was finally forced to relinquish her hand, I felt a peculiar twinge of disappointment.

Fortunately, the structure has no windows, only six long embrasures to facilitate the firing of weapons, so that, once inside, the near-darkness concealed from Catherine the blush I could feel coloring my cheeks. We stood for a moment, allowing our eyes to adjust to the dim light.

"Do you notice, Reverend Cradock, how the fireplace is built entirely inside the exterior walls?" She pointed toward the hearth. "I am told it was designed so to prevent the Indians from gaining access to the building through the chimney as they have been known to do elsewhere."

Just then, a golden ray of sunlight broke through one of the narrow slots and gilded her brown tresses. For some unfathomable reason, I found myself breathing in deep shallow gasps as though the room held not sufficient air for my lungs.

Mistaking my discomfort, Catherine laughed. "No fear, Reverend!" she said. "Since the coming of the white men, vast numbers of the Indians have died of smallpox and disease. The majority of the others have moved farther west. Father says that soon they will pose no threat at all to the colonies."

"I pray that is the case, Miss Risteau," I blurted – "it would give me the greatest pain to think that someone so lovely as Yourself might be in danger of attack by those cruel beasts!"

For a moment, it occurred to me that, in its sweetness, her answering smile reminded me of the English roses that grow along the fence of my mother's cottage in far off Bedfordshire, England. But then I realized she reminded me more of the delicate pansy-like flower called "heart's ease" that one finds growing along Saint Thomas's churchyard wall.

Trentham, 1981

"Trentham", the home to which the Reverend Thomas Cradock took his bride, Catherine Risteau, still stands on Cradock Lane just east of Reisterstown Road. It was occupied by members of the Cradock family from approximately 1750 until the 1950s. Photo courtesy of the author.

# CHAPTER 4

## 1746-1770: Catherine's Day Book

*On March 31, 1746, the Rev. Thomas Cradock and Catherine Risteau were united in marriage. We share the years following their marriage as Catherine might have recorded them in her journal.*

-/-/-/-

7 April, 1746 - My sweet and generous Papa! Mere words cannot express the gratitude I feel for his wedding gift to Thomas and me of 170 acres of land. The tract - one he recently purchased from my uncle, George Ogg, Junior - lies only a half-mile south of St. Thomas Church, so that dear Thomas need travel only a short distance to the chapel. For this first year of our marriage, we shall make our home in a small one-room cabin already on the estate while our new house is being built.

It is my most earnest prayer that our union may bring to both of us peace, happiness and felicity. I pray, too, that I may be worthy of a man who is, in every way, dedicated to the service of his King and Church.

18 January, 1747 - Construction on our new home procedes but slowly during these winter months. Each night, Thomas and I sit poring over the plans, eagerly anticipating the moment when these lines drawn upon parchment become a reality in stone and mortar. Our home is to be a one-story stone building some fifty feet by thirty feet in size. Already construction has begun on the barns, stables and dwelling houses for our slaves.

Thomas says we shall plant tobacco this spring in the south field as it is, by far, the crop which brings in the most cash. It requires, however, constant clearing of land as it has a great tendency to deplete the soil in which it is planted. Father suggested to Thomas that we not give over many of our acres to tobacco, concentrating, instead upon grain crops and forage as he has done on his land.

19 July, 1747 - My cup of joy is filled to overflowing! Today I gave birth to a son. At Thomas's suggeston, we named him Arthur for Thomas's great-grandfather, Arthur Taylor, of Trentham Parish in England.

12 May, 1747 – A most heinous charge has been brought against dear Thomas! My hand trembles even as I pen these words for I cannot believe that anyone in his right mind would consider my husband other than a loyal subject of our King. It all started with one of his parishioners who, misunderstanding statements Thomas made in two of his sermons, declared that Thomas was a supporter of James, the pretender to the throne and therefore a traitor to King George. Upon hearing this allegation, Thomas rebuked the man, but in spite of that the rumor has spread far afield, growing as it travels, until some people are now asserting that Thomas has, on several occasions, refused to drink to the king's health. So persistent has this cruel rumor become that now the Baltimore County Grand Jury has returned an indictment against Thomas for treason.

5 July, 1747 – The dreadful business is at last behind us! The grand jury has dismissed the charge against Thomas, labeling it "ignoramus". A just decision, indeed! Dear Thomas, I regret to say, is still bitterly hurt over the whole affair. This morning he announced to me his intention to publish in exactly their original form both the sermons from which his supposedly disloyal statements were taken. How fortunate that Thomas, being the scholar he is, keeps copious notes of each sermon he delivers!

21 March, 1748 – I fear that time and distance have not entirely obliterated the longing Thomas still feels for his distant home in England. When it came time to choose a name for our estate, he suggested we should call it "Trentham". I, of course, agreed.

3 April, 1748 – Now that we are established at Trentham, Thomas has confided to me that one of his fondest ambitions is to institute a boarding school for young gentlemen here in our home. As I am well aware that many in the Maryland colony either cannot afford to send their sons to England for an education, or else do not wish to do so, I immediately expressed my enthusiasm for the project. "Surely there is not a lad in the entire colony who would not benefit by your scholarly guidance, dear Thomas," I told him.

11 June, 1748 – Advertisements in the Maryland Gazette have brought us a fine contingent of young gentlemen as eager to learn as Thomas is to teach. Quite a number of the pupils hail from the southernmost counties of the Maryland Province where tobacco culture is most intense, providing ample funds for the education of the young. Thomas says he intends that this school shall be the crowning jewel of his ministry, an opportunity to impart to young minds not only Christian principles but a quality of learning comparable to that found in the best English academies.

25 January, 1749 – Our home is now doubly blest – this morning was born to Thomas and me our second son whom we have named John for my father.

24

15 November, 1751 - Today Thomas was summoned to the barrens to serve as the twelfth member of a coroner's jury. It seems a most dreadful crime has been committed there...both a husband and wife brutally murdered in their beds!

10 May, 1752 - Again I give thanks for a safe and speedy delivery. Our third son has been given the name Thomas and I pray he will be as good and godly a man as his iather.

12 August, 1753 - Thomas has been invited to deliver a sermon before Governor Sharpe and the lower house of the Maryland Assembly. At breakfast this morning, Thomas informed me that he intends to use this occasion to take to task his fellow clergymen. "Far too many of them are encouraging their parishioners to flout the King's laws by refusing to pay certain taxes," he declared. I begged him to temper his remarks so that none might take offense. Knowing how strongly Thomas feels about the allegiance we colonists owe our King, however, I realize that is a rather forlorn hope.

21 February, 1755 - With the greatest joy I record this day the birth of the daughter for whom I have longed. She is to be named Ann for Thomas's mother in far-off England.

29 April, 1755 - The usual peace and serenity of our small community have been shattered by a new threat posed by the Indian tribes. It is, of course, the French who have armed these poor, simple savages and filled them with hatred for all English colonists. All too frequently now come reports of dreadful massacres. They say that at every tavern and inn along the Great Conewago Road - or Mr. Digges's Wagon Road as it was formerly known - one encounters settlers who have abandoned their homes farther west on the frontier and taken flight for Baltimore Towne. By God's grace, we at Saint Thomas have thus far been spared, but I shudder inwardly each Sunday morning when I observe that there are loaded muskets propped in the corners oi the pews and by the doors and that neither my father nor the extra Rangers the governor has ordered stationed at the Garrison Fort are in attendance, all being occupied with the Indian threat.

2 September, 1756 - Thanks be to almighty God, the crisis seems to have passed. The extra Rangers have been recalled and the parishioners can again concentrate upon Thomas's sermons without starting at every noise from without the chapel.

1 May, 1760 - Saint Thomas church continues to grow and prosper as does the Trentham Academy. And - if it is not immodest of me to say so - my dear Thomas's reputation is also growing within the Maryland colony. Invited to deliver a sermon at Saint Paul's, he again seized the opportunity to remind our fellow colonists of where their allegiance must lie. "Let us remember what we are, whence we came and from whom we spring. Let us remember that we are Britons!" he declared. While most of the congregation were exceedingly complimentary upon the close of his address, I was amazed - and

chagrined – to discover there are a few among them who seem to resent Thomas's reminder of their obligation to remain loyal to the King. Thomas says their chagrin is of little consequence...that such malcontents will find little support among His Majesty's loyal Colonial subjects.

19 November, 1761 – When Thomas returned home this noon, he seemed unusually thoughtful. I begged him to share with me whatever matter was troubling him and learned that he is deeply concerned that a serious schism may be developing within his congregation. Inspired by the example of the itinerant preacher, Francis Asbury, who travels through the colonies promoting the principles and teachings of John Wesley, Joshua Owings and a number of others of Saint Thomas's congregation have begun to form what they call "Methodist Societies". Thomas says that although the participants in these "Societies" have stated quite plainly their intention of remaining within the framework of the Anglican Church, he fears their enthusiasm and excessive fervor may eventually lead them astray.

9 February, 1762 – More honors! Dear Thomas has been invited to Annapolis to address a meeting of the Anglican clergy there.

12 March, 1762 – Thomas returned from Annapolis tired and dejected. As he had told me he would, he used his address to urge his fellow ecclesiastics to press for the appointment of a Bishop to the Maryland colony. I felt that was an excellent idea, but it appears that a number of his listeners seized upon his suggestion as one more reason to defy the authority of the crown. Thomas said that one hot-headed cleric stood up and declared: "We've waited long enough for King George to recognize the American arm of the Anglican Church! I say it's time the colonies were managing their own affairs instead of relying upon an absent king who gives not a fig for our welfare!" For the entire week, Thomas has moped about, sadly depressed that those of his own profession should so deny the authority of their King.

14 May, 1762 – The coming of spring holds little gladness for those of us here at Trentham. I think it was the suddenness of Thomas's illness that is so disturbing. One day he was a man in full possession of his physical being and the next he was an invalid, overtaken by this dreadful illness whose nature no physician seems able to ascertain. Since Dr. William Lyon of nearby "Wester Ogle" serves as county physician for Saint Thomas parish, we have consulted him. He counsels a course of rest and physicking, saying that, in all likelihood, Thomas has merely over-tired himself. I pray that is the case.

15 November, 1762– The lassitude that grips Thomas's body grows worse. We have consulted various physicians in Baltimore Town, but none of the remedies or blood-letting they prescribe has affected any improvement. Indeed, they often seem to aggravate the overwhelming weakness.

5 June, 1763 - Today Thomas completed negotiations with Mr. Boyce for the purchase of 676 acres, a part of the Nicholson's Manor tract. Although he does not phrase it thus, I know this purchase reflects his concern that he should have sufficient land to pass on to our sons.

21 December, 1763 - Thomas's condition worsens. A paralysis is gradually denying him the use of his limbs. Dismaying to report, the illness has little effect on his appetite, with the result that he has become quite corpulent. Although at times greatly distressed, Thomas assures me he is most thankful that it is only his body that is afflicted and not his mind. "I must accept my affliction as God's will and continue to carry on with my duties as God and the King's representative to the Maryland colony," he says whenever anyone expresses pity or concern for his situation..

4 December, 1764 - Thomas's concern regarding the members of his congregation who are being attracted to the Methodist Societies continues. He also says that he is strongly disturbed by the fact that one of Wesley's teachings involves the question of slave-holding which Wesley decries as an "ungodly practice". Indeed, we ourselves are dependent upon the services of our Negroes to keep Trentham's acreage productive and I do not see how we housewives can be expected to carry out our duties without the benefit of Negroes to perform the work of the household.

Thomas says this issue is only one of many that causes him to doubt Joshua Owings's protestations that Methodists are simply a society within the confines of the Anglican Church and that he fears time will prove the differences between the two philosophies too great to bear the strain of a tandem yoke.

2 July, 1766 - Thomas suffers dreadfully with the heat. Most difficult for him to move about and he now requires the services of two strong Negroes to enter and leave his carriage.

7 November, 1767 - How it rejoices my heart that Arthur has decided to follow in his father's footsteps! Always a studious boy, he announced last evening at dinner that he intends to enter the ministry. How it thrilled me to see Thomas's face once more aglow with excitement at his son's decision.

17 December, 1768 - In spite of his many infirmities, Thomas today insisted upon traveling to the nearby village of Westminster where Arthur has begun to perform divine services as Lay Reader. As we drove home, Thomas sat back in the carriage seat with a sigh and confided to me, "You know, Catherine, in spite of the criticisms of my fellow clerics, in spite of the schisms I see developing within the parish, in spite of my increasingly bad health, I still have one element in my life that burns like a bright and glowing candle against the dark. Arthur. Our son, Arthur."

4 February, 1769 - Arthur is dead. I stood this day and watched them lower his body into the ground, but still cannot accept that our son is gone. How could such a thing happen with no warning? How could an illness snatch him so cruelly from us? How could a life so filled with piety and promise be ended so abruptly?

I try...Thomas tries...to find some reason, some moral in our crushing loss. "Was taking Arthur God's way of leading me to understand the depths of grief a parent must endure upon the loss of a child?" Thomas cried out to me as we returned from that fresh-dug grave near the church wall. "Perhaps I have grown too accustomed to seeing young lives wiped out in an instant by pox, by diptheria, by any of the cruel diseases that so frequently strike down the young...especially in this remote region where medical attention is seldom available. Is this the lesson God wanted me to learn?"

I could only bow my head and murmur, "If so, God is indeed a severe schoolmaster."

19 December, 1769 - A letter arrived this morning from Thomas's brother, John, who is now Bishop of Kilmore. All the day Thomas has seemed very sad and downcast. When I asked him why this should be so, he replied that his melancholy mood springs simply irom the realization that twenty-five years have flown, reaping for him so little in the way of honors and accomplishment. "Quite unlike the exalted situation of my brother," he said. "It appears from John's letter that he is likely to be appointed Archbishop soon. How ironic to think that I, too, once aspired to such lofty heights!"

I protested that he has not only served his Church, his King, his congregation and his family well for all these years but that, as master of the Trentham Academy, he has inspired and instructed several generations of young men of the Colony.

At that, he did, finally, seem to take heart. "It is true, Catherine," he admitted, "that if there is one thing in which I take some small measure of pride it is that...the Trentham School."

1 January, 1770 - I face this new year with fear in my heart for I somehow know that Thomas will not be here to greet the summer. Already the trembling and shaking of his limbs is so severe he must depend our faithful servants and friends to write down for him his sermon notes and the poetry whose compostion still lends some small pleasure to his days. Lately he must suffer the added indignity of being carried into the chapel and propped up to deliver his sermons "like a man stuffed with straw is propped in a field to scare off the crows", as he puts it.

I feel, too, that conducting his old friend Christopher Carnan's funeral last week placed too great a strain upon him in his weakened condition. With Christopher's death Thomas has lost not only one of the church's staunchest supporters but also a learned friend with whom he often discussed those matters of science and philosophy so dear to his heart.

3 March, 1770 - The end is very close. Just now I slipped into Thomas's bedroom and asked if there was aught I could do for his

comfort. He only looked at me sadly and whispered, "Ah, Catherine...what comfort is left? Can mere mortals such as you and I stave off the winds of change?"

It is true. Nothing is as it used to be and we have only to look about us to find ample evidence that even more changes are coming. Within the past decades, the community surrounding Saint Thomas has altered considerably with most of the desirable tracts of land already taken up and some of those being divided into smaller parcels as the land is passed on to the younger generations. Now the majority of fields are no longer planted with tobacco but with crops of wheat, corn and barley which the local farmers find more profitable and less debilitating to the soil than tobacco. On quiet nights, I can hear from my bedroom window the creak and groan of machinery turning in the mill Samuel Owings's son - also named "Samuel" - has built down along the Gwynns Falls. "Always a clever one with machinery, that second son of ours," Urath tells me. "Even as a boy he was always happiest playing with gears and machinery and such."

But such changes be the natural course of things. It is his parishioners' change in attitude toward the allegiance they owe their monarch that most distresses Thomas's mind. The winds of treason and rebellion blow ever more strongly and already the congregation is split between those who understand that the first duty of every colonist is to his king and those who would forswear that allegiance.

Speaking of that recalls to mind a day last summer when Thomas, feeling much stronger than usual, suggested that we should have Moss drive us over to the Gwynns Falls to call upon young Samuel and Deborah Owings who are building a new house for themselves and their growing family upon the parcel of land called "Timbered Level"...the tract old Samuel Owings divided between his sons, young Samuel and Thomas.

That was the ostensible reason for our visit, the actual reason being that Thomas was hoping to reason with young Samuel who is among that group of his parishioners within which there seems to be growing a spirit of rebelliousness. Young Samuel...Samuel's brother, Thomas...Cornelius Howard's son, John Eager...some of the younger Cockeys - all have vowed they will refuse to import or to purchase certain goods upon which the crown imposes a levy. Thomas attempts through his sermons to impress upon them where their loyalties must lie, but he fears his words are falling upon deaf ears and closed minds.

Our visit began well. Deborah's face sparkled with enthusiasm as she and Samuel showed us about the large plantation with its numerous outbuildings and dependencies. The house is a sturdy one-story brick dwelling situated upon a fine piece of meadowland overlooking the Gwynns Falls and the Red Run.

"Perhaps you could bless our home for us, Reverend...as if it were another Owings child for you to christen," Samuel said, half jokingly.

"I gladly offer my blessing," Thomas told him, "but even without it, I have a feeling that this home is destined to prosper. After all, I recall a day when your father predicted that the Owings family would someday populate this entire area. Considering how you and your brother, Thomas, seem to be engaged in a contest to see whether this house or 'The Meadows'" – Thomas gestured up along the Red Run to where the chimneys of Thomas Owings's plantation were just visible – "will contain the greatest number of little Owingses, I daresay his prophecy will soon be fulfilled!"

Just then Deborah was summoned by one of the house servants and was forced to excuse herself. Being great with child, she had some difficulty in rising from her seat. "It appears you are soon be a father again, Samuel," Thomas commented.

"Aye," Samuel said, "be ready to perform another christening, Reverend. Deborah says she feels certain this one is a boy and she has already decided he will be named "Samuel" after me and his grandfather."

"It will be, indeed, my pleasure, Samuel, to welcome into the parish another good Christian and into the parish registers another good subject to his Majesty," Thomas said, seeking once again to remind the recalcitrant Samuel of where his loyalties must lie.

Samuel did not take the reminder well, but scowled darkly. "Can you honestly contend, Reverend, that a ruler who sits upon a throne three thousand miles away and has never set foot upon American soil should be the one to determine the laws under which my son – the third generation of our family to be born in America – will live his life?" he demanded. "1 say it's time King George realized the American colonies are entitled to have a say in their own future! And he had better realize it soon or else..."

I could sense that Thomas was about to admonish Samuel for his treasonous thought, but he was just then gripped by a severe attack of the weakness that so plagues him. Samuel hastily summoned Moss and together the two of them carried Thomas to our carriage. "Turn the horses homeward to Trentham, Moss," Thomas gasped as he sank onto the seat.

As the carriage wheels rocked upon the stones of the lane leading from the Owings home to the Conewago Road, Thomas glanced backward across the fields toward the new house and I could see that his heart was heavy with the knowledge that Young Samuel and other hot-blooded young men like him are all too ready to join in rebellion against their King and country. I pray that terrible conclusion will somehow be averted, for I know that Thomas could not in good conscience support any plan to overthrow the authority of the King he has served all the days of his life.

# CHAPTER 5

## 1778: Blackberry Pies, Powder Flasks and English Tea

*In 1757, Nicholas Lowe, Sr., an English immigrant, purchased from a Mr. Rogers a large tract of land in Owings Mills. This holding extended a short distance east of the Conewago Wagon Road, although the majority of its acreage lay to the west of the road and included a portion of the Soldiers Delight barrens. The Lowe property also bordered upon one of the trails used by the rangers from the Garrison Fort. (The Rangers' pathway - it was scarcely more than that - was sometimes known as the "Old Church Road" as it was used by settlers of Anglican faith who resided along the upper reaches of the Patapsco River to reach Saint Thomas Church; a portion of the road still carries that name today.)*

*Nicholas Lowe, Sr. named his estate "Food A-Plenty" and it soon became one of the most productive farms in the area.*

*The estate continued in agricultural use and remained under the ownership of the Lowe family until the 1950s.*

*During the American Revolution, Nicholas Lowe's son, Nicholas Lowe, Jr., played an active part in his colony's struggle for freedom. We share the thoughts of Nicholas, Jr.'s wife, the former Katurah Baker, as she describes events on the Lowe farm to a cousin living in Hagerstown.*

-/-/-/-

"Food A-Plenty"
July 25, 1778

Dear Cousin Emma -

I take my pen in hand in hopes that these few lines will bring you some peace of mind as to our condition. I have no way of knowing, of course, if my letter will ever reach you in far-off Hagerstown; I shall simply have to entrust my missive to the hands of some traveler stopping at the tavern and hope for the best.

First off, I must tell you my good news! As I suspected - but scarcely dared hope when last I wrote to you - I am indeed with child. Nicholas and I have decided that if the baby is a girl, we will name her Merab as that name has long been in use in the Baker family. If a boy, we will call him either Amos or Alfred, both of them Lowe names.

I hope you will forgive my tardiness in replying to your last letter – now that Nicholas has been called to serve with the Soldiers Delight Batallion, my time is much taken up with supervising the farm work as well as attending to my household. Although we have two Negros and several indentured hands, I find the demands placed upon me very heavy indeed.

Today, for instance, I rose early and made up a half-dozen pies from the blackberries we picked yesterday in the barrens. Since the war prevents our getting much sugar, what with all the ships of the India trade being commandeered to serve against the British, I felt most fortunate in having on hand a good supply of honey, one of the farm boys having found a bee tree in the woods nearby. Afterwards, I rode out to the fields to make sure the hay that had been scythed was dry enough to be brought into the barn. Heaven knows I have no desire to see our animals' winter forage go up in flames as happens so often when hay is not properly cured.

Then, after preparing some of the summer apples for drying, I worked for an hour or so in my garden. Do you remember how I used to shudder at the very sight of a worm upon a squash vine? Well now I stomp upon them without a second thought, knowing how very precious those squash will be to us when the snow flies next winter.

So you can see, dear Emma, I am becoming quite an experienced farm wife. Little did we imagine, you and I, when we giggled together over our wedding plans so short a time past that my Nicholas and your Selby would both be off to war and we should be managing alone.

How I do wish these days for a good visit from you and a good gossip! Since the distance between us makes such a visit impossible, I will describe for you our situation. The home we share with Nicholas's parents consists of a one-and-a-half story house built of round logs with a one-story log kitchen in the rear. In addition, we have a log smoke house, and two log stables. Nicholas's brother, John, also dwells in a log house upon a more westerly section of the estate with his children, David and Florah. The portion on which John resides is part of the large tract known hereabouts as "Soldiers Delight" and was purchased by my father-in-law from a Mr. Benjamin Harrison.

According to what my father-in-law has told me, he chose this area for its rich soil, its excellent hardwood forests and for its plentiful water. Father Lowe says that the clay soil here has been proven to be among the richest in Baltimore County and is far superior to the sandy loam found in Southern Maryland. This is indeed so, for grain crops flourish here and are far less demanding of the soil than the tobacco which is the major crop in those lower counties. As, wheat, oats and barley as well as corn are becoming the predominant crops in the surrounding area, young Samuel Owings, whose properties adjoin our own, has recently constructed a grist mill adjacent to his home and has plans to build several more mills along the Gwynns Falls stream.

Nicholas is delighted by these developments. He says that having mills conveniently close by makes the raising of grain crops even more profitable as it is far easier and more economical to ship flour and ground meal than to ship the unmilled grain.

Lowe Homestead
Although the Lowe estate was an extensive one, the houses on it were rather primitive log structures.  Photo courtesy of Dorothy King.

We, ourselves, are not situated upon the Gwynns Falls. However, several branches of the stream known as "Red Run" water our property and we also enjoy the benefit of several fresh-water springs for drinking.  As I mentioned previously, the western-most portion of our land lies within the barrens and is of little use for cultivation, but elsewhere we are blessed with dense hardwood forests which provide an abundance of timber both for building and for firewood.

So you can rest easy, my dear Emma, that even in these perilous times we are well provided for and reasonably comfortable.  If I would have any complaint, it is that the isolation of our home makes me feel at times as if I were living in a veritable wilderness.  Even though available land hereabouts is being rapidly bought up, I cannot say that this area is becoming a metropolis by any means.  The Conewago Wagon Road, which is one of the main thoroughfares leading north and west out of Baltimore, has a few scattered dwellings as well as several taverns and inns and blacksmith shops scattered alongside it. North of us in Reisterstown, a few houses and shops are clustered close by the Wagon Road and, to the south of us, much land has been brought under cultivation by the Owings family - both Samuel and his brother, Thomas, as well as his cousins of the Joshua Owings family

33

who reside upon a more southern portion of the Old Church Road. But in general, one must mount horseback and ride for some distance in order to encounter another dwelling or another human being, an undertaking which my condition will soon make difficult if not impossible.

Of course, when one does meet with neighbors, the talk is all of the war with Britain. Last year when news arrived from Philadelphia that independence had been declared, an effigy of King George was carted through the streets of Baltimore Towne and then burned. But many - the Anglicans, in particular - still feel greatly torn in their loyalties. Some, indeed, are so opposed to the colonies separating themselves from Great Britain that they have gone back to England to live. One Tory sympathizer, the Reverend Edmiston who succeeded the Reverend Cradock as rector of Saint Thomas Church, has even been forced to flee for his life. When the British colonial government passed a law saying that any colonist who joined the militia companies was guilty of treason, Edmiston stated publicly that he agreed with the Colonial authorities on this issue and that any members of his parish who took up arms or who took the oath of allegiance the new government required were indeed, traitors. That, of course, turned many of his parishioners against him. Even though the Reverend later rescinded his words, he was forced to leave the Colony and return to England, leaving his wife and children behind.

Of course, being Baptists, we of the Lowe family were not at all sorry to see him go. Like others of our faith, we resented strongly the law that forced us to pay taxes for the support of the Anglican clergy.

Having foresworn to buy taxed goods imported from England even before the colonies declared their independence, we have become quite accustomed to improvising. I must confess, however, there is one English luxury I still sorely miss - how long it has been since I sat down to a good, steaming cup of English tea! While we brew our own concoctions from various herbs and roots, sassafras or comfrey simply fails to provide the same satisfaction.

I have not seen it for myself, but they say that Baltimore Towne is a beehive of war activity. Every day scores of new recruits arrive to join the Maryland Line company, many of them boys from the counties who have neither blankets nor shoes. The town's sailmakers have been pressed into making tents to shelter the company, and they say there is not a soup kettle to be found anywhere, all of them having been commandeered for the camps.

Unfortunately, we receive little actual news of the war and that bit we do hear is most discouraging. I suppose we should feel blessed that, while our local men were engaged when General Howe's army invaded northern Maryland en route to seize Philadelphia, they were not encamped through the winter with General Washington at Valley Forge. We hear that conditions there were incredibly bad and that many of our soldiers perished, not from enemy fire, but from the bitter cold and lack of food.

During the winter, the army quartermaster paid several visits to our local farms in search of grain to feed the troops. It is rumored that when he visited Samuel Owings's plantation, he discovered a store of wheat concealed beneath the barn's floorboards and accused Owings of planning to sell it to the British troops. How true that is I do not know. Although Owings himself is a lieutenant-colonel in the Soldiers Delight Battalion, there are some who question his loyalty to the colonists' cause since it was he who sheltered the Reverend Edmiston's wife and children when the rector fled to England. At any rate, we all pray for a speedy end to this conflict and the hardships it creates. Many feel that now that the French have agreed to assist with our cause, the situation will improve. I pray that they are right. My dearest wish is to have my Nicholas safe home again, to watch him fill his his powder flask and know that when he fires his musket it will be aimed at nothing more dangerous than a deer or a fox that roams the nearby barrens.

With all my fondest love and hopes for your Selby's safety, I remain,

Your loving cousin,

Katurah Baker Lowe

Ulm

"Ulm", the spacious home of Owings Mills' founder, Samuel Owings, presented this appearance in the early 1900s when it had become the home of the Painter family. Surrounded by barns, stables, and numerous outbuildings as well as a large grist mill, it perched on a high bank overlooking the con-fluence of the Red Run and Gwynns Falls streams. Photo from *The Garrison Church*, by the Rev. Ethan Allan, edited by the Rev. Hobart Smith.

# CHAPTER 6

## 1799 – One Summer Day at Ulm

*Ann Owings was the eleventh child and ninth daughter born to Young Samuel Owings and his wife, Deborah Lynch Owings. We encounter Ann in the year 1799 at her family home, Ulm, where she lives with her parents, her brothers Beal and William and her sisters, Frances, Rachel and Mary. Her older sisters, Urath, Eleanor, Sarah, Rebecca and Deborah are already married and living away from home as is her brother, Samuel III. Another sister, Rachel, died in 1782 at age one making a total of twelve children born into this third generation of the Owings family to live in the area.*

*Ann's grandfather, Samuel Owings, the Elder, died in 1775 and her grandmother, Urath, in 1792. Ann's father has purchased the family plantation known as "Green Spring Punch" located some four miles east of Ulm in the Green Spring Valley.*

*In this final year of the 18th century, Ann's father, Samuel Owings II, has achieved his dream of constructing a series of mills along the Gwynns Falls. He is also a respected and prosperous plantation-owner and a member of Saint Thomas's vestry. His home, Ulm, named for his Upper, Lower, and Middle Mills, has been enlarged and is now an imposing two-story structure surrounded by many dependencies. The family's nearest neighbor is Samuel's brother, Thomas, who lives with his family a half-mile farther west along the Red Run at "The Meadows".*

*-/-/-/-*

The first light is just peeping through the shutters when I hear Papa's boots on the back stairs. I slide out of bed, glad that my place is on the outside of the mattress. It would be just like Rachel and Mary to start a commotion: "Where are you going, Annie? Does Mama know you're up this early?" Luckily, neither of them wakens.

I pull on my shift and, over it, my dress and calico pinafore. How I wish I were a boy! Then I wouldn't have all these layers of skirts and petticoats to bother with. Such a nuisance!...especially when I'm in a hurry.

Carrying my slippers, I tiptoe toward the back stairs. Through the open door of the bedroom opposite, I see my sister Frances, still sleeping. The cornhusk mattress rustles faintly as she changes position.  Farther down the hall, the door to my brother's room is slightly ajar.  The low whistling snores coming from the room tell me that William is still a-bed...as usual.

I go downstairs, hoping that Mother is too busy elsewhere to notice me leaving the house.  If she sees me going out, I'll have to explain that I've promised Tadpole I will meet him down by the dairy-house this morning to help dig fishing worms and then I'll have to listen to a long lecture about how "young ladies should be tending to their embroidery and learning to knead bread properly instead traipsing about with colored children and digging up messy old fishing worms."

Mother is always fussing about things like that.  Like yesterday when she was yanking the tangles out of my hair that I got playing in the haybarn.  "You'll soon be thirteen, Annie," she scolded.  "It's time you were putting up your hair and learning to behave properly.  Look at your sister, Mary - she's only a year older than you and you don't see her chasing all over the place getting scratches on her face and rips in her clothing."

At that, Mary tossed her curls and smoothed her new pinafore.  "Yes, Ann," she said, "why can't you act like a young lady?"

I stuck out my tongue at her when Mother wasn't looking.

Luckily there is no sign of Mother in the kitchen this morning, only Melvina bending over a huge mixing bowl, stirring up a batch of flannel-cakes for breakfast.  Sausages are sizzling on a spider Melvina has set over the crackling coals in the big fireplace.  In another kettle hominy is boiling, and steam plumes from the teakettle suspended from the long iron crane.

I think the kitchen is my favorite room at Ulm.  Papa says that when he and Mama first moved to Ulm, this one big room and the loft over it was all there was.  "Where did everyone sleep, Papa?" I ask him.  "Well, at that time there weren't quite so many little Owingses, so what with trundle beds and pallets and cradles to put you all in, we made out quite nicely in here," he says.  And sometimes he talks about how even before that - when he and Mother were first married - they lived in the little stone cabin up on Berry Hill...the one our farm manager lives in now."

"Where you off to this hour of the mornin', Missy?" Melvina asks, dumping another scoop of flour into her bowl.

"Nowhere, Melvina," I tell her.  When she goes to the larder for more eggs, I grab one of the sausages from the pan and slip out the back door.

Ulm looks so beautiful this summer morning.  As I hurry across the lawn toward the dairy-house, thousands of dew diamonds sparkle from the wet grass, and the air is rinsed with the sweet, clean smell of lavender from Mother's herb garden.  Even though the sun is barely above the treetops, the whole plantation is already humming and stirring with life.  As I round the corner of the house, I can hear the huge wheel on the mill across the farm road groaning on its axle and the splash of water falling back into the millrace.  Down by the wagon shed, men are hitching a team to one of the big hay wagons and over past the barn, one of the slave boys is herding the cows out to pasture.  I gather up my skirts and hurry across the lawn, afraid that Tadpole's mother will be sending him off to weed the corn before we have a chance to dig our worms.

Luckily, he's still there behind the dairy house, digging at the damp spot where the water from the spring runs out through a trough and down to the stream. I help him sort through the clods of dirt he's turned over and we get twenty or more good-sized worms before we hear Tadpole's mother calling from their cabin - "You, Tadpole. You git yourself in here now, you hear me!"

At breakfast I ask Papa if I may go with him today when he visits the mills. Papa says 'yes', but Mother, who, as usual, is assigning each of us our chores for the day, looks up from her list with a frown. "Samuel, you just encourage her! You know I expect Annie to complete her chores just like each of the other girls."

"Oh, come now, Deborah!" Papa exclaims. "Surely it's not necessary to have the girls tending to the chickens and making the soap! You know that if you need another servant for the house you have only to say so."

"I see no reason to waste good money buying another servant simply so that able-bodied young women may sit about idle!" Mother sniffs. "Why a person can purchase a ten-acre field for what they're asking for a good Negro woman these days. Besides, I have no wish to see my daughters growing up like some others I could name...thinking of nothing but parties and balls and the latest fashions!"

"Humph!" Frances mutters under her breath, "the way Mother makes us let down the hems on last year's dresses and wear the hand-me-downs Eleanor and Sarah and Rebecca and Deborah send, there's little danger we'll become too fashionable!"

"Well, perhaps today Annie can postpone her chores until the afternoon," Papa says in a tone that makes it clear the matter is settled. "I've just installed a new gear system at the upper mill and I'm particularly eager to show it to her."

Papa turns his attention back to the newspaper he has been reading. "Ah..." he says, "I see they've run Sholl's advertisement in this issue." He then proceeds to read aloud from the *Maryland Journal* for all of us to hear:

*Ten Dollars Reward. Ran away from the subscriber living at Mr. Samuel Owings's new Mill, in Baltimore County, on Monday last, an indentured Irish Woman, named Mary Barter, about 19 years of age, and has short black hair; had on when she went away a blue petticoat made of Joan's-spinning, a check apron, a striped cotton short-gown and a pair of flat heels, lately soled; and she took with her a calico short-gown, and a new shawl; she always has hanging about her neck a piece of ivory in the shape of a heart, which she sets great store by. She has made for Alexandria, as she was seen at Elkridge-Landing on Tuesday last. Whoever apprehends said Servant-Woman and delivers her to the subscriber, at the aforesaid Mill, shall receive the above Reward, and reasonable charges paid by Philip Sholl.*

39

"Imagine!" Mother exclaims. "That a bound servant should have a new shawl!"

Papa flicks the reins across Prince's back and we turn out onto the Great Conewago Road. He points out the stakes the surveyors have planted on either side of the roadway. "Soon we'll have a regular turnpike running through here –" he tells me, "nice and straight and all properly paved with stone."

"When I was over at the Meadows the other day," I say, "Cousin Levi told me that he heard Uncle Thomas say that the Governor was going to let all the convicts out of prison to build the road and that if we don't watch out they're liable to break loose and come murder us all in our beds. He said that down at Hookstown where they've started work on the road already, the people are scared to death! They even sing a song about the convicts that goes:

Did you ever see the Devil
With a wood and iron shovel
A-digging up the gravel
On the Hooks Town Road?"

"Your Cousin Levi doesn't always get all his facts straight," Papa says. "And you must remember that I am, after all, one of the turnpike commissioners...even though it is true some convict labor is being used on the road, you can be certain they are well guarded."

Just then the wheel of the trap hits a rut and we are jolted so hard the axles creak. "Anyhow –" Papa sighs, "better the chance of being murdered in our beds than having to endure travel along this mess of mire and rocks for many more decades."

I am sure Papa is not the only one who will be grateful for the road improvements. The driver of a hay wagon that is heading toward Baltimore is cursing loudly at his team who are straining with all their might against their harness as they attempt to free the wagon's wheels from a particularly deep rut. A man and woman on foot driving a herd of yoked geese before them also look footweary and discouraged and the bottom of the woman's skirt is caked with mud nearly to her knees.

Our trap reaches the top of the hill and I can see on our left the Middle Mill and on the right, past the Gwynns Falls, the new red brick of the Upper Mill's walls. Opposite the new mill, the windows of the low stone building where barrels are made reflect the morning sun.

Papa does not stop this morning at the Middle Mill, but from the road we can smell the calcimine-like odor of the gypsum that is being ground there.

He does stop, however, in front of the row of small houses that stands alongside the road just before the Gwynns Falls crossing so that we may talk to one of his workmen, a man whose foot was crushed last week when a flour barrel fell on it. "Best let Doctor Cradock have another look at it, John," Papa advises him.

"I don' know, Sir...seems like I been getting better relief from rubbin' on that bear grease I got from Henry Baker than from any of that preacher's son's physicking," the man says, pulling up his trouser leg to show Papa that the red and purple swelling has begun to fade.

Middle Mill

The only known likeness of Samuel Owings's Middle Mill is this never-before-published painting recently discovered by John McGrain, author of *Grist Mills of Baltimore County*. Photo courtesy of the John McGrain Collection.

"Well, be sure you take care of it," Papa says and gathers the reins.

"Aye, that I will," John says. "And thank your good Missus for me for the victuals she sent us whilst I was laid up. The piece of side meat was particular welcome."

The trap's wheels clatter across the rough planks that span the Gwynns Falls. A minute later, we pull off the road into the mill yard, then continue around to the mill's rear entrance where a wagon is being loaded with sacks of flour. Robert Moale and a black man are standing beside the team. When Robert sees Papa and me, he comes hurrying over to greet us, dusting the chaff and flour from his trousers. "Good morning, Sir! And how is young Miss Ann today?" he asks.

Papa says he is quite fine but I just nod. I know why Robert is being so cordial. On account of Frances. He's sweet on her.

Sure enough, the next thing Robert asks is: "Ah...and how is the rest of your family, Mr. Owings?"

Papa winks at me as he ties Prince's reins to the hitching post and pretends to be studying over Thomas's question. "Why I think I can safely say Mrs. Owings is in fine health."

"Um...ah...yes. And the others?"

"Why young Beal had a touch of the croup last Sunday," Papa replies. "But otherwise all appear to be well." He pauses for a moment. "Except, of course, for Frances...."

"Miss Frances! I pray there's nothing wrong with Miss Frances!" Robert's voice betrays him.

"Oh, nothing *wrong* exactly." Papa's face is perfectly straight. "It's just that she blistered her finger on the teakettle last week and hasn't been able to finish hemming the new dress she's making for the Carnan's party."

"Oh!" Robert's sigh of relief has enough force in it to turn a couple of wind mills. How silly!

With Robert trailing behind us, Papa and I climb the steps which bring us onto the mill's second level. Once inside, I draw in a deep breath. I've always loved the way the mill smells...the sweet, grainy odors the wheat and corn give off when they're crushed by the stones...the smell of the huge leather belts...even the oily scent of the grease that keeps the gears turning smoothly.

Papa greets Mr. Sholl and leaves Robert to settle with the mill operator the ten percent of the flour he owes for the grinding. The water wheel on the side of the mill is running full speed this morning and Robert and Mr. Sholl have to shout to make themselves heard over the noise of creaking gears and rumbling grindstones.

We climb to the upper floor and Papa explains to me the new arrangement of gears and pulleys he's worked out for feeding the wheat into the hopper. If I were a boy, I'd be an engineer like Papa. Papa knows everything there is to know about milling and hydralic power. Even other mill-owners come by to admire the way he laid out the mill-race so that it carries water from the Gwynns Falls to all three of his mills - the Lower Mill across from our house that grinds feed and saws wood, the Middle Mill that makes plaster and this Upper one that is the grandest of all and grinds flour and middlings for cattle feed.

As we climb back down to the middle level, Papa jokes, "How much would you like to wager that young Mr. Robert North Moale is still hanging about?"

Papa is right. Even though the wagon is loaded and the driver is in his seat, Robert is standing about near the entrance, pretending to read an auction notice someone has posted. When he spots Papa and me he blushes a bright red and stammers, "Ah...sir...pray give Miss Frances my regards...."

Looking southward as we leave the mill, we see a huge dust column, hanging grayly against the vivid blue of the summer sky. "A wagon train coming..." Papa says, "more settlers heading for the West." Peering in that direction, I catch a glimpse of white canvas tops, billowing full above the heavy wagons, much the way sails swell with the wind upon the boats that travel the Patapsco River.

Earlier this summer one such wagon pulled into Ulm, its driver seeking a blacksmith to mend a broken axle. "We're heading for the Ohio territory but missed joining up with our wagon train in Baltimore," the man explained, "I had hopes of catching them somewhere before Reisterstown, but in my haste I failed to see a hole in that wretched pig-path they call the Conewago Wagon Road."

Beside him on the seat sat a thin young woman, a shawl clutched across her swollen stomach in spite of the heat. From the depths of the wagon peered four pairs of eyes, belonging to the four tow-headed children who crouched there on straw tickings.

Father explained to the man that we did not employ a blacksmith at Ulm, but that there was a forge on his brother's plantation which adjoined our own. Father offered to accompany him to The Meadows and gave Rachel and Mary and myself permission to follow the wagon as Mother was already at The Meadows visiting with Aunt Ruth.

When we reached The Meadows, Mother and Aunt Ruth rose from where they were sitting with their sewing under one of the huge oaks on the lawn. Father explained to Aunt Ruth what the strangers wanted. She immediately sent the man around to the forge and invited the woman and children to step down from the wagon and rest in the shade while their vehicle was being repaired. "Thank you kindly, ma'am," the woman replied shyly, "it's been a long trek from Baltimore and Hiram did not wish to stop as he was hurrying to catch the wagon train so we need not make that journey West alone."

"Then you must indeed be thirsty!" Aunt Ruth said, and she summoned one of the Negroes who was working in the nearby garden to go around back to the kitchen and tell Margaret Dowd to prepare some raspberry shrub for the visitors.

One of the children was a girl of about ten or eleven. "You are indeed fortunate to be going West," I told her. "Every time I see a wagon train going along the road I wish I were headed for such a great adventure."

"What nonsense!" Mother exclaimed. "Better to be thankful you have a roof over your head and a solid floor beneath your feet than to be trudging about like nomads in the wilderness!" Then she looked hard at the woman's swollen stomach. "And ought you be traveling about in your condition?"

## Cooper Shop

The huge chimneys on either end of Samuel Owings's cooper shop were used to char and to shape the barrels used in the mills. This building stood on Reistertown Road opposite Bonita Avenue until the 1950s. Photo courtesy of the Library of Congress.

"Probably not, Ma'am," the woman murmured.

"Now perhaps you can tell me," Mother persisted, "why in Heaven's name anyone with four young ones and a baby on the way would wish to set off to the frontierlands where there's every chance you'll all be massacred...if you don't starve or freeze to death first?"

The woman folded her arms tighter across her middle. "Aye, Ma'am...I know. But it's him..." she indicated with her head the direction in which her husband had gone. "No talking him out of it once he got it in his head we must go. Says there's opportunity out there beyond the mountains that we'll never find here in the East...says it's the only way we'll ever have land of our own. He sold our little house and everything we owned...paid $250 for that wagon down in Baltimore Towne and twice that for the horses. Now everything we possess in the world is what's loaded in that wagon. And I know it's true what you say about taking the children out there. The new baby will come with the winter and I fear...I truly fear..." The woman twisted her thin hands together, unable to express her fears of the terrible possibilities that lay ahead of her.

"Well..." For once Mother seemed at a loss for words. Instead she picked up the comforter she was working on and held it out to the woman. "Here..." she said in a voice several shades softer than her usual firm tone, "take this. You and the child will need its warmth more than do my own children."

But this day, as the long wagon train rolls across the Gwynns Falls, the people seem carefree and cheerful. One of the men walking alongside the horses is singing "Rooster Won't You Crow?" and I envy the children who poke their heads out of the wagons and wave merrily as they go past.

As we turn out of the millyard, I glance up at Papa, hoping that he plans to stop at the cooper shop. He grins down at me, then clucks to the horse.

Of all Papa's places of business, this low stone building directly across the Wagon Road from the Upper Mill is my favorite. Perhaps that's because the cooper shop always reminds me of the witch's house in a fairy-tale. It has little tiny windows and two huge chimneys, one on either end. Inside, there is just one long room with windowsills a foot and a half deep and fireplace openings so tall I can stand inside them without stooping. In the middle of the room a ladder leads up to the second story where the lumber is stored. When I walk across the floor I can feel the curly wood shavings crunch beneath my slippers, and the whole place has a delicious smell, like fresh-sawed lumber.

Old Enoch, the cooper, nods as Papa and I enter but he and his apprentice, Tobias, do not cease hammering the hoops down over the barrel they are working on.

Enoch is my favorite person. No matter how many questions I ask, he's never too busy to explain. Papa says I should feel honored because coopers tend to guard carefully the secrets of their trade, even making their apprentices swear an oath never to reveal exactly how the barrels are made. "A barrel's got to be put together just so, Miss Annie..." Enoch has often told me, "tough enough so when it's filled with flour or tobaccy or beer or whatever, it won't leak a drop not even when you tip it over and roll it onto a wagonbed or into a ship's hold or even roll it ten, twenty miles down the road like they do them hogsheads of tobaccy."

Today Enoch is complaining that the wood he's using hasn't cured out exactly right. "Let that pile of white oak set there drying for over a year, Mr. Owings, and she's still got too much moisture in her. See that?" Enoch points to the barrel he has upended over the iron basket filled with burning shavings that's called a cresset. Sure enough, a paper-thin wisp of smoke is curling through the slight opening between two twisted staves.

Enoch pulls out the bad staves, inserts others in their place. In a few minutes, the wood is hot enough so that he and Tobias can begin hammering on the hoops. The stone walls of the shop echo to the metallic ring as the iron hoops are forced farther and farther down the barrel. At one point Tobias stops to douse the inside of the barrel with water to keep it from catching fire. "A little charring's what we want, but won't do to burn a hole clean through," Enoch tells me.

After all the bands are in place, Tobias refills the cresset with shavings, sets it inside the barrel, and covers the top. I have learned from Enoch on other visits that this is done to set the staves so they will stay in their bent position. While Tobias tends the fire, Enoch is fitting a top onto another barrel. He has already cut the circular head with a side axe and roughly shaped the edges with a heading knife. Now he carefully bevels the edges and taps dried cattail reeds into the joints so the head will not leak even when the barrel is filled with liquids.

Before leaving, Papa orders a dozen barrels for the Upper Mill. As he heads the trap back down the Wagon Road, the Moales's wagon is just crossing the Gwynns Falls. "Silly, thing!" I exclaim as Robert blushes at the sight of us. "Why can't those Moales just leave us alone...bad enough his brother had to go and marry Eleanor and take her away from Ulm."

"Easy on the lad, Annie," Papa says as he flicks the reins to speed Prince up so we may pass the slow-moving wagon. "Someday it will be a young swain casting lovesick eyes in your direction and you'll feel quite differently about the whole affair."

The very thought causes my nose to wrinkle up in disgust.

When Papa and I return from the mills, Mother is busy upstairs, and I slip off to have a look at the new kittens. While I am up in the hay loft playing with them, Papa and Uncle Thomas come into the barn. By leaning forward and peering over the edge of the loft, I can see them quite clearly and hear what they are saying without their knowing I am there.

"What is your opinion, Samuel, of the Reverend Coleman?" Uncle Thomas is saying.

Papa rubs his head the way he does when he's thinking. "Well, seeing as how we've had nothing but ill fortune with our clerics ever since Edmiston left, I'm reserving my opinion until we can see how he's going to work out."

"Aye, 'tis no jest that Saint Thomas's pulpit has been ill served this past decade. Most of the time we've been without a rector and those who have come have stayed scarcely long enough for the Vestrymen to get acquainted with them. And that in spite of our having provided them with the new parsonage house for which you gave those four acres."

"Well," Papa said, "since our pulpit has been vacant for over eighteen months, the Reverend Coleman will certainly be welcome. As for that four acres, I felt it my duty to contribute seeing how closely involved with Saint Thomas our family has always been."

"Ah, but are you sure you could afford to part with four whole acres, Samuel?" I can tell by the tone of Uncle Thomas's voice that he is jesting. "I mean, it's likely to leave you land-poor... seeing as you've only added several thousand acres to the share of Timbered Level that Father left you."

"Well, I *did* sell off that 'Grazier's Delight' acreage to Daniel Bower recently..." Father rebutted. "That leaves me with 470 acres fewer."

"Still, I'm beginning to think you won't be happy until you've acquired everything from Baltimore Towne to the Pennsylvania border."

"Well, you know how Deborah is..." Papa sighs, "she insists we put every spare penny into land rather than 'wasting it on trifles' as she refers to any expenditure that doesn't add to our acreage."

"But better a thrifty wife that a spendthrift one," Uncle Thomas says.

"Aye," Papa agrees. "Besides, you know what Father always told us."

At that, Papa and Uncle Thomas quote in unison: "'Land!...that's where the real value lies...make sure your sons have plenty of land!'" Then the two of them laugh aloud.

"And let us not forget our daughters," Papa says. "I plan to provide well for them even though the girls, so far, have all made good marriages. But I must admit it worries me considerably that after I am gone the management of all my holdings - including my daughters' shares - will be in William's rather untrustworthy hands. As eldest son, he is, of course, entitled to inherit all this - "Ulm" and the mills, not to mention the warehouses in Baltimore Towne and my other properties. But thus far William shows very little interest in anything except gaming and carousing. As you know, that is why I bought Green Spring Punch from Mother and turned it over to young Samuel. That way, Samuel's fortunes, at least, will not be dependent upon his brother's management of the estate."

Papa's opinion of William does not surprise me. Last week when I was hiding behind the parlor curtains pretending to be an Indian chief sitting in his tepee, I heard Papa and Mother talking about my oldest brother. "I don't know, Deborah -" Papa was telling her, "Heaven knows I've done my best to interest William in the farm and in the business, but just distract him with fast horse or a pretty face and off he goes and work be damned."

"Did you hear him come in last night?" Mother asked. "Closer to three o'clock than to two it was. I daresay he was off at the cock-fights with some of his friends over in the valley."

"It's not just the hours he keeps that worries me..." Papa said. "From what I hear, he's not above wagering sums far too large for his

47

purse. It's gotten back to me that when Peter Hahn held that last horse race up at Holtzinger's tavern in Reisterstown, our William managed to lose nearly 100 pounds. I had thought that allowing him to accompany me last week when I went to Joppatowne to confer with some of my fellow county commissioners would perhaps impress upon him some sense of the duty he owes his country. Instead, I found him out behind the courthouse wagering with a crowd of the young rowdies who hang about there...boasting that his horse could outrun any of theirs."

You see? That's how it is when you're a man. Even though Rachel and Mary, for all that they giggle and whisper about their beaux, both have good sound heads on their shoulders, neither Papa nor Mama would ever consider leaving them in charge of things instead of William. I tried to ask Papa about it once, but all he would say was that according to the old English laws, the firstborn son had something called the "right of primogeniture" and that made him the heir even if he was a numbskull...or a wastrel like William.

A few minutes later, Papa and Uncle Thomas leave the barn. I climb down from the loft wishing that I were a boy. With a name like "Todd" or "Jeremy" instead of being named "Ann" after the Reverend Cradock's daughter...even if she is Mother's best friend.

If I were a boy, I could manage the mills for Papa. And when the men went hunting in Soldiers Delight I'd ride right along with them instead of being told that "girls can't go...they wouldn't know how to fire a musket!" I wouldn't have to wear my skirts longer next year when I'm fourteen, either. Horrid things! I suppose then I'll have to ride that stupid side-saddle fashion like Eleanor and Sarah instead of straddling my pony. And how do they expect a person to run or wade for tadpoles in the stream or climb to the top of the big maple tree when when she's all bogged down in petticoats and yards of muslin?

This afternoon when we finish our chores, Mother gives Rachel and Mary and me permission to walk over to The Meadows provided we promise to keep an eye on Beal.

The Meadows is quite near - in winter when the leaves are no longer on the trees, we can see it easily from Ulm's upper story windows, and the same road that passes our house continues on alongside the Red Run until it reaches our cousins' house. But today the four of us take the short-cut to The Meadows, crossing the fields and wading through the stream.

In some ways, The Meadows is much like Ulm, with an older story-and-half kitchen section at the rear and a new, two-story addition at the front. Like Ulm, it has lots of outbuildings clustered about it - some barns, a dairy-house, slave quarters, a smoke house and chicken houses. However, Uncle Thomas built his house and barns and outbuildings out of stone whereas ours are all of brick.

Inside the new front section of The Meadows, there are parlors on either side of the hall and in one of them, the shutters still have the holes in them that Uncle Thomas drilled for candlelight to shine through during the War for American Independence. Cousin Levi says that when people saw that, they knew that whoever lived in their house was not a dirty Tory.

The Meadows, 1984

"The Meadows", home of Thomas Owings, is a substantial stone farm house and was once surrounded by a number of dependencies, including two mills. The house has survived to the present time, although encroaching development presents a very real threat to its continued existence. Photo courtesy of the author.

While Rachel and Mary stroll off to the orchard with Cousin Susanna, Levi and I head toward the back of the house where the kitchen is located. Levi is the favorite of Margaret Dowd, the colored woman who rules the kitchen at the Meadows, and we can always count on her slipping us something good to eat. Today we are especially lucky – it's a good slab of homemade bread spread with her pippin preserve and an apple tart fresh from the oven.

After we finish licking the jam from our fingers, we decide to go down to the slave quarters and visit Granny Sal. Granny Sal claims to be one hundred and four years old and she tells the spookiest, scariest stories you ever heard, all about ghosts and people that get buried alive and somebody walking through the graveyard hears them screaming in their coffin and they dig them up only it's too late but they can see where the dead person was trying to claw their way out of the coffin. Granny Sal claims that's what happened to one of the people buried in the slave graveyard at The Meadows. I don't know whether it's true or not, but I wouldn't go walking past that place at nighttime for any amount of money.

After listening to Granny Sal tell about a fellow that got killed when a wagon ran over him and cut his head off and how his ghost came back and wandered up and down the turnpike carrying his head in his hands, we leave the slave cabin and hike up along the Red Run toward the mills. Like Papa, Uncle Thomas has several mills on his plantation, including a grist mill and a sawmill, although Uncle Thomas's mills are powered by the Red Run stream rather than the Gwynns Falls. We stop for a few minutes at the fulling mill where the woolen cloth is being dressed and dyed. Then we go by the forge to watch the sparks fly as the blacksmith makes horseshoes and repairs the tools and machinery used on the farm.

After that, we decide to find Susanna and Rachel and Mary and see if they will play soldiers with us in the barn. War is always one of our favorite games although we usually end up arguing about who gets to be on the side of the Patriots and who has to be the British redcoats. By promising the others that they can have a turn later being Colonel John Eager Howard, we persuade Susanna and Rachel to be the British while Levi and Mary and I are the Colonists. Colonel Howard was born just a few miles down the road at Grey Rock and everybody knows how he fought with General Washington at the battle of Cowpens and how at one time during that battle he had seven swords in his hand, all of them seized from British officers that he'd taken prisoner.

Our game ends when Levi slips up behind us with red clay smeared over his face and turkey feathers stuck in his hair, pretending to be an Indian. Mary and Rachel start screaming and running and Aunt Ruth comes in to see what all the commotion is about. She says it's time to come into the kitchen ior some nice cold milk along with slices of Margaret Dowd's huckleberry pie.

I bait Beal's hook and my own, and we both throw our lines back into the Gwynns Falls. The twig I have tied on for a float begins to bob, but the fish doesn't take the worm. Tadpole reaches in his pocket and brings out a funny-shaped stone which he shows to us.

"Indian axe-head," he says. "Found it down in the cornfield whilst I was hoeing this morning."

"Papa says that right here where the Red Run and the Gwynns Falls flow together was one of the Indians' favorite summer hunting grounds," I tell him.

"Just think!" Beal exclaims, "maybe some hateful old Indians used this very axe to whack some poor settler's head off."

"Shore am glad there ain' no Injuns 'round here now!" Tadpole says, slipping another worm on his hook. "Bad enough them ghosts Granny Sal talks about comin' after people..."

## Ten-Mile House Tavern

View from south side of Ten-Mile House Tavern, built in 1801. The spacious stone building faced Reistertown Road just north of Cradock Lane. From stagecoach days until it was demolished in the 1960s, the inn was noted for its fine food and gracious service. Photo courtesy of the Enoch Pratt Free Library.

# CHAPTER 7

## 1820 - Lessons in Hoofprints

*In the year 1819, Adam Hoover established a stage-coach line that followed the Conewago Wagon Road from Baltimore to Carlisle, Pennsylvania by way of Hanover, Pennsylvania. We encounter a typical stage driver, Iaac Dunkle, as he heads his team of horses northward through Owings Mills on a spring day in the year 1820.*

-/-/-/-

Nice, sunny day like this - can't say as I blame you for wanting to ride up here on the box with me. Like I always say, the view's better up here and besides, a person don't have to put up with the company of the other passengers. Especially when one of the passengers is an old lady in a black bonnet who squawks and complains at every little jolt and bump!

Owings's Mills, they call this section we're passing though now...most of the land around here is owned by the Owings family as well as practically all of the buildings you can see from the turnpike. That road off to the right leads back to Saint Thomas Church, or, as some still call it, the Garrison Forest Church. Off to your left - back that farm lane - you can get a glimpse of Samuel Owings's Lower Mill and his house which they call "Ulm". After we top that next hill you'll be able to see two more of his mills.

There. That sort of run-down brick building on the left is the Middle Mill. A shame. Since Sam Owings died and his son, William, took over the estate, the farm and the mill business have all gone to wrack and ruin. Rumor has it William's been speculating in flour and has lost most of his own fortune and his sisters' shares as well.

That's the Upper Mill you see now on the right...up past the stream there...that tall brick building with rows of windows facing the turnpike. The low stone building opposite is the cooper shop. Up on the hill beyond the cooper shop you'll see the fine brick house Peter Hoffman built. He's married to one of the Owings girls...Deborah, 1 believe her name is.

Once we pass the Upper Mill we've got about another two miles to go to reach the Fourteen Mile House. I daresay those six fellows and those two ladies riding inside will not object to stepping down for a bit. Especially after that bad jolt we took down near Gray

Rock...thought for a minute or two there we would be upended when the wheel sank into that deep rut. Good for a bit of a laugh, though – that dandified fellow's top hat falling off into the mud when the passengers leaned out the windows to help right the coach.

And how that old lady did take on when the rear wheel struck that tree-stump, the one that was half-buried in the roadway opposite the old Cradock place they call Trentham! Little does she know this is just the beginning...that the going will get much worse before she ever sees Hanover, let alone Carlisle. This turnpike may be one of the main roads north out of Baltimore, seeing as it's used by both travelers heading to Pennsylvania and those going off to the Ohio territory, but that doesn't make it any the smoother. The Turnpike Company claims it does all it can to keep the road in repair, but as anyone who has passed this way can plainly see, their efforts have produced scant comfort for the traveler.

Well, if that old lady didn't want to experience anything new, she should have stayed at home. Besides, if she thinks the traveling's bad in this coach, let her try riding in one of those Conestoga wagons like that one up ahead. She'd find not only a lot rougher ride but a lot rougher breed of men driving them. The fellow driving that rig-out is a perfect example of the mud-spattered, sunburned, flea-bitten lot that take up wagoneering. Listen to him now, murdering the king's English: "Yo, Beauty! What th' hell's the matter thar?"

We coach-drivers try to avoid stopping at inns where we know we'll encounter a lot of wagoneers. Table manners? – I've yet to see the wagoneer that's got any. You see them grabbing the food right off the platter with their hands or even stabbing each other with a knife over who gets the bigger piece of meat. And the ones making the return trip to Baltimore are the worst of the lot. You see, heading back, they've got some cash, and after the meal they'll start playing cards or throwing dice and then first thing you know, they'll commence brawling and fighting over who is cheating who. Oh, they can be a rough lot when they get going!

Now here along this stretch of the turnpike, they've got it easy – plenty of blacksmith shops should they need to fix a broken axle-tree or shoe a horse...plenty of inns and taverns...lots of other travelers on the road. But farther west they'll be traveling where inns are few and far between and where the roads are so bad they make this Reisterstown Turnpike look like a boulevard. Winter-time, it's brutal on both horses and men. I've heard tell of wagons getting stalled in frozen mud and having to stay there till the next thaw came. That's why every wagoneer carries with him a straw mattress and some grub as well as several days worth of hay and oats for the teams. The experienced ones also know to tote along a drag chain, an ax and a shovel, along with extra horseshoes, nails and harness leather and such.

It's a rough job, wagoneering...no doubt about it. You freeze in winter and in the summer you eat dust and bake like a hoe-cake on the hearth.

But given my choice, I'd rather be a wagoneer than to be a drover like that fellow coming towards us down the pike...the one on foot driving his herd of cattle before him. Stink! – don't ever make the mistake of sitting downwind of a drover! Why they wouldn't even look at him down at the Ten Mile House. Probably he'll stop for the night at the Seven Mile House and even there, he'll have to take his evening meal outside for there's little chance they'll serve him inside, smelling of the barnyard as he does.

Drovers and wagoneers! – both of them a hard lot. Though there's one thing I will say for most of the wagoneers – they do take pride in their rigs...keep the leather and all the trim polished...mostly have a good-looking team.

If you look closely at that wagon up ahead you can tell that it was built up in the Conestoga Valley in Pennsylvania. Those Germans up there are the finest craftsman... you can spot their handiwork right off. Their wagons all have these large, well-balanced bodies with the sides sloped inward like the sides of a well-built boat. They use good wood, too...hickory...white oak...poplar. All their wheel-hubs are of black gum or sour gum for strength. When we pass this fellow's wagon, you'll notice how neatly the tail-gate is hinged and the fine workmanship on the feedboxes hanging on either side and how the iron hoops that support the canvas top are each shaped to exactly the same degree of curve.

And take a good look at those wheels. They make the rims out of two pieces of iron, each four-inches wide by one-half inch thick and welded at both joints. To fit the rims to the wooden wheels, they have to heat the metal until it's red hot then lift it onto the wheel with tongs and hammer it into place. After that, they dunk the whole thing in cold water to shrink the iron. When they've finished, you've got a fit so tight that stones can't possibly work in between the rim and the wheel.

And size means nothing to those Pennsylvania Dutchman, which is what they call the Germans from up there...I've passed wagons on this road that were twenty-six feet long and eleven feet high and weighed as much as 3500 pounds.

Of course a wagon that heavy needs a six-horse team to pull it. I must admit it takes a fair amount of skill to handle a team that size. You'll notice that whether the driver walks beside his team or rides, he's always got a firm grip on the jerk line that connects to the bit of the left wheel horse. That wheel horse is the leader and when the driver says "gee" or "haw" and gives him a tug, that horse knows to pull the team right or left. The wheel horse also has do to the main part of the braking on steep down slopes.

We'll pass the wagon on this long upgrade from the Gwynns Falls and you'll see what a load he's carrying. Looks like some of those boxes might be full of gunpowder and there's another labeled chocolate and some barrels that look to be full of sugar. Of course those fellows haul anything from Irish linens to books to steel nails to window glass to coffee. Practically everything the folks farther west can't raise for themselves has to be carted up this road and then up over the mountains by wagon. Then on the down trip – heading back to Baltimore – these same wagons will be loaded down with skins and fur and bees wax and keg butter and tallow and flax and such.

That other wagon you see up ahead, the one up near the crest of this long hill, that one's hauling people, probably about twelve passengers.

Heading for Fort Pitt, most likely. Now that good land along the eastern seaboard is getting scarcer every day, newcomers find it to their advantage to head for the western frontier. Trip takes approximately one week and the people have to carry their own bedding and sleep at inns along the way.

Quite a nasty climb, that last hill. They call that "Pleasant Hill," but I'll wager the old lady back there in the coach didn't find it all that pleasant...especially when she had to get out and walk. Happens every spring like that...for some reason there's a boggy place down there below the crest of the hill and the stones they fill the road with sink right down out of sight.

The three-story building off to our right is the Gunbarrel Tavern. Do you notice that tin dipper hanging from a chain by the window? Now folk like yourself can go inside and order up your brew, but teamsters and other rabble have to stay outside and get their drink served to them in that dipper. In winter, when the proprietor doesn't want to annoy his guests with a draft from an open window, he pours the drinks out a small hole through an old gunbarrel.

Only two more such hills to climb and we shall be at the Fourteen Mile House. Some of the coach drivers prefer stopping at the Ten Mile House that we passed a while back. They always give their passengers a little spiel about how that fine old stone inn was built by the son of The Reverend Thomas Cradock who came here from England as the first pastor of Saint Thomas Church and how the land it's on is part of the estate known as Trentham. Makes the passengers feel like they're getting a little bit of history with their tea or their grog. Then there's others would pick Conn's Tavern that stands nearly opposite above Sam Owings's Middle mill. True, Conn's has plenty of rooms and enough stabling, but I myself like to have the worst of the hills behind me before stopping.

Others, now, are partial to "Great's" and a fine big place it is...stables enough to accomodate one hundred horses with a stream flowing through the meadow and an orchard of fine fruit trees. Just lately, though, that place has fallen on bad times. Not through any fault of the innkeeper, mind you – Michael Great was a fellow who knew how to provide what hungry travelers are looking for...a generous drink and a hearty meal. What happened was, Richard Choate who owned the inn building was appointed county roads supervisor. When he died in 1813 his accounts were so jumbled that no heads or tails could be made of the matter and over $1100 of the road funds were unaccounted for. Some said Choate used the road funds to maintain his estate during the British blockade of Baltimore harbor in 1812 when farmers were under severe financial strain because of being unable to ship their crops. Whatever the truth of the matter, the county was determined to have its money back and trustees were appointed to sell off enough of Choate's land to satisfy the debt. Well, the procedings dragged on for years, as such matters are wont to do, and it wasn't until three years ago, in 1817, that the tavern was put on the auction block along with the ninety-four acres of land it occupies and John Bausman bought it.

So, like I say, I usually pull in at the Fourteen Mile House. I always tell my passengers we're bound to get a fine meal since the inn's located on the Lowe's tract they call "Food A-plenty". Bill Dwyer is the innkeeper there...a kind of independent cuss! When it comes his bedtime, he sets a decanter of whiskey and a pitcher of water on the bar and says to the guests that are still up, "Help yourselves." That's his way of letting them know they'll get no further waiting on by him that night.

Ho, now! Will you look at that! Guess some folks can't get where they're going fast enough! Gentry those two fellows were that just dashed by us. Can tell by the fine saddles on the horses and the leather boots on the riders. Now look! They practically rode right over those two fellows plodding along on foot.

Now what's the old lady in the back squawking about? Lawks alive! looks as if one of those rider's horses flung a chunk of mud from its hooves and it's landed right in her lap. Anyhow, there's the Fourteen Mile House now...let *them* listen to her complaining for a spell. Whoa! there Lightning...Whoa! Atticus....

Gunbarrel Tavern
Photo courtesy of the author.

# CHAPTER 8

## 1824: Treasure in a Petunia Bed

*The Soldiers Delight barrens that the Indian, Grey Hawk, found so "mysterious" had another mystery to divulge. A young Baltimorean, Isaac Tyson, relates how he discovered an important mineral buried beneath the soil there and how he began a business enterprise that was to continue for a hundred years.*

-/-/-/-

My name is Isaac Tyson and I am a citizen of the City of Baltimore and of the State of Maryland. My father, Isaac Tyson, Senior, is well known about the city as he is a prominent flour and grain merchant.

Father had always planned that I should follow him into his business and, indeed, for a time, it appeared I should have no alternative. My heart, however, was not in the buying and selling of wheat and flour. Instead, I have always been strongly drawn to the study of the sciences...particularly the science of geology. It seemed to me there could be nothing more fascinating than to explore the earth's crust and to learn of the treasures that may be hidden deep below its surface.

But Father would not hear of my pursuing a career in that area. "We Tysons are businessmen," he insisted, "and I have not built a thriving business simply to have it waste away while my son traipses about peering at rocks through a magnifying lens!"

He said that if I did not care to take up a position in the company's office, it might be more to my liking to become involved with his clipper ships which sail regularly out of Baltimore, transporting goods to England. Even that more romantic role in the business held little charm for me, but in the end I was forced to accede to Father's wishes.

So it was that at eighteen years of age I put out to sea as Father's agent upon a clipper bent for England, little dreaming that this would be both my first and last such voyage.

Our crossing was an uneventful one and we were not far from making landfall when, without warning, a dreadful storm struck out of the northeast and blew our ship southwestward to be dashed to pieces upon the coast of France. I am happy to report that, by God's grace, all aboard were spared and we were taken ashore by fishermen from the small village near which our vessel had foundered.

Placing the men under the captain's command, I saw to it that the crew were returned to London to await the next ship. As for myself, I had had enough of the sea for the moment. I do not know whether it was my close brush with death that gave me the courage to do what I did next or the three thousand miles that separated me from my male parent. With great difficulty, I composed the following letter:

*Dear Father – Seeing as my arrival upon these shores is a fortuitous one and not of my own making, I take it as an omen that I should perhaps spend some time here in France pursuing the studies that have always so intrigued my imagination. The French universities teem with professors learned in the sciences, and here such studies are considered quite an acceptable occupation for a Gentleman. Therefore, I pray you will understand my taking the liberty of reserving a small portion of the funds you entrusted to my care for the purpose of furthering my education. Ever Your Loving Son, Isaac.*

Although Father's reply contained many excellent reasons why I should hie myself home at the first opportunity, distance served to dull the thrust of his message and, until my funds ran low, I reveled in my studies, being particularly fascinated by the science of mineralogy.

However the time came when my money was gone and I must needs return home. I must say, Father took my temporary defection well, referring to it as "Young Isaac's time for sowing wild oats". Grateful that he had not disinherited me entirely, I returned to the business although I made it clear that henceforth I preferred to earn my livelihood behind a desk rather than before a ship's helm.

Had it not been for our family's butler, there is no telling how long I would have continued to tally up bags of wheat and to contract with millers for their product. But then one evening at dinner, I was telling Father and some guests what I had learned of the interesting mineral called "chrome", a substance that is vital in the making of paint. "Rather ugly stuff, it is," I told them, "looks like black sand but it brings upward of a hundred dollars a ton on the market. Only found in a few places throughout the world."

"By Jove, Isaac," one guest declared, "if it brings prices like that, you'd best forget about your nice white flour and go looking for some of this 'black sand'!"

It seems the butler was listening to our talk at dinner for sometime later he approached me and said, "Master Isaac, I have something here that you might find interesting."

"Yes, Markham...what is it?" As Markham had always shown a considerable interest in gardening and frequently discussed with me his horticultural projects, I assumed he had discovered some new seedling he wished to show me.

But it was no seedling he had in hand. Instead, he held out a dark-colored rock streaked with black veins. "Would this be anything like that chrome that you were talking about, Sir?" he asked.

"By Jove, Markham!" I exclaimed. "Those veins do look like chrome." With the aid of my magnifying glass, I examined the rock and, after performing several other tests, determined that it did, indeed, contain the mineral, chrome.

"I say, Markham...where did you come upon this?" I asked.

"I found it last July, Master Isaac...when we were out at your Father's summer home at Bare Hills," he told me. "I picked it up when I was weeding the petunias simply because I thought it to be somewhat unusual."

And so it was that a patch of petunias changed the entire course of my life. I checked the area around Bare Hills and found several promising spots for the mining of chrome. In spite of Father's skepticism, I bought up a tract of land and hired a crew of workmen to begin digging. Our efforts were rewarded. Although the deposits were not as extensive as I might have hoped, there was sufficient chrome ore for me to open a small plant on Pratt Street in Baltimore where I experimented with manufacturing paints and chemicals and medicines.

Fired by the realization that the precious mineral was to be found in our region, I began to search out other nearby areas for additional deposits. I had by then concluded that chrome was most likely to be found in conjunction with layers of serpentine rock and that, since serpentine appeared to inhibit the growth of plant life, barrens areas would prove most likely to yield good results. But little did I dream on that day I traveled forth to the Soldiers Delight barrens that I should be setting foot upon an area containing some of the richest chrome-bearing ore to be found anywhere in the world.

As it happened, even before we entered the barrens area, my supposition was confirmed. We stopped to water our horses in the Red Run stream. As the animals bent to drink I espied a thick layer of "black sand" covering the stream bottom. I inquired as to where the headwaters of the steam might be found and was told that the main source is in the Soldiers Delight barrens. It required only a short excursion into the barrens to convince me that here I would find chrome in quantities sufficient to guarantee commercial success.

As the barrens is very sparsely populated, it has not been a difficult matter to buy up land or to acquire the mineral rights from those few settlers who refused to sell outright. Indeed, most are surprised and delighted to find that what they had considered to be totally worthless land can bring them this unexpected income. I purchased from John Baughman parts of the "Grazier's Delight", "Gosnell's Camp", and "Wilmot's Chance" tracts for the sum of $1,000. The following year I paid an additional $30 to William Gosnell for the mineral rights on 150 acres of his land and a little later purchased another section of "Grazier's Delight" from William Owings.

Incorporating as the Tyson Mining Company, we began operations in Soldiers Delight, setting up buddles in the stream beds to extract the chrome sand, this being the least arduous means of obtaining the chrome. The way it works is a pit or "buddle" is erected across a stream bed with heavy timbers. Chrome-bearing sand is shoveled into the buddle and the heavier chrome settles to the bottom while the lighter sand and gravel are washed downstream. Extra timbers, called "stops", are added as the ore accumulates. The ore is washed three times in all. The best-washed ore is sold as "heads", the next grade is known as "middlings" and the remains are called "tailings".

61

In addition, we have dug many test holes in what seem likely areas. When we determine the areas where the chrome is likely to be most accessible, we begin the more arduous task of digging shafts deep into the earth to extract the chrome from the rich underground seams.

Thus far, our venture has been most successful with the buddles yielding almost pure chrome ore. By now, the Ware mine has been sunk to a depth of a hundred or so feet, going straight down like a great hand-dug well. The Choate mine, more of an inclined shaft, extends westward from its mouth. I anticipate that in coming years we will continue to extend these two and to sink many more such shafts.

Once we began the underground mining, we installed a crusher mill to extract the chrome irom the ore. This particular mill is fired by steam rather than by water power. In addition to the men required to operate the mill, we keep two men on hand to cut wood for firing the boilers. After the ore is ground, it passes into a trough and is then put through a washing process which allows the heavier chrome to settle to the bottom and gets rid of the rock tailings. Mr. Eli Triplett is our mill manager and an excellent job he does.

I have brought in a number of Irish and Polish immigrants to operate the mines. To house them, I have constructed along the road that runs toward the Ward farm on the Liberty Turnpike a boarding house and some individual cabins as well as an office and a store, using the local pine lumber in their construction.

Since the great value of chrome ore has been made public – it is currently selling for up to $100 a ton – prices here in the Soldiers Delight barrens have increased considerably. One local resident paid $7,000 for some acreage in Soldiers Delight and managed to pay for the land in two years by selling to me the chrome ore he washed from the steam.

While the quantities of chrome one can obtain by the washing method is limited, it is a fairly simple matter for anyone to construct a buddle of wooden timbers laid in the steam bed and to realize a very nice profit from the ore thus collected. In fact, I daresay there is not a farmer hereabouts whose land abuts the Red Run stream who has not constructed some sort of primitive buddle or other on his land to reap that unexpected harvest.

Since production has increased so greatly, I am no longer able in my small plant to make use of all the chrome we mine. Nowadays, after it is extracted from the earth, we haul the chrome ore down to the Elkridge landing upon the Patapsco River. From there, it is shopped to Glasgow, Scotland where the firm of John and James White uses it in the manufacture of paints and dyes. We also ship to a firm in Liverpool, England.

As for Father, I do believe he is now resigned to my seeking my livelihood elsewhere than in his warehouses and ships. However, he still expresses occasional reservations about my venture. Just the other day as we were enjoying a pipe after dinner, he said to me, "Isaac, you seem to have done quite well with your mines. But tell me this – after you have taken all the chrome ore out of the ground can you plant more? Now with wheat, there is always another crop...another planting."

Choate mine at Soldiers Delight Park
Photo courtesy of John McGrain.

I told Father that so far as I could determine the supply of chrome is unlimited. Indeed, my major concern at the moment is that we have, with our Soldiers Delight mines, made such a plentiful supply of chrome available that the price is beginning to drop.

Father went off shaking his head. I sat there a moment longer, pondering how strange it was that Markham's little rock from the petunia bed has ended up affecting world finances.

## CHAPTER 9

### 1833 - Traveling God's Highways and Byways

*In Owings Mills and surrounding areas, Methodist groups, usually meeting in private homes under the tutelage of lay leaders, multiplied rapidly. By 1784, the widening rift between Methodism and the Church of England had developed into an irreconcilable parting of the ways, much as the Reverend Thomas Cradock had predicted. At the Christmas Conference held in Baltimore in December of that year, the Methodists announced their formal split with the Church of England and became The Methodist Episcopal Church in America.*

*Many of the "Methodist Societies", as they were known, had no permanent place of worship, but conducted their meetings in private homes under the leadership of lay members. In order to use to best advantage the few ordained ministers available, Bishop Francis Asbury established the custom of sending itinerant ministers to instruct and exhort these outlying Methodist groups. The eastern seaboard was divided into "districts" and the traveling ministers became known as "circuit riders" since each rode a regular "circuit" through the district to which he was assigned.*

*The Reverend Henry Smith was one such itinerant circuit-rider. Ordained in 1793, he spent the next forty years traveling by horseback throughout the various Methodist districts in Maryland, Virginia, and Ohio. He was appointed on three separate occasions to serve the Baltimore Circuit: in 1806, in 1815, and in 1833. We encounter the Reverend Smith on an autumn evening in the year 1833. He has just completed preaching to a Methodist Society meeting in Reisterstown and is returning to Hookstown by way of the Reisterstown Turnpike.*

*-/-/-/-*

Let other ministers of the gospel fear to fall from Grace...it's the possibility of falling from this poor nag's back that bothers me at the moment. 'Tis not that I begrudge Brother Reister his ability to pray long and fervently, but surely if he realized how painfully the rheumatism throbs through my body with the coming of nightfall, he would have spared us so lengthy a benediction.

But there! Instead of complaining of Brother's Reister's fervor, I should be down on my knees thanking God that our local Methodist

65

Societies are blessed with dedicated Christians such as himself to serve as lay leaders, opening their homes for services and their hearts to the Lord. Otherwise, we itinerants would have a hard time indeed holding the flocks together, seeing as we are spread out upon the circuit so thinly that we can scarce visit with the individual groups twice a month.

While giving thanks, I should rejoice also that my own situation has changed. Now – for the first time in my forty years of itinerating – I can look forward at each journey's end to a bed of my own and a wife to greet me. Not that I fail to realize there are those who made sport of my decision to marry – "Here's old Smith...one foot in the stirrup and the other in the grave...taking himself a wife at his age!"

Well, I do not feel called upon to explain myself and shall assign no reason for changing my state so late in life. Suffice it to say that although my feelings for Rebecca never faltered during the twenty-three years of our acquaintanceship, I refused to allow this tender and loving woman to endure the hardships itinerating imposes upon ministers' wives. Often have I observed that the wives of itinerants are caught between two grindstones – those whose spouses travel without them must endure guilt and loneliness, and those who go along with their mates upon the circuit must needs struggle to make a home for their families in the most uncomfortable of circumstances.

At least our good bishop took my advancing years and my newly-wed state into account when assigning me to a circuit this year. Always I have considered this Baltimore circuit to be the best, not only for the short rides between preaching places and the good accomodations but for the sure pay as well. Compared to some assignments I have received, the sixteen weekday appointments and four regular Sunday services each month seem light duty indeed, even with occasional afternoon and evening sessions thrown in.

I do wish, though, that the Bishop had assigned me to a settled parish where I need not heave these old bones into the saddle by day and by night. "I am an old man..." I told him, "an old man, tired, sick and weary and yet you wish me to do a young man's work!"

"Not so, Brother Smith," the Bishop insisted, "you are truly needed out upon the circuit."

Needed – hah! As I said to Rebecca afterwards, "An old worn-out man to be palmed off on a circuit is an affecting sight. The people may say they love an old preacher for what he has done for them in the past, but in truth they are looking for a 'pusher'."

Have a care, Old Friend! One more stumble like that and we will both be in yon ditch. Were it not for the moon's light, 'twould be dark indeed upon the turnpike this evening. Soon now the lights of the tavern house at the fourteen mile marker will be in view. Already my nose senses the smoke from its kitchen fire...a piece of venison turning on the spit from the smell of it. No need to stop there tonight, however, since the Reisters saw to it that both my mount and I were well-fed for our long ride home to Hookstown.

Not that I am much giving to stopping at taverns. Many's the night I've bedded down upon the hard ground or ridden past midnight to get to the home of some brethren who offers a harbor house rather than spend the few coins I carry to buy a bed and meal. Why, I recall one time I traveled from Chilicothe, Ohio, to Baltimore on less than five dollars!

But I must be honest – 'tis not just the lack of funds that causes me to avoid such places. It is the rough nature and often cruel humor of their clientele that causes me to shun them even though there are those among my fellow ministers who seize upon the heckling and razzing as an opportunity to bring God's word to those most in need of salvation. Were I, like them, both bold and gifted, I, too, could exult in my ability to bring swearers, liars, cock-fighters, card-players, horse-racers, and drunkards into the fold. Unfortunately, when I am confronted by such ruffians, I can only seek a dark corner away from the fire and pray that I will be allowed to take my meal in peace.

However that may be, I do think this night's meeting was a goodly one. Although I must say I found it a bit unseemly that Sister Bowers and Sister Gore found it necessary to vie with each other as to whose conversion had been the most powerful. Indeed, had Sister Bowers declaimed: "How the Lord has brought me!" one more time, I should have found it in me to wish the Lord would *take* her! I daresay one of my more eloquent co-workers could have turned their competition to advantage, calling forth chapter and verse to demonstrate to the two ladies that even religious fervor may be only a concealment for the sin of Pride. I, however, could only stammer and congratulate the two upon having been called with so clear a summons.

It is times like those that make we wonder why He whom I serve chose such a poor, weak vessel as I to do His bidding. While my brother ministers call forth fire and brimstone and move men to shouts or weeping with their oratory, I can only pray my modest talents will see me through the next preaching.

It was ever thus. Even these forty years later, I remember well the ordeal of my ordination...how when I was called before the bishop and the other ordained ministers I was shaking so hard I could scarce stammer out an answer to their questions and finally – to both my mortification and theirs – broke into tears. To this day I do not know if they allowed me to pass because they were convinced of my sincerity or because they took pity on so poor a specimen of a preacher.

Now, after all these years of itinerating, I am still too often that same, weak, trembling fool. And still traveling up and down God's highways and byways, trying to bring His Word to those who would hear it.

Yon lantern must be the light on the tollgate keeper's house at Nicodemus Road. Ah, good! – he waves me on. Tis not always a Methodist preacher can count upon such courtesies, for there are those who disparage us still for our Tory sympathies during the war with Britain.

Now that we are past the Fourteen Mile House the road grows darker once again. Do not stumble, old Friend, for should you break your leg this night, I am too weary to pull the trigger to put you out of your misery.

At least it is not raining. Worse than snow I hate those chill rains that soak into every crevice of one's body...right through to the very soul. That time I was caught in the rain with only light stockings and no cape, how the chill and rheumatism did set in! It was then that

Doctor Wilkins, who married one of Samuel Owings's daughters, advised me to get "electrified", a treatment that proved worse than the ailment itself and of little avail besides.

Ah, well, my rheumatism serves one good purpose – it provides to me a feeling of kinship with that most beloved of all itinerants, the late Bishop Asbury. 1802 it was, when I had the honor of traveling the wilderness roads with that saint among men. Ah, those early years! How trivial are my present discomforts compared to what I endured then! Traveling over Indian trails or where there were no roads at all...through swamps and bogs and over mountaintops...rattlesnakes and mocassins slithering across my path...

And how well I remember that night in a little backwoods settlement...no more had I bedded down in the home of one of the parishioners than the village was attacked by Indians. Had it not been for a barking dog, all would have been slaughtered as we slept. As it was, the Indians shot the dog and stole several cows before slinking away into the forest.

When we knelt together afterwards to give thanks for our deliverance, I was actually grateful for the dirt floor for I knew that my quaking knees would have rattled the sturdiest of floor boards.

Of course, when one must make one's bed where God wills it, there is always more than the threat of Indians to keep one awake. Many's the night I have been driven from my borrowed bed by the fleas and bugs who claimed prior occupancy. Fortunate for me that early in my travels a kind old lady whose name I have forgotten taught me how to deal with flea bites as well as with the itch which afflicted me badly two or three times a year. The salve she prepared for me – a mixture of sulphur and rosin and black pepper and hog's lard – may smell like the very pits of Hell, but it invariably works and a tin of it always reposes in my saddle bag right next to my Bible.

Just over that next hill now and we shall see the lights of the tavern John Murphy operates upon the hill opposite Samuel Owings's upper mill.

Thanks be the old bridge across the Gwynns Falls has been replaced with a more solid one. Well do I remember the time some twenty years past when my horse's hoof broke through the rotten timbers and both of us were thrown into the stream below.

Ah...candles still burning in one of the little houses down there past the Gwynn's Falls. Pray God it is some joyful occasion and not an illness that causes the occupants to be about so late.

Up the hill now and past the middle mill. A pity that the business Samuel Owings worked so hard to build has fallen upon hard times. I see by an advertisement in the *Baltimore American* that the mills and the Ulm estate are being offered for sale.

Whoa! Have a care for ruts like that one or you'll have me out of the saddle yet, Old Friend. I daresay, now that the Greenspring Valley railroad line is operating from Baltimore to Owings Mills, local residents who have business in the city will gladly avoid the turnpike altogether. It is even rumored that the railroad company is to build a grand hotel close by the Chattolanee Springs for the convenience of city residents who wish to enjoy the benefits of country air and water during the heat of summer. A blessing for the gentry, perhaps, but hardly likely to be within the means of such as myself.

If the dim light does not deceive my old eyes, yon road to my right is the one that leads from Samuel Owings's mills to the Waters Camp Ground a mile or so west of here. Come summertime, that old camp ground will again be the site of many conversions and many blessings. I often think the Lord provided those wonderiul freshwater springs in that exact spot to bless the multitudes who flock there to hear His Word.

And some few miles northwest upon the Liberty Turnpike the Ward's campground will likewise offer a haven to those who come to sing and worship and pray in God's own outdoors. A joy indeed, to be serving that congregation again and to observe how they grow in numbers and in strength. I remember upon my first being assigned to the Baltimore Circuit in 1806 the group had just outgrown its meeting place at the home of John Ward and had begun holding its services in the New Tavern built by Robert Ward. Now they speak seriously of erecting a chapel of their own and I daresay that will be accomplished before many more years have passed.

Had I no place of my own to rest my head this night, I would turn off here at the Saint Thomas's road and head for the dwelling of that good old Christian gentleman, Robert North Carnan. I doubt there is an itinerant to serve this circuit this past fifty years who has not availed himself of the Carnan's hospitality. Pillars of the Stone Chapel congregation, the Carnan family. 'Twas they who negotiated with Dr. William Lyon to rent for ninety-nine years the acre of land upon which the Stone Chapel church is built, the annual rent being exceedingly modest...the payment each year of one grain of peppercorn.

Aye, this little village that clusters about Samuel Owings's mills would seem but an insignificant dot upon the map and yet it and the Owings family have played an important role in our Church's history. I remember how glowingly the good bishop Asbury always spoke of that family. "Often, Henry, have I rested my weary head at the home of that good Methodist, Joshua Owings," the Bishop would reminisce as our horses' hooves clanged out a rhythm over some rocky path. "Ah, the man was an Israelite indeed! He began as an Anglican, a communicant of Saint Thomas, but was always a serious churchman who sought for the truth and God revealed it to him. And how the Lord has blessed his family! His son, Richard, was one of our ordained ministers and a close associate of Robert Strawbridge, that fiery Irishman who lit the torch of Methodism throughout the western shore of Maryland. When Stone Chapel was dedicated in 1786, it was none other than Richard Owings who performed the dedication service."

The bishop always lauded Joshua Owings, too, for his refusal to employ slave labor upon his acres, even though it had been the custom of others in the family to do so.

A perennial issue, the question of slavery, one that causes as much dissension within the church as it does in society as a whole. Bishop Asbury always spoke eloquently against the practice and often reiterated his stance that no man could, in good conscience, hold another human being in bondage. I've heard it told many a time how, back in 1783, Bishop Asbury stopped by John Worthington's place and saw a negro being so cruelly treated that he announced he could no longer accept his old friend's hospitality and, with that, called for his horse and departed.

Well, some fifty years have passed since that time, and I do not see that matters have improved much. Just recently – at the 1828 General Conference – a resolution was introduced requiring that anyone who treated slaves inhumanely should be expelled from the church. The resolution did not pass.

Only last year in Southern Maryland where the land-holders rely heavily upon slave labor to raise tobacco, I was accosted outside the meeting house by an angry group of parishioners who wished to take issue with my sermon in which I had reiterated my firm belief that slave-holding is a sin against nature and against one's fellow-man.

"And just how would you suggest, Reverend, that we make our tobacco crops without our negroes?" one burly farmer demanded.

"Perhaps if you made freedmen of your slaves and paid them decent wages they would work just as hard," I suggested.

At that, the man simply sneered, "No use talking about this with a preacher fellow...all he's ever done is stand up there in the pulpit and talk. How can a man who ain't ever got his hands dirty with a day's work know anything about tobacco raisin'?"

Knowing in my heart that slavery is an evil practice and one that could eventually bring destruction upon the very ones who now defend it, I continued to try to persuade the group of their Christian duty. But in the end 1 could see that they were, for the most part, unswayed. Indeed, the men made it clear I would no longer be welcome in their community if I "kept on harping on the slavery question."

I rode off with a heavy heart, their disparaging words still ringing in my ears. Once more I was reminded that my frequent prayers asking for a little of Bishop Asbury's powers of persuasion to rub off on me have remained unanswered.

Perhaps I must simply pray for the Grace to accept the fact that I shall always be as I am...no more than a weak and weary journeyer traveling God's highways and byways...trying to complete the errand upon which my Master has sent me.

# CHAPTER 10

## 1848: Eureka!

*By the mid-1800s, the three mills from which the Owings Mills community took its name had changed ownership several times. The Lower Mill and the plantation house, Ulm, were ultimately purchased by William Painter whose family would continue occupy the premises and to operate the mill until the mid-1900s. The Middle Mill appears to have been demolished sometime before 1850, although the stone house which was probably the miller's residence remained standing until the Western Maryland Railroad built its coal chute on the premises at the turn of the century. The Upper Mill was still operational but its owner had listed it for sale.*

*Since a large percentage of Owings Mills's population consisted of residents who had migrated into the area from Pennsylvania, it is perhaps fitting that the Upper Mill should be purchased by a family whose American roots had been planted in the very heart of Pennsylvania Dutch country - Lancaster, Pennsylvania. In 1848, having inherited their share of their father's estate, three Groff brothers traveled south toward Baltimore with the intention of buying farmland. We join them at the Gunbarrel Tavern near the crest of Pleasant Hill where their expedition has met with a delay.*

-/-/-/-

I told Abraham and Jacob before we left home that this was a ridiculous expedition. "If it's more land we need, why not purchase some fine big farm right here in Lancaster County instead of traveling all that distance on what may be a fool's errand?" I asked them.

"I explained it to thee before," Abraham said. "Land hereabouts has all been taken up and, on the rare occasion a farm is sold, it goes for too dear a price. Judging by the advertisement that was sent to me, this particular farm I have in mind lies within a mile of Baltimore Towne's northern border and is quite reasonably priced."

Like all the Groff's, once Abraham makes up his mind to something, he is hard to dissuade. So I had no choice but to join them. Of course, young Benjamin Franklin thought we were setting out on some glorious expedition. I could see by his sad expression as we left that our younger brother remained unconvinced that he was better off stay-

71

ing behind. And now here we are...stuck halfway to nowhere until Abraham can locate a blacksmith to mend the wagon.

They call this the Reisterstown Turnpike. More like a pig wallow if you ask me. Heaven knows what obstacle we struck in the dark or how much damage it has done.

As usual, Abraham counsels patience. "Be thankful, Brother, that we have met with our misfortune where there is an inn adjacent, otherwise thou might have spent this night sleeping upon the cold earth instead of in a bed."

To call this wretched place an inn is to give it more credit than it deserves. Indeed, I suspect the rough lot who frequent this "Gunbarrel Tavern" are more to be feared than any wolves we might encounter in the woods. As for sleep – I could not see how the three of us sharing one bed was a situation in which one could hope for much repose...especially considering that Jacob's snores are enough to rouse the dead from their very graves. Between the curses of those two teamsters who engaged in fisticuffs behind the tavern around midnight and Jacob's trumpet blowing in my ear, my head this morning feels the size of a watermelon.

And now Abraham has decided we should not be in any haste to move on, but should consider the proposition presented to us at breakfast this morning by one of the inn's other occupants. "What is it you three gentlemen are here for?" the fellow inquired as we were finishing up our meal.

Abraham explained our errand.

"Land it is you're looking for, gentlemen? – in that case I propose you tarry a bit and take a look around you. Within sight of yon little chapel" – he pointed southward where I had noticed a crude log church perched upon the hilltop – "within sight of the Pleasant Hill Methodist meeting house you will find five excellent tracts of highly productive farm land...every one of them for sale."

"Nay, it is our intention to continue on toward Baltimore Towne," I said.

"Not so fast, Brother," Abraham said. "It would do no harm to at least have a look. Indeed – " he gestured with his hand toward the window, "what I can see of our surroundings gives me reason to think we might profit by following this gentleman's advice."

"Indeed, you might go far and do worse," the fellow said. "The soil hereabouts is noted for its richness and one parcel that is being offered for sale includes one of the finest gristmills in the county, a mill that can produce between 15,000 and 20,000 barrels of flour each year. It is the newest and best of three mills that were constructed by Samuel Owings and has lately come under the ownership of a Mr. Louis Lewis who now wishes to sell both the building and the twelve or so acres upon which the mill and its race are situated."

With that, he insisted upon accompanying us to the adjacent hilltop from which he pointed out the tracts that were for sale. "All the land from here at Pleasant Hill down past the Gwynns Falls and on beyond the lane that leads to the Painter farm is for sale. Some of the tracts extend back into the Caves Valley on the east and to the Red Run stream on the west."

Thus it came about that we have spent this entire day tramping about over fields and woodlands and hills and valleys. Jacob was particularly interested in examining the mill. A Mrs. Nicholson showed us about the place...it seems her husband had been managing the mill and when he died she had taken over. But now, apparently, she has decided to marry her miller and has plans to move elsewhere.

I still feel we should at least inspect the land nearer Baltimore Towne, but, by this afternoon, I could see that both Abraham and Jacob were convinced they had found what they were looking for. As we came away from the mill Jacob remarked, "Some fools are setting off for California in search of gold. I say there's treasure to be found right here." With that he picked up a fistful of wheat and let the golden grains sift slowly through his fingers.

"In that case," I said, "we should do as the gold miners do when they strike a particularly rich lode – I have heard it said that they cry out 'Eureka!', meaning 'I have found it!'."

I spoke thus only in jest, but Jacob failed to catch my intent. "Just so!" he exclaimed. "We shall name this place 'Eureka Mills'...have the name printed on all our barrels and sacks..."

Abraham, too, took my words seriously. "An excellent suggestion," he said. "Eureka Mills...I like the solid ring of it."

As we hitched the horses to our now-repaired wagon, I could see that it was going to be a long ride back to Pennsylvania. For every mile we passed, the name 'Eureka' would echo in my ears as my brothers continued to plan for their new purchase. Ah well, at least it is better than listening to Jacob snore.

Upper Mill

This early photo pf the Upper Mill shows it unchanged from the original 18th centruy building constructed by Samuel Owings. Now known as "Groff's Mill", it still stands on Reisterstown Road at Bonita Avenue and presents much this same appearance today. Photo courtesy of William D. Groff, Jr.

## CHAPTER 11

### 1857: Running for Freedom

*The slavery question that had so troubled the Reverend Henry Smith remained like a barbed arrow stuck into the very flesh of the nation. For those who suffered under the yoke of slavery, life offered little hope; the only promise of a better future lay in escape to the North where abolishionists provided shelter. Considering the difficulties of escape and the severe penalties – including possible death – they would face if captured, only the very brave and the very desperate undertook that journey.*

*The following narrator was among the few who successfully left a slave existence behind. His story is based upon a former slave's account of his flight to freedom as it was related, many years later, to E. Bennett Bowen.*

*-/-/-/-*

I can't tell you my real name because if I did, some of the folks that have helped me out could get in trouble. Let's just say that my name is "John" and that I was born a slave. It was on this big plantation in either Virginia or North Carolina...I ain't exactly sure which. My Daddy was a field hand and my Mamma worked in the "Big House". Me and my brothers and sisters was put to work in the fields as soon as we was old enough to lift a hoe. Hard labor it was, too! Many's the day we hoed corn or cotton from sunup to sundown and by the time I was seven my hands were blistered and callused like an old man's.

Maybe I could have put up with that if something real bad hadn't happened. The way it was, I come into the cabin one summer evening and I find my Mamma rocking back and forth on a stool...this awful look on her face like if somebody be dead...tears streaming down her cheeks. "Mamma! What's wrong?" I ask her.

"It's your brother..." she say, still rocking herself back and forth, "they done sold him...sent him down to the slave market in Charleston."

When I hear that, I get so furious mad when I hear that that I want to go kill somebody. But my Mamma stop me. "You only bring more trouble on the family, you do something rash like that," she say.

I knowed she was right but the hatefulness of what they done burned in me like a field fire. "I tell you one thing, though, Mamma" I say to her, "I ain't never gonna let them sell me!"

Mamma look at me hard. I can see by her face she done made up her mind to something. But all she say is, "If that time come, son, I'll do all I can to help you."

After that, the family all begin to listen whenever there's talk among the other hands about "going North". We learn the names of some places where it's supposed to be safe and the names of some people they say will help anybody that's running for freedom. My Daddy, he teach me how to tell the North Star and show me how moss grows on the north side of trees. We go over and over again the things you supposed to do and the things not to do.

It's over a year before I get my chance, but one night my Mamma wakes me up off my pallet and says it's time to go. "I heard The Man talking today about how crops be bad this year and how he be planning to send some more young people to the market because he be short on cash," she say.

I rouse up from sleep, hardly knowing what's happening. "You mean right now, Mamma?" I mumble.

"Come on, Son," Mama urge me, shoving a bundle of food and clothes into my hand, "you got to get going before the moon comes up." And before I can do more than give her a quick kiss, she done shoved me out the door.

I set off across that corn field with the salt of my Mamma's tears drying on my cheeks. Like we planned, I make my way to the nearest stream, then get down into the streambed and start walking north. The water it be cold and the rocks they be slippery and a couple of times I go in over my head in a deep hole, but I keep right on going, always holding my gunny sack up high so my rations don't get wet.

Daylight come and I find a hole to crawl in and eat a little of my grub. I lay up all that day and from time to time I hear dogs barking off in the distance, so I know they be looking for me. Finally, I fall asleep for an hour or so, and when I wake it's pitch-y dark out, but that old North Star be peeking right down through the tree-tops like a good omen.

I don't dare leave the stream beds yet, for fear the dogs will pick up my scent if I travel over dry land. By the third or fourth day, my boots done be falling to pieces from staying wet all the time. I'm holed up one afternoon, wondering how I'm going to make it barefooted when all of a sudden I hear voices...people talking...coming closer and closer.

At first, my heart stops beating, I'm that sure I been found. Then I peek out and see it's a bunch of young people. They be carrying picnic baskets and laughing and talking amongst themselves and I figure they done come to swim in the stream.

Sure enough, soon they is all in the water frolicking around, their clothes scattered along the bank and hanging from the bushes. When none of them be looking, I slip out of my hidey-hole and grab the first pair of boots that looks like it might fit me. Just then one of the young fellows looks around and sees me and yells, "Hey! You there!"

I light out running for all I'm worth. Barefooted or not, I keep going till there ain't an ounce of breath left in me. Finally, when I can't go one more step, I stop and listen but I don't hear nothing so I figure they done give up with chasing me. Them boots ain't the best fit in the world but if it wasn't for them, I sure would have been a goner... wouldn't been able to keep on going.

I try to make the fatback and cornpone Mamma packed for me last long as possible, but all that walking makes me powerful hungry. At times, I manage to slip into an orchard and grab a few apples or to snatch some turnips or potatoes out of a garden and eat them raw. Once I find myself an old bucket and I clean it up. Whenever I come upon a herd of cows out in a pasture at night, I slip in and help myself to some fresh milk.

One night when it be pouring rain, I take a big chance and hide in the haymow of a farmer's barn. I ain't had nothing but a couple of turnips and a little bit of milk that whole day and my stomach be growling loud enough to keep me awake. Next morning I smell fresh bread baking and it's more than I can stand. I hunker down amid the hay and wait until the farmer's wife sets the bread near the window to cool, then I slip up as quiet as I can and reach in and take me a loaf. If I said my feet had wings on them while I was beating it away from there, I wouldn't be exaggerating none. Luckily, nobody be chasing me and when I finally set myself down in some bushes to eat that bread, I'm crying because it tastes so good!

Walking by night like I'm doing, gets pretty rough when the moon ain't out, and after while I take the chance of sometimes traveling by day. That was almost the finish of me because just after daylight one morning I be walking along through a woods and I hear a man's voice behind me say, "Hold it right there, Fellow!"

I turn around real slow and see that it be a white man and he got this big old double-barreled shot gun hanging in the crook of one arm. "Where you headin' for, Boy?" he ask.

I be shaking inside so hard I'm sure he gonna guess I be on the run, but somehow I manage to grin at him and say in this kind of muddle-headed voice, "I'se jus' comin' over to see 'bout the raspberries, Suh...find out whether they be ready for pickin' yet..."

The man frowns for a minute then he says, "Oh...yes...the raspberries. Well you go on up to the house and ask Miss Sally...she's the one will know if they're ripe or not."

"Yes, Suh...I surely will do that, Suh..." I tell him and walk away just like my knees ain't knocking themselves together with every step I take.

A few times when I spot folks working out in the fields, I take the chance of talking to them. Most times they slip me into their cabins after dark and see that my belly gets filled with hot food. One such bunch of folks warn me that I be getting near the Potomac and that crossing won't be easy. "These-here Virginia planters always say the river be their best guarantee against any of us taking off for the North," they tell me.

When I get to the river, I see what they mean. It be over a mile wide and the only way a person's gonna get across is by boat. I lay up along the river banks for a day or so, wishing I knew how it was old Moses managed to get them Red Sea waters to part like he did. Finally, I spot this old man trying to get his skiff into the water.

77

Mustering up every last ounce of courage I got left in me, I walk toward him and ask if he needs any help.

"Who you, Boy?" he demands, peering up at me.

"Me?...oh, I'm jus' John...Mist' Amos's John...from over there." I point toward some farms off in the distance.

"Well, git aholt of that other end and help me slide her into the water then," he orders.

We get the boat in the water and - trying to act like it don't make no what's-the-difference to me - I say, "You want, I could row you across...Mist' Amos say we can't cut tobacco this mornin' cause of the rain last night."

"All right then, Boy...don't just stand there, start rowing!"

I set to the oars and across the river we go. Soon as I see we're close enough to the north side that I can make a run for it, I drop both oars in the water and take off swimming like there was a big old water mocassin after me. I hit the shore and I head off through the woods. All the while the old man's standing there in the boat screaming and yelling, "You come back here, you John!"

I keep right on traveling.

I been told that after I cross the Potomac I shouldn't head due north but go a little to the west so's not to fetch up smack dab in the middle of Baltimore City. I do that and finally make my way to a farm where I been told I'll find help. I can tell you now, it took all my courage to come out of hiding and show myself to white folks after being on the run for close to two months! But, sure enough, they take me in and give me food and clothes and tell me about another place farther along where I'll find help.

At the next place, they feed me again, and before I set off they tell me which direction to take. "Keep on until you get to the Liberty Turnpike." they say. "After you walk down a big hill where there's a mill at the bottom, keep going for about two miles more." They tell me what kind of house I should look for and that I should ask for a certain farmer.

I follow their directions and when I get to that farm, the people there take me in and hide me for a few days. Then one night they take me to another farm over near Harrisonville and that's where I been ever since.

I work for the farmer and he's done give me a little cabin to live in. Pays me my wages every Saturday night, regular as you please. I done met this girl I like quite a bit. Soon as I save up enough from my wages, we be thinking about getting married.

The farmer I work for, he say that pretty soon now, Mr. Lincoln is going to make me a free man. I can't tell you how proud it's gonna feel when I can walk down the street just like anybody else and maybe someday even get to vote for who gets to be the next president. But when that day comes, I'll be rejoicing most of all for my Mamma and my Daddy and all the rest of my family that I left behind.

# CHAPTER 12

## 1862: "I Am Tired of Hearing Cannon"

*By the sixth decade of the 19th century, the festering boil that was the slavery question had erupted and the United States found itself plunged into a bitter Civil War whose consequences would continue to be felt generations later.*

*William Henry Harrison Campbell served in the Confederate Army throughout the four-year duration of the War Between the States, now known as the Civil War. He was born near Winchester, Virginia, but would spend the greater part of his life in Owings Mills, where he would serve as the community's physician for nearly fifty years.*

*The community's future doctor enlisted in the Confederate Army on May 20, 1861 at Woodstock, Virginia and was detailed to serve with General Stonewall Jackson's forces. He continued with his company until he was captured near Petersburg, Virginia, on March 25, 1865. He was interned at Point Lookout prison in Maryland for nearly three months and was released on June 7, 1865.*

*The following letter was written by him in 1862 and is addressed to his father who had apparently visited him in camp some time previously.*

-/-/-/-

Camp near James River,
July 5, 1862

Dear Papa:

Although the chances are very poor of your getting this letter I have determined to try the experiment. We have been marching with the exception of three or four days ever since you left us at Strasburg.

The Yankees annoyed us every day on our retreat up the valley until we reached Port Republic. There Jackson made a stand and defeated them in both the battles that were fought there. We captured between four and five hundred prisoners on the second day. My regiment was not engaged in either of those fights, although we were exposed to the firing of the enemy's battery. I forgot to say we captured eight pieces of cannon.

At Port Republic we rested, I think, three days. This was necessary as we were almost broken down. On the third day the order came to cook three days' rations. We were all speculating as to the direction we would take, but our doubts were all removed when the wagons were sent across the Blue Ridge.

We were six days coming down the valley to Hanover County [Virginia]. Our brigade and the Stonewall brigade were in the rear of Jackson's army. We arrived on the battlefield Friday 27th of June about an hour before sunset. You haven't any idea of the excitement that existed. Generals Lee, Hill, and Longstreet were all present. General Lee said he had come over to see Jackson's men fight. Of course we would have fought then if we ever would fight, but as I said before, the battle was nearly over and all we did was run and halloo.

The tenth regiment didn't lose a man. Colonel Fulkerson commanding our brigade was killed. He was a valuable officer. Elzey's brigade suffered very badly in this battle. The thirteenth regiment had 125 killed and wounded out of 300 engaged. Frank [Campbell, a cousin] had a very lucky escape. He was with the colors; a shell came along killing one man, wounding another and knocking him down. Bob Streit and Henry Gilbert were killed. Captain Shearer and Ed Legg were wounded. Those whom I have named are all the Winchester boys that were killed and wounded in the boomerangs. General Elzey was wounded - it is supposed not mortally.

This was one of the greatest battles that was ever fought. Our loss was very heavy. The Yankees' loss including the prisoners was far greater than ours. We had been fighting for six days. Last Tuesday the second great battle was fought. The fight lasted until ten o'clock at night. The hardest fighting was on our right. We on the left were exposed to a very severe shelling. Louis Knicely was wounded in the back, but not mortally. He was the only one wounded in our company.

I hope I shall never be under another such fire. I am very tired of hearing cannon. Today there is a calm and you don't know what a relief it is. From present appearances we may have another battle tomorrow. I hope we will not, for I have seen enough in the last week to satisfy me for life.

We are about twenty-five miles from Richmond, Charles City County, and three miles from James River. I hope we will be in the valley before long. This is miserable country.

The loss of Yankees in killed, wounded, and prisoners is estimated at between thirty-five and forty thousand. The Yankees have been defeated at every point.

Give my love to mother and all the family. Hoping I shall see you all soon,

I remain your affectionate son,
Wm. H. H. Campbell

# CHAPTER 13

## 1866: A Man Worth Thirty Acres

*For five long and bloody years, Civil War raged throughout the southeastern United States. By the time the conflict ended, over 300,000 men were dead and even more bore scars and mutilations that would remain with them for the rest of their lives.*

*While Owings Mills was spared the devastation experienced by nearby areas such as Gettysburg, even here the war delivered its impact. Oliver Disney, Senior, a farmer whose land lies along the Red Run stream, looks back on the war years and upon the effect the conflict has had on his family and on his community.*

*-/-/-/-*

They stole it from me! Thirty acres of good land along the stream bed...land that I sweated to clear and plant and harvest! And now our own government just up and snatched it right away from me!

I tried to explain to them that I couldn't afford to pay again. "Look here," I said to the recruiting officer, "you fellows have already tried to draft me twice and both times I've paid up the $300 for a substitute to fight in my place."

"That's all well and good, Mr. Disney," the man said, "but the law is clear. You are an able-bodied man and our army needs every recruit it can get if we're going to whip these Johnny Rebs."

"But, hang it all, man! I'm a fellow with seven children to support and a farm to look after," I told him. "My wife's expecting another child come Spring...by no means can I go off and leave her to take care of everything!"

"I'm sorry, Sir, but I have my orders. Either you join up or pay for a substitute again."

"But I've already told you! I can't leave here...and paying twice for substitutes has drained every cent of my cash money. The only thing I've got left is my farm."

"In that case, Mr. Disney, the government has no choice except to seize from you acreage equal in value to the cost of buying a substitute."

Now I'm as much a patriot as the next fellow, but I can't tell you how it hurt me to have them come in and take away that thirty acres. Ten dollars an acre! -- that's all the government would allow for that fine parcel along the Red Run.

When I told Eliza what had happened, she tried to make me feel better by saying, "Maybe the price was cheap at that, Oliver...to me you're worth a lot more than thirty acres."

I don't know whether that made me feel better or worse. Then, to top it off, the war ended just a few short weeks later. In fact, by the time our eighth child was born, President Lincoln had already been assassinated and Andrew Johnson had taken over.

But I don't hold what happened to me against the new president. In fact, we named the baby after him. You can see right here in the family Bible where I wrote it down: Andrew Johnson Disney, born April 28th, 1865, Owings Mills, Maryland, United States of America.

I, myself, wasn't born in Owings Mills. Actually, I grew up at Hookstown. That's down around Coldspring Lane...down the Hookstown Pike toward the city. Wasn't city by a long shot when I was growing up there....nothing but farmland all the way north of Druid Hill, fields and barns stretched along either side of the pike.

But I could see that the city was going to come crowding in, so along about 1850 I saw my chance and bought this 100 acres of wooded land here in Owings Mills. You might be interested in hearing how I came by the money to buy the place. You see, when gold was discovered out there in California in 1848, lots of folks here in the East got what we called "gold fever" - up and sold everything they owned and went rushing off to the gold fields, thinking they were going to strike it rich.

Well, I've been a farmer all my life, and the only thing worthwhile I've ever seen come out of the ground is what's been planted in it, so I wasn't about to go running off like that. But I did see a way to make a tidy bit of money out of the situation. I'd buy up the farm equipment and household goods the 49ers were selling dirt cheap, fix the articles up a bit and end up getting a good price when I re-sold them. That's how it was I was able to save up enough cash to buy myself a farm.

Now, some folks probably thought I was crazy for buying land so far back off the main road. "Oliver," some of them said, "there's hardly a trail fit for a horse from the turnpike into your place -- how are you ever going to get to the store or to church?"

At times, even my good wife Eliza questioned the wisdom of giving up everything we'd known and moving to what was practically a wilderness. She worried especially about how a doctor would ever get to us if one of our children fell sick.

But, in spite of all that, I could see that the piece of land I'd bought had the makings of a fine farm. The soil was as rich and fertile as you could ask for and the meadows along the Red Run stream would be ideal for grazing dairy cattle. As for clearing the woods, well, I knew it meant work with endless felling of trees and dynamiting of stumps, but at least there'd be plenty of timber for building our house and barn.

Another thing I thought about - there's plenty of lime kilns nearby, like the one over on the old Lyon property by the Gwynn's Falls and others back on John Berryman's farm and on Solomon Choate's place in the Soldiers Delight. That meant it would be no problem to get burnt lime for sweetening the soil, and, at the same time, I'd be able to sell off any extra wood to the kilns.

82

My father and some other close relatives helped with clearing the land. As I'd foreseen, the dense woods provided plenty of substantial oak and chestnut timbers for building. We cut the smaller "lap wood" into cord lengths and hauled it down to Hookstown to sell for firewood. The brush and twigs we heaped into great piles and when they were sufficiently dry, we burned them.

But stumps were a problem. Even after the trees were cut, the stumps still stood so close together that you couldn't drive a wagon between them. And there was no easy way to get rid of them...it was either pull them out with the horses or blast them out with dynamite. But we did manage to make one good use of all those tree-stumps - we built our house right on top of them...used the stumps for a foundation. Some time later, a stone mason, Mr. C. Cornelius Hopkins, took up residence out on the lane that leads back to the Ritter farm - "Ritter's Lane," as they call it - and I engaged him to build us a stone wall under the house to support it better. He built a fine strong foundation, all the while humming "Scissors Won't You Cut?", a tune he hums so constantly it's become his trademark.

While I'm thinking about him, let me tell you a little bit more about Cornelius Hopkins. In addition to being a stone mason, he is also considered a pretty fair doctor and the salves and liniments he concocts are very much in demand. Occasionally, he's even called upon to set broken bones.

Besides that, Mr. Hopkins is a man who can bed himself down and sleep outdoors just like the scouts did back in colonial times. He told me once how he got caught in a blizzard and sat out the storm for an entire night. "Next morning my friends came looking for me, all the while fearing the worst since the night had been bitter cold," he said. "You can imagine how surprised they were when they found me digging snow from under my horse! The animal was only slightly frostbitten and I didn't even catch a cold." Cornelius credited his luck to the linement which he had soaked into his shoes to prevent frostbite.

Each spring, you'll find Cornelius wandering about the hedgerows, budding or grafting seedlings that he thinks are growing in a favorable spot to become full-grown trees. Fifty or a hundred years from now, I daresay, many a person will stop to rest in the shade for a moment without ever realizing they're beneath one of the trees he started.

Be that as it may, Cornelius Hopkins strengthened our foundation wall with stone, although our house never has had a cellar. But cellar or no, our house is a fine one. Eight rooms, it's got. "Salt-box" style, they call it, like the New England houses with a roof that peaks high in the front and dips low in the rear. Sits right on top of a nice high hill overlooking the Red Run. As you can probably tell, I'm right proud of that house and expect it to serve us well for many a year.

Soon as the house and a few of the outbuildings were finished, we moved in, although Eliza said she felt like she was going into the wilderness and might never come out again. I have to admit the dirt trail that worms its way through the woods from the tollgate on the turnpike is nothing to brag about - full of ruts and mud-holes, sassafras bushes and blackberry brambles growing so thick on either side, you're lucky to make your way through without the horses getting scratched up.

And I can't deny it's been back-breaking work to farm these hillsides and drain some of the swampier meadowlands. Often all our work of clearing the hillsides goes for nothing when the spring rains come and tons of rich topsoil get carried off down the Red Run or deposited in the meadows below.

When we first moved to what Eliza still refers to as "our wilderness", the children wanted to know where all the neighbors were. I had to tell them there weren't any. In fact, we lived in the woods for several weeks beiore we ever saw a single living soul and long as we lived there, it never did become an easy matter to visit back and forth.

Eliza has missed being close to the city something fierce. "Even if we go out to the turnpike there's not all that much out there," she complains.

I must say she is right. Of course there is Joseph Benanzar's blacksmith shop and another smithy run by John King. I'd say John Harmon's store has a fair line of general merchandise...you can buy anything there from a horse-collar or a plow-share to a tea-kettle or a piece of calico for making an apron. And then there's the mills -- Groff's grist mill and the mill down at the Painter farm which used to be known as Ulm when the Owings family still owned it.

And speaking of Painter's mill, they had quite a nasty accident down there not too long ago. Fellow name of Morningstar is managing the mill for the Painter family now, and he hired this new fellow named Jim Cowan. Seems Cowan didn't know too much about mill operations or else didn't have sense enough to stay out of the way of that powerful machinery. Anyhow, he managed to get himself caught by one of the main shafts that was spinning at a right good rate. The thing carried him round and round until his coat gave way and he was flung clear across the mill. They say he broke a leg and an arm and a couple of his ribs in the bargain, but that he's got a good chance of recovering.

Anyhow, like I was saying, Owings Mills isn't altogether the way Eliza sees it. Up and down the turnpike there are a number of inns and taverns -- there's Conn's or the Twelve Mile House down near the Gwynns Falls and halfway up Pleasant Hill there's the Octagon House which some folks call the "Eight-Square House", not to mention the Ten Mile House down by Cradock's and the Fifteen Mile House up at Delight. Still, all in all, I suppose it's reasonably accurate to say Owings Mills is a pretty quiet little town.

Eliza's right, too, when she complains that it's no easy matter traveling the two or three miles from our place out to the mills. It would be a help if there were bridges over the Red Run. As it is, we have to depend on poles and felled logs laid across the stream for going on foot. For horses and wagons, it's a wet splash through the water, with slippery rocks to make the footing doubly treacherous. A broken axle or a wagon turned over is nothing unusual, and it's not un-heard of for a horse to break its leg and have to be shot. So you can see why a trip to the general store or to the doctor's or to the Morrow Chapel, as they call the new Methodist church at Pleasant Hill, isn't something we undertake lightly.

Of course the government doesn't give a fig for us farmers. "You want to use the roads, you'll have to maintain them yourselves," is their attitude. Only one consideration do they show us - those of us who haul stones for the turnpike roadbed get excused from paying the tolls. Every spring we fill wooden sledges - "drags", we call them - with stones we pick from our fields, and haul them off to be dumped into the larger mudholes and boggy spots. It takes plenty of muscle to break up the larger stones with heavy mauls and sledge hammers. We also have to shovel earth from the roadside banks over the rougher stones so the horses' hooves will have some protection.

In winter when the blizzards come, it's sometimes a week or more till we can shovel our way out. That's my snow-plow sitting out there in the shed...that V-shaped box made out of planks. Before we start plowing snow, we pile the inside of the box high with stones for weight. The heavy cable that's passed through the holes on each side of the planks has the end twisted together and hammered into a tight knot so we can hook onto a single-tree or double-tree, depending on how many horses it's going to take for digging out.

Yes, life along the Red run is hard, but in spite of all that, I believe I chose the ideal spot for my farm and my family. My dairy herd's got good fresh running water from the stream and all the meadow grass they need for grazing and nice big sycamores to shade under, to boot. Richest soil in Baltimore county, they say...a person can just sit here on the porch and watch the corn and wheat and barley and hay flourishing on those hillsides. Those woods over across the way are full of hundred-year-old oaks and chestnuts and hickorys...more timber than a person could use in a lifetime.

And where else could a person put meat on the table with so little effort? Just peek into Eliza's cooking pots and chances are you'll find deer or rabbit or squirrel meat simmering away. Look on our table and you'll see a huge platter of quail or pheasant. At night when thousands of passenger pigeons roost over yonder in those thick sassafras groves, you can practically go out and knock them off the branches with a broom. Then there's the stream to provide fish and frogs and the snapping turtles Eliza makes into the best soup you ever set your spoon to.

Want blackberries or dewberries or wineberries or huckleberries? -- all we have to do is hike a mile or so west to the Soldiers Delight and fill our pails and buckets. For apples and pears and cherries and peaches and such, we've got a fine orchard started over there on that north slope.

In winter, we farmers set our traps along the streambed and add a few dollars to our income by selling the pelts of muskrats, minks and raccoons and the foxes that live up in those rocky outcroppings along the stream.

I'm proud to say, too, that our family has grown and prospered since we moved to Owings Mills. Our seventh child was born about the time of the Battle of Gettysburg and since we wanted to show clearly which side our loyalties were on - not all the Disneys were for the Union side, a fact that has caused a great deal of hard feelings within the family - we named him "George Washington Disney" after our nation's founding father.

Speaking of the war, I must say I'm just as happy we never saw any actual fighting here in Owings Mills. They say it was something fierce up there around Gettysburg and Antietam.

Of course the war didn't entirely pass us by -- in 1863 and 1864 bands of Reb soldiers came sweeping through here, scouring around for whatever they could get to eat and for fresh horses to replace their tired-out mounts. We farmers especially feared to see the Confederate troops come, knowing they lived off the land and didn't care whose livestock they confiscated. In 1863, a bunch came through our place and butchered one of our cows and killed all the geese and chickens they could catch. And there was nothing I could do but bite my tongue and hope they didn't take a mind to burn down my buildings.

But we made sure those Johnny Rebs didn't get their hands on our horses. When we heard the Confederate raiders were on the way, a bunch of us - Mr. Lockard who lives across the way...Alfred Lowe...myself...several others - we all got together and fixed up a hiding place for our horses. We put up this corral along the upper branch of the Red Run...up there in that dense part of Lowe's woods we call "Egypt". When the soldiers got too close for comfort, we would walk our horses up there.

Those Rebs were smart, though, especially that Confederate Colonel, Harry Gilmore. When Gilmore suspected horses were being hidden, he'd ride a stallion into the vicinity, trying to get the mares excited so they'd give away their location. But we farmers weren't so stupid, either - we took the precaution of tethering the mares with their heads tied low so they couldn't raise up to whinny.

We were extra cautious at feeding-time, too, and we took turns keeping lookout with our guns loaded and ready to use. This one time Harry Gilmore rode so close to where our horses were hidden that I could have gotten off a shot at him easy as knocking a squirrel off a branch. I thought better of it, though - I decided my horses were worth more to me alive than Harry Gilmore would be dead.

Besides, to have killed Gilmore would have created a lot of hard feelings here in Owings Mills. I can tell you for a fact that there are plenty - especially among the ladies - who look on him as a hero. One time Gilmore was courting a young lady who lived up at "Cedarmere House", which stands close to the turnpike just south of the Fifteen Mile House Tavern. A bunch of Union soldiers staked out the house and sat out there by the turnpike all night, thinking they had him surrounded. It wasn't until morning they found out he'd slipped out through a passageway from the house to the dairy and was already as far away as Liberty Road. It was stunts like that that made even those who don't agree with the Confederate side think of him as kind of a dashing scoundrel.

Speaking of Harry Gilmore, I guess nobody in Owings Mills is likely to forget how on July 11th of '64, Gilmore sent Captain Nicholas Owings to escort a bunch of prisoners - Union Major General William B. Franklin and several of his staff - to the Oliver farm down there west of the Cradock estate for safekeeping. But by the time Gilmore and the rest of his troop got there, Owings's men had fallen asleep and the prisoners had escaped. You should have seen those Rebs beating the woods and bushes trying to find them.

An even funnier sight was when a bunch of Confederate soldiers under command of General Bradley T. Johnson passed through on the Reisterstown Turnpike. They came to the old Samuel Owings farm which has been sold a half-dozen or so times in recent years and is now owned by William Painter. Painter's dairy herd produces a lot more cream than he has use for, so he's turned one of the buildings on the place into an ice-cream factory. After the ice-cream's made, they ship it by railroad down to Baltimore where the Painters have a store on Charles Street. Well, those Rebs spotted these big containers of ice-cream sitting on a railroad flat-car, and they figured they'd sample the stuff. Funny thing, though, some of those West Virginia mountain boys had never seen ice-cream before. They called it "frozen milk-mush", and when they couldn't figure out what to do with it they just waited till it melted and poured it into their canteens.

Over on Chestnut Ridge at Caves Road and Greenspring Avenue, George Scott was flying the Union flag, and when he heard the Rebs were coming through, he spiked the lower six or eight feet of the pole figuring the Confederates wouldn't be able to cut it down. But when a Confederate officer gave Mr. Scott the choice of either taking it down or having his house and barn burned, it didn't take Mr. Scott too long to figure out that it would be easier to get a new flag than to replace his buildings.

Now that the war's over, things are changing fast around here...too fast, some of us think. Take the railroad line. Ever since back in '32 that little old Greenspring line has came out past the Chattolanee Springs, crossed the turnpike and stopped dead at what they call Kirk Station, right in the middle of that big empty field south of the Painter farm. Never was much of a railroad - a mud roadbed...wooden rails...horse-drawn carriages at first...then this little engine they brought from England. Finally, the line got to be in such terrible condition that the locomotives couldn't run in winter and then the track got so bad they were afraid to run the engines over it at all. Only ran horse cars and that only in the summer so city folks could come out to the Chattolanee Hotel and the fancy new summering place they call "The Greenspring Hotel".

Anyhow, right before the war, the railroad directors hired an engineer, George Worcester, to survey the line. He said that in his opinion that the line ought to be put on through at least as far as New Windsor as it would draw freight from the flour mills at Owings Mills, the chrome mines in Soldiers Delight, the bark mills and the tanneries at Finksburg as well as the iron mines, mills and quarries at Westminster. In fact, he predicted that if the railway was extended clear through to Washington County it would handle each year about 400,000 barrels of flour, 200,000 of corn, 6,000 of whiskey and 10,000 fattened hogs.

They started putting the line on through in about 1857, after the Baltimore and Susquehanna sold the line to the Western Maryland Railroad Company. Like practically everybody else in Owings Mills, I was there the day the foreman, Henry Waters, and his construction gang took up their picks and shovels and broke ground down by the

Kirk station. Actually, they had two gangs of men working – one of them between Groff's mills and Reisterstown and one between Union Bridge and New Windsor. By the end of '58 there were seventy men working on grading for the railroad. At Reisterstown, they set up a steam sawmill for cutting the seven-foot chestnut and oak crossties. The iron for the tracks they shipped over from England.

In the meantime, the horse cars from Relay House to Owings Mills were discontinued while they rebuilt the entire line over that old mudbed from Owings Mills clear back to Relay House on Swan Lake, some ten miles altogether. Finally, by late summer of '59 that part of the railroad was ready to re-open. They had this big celebration on the day the first trains ran –- August 11th, it was. We all went out to the mills to see the special train carrying 150 guests that came out to where the tracks ended at Reisterstown Road. The passengers got off there and marched to the Eagle House for refreshments and then they were taken back to the Greenspring Hotel where they say they had quite a lay-out with soup and fish and roasts and all kinds of vegetables and fruits and pastries along with ice cream not to mention plenty of champagne and brandy.

By December of that year, the line was open to Reisterstown and trains were operating regularly twice a day each way. In '61, the line opened all the way to Westminster. Of course, there were some who didn't think too highly of the railroad service and called the Western Maryland a "one-horse concern". They started complaining right off the bat that half the time the mail for Westminster got thrown off in Finksburg...that the track was too often closed for repairs...that engines ran off the rails...that the trains didn't run on schedule. Already there have been several people struck by the train and either hurt or killed. Not too long after the line opened, James Schaffer, the baggage-master at Owings Mills was uncoupling some cars when they moved and caught him between them. Another fraction of an inch and he could have been crippled for life. The *American Sentinel* newspaper published a big article about it and said that there was bad management that needed correction at once.

Of course, to people like us, the railroad seems like a kind of miracle. Lots of times when we've got business out at the mills, we just wait around till train time so we can watch the engines go by. Everybody in Owings Mills knows those first two engines they put on the line by sight – "The Canary" and "The Greenspring." Nowadays, they've got a bunch of new engines and my boys can call off their names – the "Maryland", the "Patapsco", the "Pipe Creek" and the "Monocacy" – just by the sound of their whistles as they come down the track.

Most of us have gotten to know by sight the chief engineer, William Morgan, who used to be on the B&O line out of Baltimore. During the war, a bunch of Baltimoreans who wanted to join up with the Confederates came out to Owings Mills and captured Morgan and the Canary. One of them stood right there with a gun pointed at Morgan's head and they forced him to take them to the end of the line near Westminster.

During the Battle of Gettysburg, the government took military possession of the road for five days and used it as a supply line for

General Meade's troops. They brought in locomotives and cars and fuel and operators from down in Virginia. From here to Westminster there was practically a continuous line of cars carrying troops and supplies. Up in Westminster they set up a hospital to take care of all the wounded they carried back down there. After the battle you could stand by the tracks and watch these cars full of wounded Confederate prisoners being hauled back to Baltimore.

The railroad was used to haul the dead, too. On the morning of July 2nd in '63, we saw the train with the body of Major General John F. Reynolds and his honor guard pass through Owings Mills. The next day, fourteen wounded Union soldiers who had walked all the way from Gettysburg to Westminster rode through on their way down to Baltimore.

After the war, they took the old Canary off the line...just kept her around to fill in when needed for special excursions. Last I heard, she was being used for a trip some folks took to Westminster to see the circus. That was the same night Lincoln was assassinated. I don't know what happened to the Canary after that.

Come to think of it, I don't know what's happened to Harry Gilmore, either.

One thing I do know, though – that was my thirty acres the government took away from me and I'm not likely to forget it!

# CHAPTER 14

## 1880: Beholden To No Man

*The Soldiers Delight barrens, lying along the western borders of Owings Mills and extending to meet the eastern borders of Harrisonville and Randallstown, were never settled in the sense that other lands in the area were put under cultivation or developed for homes and businesses. The area's geological structure – now known to be the dome of an extinct volcano – made it inhospitable to farming; the rocks that lay only inches below its sparse topsoil made it difficult to either put in a foundation for a house or to dig a well.*

*There were, however, a few hardy and independent souls who established their homes in what remains, to this day, largely a wilderness area. In an essay read before the Historical Society of Maryland in 1881, Edward Spencer described the early settlers of Soldiers Delight as "...a very different class irom the slave-holders and tobacco-growers who settled the fertile valleys. They were somewhat rude, independent, simple-mannered, fond of keeping their own counsel, plain and old-iashioned in dress. Taken altogether, they were the most primitive people within fifty miles of Baltimore."*

*Abner Baker is a descendant of those early settlers. He lives upon a portion of the land known as "Ford's Range" and displays many of the unique characteristics developed by those who chose to make their homes in the seemingly inhospitabie barrens.*

*-/-/-/-*

You might have heard the old saying they've got about us folk who live in the Soldiers Delight -- that we only come out to town once a year to vote and it takes us until Christmas to find our way home again? Well, that might not be too far from the truth.

Actually, it's always been considered so little of an honor to say you lived in the barrens that most people, when asked, claim they live "just on the edge". That goes back to when the first settlers came and if they had a mite of sense they took up the good farmland outside the barrens. Like Joshua Owings who settled over there to the west of the road that leads to the Lyons's mill - built that big house they call "Harmony Hall"...where his son-in-law, Thomas Worthington, lives now.

Now me, I was born right here in the very log house you're sitting in. I won't say this place is anything fancy, but I can tell you this – my granddaddy built it with his own hands and it's still standing.

Some folks think this is no fit place to live, but it suits me right well. Anytime I got the appetite for a squirrel pot-pie or for a few quail on the table, I don't need to go more than twenty yards outside my back door to find more game than any one family could use.

Come nighttime, we got thousands of passenger pigeons roosting out there in those scrub oaks. Lots of time boys come over from Owings Mills and just beat them out of the trees with clubs. Next morning we go out and find the ground covered with birds they didn't even bother to take with them. I usually gather up the dead birds and feed them to the hogs.

Want to know the first thing the Soldiers Delight was ever famous for? Well, I'll tell you – they went and hung a fellow here.

That's right – hung him and left his body swinging from the scaffold 'til the buzzards ate his flesh and his bones rattled in the breeze. No, I wasn't there to see it...happened well before my time, back in 1751. But I can show you the exact spot. Berry's Hill, we call it. Right over there off the Ward's Chapel Road.

Back then, this family named Clarke lived on the place they call nowadays the "Bailey Farm". There was the husband, the wife, a step-son, John Berry – usually called him "Jack" – and two indentured servants named Mary Powell and Martha Bassett.

They say the farm originally belonged to John Berry's real father – the man his mother was married to before she married Clarke. Then, it seems, Berry's mother died and Clarke married a Miss Wheatley, so it ended up that neither the husband nor the wife of the couple that now had possession of the farm was Jack Berry's natural parent.

The way I've heard it told, it was gnawing away at Jack Berry that the farm he felt ought rightly to be his had passed into the hands of his step-parents, folks that was no blood kin to him. However the right of it might be, on a November morning in the year 1751, Clarke and his wife were attacked whilst they were asleep in their bed...their heads all cut and gashed in a fearful manner.

One of the servant girls ran screaming for help to the next farm where Mordecai Gosnell lived. Gosnell, who was a Baltimore County deputy sheriff, had a look at the bodies and announced that Mrs. Clarke was deader than a stone, but said that he could still hear a faint heartbeat in Mr. Clarke's chest. Jack Berry was sent to hotfoot it off to Baltimore, some sixteen miles distant, to fetch the doctor.

As the story has it, Jack was in no hurry to get to town...made a few stops at taverns along the way. Actually, it must have been more than a few stops, because he got so drunk he didn't come back home for several days.

The next part of the story varies a bit depending on who's telling it. Some say that Mr. Clarke pulled through all right, while others claim that both of Berry's step-parents died. I tend to favor the latter version, since, if Mr. Clarke had lived, he would likely have been able to tell who it was that went after him and his wife with the axe.

As it was, they had to call in a coroner's jury. Now back in those days, wasn't more than a handful of people living in the Soldiers

92

Delight and only eleven men could be found. Finally, the Reverend Thomas Cradock, who was, at that time, rector of Saint Thomas Church, some five miles away, said he would ride over and serve as the twelfth juryman.

Well, the jury started looking into things and right off suspicion fell on the two servant girls. Neighbors testified that Mary Powell was wild and wayward, while the other, Martha Bassett, was a bit muddle-headed. Whether that was so or not, who can say?...you know how folks like to embroider the truth when something big's going on.

Anyhow, maybe Martha Bassett's brain wasn't as sharp as it might have been. Chances are, the poor befuddled thing didn't even understand the consequences when she broke down and admitted that, while she and Mary Powell had done the killing, it was Jack Berry who had set the whole scheme up.

Berry's plan itself was simple. Or simple-minded, depending on how you look at it. Martha was to whack the pair with an axe while Mary Powell held a candle for her to see by, and all the while Jack would claim he was out coon-hunting with some friends.

When the jury asked Martha why she went along with this scheme, she told them that Mrs. Clarke had gone back on her promise to give her and Mary their freedom. As for Jack Berry, the two girls' testimony made it plain he had schemed up the murder to get a-holt of the property he considered to be rightfully his.

By the time Jack Berry got back from Baltimore, the servant women had spilled the beans. He was arrested and the three of them sent to jail to await their trial.

Their case came up at Joppatown that December, and, throughout the whole rigamarole, Jack Berry refused to say he was guilty. "I didn't want to wake up the household when I came in from hunting," he told the court, "so I just threw myself down on the cot in the kitchen and went to sleep." Berry declared he never woke up till he heard somebody yelling "Murder!" He also claimed that Martha's testimony wasn't worth a plugged nickel...that she didn't have wits enough to know what she was talking about and that it was his opinion that somebody had broken into the house to rob it and then when the Clarkes woke up and caught them at it, they added murder to their other crime.

Berry's story didn't carry water with the jury. They wasted little time finding him guilty and the two women as well.

The judge sentenced Mary Powell and Martha Bassett to be hanged at Joppatowne on the 10th of the following January. Then he called Berry to the bench and pronounced, "John Berry, because your crime has been such a dastardly one and because it led not only to the deaths of those two persons who were your parents but also to the downfall of two ignorant servant girls, I sentence you to be hanged at the highest point from which the scene of your crime can be viewed and order that your body shall remain there hanging in chains until it rots."

And that's how it was. They put up this high scaffold on top of that hill over by Ward's Chapel Road and hung John Berry and left his body dangling there until his bones rattled with every wind that blew across the barrens. Finally, even the scaffold itself rotted and fell to the ground.

I'm not saying it's so or not so, but there's many a person here in Soldiers Delight that will tell you there's funny things go on over at that hill...chains clanking and weird moans late at night. I do know one thing - whenever I've got to travel that way at night, I go the long way around.

Hearing all this, you might get the notion that the Soldiers Delight is some strange, spook-ridden sort of place. Actually you wouldn't be far wrong. At any rate, things do seem to happen different here from anyplace else.

Take even the name - no two people ever agree on why it's called "Soldiers Delight." There's those who claim that when the Englishman, Captain John Smith, sent his soldiers to scout out the land up around the headwaters of the Patapsco, they got lost in here. When they got back to their companies and went on and on about about the treacherous bramble thickets they could hardly make their way through, the other soldiers twitted them and said they must have been wandering around in "Soldiers' Delight".

Then there are those who say that soldiers from Fort Garrison had to patrol this section and when they found the hunting especially fine here, they called it "Soldiers' Delight".

Still others say that way back, a German immigrant by the name of Sollers got himself euchred by a land dealer in Baltimore. Fellow persuaded him that this place would be a lot like the hills near his home in Germany so he bought up 2,000 acres, sight unseen. Of course he soon found out the land wasn't worth a dime for farming...just thin, poor soil of cold clay. Not only that, you put a plow in the ground most anyplace and you'll strike rock just an inch or so below the surface. Sollers didn't give up easy, though, and he kept trying to raise crops on it. I guess it was his stubborness that started the farmers who owned the good, productive land nearby poking fun at him by calling the whole area "Sollers's Delight".

One of the more far-fetched local stories is that soldiers were camped out here during the Civil War and that some of the local young ladies came and brought them ice-cream to eat and that the men enjoyed the attention so much they started calling it "Soldiers' Delight". That one's just plain loony! - place was called Soldiers Delight long before Abraham Lincoln or Robert E. Lee either one was a pup!

Another thing nobody agrees on is exactly *where* Soldiers Delight *is*. You take the government, for instance. For years now we been asking them to set up a post office that would be handy for us. Well, they argued back and forth about it and finally last year they did give us one, but they wouldn't use the name "Soldiers Delight"...they just called it "Delight". Then, wouldn't you know, they went and stuck it clear out there on the Reisterstown Turnpike and appointed Charlie Griswold for postmaster.

I had it explained to me once why it is folks are so unclear about where the Soldiers Delight is located. Seems that back in the days they were first laying out the boundaries of the Maryland Colony they divided each section into what they called "hundreds", a hundred being the amount of land that had on it one hundred families. Soldiers

Delight Hundred was the name they gave to an enormous stretch of land beginning at the Patapsco River near Elkridge Landing and following Old Court Road east to Joppatown and from there northwest to the Pennsylvania border and south to the Potomac River. It took in a good portion of Carroll County, parts of Baltimore County and ran clear over into Frederick and Howard Counties. Which goes to show you how few people there were living hereabouts back in those times.

Later on they started carving Carroll County and Frederick County and all different places out of the Soldiers Delight Hundred till, by now, it's shrunk down so that there's only a couple of thousand acres that goes by that name any more. What folks who live here mean when we say "Soldiers Delight" is the barrens that stretches from the main headwaters of the Red Run just about over to Ward's Chapel Church. It lies along both sides of the western end of the Dolfield Road and both sides of the Deer Park Road from Dolfield north to Berryman's Lane and westward along the Ward's Chapel Road almost to Liberty Road.

But you don't need no map to tell when you're in the barrens. No place else I know of you'll find mile after mile of scrub oak and moss and sedge grass. You ever seen a piece of rock that's red and looks like a honeycomb? Or grass that smells like vanilla? Or a little fringed flower the same shade of blue as an October sky? We got all those things. Not to mention the loudest whippoorwills you ever heard and practically every kind of bird and bat and snake and lizard that there is.

Up by Oakland Mills...up there on that little fork of the north branch...the Ware family has got this flint mill where they take the quartz rock folks from the farms hereabouts haul in and grind it for flint. I recollect that the Wares hired Henry Connery to make the water wheel for that mill. Now Henry's a good carpenter, but slow! why Christmas has come and gone before he's halfway through December! So here's the Wares, wanting to get the mill started up soon as possible, and here's Henry, cutting out this part and that part, particular about it as an old maid schoolmarm. Finally, the Wares figured they couldn't wait any longer and they hired this other fellow to get the job done. But, as it turned out, the new fellow couldn't begin to figure out how the thing went together and they had to hire Henry back in the end.

I tell you, though, I'd rather be carpentering like Henry than working in the Wares's mill. From what I've heard, everybody that works there ends up with flint lung from the stone dust.

Speaking of rocks, this geologist fellow came through once...said he was making a survey of the area. He told me these barrens got the way they are because they're sitting right over top of an old volcano. I asked him were it likely we was going to blow up one of these days, but he said he didn't think so...that the volcano had been dead a long, long time. He told me, too, that underneath this grayish-green rock you find cropping out all over - "serpentine" he said they call it, same kind of rock they used when they built that new Mount Vernon Place Methodist Church down in Baltimore - he said that under that rock you'll find huge beds of iron chromate. I can believe that, because when folks ride horseback over the trails through here, you can hear this metallic kind of ring from their horses hooves...sort of like when a blacksmith pounds iron out on his anvil. And down in the mines, you can see the different layers...first the green serpentine and then the red iron and the black of the chrome running in layers.

I didn't tell you about the mines? Don't see how I could have over-looked that! Fact is, if that Tyson fellow hadn't come along and found chrome ore in the barrens, there'd still be only a handful of people ever heard of this place, let alone lived here.

For over fifty years they've been digging it out of the mines back here - the main ones being the Choate mine, the Ware mine and the Harris mine. I recollect how right after the War Between the States these barrels were piled all up and down Reisterstown Road and from one end of Owings Mills station platform to the other. When you con-sider that each barrel holds 400 pounds of chrome ore, you can see what a big operation the mines are.

Back here along the Deer Park Road and the Ward's Chapel Road you'll find these big mine pits. Lately, though, they've been having a heap of trouble with the mines filling up with water after they dig down so deep. They're always having to rig up pumps to clear them out and a few of the pits they've just plain had to abandon.

But there's still plenty of chrome to be had. I daresay there ain't a stream hereabouts that don't have its own buddle for taking out the chrome sand. Main one is the Triplett Buddle down there below Wards Chapel Road. That's the place most people haul their ore to have it washed. Tripletts been working in that stream ever since I can remember. Pretty little place it is, a little grove of box oaks and the grass so green you just want to lay down and roll in it. Mr. Triplett says it's getting so now most of the best chrome has been taken out and it's a lot harder to fill a barrel than it was twenty, thirty years ago.

Tripletts haul their chrome out to the railroad siding at Owings Mills. Then, when there's enough for a carload, the Triplett boys all go over to push the heavy barrels up onto the skids and into the box cars. I went with them a couple of times and the worst of it is, the railroad's built up high there, so loading's no easy job. But at least with all that hard work we had a plenty good excuse for stopping off on the way home at the tavern on the old David Slade place that Daniel Lutz just bought.

Lots of the folks living here in the Soldiers Delight work in the mines. Some of 'em are Catholic and so's Missus Betz Harker whose family owns the New Tavern out on the Liberty Turnpike. Since she found out some of the mine workers are Catholic, she's set about ar-ranging for some of the Jesuit priests from Woodstock College to come to the tavern and hold Sunday services for the miners and their families.

Speaking of churches, that's one of the few things we have got here in the Soldiers Delight. Besides the Wards Chapel up on the Liberty Turnpike, there's this old Presbyterian church Paran over the road that goes from the Lyons' mill over to Liberty Turnpike. That church got started way back in George Washington's time or even before. At first it was called "The Church of Soldiers Delight" but for the last forty or so years it's been known "Mount Paran."

Long about 1815, Mount Paran's congregation sort of dwindled away and the church stood empty for about fifteen years. Somebody was even using it for a sheep fold.

Like most other buildings hereabouts, the Mount Paran Church is built out of logs and right now the congregation is collecting money to raise the height of it and to cover the outside with weatherboarding and to put on a new roof. I understand they're also taking down the old crow's nest pulpit and the box choir and building a gallery across the back of the church. Being Calvinists like they are, folks at Mount Paran don't hold with the idea of an "altar" but call theirs the "communion table". They don't tolerate any cross or candlestick, neither, which is something even the Methodists will allow.

Speaking of the Methodists, we just got ourselves a new Methodist Church right here in the Soldiers Delight. Out along Deer Park Road. Up till recently, that congregation's been meeting in different folks' homes. Fact is, their Sunday School classes was held all about - Finksburg...Oakland Mills...Owings Mills, in addition to various houses here in Soldiers Delight. But now Charles and Ann Griswold and Elias Stocksdale have donated a parcel of land facing on Deer Park Road so the church can have its own building. Some of the local farmers hauled in logs to put up the building and the bricks for the two chimneys on either side were made locally, too. The trustees they've appointed are all good local people - Washington Aler, Ephriam Triplett, Charles Griswold, Greenbury Cook, William Reed, George Stocksdale and Ernest Cook.

And over on the road leading from the Lyons's mill to the Liberty Turnpike you've got the Water's campground - that's where they hold the big Methodist camp meetings. Every summer thousands of people flock out there for the preaching and the singing and the sociability. Come by railroad or bring their wagons and set up tents and have themselves a grand old time. Dinner time you can smell the chicken frying half a mile away.

Me and my brother walked over there one Sunday afternoon this past summer. They were having what they call a "Sunday School Jubilee"...must have been at least a thousand young folks of all ages on hand. When them children all marched around the campground singing "We Are Marching To Zion", the line stretched for over half a mile. That afternoon, there was over 2,000 folks gathered in the grove to hear Professor Harry Sanders play the organ and to listen to the preaching. But what my brother and I remember best is the homemade peach ice cream they churned right there on the spot. Had two big dishes of it, myself, and would have gone back for a third if Henry hadn't poked me in the ribs and said these folks might think we people from Soldiers Delight don't have no proper manners.

Only part of the services over there at the campground I don't care for is the taking of the collection. I recall this one Sunday back in '67 we wandered over there and this preacher fellow stood up and told everybody to dig deep into their hearts and into their pockets because the rain earlier in the week had made the collections awful puny. Well, here was Henry and me with scarcely a dime between the two of us and some of those city folk were putting folding money in the plate! Would you believe! - when they got done counting, they announced that for Saturday and Sunday alone, they had taken in $217. Why a person could buy half of Soldiers Delight for that amount!

Folding money is something you don't see much of around here. Never did know anybody in the barrens to have more than fifty dollars between them and bankruptcy. You take the Fords - their farm has just lately been put up for public auction. Husband died and Mrs. Ford's got to sell off the place to pay off what was owed. A shame! The Ford's were hit bad when the hog cholera struck last fall. Over a hundred hogs died of it hereabouts and more than one farmer has found himself barely scraping by this season.

Folks here have got to be pretty tough - we ain't got no doctors close by...no firemen...no hospital. We did have this Doctor Ward but then one dark, rainy night he was going through the barrens on a house call and him and his horse fell into an open mine pit that was close by the road. Got pneumonia from spending the whole night in there, and a few days later he died.

But that's the way it is here. Folks got to look out for themselves because ain't nobody going to do it for them. Best way, my Pappy always told me, is to take care of your own wants and not to want what you can't have. That way, he said, you'll be beholden to no man.

Ford Homestead
The log structure of the Ford homestead was typical of houses in the Soldiers Delight area. Photo courtesy of Dorothy King.

# CHAPTER 15

## 1885: An Evening at Henry Fitch's

*From the earliest years of the Owings Mills community, inns and taverns for the accomodation of travelers were established along the turnpike. Since the only modes of travel were by foot, horseback, or horsedrawn vehicle and, since the poor condition of the thoroughfare made travel excruciatingly slow, Owings Mills, some twelve to fourteen miles from the heart of Baltimore City, was a frequent overnight stop for travelers journeying north to Pennsylvania or to the western territories by way of Pittsburgh as well as those traveling south to the city.*

*One of the early Owings Mills taverns was Conn's, located at the 12-mile stone on the Turnpike, almost exactly where the present-day Western Maryland overpass stretches across Reisterstown Road. Conn's Tavern appears on the 1803 tax list of the Soldiers Delight Hundred as being the property of William Owings, heir to Samuel Owings of Ulm. Later it was deeded to Peter Hoffman who married Samuel Owings's daughter, Deborah, and even later the inn became the property of their son, Samuel Owings Hoffman.*

*An inkeeper named Conn leased the premises for many years, then sold his business to Henry Fitch who continued to lease the building for a time before purchasing it in 1880. By that time, the inn had become a commodious hotel and tavern, offering rooms and food not only to the many travelers along the turnpike but also to those who reached Owings Mills by railroad. We join Henry Fitch as he sits on the front porch of his inn on a September afternoon of the year 1885.*

$$-/-/-/-$$

Well, they caught the scoundrel, at least! An Officer Beckley up there in Carroll County captured him with the goods still on him...Alice's gold watch, her chain, her bracelet, several of her rings and my money.

Oh, he was a cool customer, that Myers! Came in here from the railroad station that night and asked for a room...said he was on his way to Westminster and that he was stopping off to look at a piece of land that's for sale back along the Red Run. Then, next morning, he slipped into our room and cleaned out Alice's jewelry box and took the money I had hidden under my socks.

Came downstairs afterwards just as unconcerned as you please. Sat himself down to a breakfast of beefsteak and fried potatoes and sausage and hominy plus a couple of fried eggs and some cold apple pie with milk and sugar on it just like there wasn't a thing on his mind but the weather!

But Alice, now...she said all along there was something about him wasn't quite right. I thought that was just woman talk, but when I saw him go over to the station and hop on the train right after breakfast without ever bothering to look at any land...well, that's when I got suspicious myself. But it wasn't until we found the stuff missing that we put two and two together.

Only thing more brazen I've ever heard of was a couple of years ago when those horse thieves stole a horse and wagon and harness from Russell Brothers' stable up in Reisterstown and then had the gall to go down to George Shugars' barn and load up with wheat and oats. Drove right on down the turnpike with it. Tollgate keeper up the road here said they passed through about three in the morning and paid their toll just as cool as anything. Of course you can count on it that William Bleakly would be out there at that hour collecting his fee...not like some tollgate keepers who just leave their gates open and go on to bed after a certain hour.

That's the tollgate keeper's house you can see part-way up the hill there...the two-story house with the red tin roof setting close to the turnpike. When they decided to move the tollgate down here from Nicodemus Road, the tollgate commissioners bought an acre of ground from Mr. John R. Reese, the fellow who bought the big old Owings farm up on the hill. The front room is the gatekeeper's office, and, if you look close, you can see from here the long beam he swings down to block off the road. That box of stones nailed to one end is for balance...so the gate can be raised and lowered easily. At night you can sit right here on the porch and see the glow from the two big lanterns that light up the barrier.

There's one bad thing about that tollgate house - the stream runs right under it. Come high water, the whole first floor floods. Daniel Weaver was the first gatekeeper to live there and then after him, there was a German, Conrad Bork. John Logsden took over the job in '70 and his son Nimrod came after him. Nimrod was also a Baltimore County justice of the peace. Since 1880, Bill Bleakly has been the gatekeeper.

Of course, I don't want you to get the idea we've got crimes taking place every day here in Owings Mills. No...for the most part, this is a pretty quiet place. I've been running this hotel and tavern for quite a while now. Came down from Finksburg where I used to run a general store alongside the Western Maryland tracks. Actually, I got my start over near Mount Washington where I had a tavern and ran a stage-coach line from Riderwood to Towson for the convenience of passengers that rode the Northern Central. During the war, I was carrying on a business in Riderwood...had a blacksmith shop, a hotel and a store, all right close together.

I was taken right off with this spot, what with the train station being so handy. It's that three-story stone and frame building next door...over there to your left. Front of the building is the side facing up the hill toward the tracks. The station was built on part of the old Owings property that's now called "Five Oaks". They tell me the building was first used for a store house and then later part of it was made into the railroad station...that was back when Charles Painter owned it. When Mr. Painter died a couple of years ago, it was sold to settle his estate. His son, Milton Painter, bought it and he's kept on leasing it to the railway for a station.

Anyhow, like I was saying, I was real taken with this place. Used to ride past here on the railroad and admire this big, fine hotel with the porches all around and the nice roomy stables and plenty of space up there on the north side for wagons to pull in off the road, and I'd say to myself, "Henry, someday that place is going to be yours!"

Everybody that stops here says it's a right peaceful spot, what with that cluster of willows and the Gwynns Falls stream flowing by. They like the porches, too...a place where they can sit out of an afternoon and watch what's coming up and down the turnpike. I'd say this hotel is particularly fine in that respect, since it has porches on both the first and second floors and that iron grillwork that reminds a person of New Orleans. Summertime, with the ivy and Virginia creeper growing up along the grillwork, the porch stays nice and shady all day.

You'll notice my pigeon house I built along the south side of the stable. I keep close to a hundred birds now. Over there by the driveway is my martin house. The birds always come back each summer and they do a fine job of keeping the mosquitoes in check.

A right profitable location this has proven to be, too. Especially since the Western Maryland has turned that old Greenspring line back to the Baltimore and Susquehanna and put its own track through to Fulton Station instead of folks having to get off at the city line and take the horse-car tramway downtown. Work on the new direct line was slowed considerably by the builder's dawdling and by the epizootic that hit during the summer or '71, but they finally got it finished and a person can go straight on through now without transferring. The railroad company has also spruced up the old Painters Store a good bit...made it into a regular station with a telegraph office and everything.

We've got four locals and one express that stops here on weekdays and two locals on Sundays. Now that they've changed over to standard time, it's a lot easier for people to cipher out the schedules. Used to be the trains left Baltimore on Baltimore time but then at other places along the line they went by Philadelphia time till nobody could figure out what was going on.

Since the railroad company has built that fine resort up there at PenMar, a person can get on the train here in the mornings and by afternoon be rocking on a hotel porch up there at Blue Ridge Summit. They've put on a new engine expressly for the PenMar run...one that can haul eight coaches at a time up over the mountains.

The president of the Western Maryland, Mr. John Mifflin Hood is doing everything he can to get more regular commuters. He's announced that the railroad will transport building materials at half rate for anybody that settles along the railroad line between Baltimore and Glyndon. Besides that, he's offering to give the head of the family free transportation to the city for one year for each $1,000 he invests in his house. Of course, they set a five year limit so those that put over $5,000 in their properties wouldn't be riding free forever.

Actually, a year's commuting doesn't amount to all that much in cash...only about $14.40. The fare for a round-trip ticket from Baltimore to Owings Mills is only forty-five cents and a commuter ticket good for a whole month sells for $1.20. Or a person can buy a nine dollar commutation ticket that's good for thirty single trips for everybody in the family including servants.

I guess that family commuter ticket is what Alex Dolfield travels on - I see him and his wife and the cook and the maid all get off the train here on Fridays. Fellow that farms Mr. Dolfield's big estate back there on what they now call Dolfield Road...back along the Red Run opposite Oliver Disney's place...he meets the whole bunch of them at the station with a buggy or a coach.

From June through August, though, the Dolfield family stays right here in Owings Mills...makes it their summer home. I can tell you everybody on the station platform turns their head when Mr. Dolfield drives up to catch the morning train into the city, his man holding the reins of that high-stepping stallion and him smoking these big expensive cigars and wearing these suits with gray pin-stripes just like you'd expect a big-city banker to do. Same when Captain John Sherwood - he's the one that runs the Old Bay Line steamship line out of Baltimore - same when he comes driving out from his summer place back there next to the Dolfield's place.

Can't say as I blame the Dolfields for wanting to get away from the heat and dirt in Baltimore, not to mention the disease epidemics that always seem to be going around the city during the hot months. The railroad brings a lot of city people out to Owings Mills for the summer...boarding houses around here are always filled up in July and August. Besides my hotel, there's Mrs. Pollett over at Ulm... she takes in up to nine boarders at a time. Mrs. John Marshall up by Pleasant Hill takes in boarders as does Mrs. Phil Tilyard up at Denewood. Across the way there, Mrs. Fannie Harmon runs what she calls "The Poplars" for summer boarders.

Trouble is, having the railroad this handy makes it too easy for hoodlums and con men to light here. You take this fellow came through a few months ago selling White Washing Machines -- offers a brand-new machine dirt cheap. "Just sign these papers," the fellow tells the housewives, "and you can throw away your scrub-board for good!" What they don't find out until later is that they've gone and signed a promissory note. By the time they do get wise, the fellow has skipped town and sold off the notes to some broker, so there's nothing the victims can do but pay up.

Another swindle that's been worked hereabouts is selling lightning rods. Guess you can't blame folks for being nervous about lightning, seeing how often a barn or house burns down after being struck. Only trouble is, these salesmen talk a good deal, but then when they get their "down payment" that's the last a person ever sees of them. Same thing with windmills which a lot of folks hereabouts depend on to pump their water. This bunch goes around peddling windmills and they'll tell a farmer that if he gets three of his neighbors to buy one, he'll get the money back he paid for his windmill. Of course none of them's ever yet seen that refund.

Some folks will fall for anything. Like ever so often you hear a rumor that gold's been discovered in Owings Mills. They even printed it in the Union News as a fact. Now I do know there's been a couple of fools prospecting and digging holes near where the Methodist camp meetings were held till they opened up Emory Grove...over on that hill just this side of the old Waters place. They call it "Gold Hill", but if you ask my opinion, all they're likely to get for their efforts is a batch of blisters and a sore back.

Of course, not all the scalawags come through Owings Mills by railroad. There's the turnpike, too, and here at the inn we do get some rowdies now and then...no denying that. You take the drovers and wagoneers coming back from long hauls, they're usually ready to cut loose a bit. That's one reason they had to pass that new Baltimore County ordinance limiting the speed for wagons to 15 miles an hour. Those wagoneers would pull in here and after they'd got a few drinks in them, first thing you know one would be challenging the other that he could beat him to the Ten Mile House or down to Tobin's store.

Oh, we do have an occasional bit of excitement around Owings Mills! A couple of years back the Sears home, "Cedarmere", was burglarized...that's the place they say Harry Gilmore got out through some secret passage when he came through here with his rebel troops. And I heard recently that a thief broke into Henry Cronhardt's meat house over on the Chestnut Ridge and took off with two big hams and thirty pounds of pudding along with some soup beans and corn meal.

And then there's always accidents along the railroad. A few years back this young lady from up around Trenton that they said had had a sunstroke wandered onto the tracks right above the inn here and got run over by the east-bound five-o'clock train. They brought her into the Harman's place and called a doctor to have a look at her. Had her left arm cut off above the elbow but they say she's going to be all right.

Now I don't want you to get the idea folks around Owings Mills are a bunch of rubes and ignoramuses. We've got some fine productive farms around here. Why, a person would hardly believe that a little over a hundred years ago there were nothing but Indians running around here. And speaking of that, I saw by a piece in the *Union News* some time back that these fellows were digging for a house foundation over in the Green Spring Valley and what should they come upon but a bunch of old Indian graves. Paper said they were probably Susquehannas...that the whole area was infested with them at one time. I know that's a fact because my wife's grandmother used to always tell how when she was a girl the men carried their guns with them right into church in case the Indians should come.

They say once the settlers came, the Susquehannas got dependent on trading with the white men and forgot how to fight. Then the Senecas came and pushed them down into Southern Maryland and the government had to give them some land to live on -- stuck them in Zekiah Swamp near Laplata. People down there started complaining, so just this past year they rounded them all up and marched them up to Carlisle where there's another reservation. They came through here on the way to Pennsylvania...camped right in that stone quarry up on the west side of the Turnpike...about half-way between the railroad and Pleasant Hill Road. A sorry-looking bunch they were, too. Funny to think anybody could ever be afraid of them.

Anyhow, like I was saying, it's all farmland here now. You take that big place up there on the hill...the one I pointed out to you a while back - that belongs to Mister John B. Reese and I daresay you won't find a better-run, more productive farm in this part of the county.

Reese Farmhouse

Another Owings residence became the home of John B. Reese, a prominent local farmer. The house still stands just west of Reistertown Road in the community known as Tollgate. Photo courtesy of Somerset Waters.

Like a lot of others hereabouts, Mister Reese comes from good German stock - or what we call Pennsylvania Dutch - on his mother's side at least, although I believe his father was Welsh.

Anyhow, he was born up at Westminster in Carroll County and after he married his cousin, Elizabeth Roop, the two of them moved down here to Owings Mills.

That was back in about 1850. Mr. Reese first bought a parcel off the old Sam Owings farm from David Lightner...176 acres that was and it includes the big brick house you're looking at and most of the farm buildings. A couple of years later, Mister Reese bought another hundred or so acres off the Owings farm from Edmund Addison. They say there's a cloud on John Reese's title to his land...seems the Owings heirs never did come to any agreement about the way William Owings divided things up after old Sam died.

Anyhow, like I was saying, Mr. Reese is a good, thrifty farmer. Most of his land that lays along the Gwynns Falls is in pasture and the rest he has planted in grain crops and forage. Runs a little sorghum mill where other farmers can bring their sorghum to be crushed and keeps a little general store in his house where he supplies his neighbors with eggs and butter from the farm along with sugar and salt and a few other staples. Raising a fine family, too, Mr. Reese is. There's Charlie and Francis and Mary and young John B.

Yessir...good farmers, the Reeses. You can tell by their fine livestock and the pride they take in keeping their harnesses and farm equipment just so. I'd say practically every big farm in the area is now owned or run by Germans or Pennsylvania Dutchmen. Back along the Red Run there's the Zimmers and the Roses and over on Gwynbrook Lane and over toward Chestnut Ridge there's the Mosers and the Schmidts and the Baublitzes and the Uhlers just to mention a few. Come Shrove Tuesday, you can smell the fastnachts cooking from one end of Owings Mills to the other.

The Reeses happen to be Episcopalians, but a lot of the German families hereabout are Lutherans. Take the Bates family, for instance - or "Batz," as some spell the name - back in the '60s they settled on a piece of land up toward the northern branch of the Red Run and they attend the German Lutheran Church over on Chestnut Ridge. I find it a little hard to understand Mrs. Bates as she speaks with this heavy German accent.

Speaking of the Lutheran church over on the ridge, they sure know how to put on the oyster suppers. I read in the Union News that one fellow over there went to an oyster supper and put away thirteen platters of oysters all by himself! Oh, those Germans sure do like to eat!

Like the Hoffs, who came here from Germany right after the Civil War. They lived back along the Red Run for a while on that thirty acres the government took from Oliver Disney when he couldn't pay for a substitute to fight for him. Now they've sold that land to a fellow name of Hooper and moved out here to the Turnpike. The Hoff's son, John, is a real go-getter. Set up his own blacksmith and buggy shop - you can see it right across the road there from the inn.

That stream you see running behind the Hoff's Buggy Shop is part of the old mill race. It runs from up there on the Cwynns Falls above the Upper Mill down the hill and under the road right on past the Middle Mill and down to the Painter Farm which some folks still call Ulm.

If you look directly across the turnpike and up to your left just a bit, you can see the stuccoed stone building that used to be the millers house for Sam Owings's Middle Mill. It's Harmon's store now and it's also the post office, Mrs. Fannie Harmon being the postmistress.

And speaking of Sam Owings and his mills, if you look up there past the Gwynns Falls you'll see a low, white-washed stone building with big chimneys at either end. That's the cooper shop. The Fleighs live there...Mr. Fleigh's the cooper now...makes all the barrels for the Upper Mill, which most folks now call "Groff's Mill" or "Eureka Mill" and the Lower Mill, or what they now call "Painter's Mill".

Being right on the Gwynns Falls and the Red Run like it is, Owings Mills has always been known for its mills. Back along the Gwynns Falls, not too far from the Gwynnbrook Station, there's another mill run by the Schnavely's. Over on Lyons Mill Road you'll find another old mill and down a little farther along the Gwynns Falls there's the Howard mill, not to mention a few smaller mills that farmers have for their own use.

Just the other day, a couple of fellows were sitting up at the bar here chewing the fat, and they got to talking about the steam-powered wagons that went through here on the way to Westminster...that was when they were having the state fair up there. Everybody in Owings Mills must have been out on his front porch that morning, watching as they went by. Anyhow, Guy Groff was saying that a few years from now, instead of depending on water to turn the mills they'll be using steam power.

At that John Hoff slapped his hand on the bar and said, "And I guess, Guy, the next thing you'll tell us is that one of these days we'll look out that door over there, and, instead of horses pulling wagons up and down the road, we'll see nothing but steam cars going by!"

"That's the way it will be in the future," Guy insisted. "All a fellow will have to do is sit back and steer and the steam engine will do the work."

John Hoff slapped his knee at that and laughed fit to kill. "The day they come up with a contraption that will pull a wagon up these hills and it doesn't have four legs, a tail and a mane," John says, "that's the day I'll give up blacksmithing!"

# CHAPTER 16

## 1891: An Excellent and Worthy Citizen

*As noted in Chapter 12, Doctor William H. H. Campbell served in the Confederate Army throughout the Civil War. Between the end of the war and 1870 he attended the University of Maryland medical school. During this time he met Miss Jessie Gorsuch of Baltimore, and in 1872 they were married. Doctor Campbell and his bride took up residence in Owings Mills, and he began the medical practice which he would continue until the 1920s.*

*The Campbell's first home, "Wilton" was the house still standing on Reisterstown Road at the southwest corner of Pleasant Hill Road. Their first five children were born there but only two survived, John Gorsuch Campbell and Robert Madison Campbell. In 1883, they moved to a house farther south on Reisterstown Road, approximately where the exit ramp from Reisterstown Road to the Northwest Expressway is now located. By the year 1891, three more children had arrived to fill the rooms of the new home which they called "Sunshine": Thomas Gorsuch Campbell, Francina Hollingsworth Campbell (known as "Fannie"), and Douglas Preston Campbell (sometimes referred to as "Preston").*

*In addition to the community at large, Doctor Campbell served as physician to the McDonogh School, the Hannah More Academy in Reisterstown and to Rosewood, an institution he had been instrumental in founding. Rosewood was, at that time, designated for the care of mentally retarded white children between the ages of 7 and 17.*

*The following are excerpts from an actual pocket ledger which Doctor Campbell, always a meticulous record-keeper, carried with him on his rounds in the year 1891.*

-/-/-/-

Thursday, January 1, 1891 - Foggy with rain today. All well. The children have been enjoying themselves indoors. Mr. Reese allowed me to cut the remainder of his ice today. About 4 inches thick but not very good, mixed with snow.

Saturday, January 3 - Clear, pleasant day. Was called to see Mrs. Mary Ward. Went to McDonogh. Mr. Lyons sent me a load of hay.

Sunday, January 4 - Cloudy with prospect of snow. John Betz's (possibly "Batz" or "Bates") wife had a fine boy this morning. Mrs.

107

Noyes, nee Miss Clem Uhler, had a fine little girl in the evening. All well at home this Sabbath day. *Thank God.*

Tuesday, January 6 - Cold. Fine skating which the boys enjoyed on Mr. Painter's pond after school. Henry Hoff had an addition to his family, a fine little girl.

Friday, January 9 - Warmer today. Andrew Tase commenced hauling ice again. About 4 inches thick and good quality. I took the boys at night to see Mrs. Bailey's wax works. We enjoyed the exhibition.

Tuesday, January 13 - Snow squall in morning. Called to attend Mrs. Moran at night. Also called to see Mrs. Frank Reese. Another fine boy.

Sunday, January 18 - Cloudy. Called to see Mrs. C. Fangmeyer. A fine boy. Went to see Britton, a McDonogh boy, in the afternoon. Stayed to service which I enjoyed.

Monday, January 19 - Pretty mild day. Britton quite ill. Pneumonia developed. Attended the Confederate banquet at night. General Wade Hampden and General Hooper and others present. Had a pleasant evening. Came back on midnight train.

Tuesday, January 20 - Pretty day. Britton about the same. Applied a blister. Went in the afternoon to see the opera for the benefit of Confederate Home. It was charming. Do not wish to become too fond of such things.

Wednesday, January 21 - Warm with indications of rain. Britton a little better, I think. Went to Carroll County in the afternoon to see a patient.

Sunday, January 25 - Rain turned to snow during the night. This morning it was several inches deep. Found Britton better today. John and I went to hear Mr. Smith (Reverend Hobart Smith, Rector of Saint Thomas Church) preach. Mrs. Moran this evening delivered a fine boy.

Thursday, January 29 - Foggy day. I have a very ill patient at the asylum. Membranous croup. I think she will die tonight.

Friday, January 30 - Clear, rather warm day. The little girl, Hester, at the asylum died last night about half past ten. She was an interesting little child, far beyond any of those around.

Monday, February 2 - A clear, mild day. Douglas and Fannie both in bed with cold, influenza. Found the little boy at McDonogh better today. The groundhog saw his shadow.

Thursday, February 5 - Clear, very cold. Fanny had the catarrh last night. The dear little girl is better today. Douglas had a severe fall on his face. His cold much better. Did not snow.

Saturday, February 7 - Rained hard most of day. In the afternoon went with Jessie, John, Rob and Tom to Hannah More Academy to see the McKado (Mikado), an opera. The young ladies did well. We all enjoyed it.

Sunday, February 8 - Cloudy. Went to Saint Thomas Church. Mr. Smith preached an excellent sermon. I am often reminded on Sunday how lonely I am situated here as regards attending church. [Although Mrs. Campbell was Episcopalian, Dr. Campbell had been raised in the Presbyterian faith, of which there was no church nearby.]

Dr. Campbell, circa 1912

Dr. William H. H. Campbell served as the community's physician for nearly fifty years. Photo courtesy of Minna Campbell.

Tuesday, February 10 - Cold and windy. This is John's thirteenth birthday. I hope the dear boy will grow to be useful and honored. May God grant he may be a Christian gentleman.

Wednesday, February 11 - A beautiful day. Ash Wednesday. The boys had a holiday and they drove to the city. Jessie went along. I went in the afternoon to Pikesville. Attended a grange meeting. Heard an interesting lecture on tree pruning and cultivation.

Thursday, February 12 - Cloudy with indications of rain. Our roads are in a dreadful condition. I am sure they were never in a worse state.

Saturday, February 14 - A clear, mild day. Mrs. Glaum's little girl is very ill with diptheria. I fear the worst in her case. This is Saint Valentine's day. The children have received a number of them which pleased them.

Monday, February 16 - Cloudy and rather warm. I have a bad cold and sore throat all day. Tooth ache besides. I feel miserable. Hope I will not be called out tonight.

Thursday, February 18 - Warm and fair. The frogs have been heard yesterday and today. Tomorrow promises to be quite cold. My tooth aches tonight. What a great nuisance. Mr. Warfield saw a garter snake this afternoon.

Saturday, February 21 - Rainy. Muddy roads. Was called in the morning to see Mrs. John Buckman. Result, a fine girl. Went to see a patient in Worthington Valley. Came by Miss Hall's. Returned home 3 am.

Monday, February 23 - A little colder. Met Dr. William Lockwood in consultation. He is a perfect gentleman.

Tuesday, February 24 - Warm day. I took Mr. Warfield to Worthington to catch some trout, but he did not get a bite.

Wednesday, February 25 - Rain most of day. The frogs have been making noise, more like Spring than Winter. Bob says I must note the fact that Mrs. Pigeon has laid one egg.

Thursday, February 26 - The day was ushered in by a cold rain which turned to snow. The ground tonight is covered. Jessie treated us to snow cream which we all enjoyed.

Saturday, February 28 - Clear and cold. Went in the morning to see Miss Hall and other patients. In the afternoon called to see patient at Burnside, Mrs. Shoemaker's place.

Monday, March 2 - A bitter cold day. Jessie has a hen with ten little chickens in the kitchen. Brought in today. Bad roads.

Wednesday, March 4 - Cloudy. Bad sleighing. I did not take my sleigh out. Saw one or two on pike.

Tuesday, March 10 - Clear, not very cold. Was called to the Dover Road during the night. Returned about 12 noon today. Had a dark, disagreeable ride. Had to use instruments to relieve the woman. Assisted by Doctor Naylor. Late in the day was called to see a McDonogh boy.

Friday, March 13 - Hard shower. Went this morning to McDonogh then to Mrs. S. M. Shoemaker's place then to Mr. Carroll's place and other places. The roads are about as bad as they ever were.

Tuesday, March 17 - St. Patrick's Day. Clear and cold. John and Mr. Warfield went out in the afternoon and killed a few robins.

110

Thursday, March 19 - Cloudy. Mr. Harry Fox ploughed my potato patch today and commenced the field for oats.

Friday, March 20 - A rainy day. I have been out most of the time. Paid two visists to Miss Buchanan at Hannah More Academy. She is very ill, but I hope a little better today. She is a relative of the President Buchanan.

Monday, March 23 - Cloudy and raining. Mud. Mud. Mud. I visited patients most of the day. Miss R. Slade came to see me this morning.

Thursday, March 26 - Clear day. Saw one or two butterflies today.

Friday, March 27 - Snow commenced falling about 5 a.m. which turned out to be the most violent snow storm of the winter. The snow drifted considerably. I have been riding all day.

Saturday, March 28 - The storm continued steadily all last night and most of this day. I had to ride most of the day.

Monday, March 30 - The snow has melted rapidly. Mud, mud, everywhere mud. I have been riding in it most of the day.

Tuesday, March 31 - Hard rain about 3/4 of the day.

Wednesday, April 1 - Cloudy, chilly. The Easter flowers in the yard are blooming. There remains a good many snow drifts in the country.

Thursday, April 2 - Windy, cold. I was called out last night to attend to old Mr. Moran near the 14 Mile House. Found him suffering from retention of urine. The catheter relieved him.

Wednesday, April 8 - A bright day. Commenced planting potatoes today. Attended Henry Gingrich's sale in the afternoon.

Thursday, April 9 - Fair, cool. Finished planting potatoes along the side road. Burnt brush in the orchard. The children helped. Planted onions in the garden.

Friday, April 10 - Cloudy with slight rain. Went to see Henry Bennett on the Patapsco. Snow can still be seen in sheltered places.

Sunday, April 12 - Jessie, John, Bob, Tom, Fannie and I attended service at St. Thomas. The day was bright. I was called to attend a special case in Soldiers Delight. Left the mother and a little girl doing well. Our precious little girl's birthday.

Tuesday, April 14 - A bright warm day. Went without my coat for the first time since the winter began.

Wednesday, April 15 - A bright, warm day. Mrs. McCubbin presented her husband with a fine girl today. Jessie, Bob and I went in the evening to Reisterstown to see the play, "A Watercure", Greek, by the Ladies' Aid Society of the Parish.

Wednesday, April 22 - Bright, cool. Dan Tucker, Mr. Ward's dog, died this morning. The old gentleman decorated his grave and our family except Douglas went up and each placed a flower on it.

Monday, April 27 - Bright, warm day. Jessie and I called to see Dr. Frank Rich and his bride. The apple trees are in full bloom as well as all the fruit trees.

Wednesday, April 29 - Fair, warmer. Roads dry and dusty.

Thursday, April 30 - Warm day. Need rain. Planted corn field.

Monday, May 4 - Cloudy, cool. Mrs. Henry Nelson very ill. Joshua left today. William, a German man, has taken his place. The man will not suit me, but I hope he will be better than nobody.

Wednesday, May 6 - Colder today. Slight frost. Sent my German man away today. Did not suit me although he tried to do his best. Have engaged Sewall Fax to take his place. Snow fell this morning.

Friday, May 8 - Warmer. Rain needed very badly. Attended Mrs. Samuel Tagart's funeral. The McDonogh boys were present. Several of them fainted at the grave. The long walk was too much for them.

Sunday, May 10 - Dry and dusty. Was too busy to attend church. God be merciful to me a sinner.

Thursday, May 14 - Cool, pleasant day. No rain. Mrs. Nelson is slowly improving. Found Mr. Shoemaker's little girl better.

Saturday, May 16 - Cloudy. Was called to attend girl in confinement. She is now married. 18 years ago, I attended at her birth. How time flies.

Wednesday, May 20 - Another pleasant day. Was called in the evening to Harrisonville by Mr. Naylor of Pikesville. Mother and baby both did well. Returned from Harrisonville 4 am.

Monday, May 25 - Cloudy, cool. Mr. William Seymour of Glyndon was buried today. He served in the Confederate Army. I attended by request. Was one of the pall-bearers. He was buried at the Episcopal cemetery, Reisterstown.

Saturday, May 30 - Warmer. Commencement day at McDonogh. Jessie went with me. We enjoyed the exercises. The address was particularly fine. Dr. Babcock of Baltimore was the speaker.

Thursday, June 4 - Warm day. Went to the Confederate Home (in Pikesville) in the afternoon with Jessie and the children except John. Were caught in a violent rain storm.

Wednesday, June 10 - A delightful day. Plenty of cherries in the country. Mr. Ward very kindly allows us to get them from his trees.

Saturday, June 13 - A bright, warm day. Drove to the Ivy Paper Mill to see a patient of Dr. Slade's.

Thursday, June 18 - The rain last night has refreshed vegetation. All the family except Douglas and Grandma went to the Ivy Paper Mills on the Patapsco. A picnic excursion. Randal Belt and Checkly Shaw went with us. Returned about 4 pm.

Sunday, June 21 - Heavy showers. Was called to see Mr. Rodgers little boy who was bitten by a dog. Cauterized the bite. Do not think the dog is mad.

Tuesday, June 23 - A clear, warm day. Charley Marshall fixed a new water trough in the dairy. Had a case of snake-bite today. Copperhead. Prescribed whiskey and injected ammonia into the part bitten.

Saturday, July 4 - Cool, pleasant. The boys had some fireworks at night. Freddie Foster and his cousin were present.

Monday, July 6 - Another pretty day. Had my wheat threshed today. It turned out fairly well. Quality first rate.

Thursday, July 9 - A delightful day. Henrietta, colored, came today as house girl.

Sunday, July 12 - A pretty summer day. Mrs. G., Tom and I went to St. Thomas church. Mr. Reese of Westminster preached an excellent sermon.

Friday, July 17 - A warm day. Miss Patton at Burnside is better. Mr. Barker's baby very ill. Died about 6 pm.

Saturday, July 18 - A rainy day. Primary election at Reisterstown. I voted after my return from city.

Thursday, July 30 - Rain in morning. Jo Colman has unfortunately taken Sewall Fax's place. The latter I discharged.

Saturday, August 1 - Rain. Rain. Rain.

Friday, August 7 - Clear, hot. Two consultations today. Dr. Slade and Dr. Brooks called on me to see their patients.

Tuesday, August 18 - Cloudy. Foggy. Rain in the morning. To Emory Grove Camp. Bishop Wilson preached a fine sermon. After dinner went to the Dover Road to see a patient.

Saturday, August 29 - Cloudy, cool. Went to Baltimore with Jessie and the boys to see a game of baseball. My first game. I enjoyed it but very likely will not go again.

Tuesday, September 1 - "The melancholy days have come."

Wednesday, September 9 - A bright, cool day. Miss Annie Disney rode out with my colt, "Red Eye", today. She has decided to buy him. Mr. and Mrs. Foster spent the evening.

Friday, September 11 - Bright morning. I have a number of cases of bilious Remittent fever at McDonogh. All doing well.

Saturday, September 12 - Bright day. The boys took some apples over to the asylum farm to make into cider.

Wednesday, September 16 - A bright, pretty fall day. I drove to Glyndon to see Dr. Rider who is staying with his son, Arthur. Also called to see Col. Norris. The Col. gave me a nice basket of peaches. Tom and Fannie went along.

Monday, September 21 - Foggy. Miss Annie Disney returned the colt today and took Charley, my valuable bay horse. The colt had some faults which she did not like.

Thursday, September 24 - Hot and dry. A collision occured on the Railroad last night near Timber Grove. Was called to attend one of the injured.

Friday, September 25 - Another hot, dry day. One of my rides was over to Soldiers Delight and Fannie and Douglas went with me.

Saturday, September 26 - One of the hottest days. Another collision occured near Owings Mills. Two freight trains. One (person) badly but not fatally hurt. I was called to attend.

Wednesday, October 7 - Bright and cool. Jessie took Annie, a colored girl, away today. She came from an institution near Baltimore. The ice (in the ice-house) gave out today.

Thursday, October 8 - A busy day. Started on the 6 a.m. train to the city. Went to Locust Point to meet the steamer just arrived from Europe. Object was to obtain some female help. Was disappointed. Grady very ill at McDonogh.

Saturday, October 17 - A pretty fall day. Grady died this morning at 6 o'clock. During his illness of six weeks he was always patient.

Monday, October 19 - A downpour of rain. There has been since about the 1st of Sept. an epidemic of Typhoid fever at McDonogh. So far one death. Those at present sick are doing as well as could be expected.

Wednesday, October 21 - A clear day. Very busy. Was called out in the evening, did not rest till after midnight. Mr. Shray put in a new pump.

113

Thursday, October 22 – Hard rain. Have a bad tooth ache.
Saturday, October 24 – Warm. Spent last night at McDonogh. The boys perhaps a little better today.
Tuesday, November 3 – Cloudy, chilly. Indications of snow. Went to Reisterstown and voted for state and county officials.
Monday, November 9 – A bright day. Finished husking corn today. An excellent crop.
Thursday, November 12 – A bright morning. Went to Baltimore. Miss Hall died early this morning of old age. I attended her for years. She was one of my warmest friends. She lived near the Hannah More Academy.
Saturday, November 14 – A bright day, warmer. Attended Mrs. Charles Berryman. A fine boy.
Saturday, November 21 – Warmer. Founders Day at McDonogh. The exercises were very interesting. A marble bust of Col. Allan was unveiled. The address was delivered by Charles Lanier and a poem read by Mrs. M. J. Preston.
Thursday, November 26 – Thanksgiving Day. Mrs. Allan took dinner with us. I attended services at Hannah More Academy.
Tuesday, December 1 – Warmer today. Went to Towson to give testimony in the Carroll Horner case.
Wednesday, December 2 – Warmer. Have a very bad cold. Something similar to La Grippe.
Monday, December 7 – Rainy morning. Had my hogs butchered today.
Friday, December 25 – One of the foggiest days I ever saw. The children all well and happy. Henry Colman, colored, was shot in the leg above the knee by another colored man who fired a shotgun. The wound not dangerous.
Wednesday, December 30 – Windy and cold. Mr. Edward Hook died yesterday evening of pneumonia following La Grippe. He was an excellent and worthy citizen.

114

PART II. VOICES PRESENT

Introduction to Part II

The material in this section is taken from more than sixty oral history interviews conducted between 1980 and 1988. Most of the narrators were long-time residents of Owings Mills and all had some connection with the community's current or past history. Interviewers were the author and other volunteers from the Owings Mills History Council. Interviews were tape recorded, transcribed and indexed and are contained in the files of the Owings Mills History Council. Also included are materials taped at council meetings, including commentaries by both guest speakers and council members.

In circumstances where personal interviews were not feasible, narrators were interviewed by telephone. Letters and published articles have been included as oral material in those few instances where they seemed to add a fresh dimension to the subject. For instance, Francis Sydney Reese's "Lone Hickory Farm Notes" presented many delightful glimpses of life on a farm that would be impossible to convey otherwise.

I feel extremely fortunate in having gained access to such a wide spectrum of narrators, each with a particular relationship to our community and its past. What emerges from their recollections is not so much a precise photograph of our community's past, but a delightful and endlessly varied mosaic of Owings Mills and the times from which it has emerged.

Unlike Part I, in which material was presented in chronological order, the recollections of our narrators seemed to fall most logically into groupings according to subject matter. As the various voices contribute their remembrances of how we ran our homes and businesses, what we did for fun, how we cared for the sick, who among our citizens was unusual or unique, and a wealth of other topics, we obtain not just a narrowly focused view of life in the Owings Mills community but a widely-angled perspective.

In using oral history interviews as a basis of research, it is inevitable that certain misconceptions and inaccuracies should color the narration. In some instances, I have included opposing views of the same event in order to show how rumors and suppositions color our recall of the past; in other instances, several similar recollections serve to confirm a particular fact.

Oral communication, by its very nature free-flowing and uninhibited, differs grammatically and structurally from written speech. In order to present these narratives in written form, it was sometimes necessary to alter verb tenses to reflect the proper time element or to re-structure sentences to accurately present the speaker's intended thought. However, care was taken not to delete the delightful colloquialisms and ungrammatical usages that reflect the patterns of everyday speech.

One difficulty I confronted was the question of how to handle the racial and sexual stereotyping the narrators' words often displayed. My solution was to delete any egregious examples, but, where such comments typified the ethos of the period of which the narrator was speaking, to allow them to remain. It is hoped they will be viewed as evidence of a mind-set we have finally discarded and of the considerable progress we have achieved in these areas during the past decades.

Likewise, incidents that seemed too personal or potentially embarrassing to either the narrators or to the persons of whom they were speaking were deleted. While narrators are sometimes quoted discussing the foibles of their fellow-townsmen and townswomen, such material is presented with love and empathy and never with the intention of causing distress or pain.

Other difficulties I encountered in using these oral accounts were generated by a lack of precision on the part of the interviewers. For instance, we often failed to elicit exact dates or exact spellings of names or places. At other times, we allowed our personal conceptions and misconceptions to steer the narrators' responses. Having provided our interviewers with the guidelines they used in conducting interviews, I must assume total responsibility for those lapses.

I am also solely responsible for failure to include in this narrative other persons, places and events of equal importance to our history. I can only plead the lack of time, energy and volunteer help in tracking down all facets of the community's past. It is my hope that readers who are aware of such gaps in this narrative will call them to my attention and that, at some time in the future, this book may be revised to include such fresh material.

Ultimately, however, the selection process I, as author, have exercised determines this book's tone and focus. While I have listened to the most articulate and precise voices - like that of John McGrain whose research into the grist mills of Baltimore County is scrupulously authenticated and eloquently expressed - I have also listened to the sort of neighborly gossip that took place around the stove in Garner's store or the chit-chat that passed back and forth to the creak of a porch rocker on summer evenings. So if you suspect there's a splatter of tobacco juice or the smell of ginger cookies baking mixed in, I hope you'll understand it's only because that is the way we human beings remember our past...as a meld of actual events and the supposition and conjecture we weave around those events.

# CHAPTER ONE

## All Around The Home

*The lives of our narrators share one common thread – each of them has carried down through the years strong, vibrant memories of their early home life. For this reason, it seems appropriate to begin our narrative with some recollections of typical Owings Mills households at the turn of the century.*

*If we could glance through the windows of any typical home of a hundred years ago, we would marvel at the many changes time has wrought. Our feelings as we stared through that window-pane would no doubt be strangely mixed ones – nostalgia for some of the simplicity and family closeness we seem to have lost, gratitude for the technology that eliminates much of the drudgery housekeeping entailed at the turn of the century.*

-/-/-/-

### Kerosene Lamps

[Kerosene lamps] were all that was known then. You'd have these old lamps to fill and wash those old globes. They broke so easy and a little gust of wind would come along and they would smoke up for you.

If you had a very tiny [kerosene lamp] – I had a couple of little ones for my bedroom when I was a kid – they'd burn out quicker. The larger ones with bigger bowls would probably last a week [without refilling]. Some of them were very pretty...beautiful. *-Margaret Clark Hoff*

You had to fill the lamps, wash the globes, clean the wicks every day. Sometimes you had to scrape the wicks a little, sometimes you had to cut them. And we had the lanterns, too, that they'd carry to the barn. You had to do the same with them...wash and fill them. *-Elsie Moser Bates*

Electric didn't come up here until about 1918. There was a coal-oil lamp that sat in the upstairs hall [at night], and after something happened to it, it was a lantern that sat at the top of the stairs. We did have a candle with a globe but I didn't read in bed by that. *-Dorothy King*

117

## Linoleum Floors and Rag Rugs

We had linoleum on all our floors. I mean those floors were cold when you got up in winter! We used to make our own rugs - plait rags together. *-Mary Robinson Sprinkle*

Rags were also sewn into rag carpets which were woven with bright-colored cord. When a woman had filled several guana ["granny"] sacks with balls of strips, she sent off a postcard to Mr. Kittle, a weaver who lived at Hernwood who came and wove the strips together. Mr. Kittle charged according to the quantity and brightness of the cording that he used. The cord made the rugs last for years.

Rag carpets were tacked to the floors. Whenever a length of carpet was soiled, it was taken up, soaked in a tub or water for a day or two, then scrubbed until it was clean. After being thoroughly rinsed, it was hung on the line or over a fence and dried. Afterwards, it was stretched and tacked back into place. *-E. Bennett Bowen*

## Quilts and Feather Tickings

One room was all we ever had heated -- a big kitchen. Of course, that made the upstairs kind of nice because it made the floors warm. But my brothers slept between feather-beds, one under them, and one on top of them. One time it snowed in on my mother's bed...snow sifted through the window onto her bed, so you know that was cold. You'd get up and break the ice on the water bucket in the kitchen. *-Elsie Durham*

We used to have a straw ticking, a big tick that was filled with straw. That was in place of the mattress and springs both -- it sat right on the bed slats. *-Elsie Moser Bates*

Mothers made most of the bed clothes. Light spreads with appliqued patterns were made to "dress up" the beds. Quilts were made from small pieces sewed together to form patterns. They were placed on special "quilting frames" and filled with either raw cotton, wool or feathers and lined with plain muslin. Old covers and old blankets were also re-cycled to line and fill quilts.

Goose feathers were used to make feather tickings. The feather bed was "beaten up" when the bed was made each day. In earlier times, feather pillows and a feather tick were regarded as necessities for a girl's hope chest. *-E. Bennett Bowen*

## The Kitchen Stove: Heart of the Home

We had an old black cook stove. We would take our baths in a washtub beside the stove. *-Mary Robinson Sprinkle*

On Saturday nights, the old wooden tub was rolled out onto the kitchen floor. And the little out-house -- as we remarked in those

days, "Four rooms and a path." But we had no feeling of being under-privileged. We never felt any need for or serious lack of plumbing.
*-Wilson Herera*

About 1890, a kitchen range salesman visited farm homes in the area. He was selling a new range called "The Home Comfort." This stove had a copper water tank called a "reservoir" attached to the side of the stove next to the firebox. Two large black preserving kettles came with each range.

Cooking utensils were still made of iron at this time and they were heavy. There was nearly always a supply of hot water in the iron teakettle. Coffee ground from whole beans -- "Lion's Coffee" and "Levering's Coffee" were the two popular local brands -- simmered in a coffee pot on the back of the stove. All people did not make coffee the same. Some boiled the ground coffee until the liquid was thick and black, then dropped in egg shells to clear the coffee. Others thought the best way to clear a pot of coffee was to add a cupful of cold water just before serving.

Housewives prided themselves upon keeping their ranges shined with blacking and they polished the nickel trimmings to keep their stoves looking brand new. A rocking chair near the stove served for little jobs like peeling potatoes or shelling beans or mending clothes. Near most kitchen stoves you would also find a spitoon, since most men chewed tobacco.

The fire was kept alive overnight by banking the wood with coal. Each morning the ashes were shaken down into the ash-box.

In winter, soap stones heated in the oven were used as [bed-warmers between the icy sheets] or as foot-warmers on long, cold winter drives.

The kitchen range had one great disadvantage -- it heated in summer as well as in winter. Some farms had two ranges -- one in the kitchen for winter, one in the summer kitchen for summer. The second range was also used at butchering time and pressed into service for the extra holiday baking.

Some used oil stoves in summer. They did not make much heat and they did not require a chimney. A popular brand of coal-oil stove was "The Perfection." There were two-, three- and four-burner stoves. The burners were shielded with small isinglass-fronted doors so a watch could be kept on the flame. The oil stoves were filled from a tank on the side. The wicks of the oil-stoves had to be cleaned regularly and the carbon thoroughly removed.

[For safety's sake as well as for cleanliness], stoves usually stood on a large square of zinc and a second square was often tacked to the wall behind them. Users purchased coal oil from one of the local general stores, although, for users of large quantities, horse-drawn tank wagons delivered fifty or more gallons.

But oil stoves often proved very dangerous. The most important rule was to be sure and not fill the fuel tank while any burner was lit. Miss Emma Knetzer of Meadow Road neglected this detail, her stove exploded, and she was burned so severely she died.

Oil stoves were in demand until gas [was piped] out Reisterstown Road in 1930. They were used in farm homes until a much later date. *-E. Bennett Bowen*

## Home-made Pies and 1-2-3-4 Cake

We had a wood-burning stove [Mom] used for baking. She made 15 loaves of bread a week. She made pies -- never less than four or five at a time. She made cherry, peach, apple, coconut and grape pies. They were cut in four pieces -- not like we cut pies today. Everybody at my house ate a quarter of a pie or a half. *-Helen Kendig Bowers*

[My mother] baked all kinds of pies. Any kind -- apple pie, cherry pie, custard pie, sweet-potato pie -- anything you could make a pie out of, she made it. Made her own mince-meat. She made green tomato pies, but half of us didn't like them, so she never made too many of them.

She had one of these long griddles she cooked [pancakes] on. She used to make pancake batter and then take a raw potato and grate it and put it in the batter and stir it up. Then you got potato pancakes, you see.

My mother got sick one time for about five or six weeks. She got me to do the cooking. I says, "Mom, how about bread? - I can't make bread." She says, "Yes, you can." So she told me what to do - she was laying in bed hollering down the steps telling me what to do.

You had to make your own yeast...with potatoes. You take the potatoes and cook them and mash them up real fine. Then you take the water you cooked the potatoes in and take some of your old yeast and pour in with them. That would start it working right away.

She told me to put a cup of that [yeast mixture] in. That would make ten or twelve loaves. I had a great big pan and I worked it up. I said, "It's sticking to my fingers." She said, "Sift more flour in it." After I'd done that, she told me how big a loaves to make for each pan -- some of them held two loaves, some four loaves. Then I had to leave it set a while to raise. She told me when to put it in the oven.

You had to run the oven by guess, because you didn't have [any controls] to set it on. She hollered down and said, "Every once in a while [open the oven door], but don't leave it open too long. Then take a stiff broom straw and stick it inside the bread then pull it out and feel it. If the straw's wet, the bread isn't done. If it comes out dry, it's done."

I kept watching it, and after a while I said, "Some comes out dry and some ain't dry." She says, "Well, them that's dry, take out, and them that's not leave in five or ten minutes more." [After I took them out] she said, "Now leave them out a few minutes so you don't burn your fingers and then cut off a piece of that fat meat" -- we had a ham hanging -- "and grease the top of the bread." That made the crust nice and moist and gave the bread a flavor. Same way if you make rolls, you rub the grease over them and that softens them. *-Joseph Brown*

[My mother] baked all her own bread all the time. Take the wheat to the mill and they'd grind it, take out the flour. We always took a good clean bag and they'd save a bag of the middlins. That's in between the wheat and the bran. We made bread out of it, made biscuits out of it, made hot-cakes out of it. It was something like whole wheat, only it wasn't quite as dark and didn't have the bran ground up in it. But you talk about hot-cakes! You've never eaten any hot-cakes until you've eaten them! *-A. Franklin Parker*

We all knew the "One-Two-Three-Four" cake that was baked on Saturdays. The variety of pies was amazing. One that helped fill many a lunch box was the Crumb Pie" introduced by the Germans. *-E. Bennett Bowen*

I used to go up there [to Sidney Reese's house] and they always used to give you hot chocolate or some kind of cakes or something. They made thick ginger cakes, they made thick ones and real hot. Like that big...[four-inch diameter] around. *-Viola Clark Nesbitt*

## Meat and Potatoes for Breakfast

A great deal of fun and amusement was around the home and around the dinner table. *-Catherine Dimmling Morris*

You most always had heat in the kitchen, so that's where you'd eat. Wouldn't eat in the dining room unless we had company coming. *-Joseph Brown*

Oh, breakfast was like our dinners! Meat and potatoes and everything! *-Paul Englar*

For breakfast we might have fried potatoes, eggs, oatmeal, pancakes, toast. Once in a while there'd be beef and gravy. Hardly ever dried cereal like you have now. *-Bessie Moser vonGunten*

Mother's recipes were woven into the fabric of our lives. She has a well deserved and wide reputation for her cooking. Charles, Frank, or I was often dispatched with a platter of goodies to take to a neighbor. With the orders to deliver them always came the admonition, "Now, if they offer you any of this, say 'No, thank you'."
Mother's fame for her Butter Creams spreads over an amazing distance. They are truly the "best you ever ate".

## BUTTER CREAMS

| | |
|---|---|
| 1/2 lb. butter, melted | 2 pts. cream |
| 8 c. sugar | 2 tsp. vanilla |

Melt butter. Add cream. Stir in cream over medium heat. Add sugar while stirring. Stir until dissolved. Insert candy thermometer.

121

Then do not stir anymore. Cook until thermometer reaches 238 degrees F. Watch that it does not boil over.

Pour on marble. Add 2 tsp. vanilla to center. Allow to cool. Work until white with wooden paddle first, then by hand. If sticky, add 10-X sugar. You can make different flavors (coconut, chocolate, walnut). Shape and dip. (There was no recipe for dipping). *-Helen Hewes Nussear* from her booklet, *We Call Her Mother*

Those young white people out there in the country, they ate food at our house many a time. My mother made bread and stuff for them. To tell you the truth, my mother fed better than most of them. The Coles were in bad circumstances...I don't know what he did, but she had children so fast. And my mother fed those children many a time, those Cole children. *-Minnie Clark Hebron*

Sunday morning we usually had buckwheat cakes [my mother] would make from scratch. Put yeast in them so they'd raise all night. [After they were cooked,] you'd put King Syrup on them or sometimes that old black molasses.

You would soak [hominy] overnight. [My mother] used to put it on early in the morning. Then it cooked all day on the back of the stove. Every Saturday night we would have hominy and fresh sausage and hot rolls [for supper].

I had to eat whatever was put on the table or I didn't eat. I've even carried cabbage sandwiches in my lunch. *-Mary Robinson Sprinkle*

### "Smearcase," Fresh-churned Butter and Home-made Ice-cream

[To make cottage cheese], you set the milk on the back of the stove, and when it started separating, you had a regular white bag you poured it in. Then you hung it up to drain until it got firm. Then you mixed it with cream. Some people called it "curd". "Smearcase" was another name. *-Bessie Moser vonGunten*

We had one of these swing churns and churning the butter was my job. When the butter came - and it always seemed like it took forever - the cook would come out, take the churn contents and press it to get the butter together and [to get] the water out of it. Then they put it in wooden molds with a design in the top of them. *-George B. P. Ward*

We made ice-cream. You'd get ice from whoever had an icehouse. Then you'd get the cream from people who had cows. *-Dorothy King*

We lived in the brick house that's now on the Gwynnbrook State Game Farm. We kept all our milk and butter in the springhouse that sets on the opposite side of Gwynnbrook Avenue, right next to Bonita. Oh, I tell you on a hot day that springhouse was the coolest, nicest spot! Back then they never knew what pasteurization was. We used to take all that cream, and we'd put that over oatmeal for breakfast.

We'd make ice-cream, and the best kind of all was when there were
fresh strawberries. There's nothing in the world better than fresh,
home-made wild strawberry ice cream! But then again, it was nothing
but cream -- we used a little milk, but mostly all cream. *-Catherine
B. Moser*


## How Did Our Gardens Grow?

The Knatz home was noted for its fine garden with its rows of
strawberry plants and its banked rows of celery which Mrs. Knatz
generously shared with neighbors.

The residence where the Colonial Inn now stands was also noted for
its fine garden. In fact, orchards and gardens could be seen all along
the turnpike. The Joshua Clements family always had acres of garden. Mr. Jesse King's garden closely paralleled the streetcar tracks
and was inviting to the "night hucksters" who sometimes made off
with his cabbage and pumpkins. *-E. Bennett Bowen*

We had a very fancy garden...it would take up better than an acre.
One of the things I particularly remember was the celery. That had
bundles of fodder alongside of it and they put leaves around the stalks
and packed them down to blanch the celery. *-George B. P. Ward*

Most of the [people who moved from Virginia and settled in the
Deer Park area of Owings Mills] had their own gardens. Since the
nearest large stores were at Gwynn Oak Junction, a home supply of
food was a necessity. *-Valley Shipe*

[My wife] Annette and I would visit the Dolfields quite frequently.
On Labor Day, they would have a party at the farm and they'd have the
best darn food! Right out of the garden -- tomatoes and lima beans.
And they had a long bed of asparagus. I got bawled out for pulling up
some spring onions. *-William F. Stone*

We would always plant ahead in a hot-bed. We would dig it out,
put boards around. You put in a few wheelbarrow loads of horse
manure then cover it over... put a glass over it.

The main thing with peas is to plant them early - they like cold
weather. We'd plant peas and potatoes on Saint Patrick's Day. A lot
of people used to plant a second crop of peas in the fall. Turnips,
cauliflower and cabbage - you didn't have too much trouble with
worms when you planted them late. You always planted late potatoes.
They'd stay in good shape until the early potatoes were ready.

The moon has a lot to do with planting times. Raymond Moser and
my mother knew all the signs for planting. My goodness, Raymond
[Moser] knew the almanac by heart! If the signs said to plant corn
he'd go ahead and plant it.

In the almanac, every day of the calendar has a different name.
Your grandmother [Priscilla Shorb Moser] always said Boniface was
the best day to plant lima beans. That day usually comes the first
part of June. The lima bean is from South America...from Lima...and

he needs hot weather.  Fact is, he won't come up if it ain't warm...he'll rot in the ground.

Old Lady Terkel once said to me: "Ain't no use planting [vegetables] yesterday and today...it's "Esther" and she's the "Flower Girl" -- all you'll get is blossoms."

They went by the different [zodiac] signs, too.  Pisces is a really good sign.  Taurus -- he's a good sign.  The Crab, he's a good one.  Aquarius , that's a bad one.  Some signs are better for root vegetables.

In May this year, the 26th, 27th and 28th are the best days of the whole year for planting vegetables that grow on top of the ground.  But we don't plant on the 28th.  That's Ascension Day.  People used to take off in spring on that day and most of them went fishing.

The almanac also shows you the days to work on the weeds and get rid of them and the days to harvest.  Here in May, the 29th and the 30th.  We could be cutting hay then...it'll be ready.  Cut it on Saturday and rake it up on Monday.

If you just go by what it says here, you don't go far wrong.  You see, if some of those old timers planted things on a certain day and that turned out good, well...that was a good day.  But I know the moon has a lot to do with things.

I plant the signs and I still goof up.  I set my lima beans out of the greenhouse the other day and the plants looked just beautiful.  And darn! - the sun cooked the leaves on them. *-Carl A. vonGunten*


## Food From the Woods and Streams

Mrs. Burkholder used to like snapping turtle.  So I always had a little something going with her -- whenever she wanted a snapping turtle, I'd get her one and she'd give me a dollar for it.  I'd always say, "Mrs. Burkholder, they're kind of hard to get."  That kept my business going.  But, [actually] the Owings Mills Fire Company dam back on Ritters Lane was full of snapping turtles.  All I had to do was take my bushel basket and go back there and I had my turtle.

No problem at all [to catch one].  I'd take a stick and tease the old snapping turtle until he'd get mad and snap on my stick.  I'd just yank him out and put him in the basket.  I'd take it to Mrs. Burkholder and she'd put it in a barrel behind the store and fatten it up.  Then she made snapping turtle soup. *-John Kellar*

One of the best times of the year was chestnut time, about September 25 to October 15.  We picked up several bushels under the trees which had been left on the top of hills in each field as shade for cows.  The chestnuts in the woods were hard to get, due to squirrels and too many leaves and bushes.

Every night in the fall we sat round the table after supper peeling and eating a big bowl of boiled chestnuts.  Soemtimes we buried crocks of them in the garden to keep them fresh for later use.

Beginning about 1910, all the native American chestnut trees died from Japanese chestnut blight which wiped them out.  So the U.S. Department of Agriculture has introduced Asiatic chestnuts.  That is my hobby today.  I have about 60 trees and in 1955 I got over a half bushel from the older trees, now 25 feet high. -from *Lone Hickory Farm Notes*, October 16, 1955 by Francis Sydney Reese

You would take a stick and tie binder twine to it and throw that up and try to hook it over a limb. Then you'd shake the limb and the chestnuts would come down. The job was to get them out of the burrs before the worms got to them. *-George B. P. Ward*

We used to have black walnut trees and I'd hull two or three bushels of black walnuts every year and dry them. I used to just step on them [to hull them] and then I'd carry them in and put them on wires, like. I would carry them out every day and spread them out until they'd dried, and then we'd crack them and make cakes and candy.

Mom used to get hickory nuts and we had a hazel-nut bush behind the house. *-Helen Kendig Bowers*

Wild cherries, plums, fox grapes and chicken grapes were abundant. They said the Yox family were especially good at making grape juice and grape wine. We had a lot of persimmons. We also had haws, wild raspberries, dewberries, wine berries and blackberries. *-E. Bennett Bowen*

Poke -- that's what we'd go for where there was new ground. If it was new ground or had burned off, you'd find it there. When it comes up [in the Spring], that's good with butter. [You cook it] in plenty of water. First I would pour boiling water on it to take some of that -- pretty strong, you know -- take some of that [strong flavor] away.

And dandelion greens. Mom would send us for those. We'd go in the fields. Mom would say, "Go where there's no dogs." [We ate those] raw. Like with bacon and vinegar and a little bit of sugar.

Hickory nuts and black walnuts. That was quite a thing, too. The boys hands would all be stained from hulling the walnuts.

And we used to get persimmons. They were full of seeds but they were good after the frost. We'd put them on a shingle. We'd put them on the porch roof to dry and we'd say that was taffy. Picture putting them on a shingle today for children and that would be taffy! *-Dorothy King*

The huckleberries [in Soldiers Delight] would be at the foot of the scrub oaks. All of our families would get together and when we went up there it was about ten or twelve of us. My father used to take the berries to market and sell them. *-Eva Triplett Boyd*

Another boy and I picked forty boxes [of blackberries] in an hour and a half. It was [from] a patch that nobody would touch. We thought there was something funny with all those blackberries there, so we got to snooping around and there was a big hornet's nest. We waited till about ten o'clock at night, and we went back there, and when Mister Hornets woked up they were in a bag all tied up good and strong and laying in the creek. So next morning, we were back there picking berries and we picked forty quarts.

I've picked huckleberries till I didn't even know I had a back! There were different men around who ran routes in Baltimore, so we could sell them. I've picked many a box for about three cents.

At one time we used to gather chestnuts by the bushel. If there'd come a little sprinkle of rain with wind, we'd be out there, because that would knock them. We'd take a bag full and lay them up somewheres where it would freeze a little bit. They'd keep all winter just as sweet as honey.

My mother would get poke and cook it like asparagus. And dandelions, wild mustard -- all those greens we ate in the Spring. She'd cook them like you'd cook kale. Dandelion you can use for salads or just pull it up and eat it. The mustard they always cooked. *-A. Franklin Parker*

All the children had to go out and pick blackberries. I started out black-berry picking when I was about five years old. Used to wear long pants...you'd get all scratched up but it didn't make no diiierence -- you still picked blackberries.

Plenty elderberries. Elderberries didn't sell too good, but there was a couple of customers we used to pick a half-bushel for. A few wild strawberries...not too many.

When we were kids, my father used to make dandelion wine in five-gallon crocks and set it out on a bench beside the well platform. It got right powerful. Before it got finished making, I'd sneak out there and taste-sample it. Pretty good stuff! Grow hair on your chest! *-James L. Bowers*

[We picked] huckleberries, raspberries, black-berries and even wild cherries, both black ones and the small red ones that grew in the woods. Soldiers Delight [was the best place] for huckleberries. Lordy days! we picked a bushel back there one day. We used elderberries for jelly and a lot of people made wine out of them. Fox grapes were a big thing, too.

Some people made pudding and stuff from persimmons, but we mostly just ate them off the tree. You had to wait until after a good, hard frost to pick them or they'd pucker your mouth. *-Bessie M. von-Gunten*

### A Bee Tree Was a Good Thing

[If you found a bee-tree], that was a good thing. Sometimes they'd get...oh, I don't know how much honey. Look up in a tree and if it's an old tree you might see the hole. Sometimes the honey would run out at places. We were back there at Gore's one time -- John Frank and [my brother] Dutch and I believe Gore went with us. [We found this big bee tree] that was leaning over Gore's fence and I said, "Well, we can't cut this one...it'll fall right over that fence." Gore says, "Cut her down! Throw it right over the fence and we'll leave it right there. Cut her down!" *-Carl A. vonGunten*

Some trees yielded ten or twelve pounds of wild honey, rich from the pollen of many blossoms. The honey was several shades darker than the commercial honey of today and sometimes had a bitter tang. This was said to be due to the bees collecting honey from golden rod. Honey was a good substitute for sugar and was also used in making cough syrup. Mr. Simon Klinefelter was said to be very good at locating bee trees. -E. Bennett Bowen

[To get the honey out], you'd have to cut the tree down and drill a hole in it and kill the bees with sulphur. You take sulphur and wrap it up in a rag, or you have a smoker and put a rag with sulphur in that, and set it afire and then pump the smoke into them.

My cousin, Gus Curtis, and I found a bee-tree down at Shawan Farm. It was a big chestnut. There was a hole under a big branch where the bees went in. We had the axe and cross-cut saw and Gus took the butt of the axe and hit the tree a couple of times. He said, "Them bees are down here in the trunk, too -- this tree is hollow."

So we throwed the tree and that tree had a hollow in it that big around, and we took 300 pounds of honey out of that tree -- prettiest honey you ever saw.

I says to Gus, "Gus, we ain't gonna kill them bees. Let's let them stay in there." So we left them stay in there with enough honey to keep them and we got boards and nailed over the bottom of it so nothing could get in.

So they stayed in there all that summer, and we went over there again next fall and somebody had cut the tree and busted it open and took the honey that was in it. -Joseph Brown

**If the Snow Came That High, You Had Food**

We used to get King Syrup in big cans. When [my mother] canned tomatoes -- she always open-kettled them -- she'd put them in these cans and put the lid on with sealing wax. She had a special little cup she heated the wax in and ran it around the rim of the can. She used to make a lot of ketchup, too. We didn't have bottle caps then, so she would just take a piece of cork and put over the top of the bottles and seal it with wax. The wax was red and it came in a block similar to paraffin wax. -Helen Kendig Bowers

Superstitions persisted about the use of foods from tin cans. As late as 1910, neighbors declared that the father of one family had died from a stomach ailment because his wife served food from tin cans.

The invention of glass Mason jars introduced canning to the home. But it was an improvement in the rubber jar rings that finally brought success to home canning in the late 1890s.

Canning did away with the old practice of salting string and pole beans which had to be soaked over and over to remove the salt before they were cooked. At first housewives doubted that the food would keep [in jars]. Two rubber rings were placed on each jar and the housewife made the top as tight as she could, then asked one of the men to see that each top had a firm setting.

Jellies of fox grape, currant, quince, etc., were often enjoyed on our tables. Splendid pickle recipes. Some fruits, such as seckle pears and watermelon rinds were sweet pickled. *-E. Bennett Bowen*

My mother canned vegetables for soup -- tomatoes, corn, lima beans. After the vegetables were cooked together, they were put into quart jars, hot jar rubbers put on them and then a large screw-top lid. After that they were put in a boiling bath. To lift the jars out of the water required the use of both hands and a large metal clamp.

When I started to can about 1938, I did tomatoes, tomato juice, lima beans, string beans and corn. But I used a pressure cooker. By 1947, we were freezing vegetables [to preserve them]. *Genevieve Berryman Kelley*

We had to lift a trap-door in the kitchen floor and walk down some steps to get to the cellar. We put paper over the crocks of apple butter and stored them down there. [We also stored down there] potatoes, canned fruits and vegetables -- string beans, corn, tomatoes, peaches, apple-sauce, all kinds of jellies. *-Elsie Moser Bates*

Mrs. John Hoff was one who complained about the difficulty of removing corn from the cob, and her husband, the Owings Mills blacksmith and wheelwright, decided to see if he couldn't help save his wife's fingers. He cut a rectangular piece of sheet metal so as to make a number of strong triangular teeth, and below them he cut a straight metal bar to serve as a scraper. As the ear was drawn back and forth, the teeth split the grains and the bar extracted the pulp and kernels. The grated corn dropped into a bowl. Mr. Hoff obtained a patent for his idea and sold quite a number of graters. *-E. Bennett Bowen*

Sauerkraut was made in a big crock. You [shredded the cabbage] like you were making slaw and put it down in that crock with salt. Then, on top, you would put like a plate and a nice, big, clean stone to weight it. You'd make that in summer and you wouldn't start using it until cold weather -- maybe Thanksgiving or some time like that. We made it a couple of times up there at the yellow house, and one time it was really good and the next time the plate cracked and it wasn't good...it got soft. *-Bessie Moser vonCunten*

In the winter time, my mother's shelves were just loaded. Tomatoes...corn...all kinds of preserves. If the snow came that high, you had food. *-Minnie Clark Hebron*

**Burying the Cabbage**

Up in the field there is a ridge, and I'd go up there and dig holes and bury the root vegetables -- turnips and rutabagas and potatoes and all that. We'd bury them back in there and put a big load of fodder over them. The cabbage we put all together in a row with the roots in the ground and then built [fodder] over it like a tent. It kept good and crisp. You could go up there most any time in the winter and get out one just the same as if you'd picked it. *-A. Franklin Parker*

Eventually, we cut a door into the side of the stone ice-house under our carriage house and made a place to put apples and potatoes...a marvelous place for storing stuff like that. *Wilson Herera*

## Drying Fruits and Vegetables

In about 1918 to 1922, I watched my grandfather dry corn and lima beans. The corn was cut from the cob and the lima beans were shelled. They were then laid on clean white bags that were placed on the roof of the porch. The vegetables were covered with cheesecloth. [From time to time,] Grandfather would uncover and turn the vegetables and then re-cover them. *-Genevieve Berryman Kelley*

Women of this area dried apples, peaches, cherries and plums. There was much work involved in drying any fruit successfully. The fruit had to be exposed to direct sunshine. When one side of a plum dried, the fruit had to be turned. It could not be exposed to the dew, therefore, it had to be picked up and stored in a dry, breezy place each night. When three or four humid or rainy days came together, the fruit was often lost. *-E. Bennett Bowen*

[My mother preserved] anything you could can, dry, or store. The old kitchen was a shed kitchen and it had poles going across. I think she'd heat the fruits a little first to shrink them, and then she'd put them on big, round wire screens and set them up on the rafters above the kitchen stove. Every day she'd have to stir them up. *-A. Franklin Parker*

We cut the apples in "snits" and spread them out on a long tray. We'd put a cheese-cloth over them. [Ever so often] we'd have to shake them around. Same way with corn, although we put the corn on plates because it would stick. It would take at least a week to dry. *-Elsie Moser Bates*

Apples and corn were the chief things that were dried. Sometimes peaches were dried, also. The apples were peeled and cut into small half-quarter sections then spread out on a big steamer that was kept on the back porch. The water underneath was heated by an oil stove. [The apple sections] were turned frequently. When they were properly dried, they were put into jars in the pantry. They were made into pies or applesauce. Corn was cut off the cob and spread out on the same steamer/dryer. It was also turned from time to time so as to dry thoroughly and was then put in jars. *-Waiva Dean Reese*

129

## Apple Butter Stirrings

The family gathered at my Grandfather King's [house] at apple butter making time. Five of his six girls and a couple of daughters-in-law started on Friday night peeling and slicing apples from his orchard. Early on Saturday, cider was put into a large black kettle that was hung over an outside fire. The apples and other ingredients were gradually added.

[The mixture had to be] stirred all the time. The stirrer had a long wooden handle with a solid wooden piece on the end like a hoe, only larger. The butter cooked all day, with family members taking turns to stir. [When the apple butter was finished,] it was put into crocks and large jars. *-Genevieve Berryman Kelley*

The job of peeling the apples for apple butter was often made easier by the use of a hand-cranked apple-parer attached to a table. After peeling, cores were removed by a round cutting gadget. The apples were inspected for any specks, bruises or bits of peel the parer had missed. Slicing began. Soon large dishpans were filled with sliced apples. These preparations often went on all day and into the night.

Girls usually assisted their mothers while the young boys gathered firewood, carried pans of apples and apple peelings, and washed the stone crocks that would be used for storing the apple-butter.

At daybreak, the men hung the large copper-lined black iron kettle [outdoors on a tripod] and kindled the fire under it. Cider or water was heated first, then the apples were carefully dropped in and the stirring began. More cider, apples and water were added during the day to keep the mixture at the right consistency and to replace the bulk that had "cooked down". The kettle was kept boiling, and all strong arms participated in the stirring which never stopped, otherwise the mixture would burn and the apple butter would have a "burnt taste."

Sugar and seasonings were added as the mixture began to thicken. The butter was tasted frequently -- a little of the mixture was cooled on a plate and tasted by several authorities who judged not only its flavor but its density and texture as well.

About 8 o'clock in the evening the cooling started. When the fire was only a few embers and the glimmers from coal-oil lanterns cast a shadowy light, the new apple butter was slowly dipped. Jars were partly filled at first to speed the cooling. Finally, they were filled to the brim and capped with tight-fitting paper caps before being carried to a cooling shelf in a nearby shed or cellar. *-E. Bennett Bowen*

## Cider Making

We used to make a great big barrel of cider. When you first make it, it's sweet. Then it gets bitier and bitier until, eventually, it's vinegar. *-Mary Robinson Sprinkle*

## Hog Jowls and "Ponhaus"

An old gent by the name of John Zeigler was the boss butcher and I was foreman and then whoever else we could get. He went around all over the country and I'd trail behind him.

I made many a dollar those days shooting hogs. I think maybe I was eight years old when I started shooting hogs. An "X" between the ear and the eyes and where that crossed, that's where you got him. Either that or right down through the back of the ear. I shot plenty of them and never a one of them hollered yet.

Soon as [the hog] hit the ground, you stuck him right there while he was still moving. Then we'd scald them. You'd build a fire full of iron -- old plow-shares or anything you could get. When [the iron] got red-hot, you'd put it in this barrel of water. That would get the water hot enough to take the hair off of Mister Hog.

They hang him up and wash him down good. Use warm water and rags and a scrubbing brush. That's to wash any dirt off and also to get any hair you might have missed. What you don't get off, you eat.

Then you get the insides out and hang [the carcasses] up and let them cool. When the meat's cooled out, you cut it up.

My likings for a butchering day was about twenty-eight to thirty [degrees]. Then it didn't get sloppy. If it was above freezing, then you had a mess on your hands. -A. Franklin Parker

They always had a boss butcher. In later years, it was Raymond Whitcomb. He told everybody what to do and everybody obeyed him. He was a very careful supervisor. He often sent the pig's ears back to be re-scraped. -Waiva Dean Reese

At butchering, the ladies in the kitchen would be given the delightful jobs...such as cleaning the [pig's intestines to make sausage casings]. We'd have a wooden shingle...you'd take the intestine [and stretch it out on the shingle] and scrape and scrape and scrape all the way to the end. Then you'd turn it inside out and do the same thing. Then you'd blow through it to see if there were any holes.

There were other delightful jobs, such as scraping the ears ... chopping up the brain. -Jean Reese Worthley

The hog brains were removed and cleaned. They would be breaded and fried and served as a breakfast delicacy. -E. Bennett Bowen

You grind up and make your sausage out of those parts that you can't store to keep...the lean [trimmings] and all that you cut up from shaping the hams and shoulders. When you want to have the sausage in long links, you use casings from the intestines of the pigs. You [thread] those casings on a little tube on the sausage stuffer, and one person turns the handle and another person holds the casings and guides the sausage to make them even.

People would fry [the loose sausage] down and put it in a crock and pour lard over it. It would keep for months. Some people fried the loin and put that down in lard, too.

When you cut the meat off for sausage, you saved all those bones, and you cleaned the head -- the hog jowls -- and put all that in a big kettle to cook for your pudding meat. The liver and heart was cooked, too. They ground that up and made the pudding, and then that liquid was saved and strained and used to make the scrapple -- some people call it "ponhaus". You'd take corn-meal and a couple handfuls of flour and salt and pepper and that's what goes into your scrapple. That has to be stirred until it starts rolling away from the sides of the pan, and then you know it's getting done enough so it will firm up and you'll be able to cut it [after it is poured into bread-pans and cooled.]

Some people used the ears to make souse, but we just mostly used the feet. They really have to be cleaned and scraped and the toes cut off up so high. You boil them off once and throw that water away. Then [you] cook them until the meat starts falling off the bone. Then you pick the meat off and put your meat and vinegar back in the liquid and let it set until it firms up. From the bones and all, it gets [jelled] like aspic.

There were a couple of different ways of curing hams. Some people put them in what they called a brine and others salted them. After so long, they would smoke them some, then put them in paper bags and tie those shut until they used them. *-Bessie Moser vonGunten*

We used to get Mr. Raver to come help us butcher. He lived over on Greenspring Avenue. He was a dear old butcher -- wasn't much about butchering he didn't know.

It used to be cold enough to butcher by Thanksgiving. We would usually have the hog killed when he came. He would help us get it cut up and get the lard made and the pudding and the sausage and all that. It was terribly messy, but oh, it was so good.

When you cut up your meat, you cut all the fat off. You kept that separated, and then you put it in a great big kettle outside and you'd put fire under it. You'd stir it and keep fire under it until it cooked enough so that all the lard, all the running lard, was out of the pieces. Then you'd put it in a lard press and turn [the screw] down and [the lard] would run out a little spout into your can. The cracklings were what was left [after all the lard was pressed out].

Some of the head would go into the pudding and some of it would go into the lard. A lot of people used the tongue just like it is, but we used to put it in pudding. *-Elsie Durham*

For a day or two, the fresh pork was placed in salt water. Salt and seasonings were rubbed into the cut surfaces of the hams and shoulders and loins which were to be smoked, as well as some of the sausage. Other cuts were soaked in brine. After the meat had dried for a few days, the smoking process began.

Each farmer had his own secrets about curing and storing meat. Some added brown sugar by hand. Some dipped the cuts into sulphur solution to keep away insects.

The smoke houses were made as air-tight as possible, with all the chinks sealed to keep the smoke in and to keep out rodents and in-sects in the months ahead. Wood...was carefully chosen. It had to be slow-burning and give off lots of smoke. Knots of apple, sassafras and pieces of swamp growth which the farmers called "spice wood", and occasionally a piece of cedarwood were especially prized for the flavors the smoke left in the meat. The smoking continued for days, until the meat was...properly "cured." *-E. Bennett Bowen*

I know they burnt a lot of corncobs to smoke the meat because it was just at about the time of year when you'd have a lot of corncobs. *-George B. P. Ward*

## High-button Shoes and Feed Bag Dresses

[Our shoes were the high-button kind.] We all wore them. [And we wore] gingham dresses. Just made plain. My sister used to make some of them. Then, when I got older, I made my own. *-Mary Kendig Gettierre*

You remember those bags you'd get chicken feed in? Mother made my clothes right out of those. The dresses buttoned down the front and you had panties with ruffles on. And high-button shoes. You had two pairs of shoes -- one for Sunday and one for school. *-Mary Robinson Sprinkle*

In winter time we wore long underwear and black stockings. We wore what I guess you'd call gingham dresses. For Sundays we had a white dress...white embroidered skirts. My mother made the clothes. *-Elsie Moser Bates*

Of course, then, you never had nice warm things like you do now...boots and all. Then you had long underwear and you stuffed them down in your stockings and tied up your feet with bags. *-Elsie Durham*

In winter, children were sometimes sewed right into their underwear. When I was teaching on Chestnut Ridge, I had to send for some parents to tell them that a child's underwear which was sewed on for the winter would have to be changed and washed as the odor was making the classroom uninhabitable. *-E. Bennett Bowen*

My mother made everything we wore. [For underwear,] you wore drawers and they were buttoned on to what you call a "drawers body". She made those, and all the buttonholes had to be made by hand. There was no [sewing machine] attachment [to do that job].
She made our coats and all. In those days, we wore long pants down [to our ankles] and long stockings. We wore undershirts with long sleeves and our winter petticoats had bodies to them and they were flannel. I don't know how we moved. No snowsuits, nothing like that. We wore high-top shoes and rubbers -- that was all we had for our feet. We had enough upstairs to take care of the downstairs. *-Belle S. Zepp*

The Trout's mother was a quaint old lady, dressed real old-timey. She wore a real long dress for housework, usually dark, but with an apron...always had an apron on. *-Genevieve Berryman Kelley*

When Miss Painter's brother was killed by the train, she sent for Mother [Annie Disney Cox] right away to come make her mourning clothes. All black. If there was any trim on it, it was white, and that was [only] some piping around the neck or something like that. They wore [the mourning clothes] for a year.

[The dresses in those days took a lot of material.] I have some of the dresses Mother had in her trousseau that were eighteen yards around the bottom. Tight sleeves and puffs all up here. The ones I have are silk. One is black net and had a ruffle around the bottom. It had an under-foundation so you couldn't see through. *-Sarah Cox Hewitt*

### Needles and Pins

At first, we didn't have a machine and we sewed by hand. *-Mary Kendig Gettierre*

[My mother] had an old-time sewing machine. This tip would go up and down and it would sound like a threshing machine -- Bup-te, Bup-te, Bup-te, Bup! She would make the underwear, she'd put lace on it. Cut out of flour bags, stuff that flour or sugar came in, mostly. She'd wash them and put them down with a little lye or something...come out white as snow. Cut them out and put lace on them. *-Minnie Clark Hebron*

[Aunt Minnie Pfoutz] darned all the socks and mittens and coats and sewed on buttons and patched pants for the family -- kept them all neat and orderly. *-Waiva Dean Reese*

I don't think we ever had any ready-made clothes -- everybody made their own. We had to take sewing in high school, but I never turned out anything outstanding. *-Elsie Marshall Hooper*

### Hard Soap and Soft Soap

There is a hard and a soft kind of soap. [To make homemade soap] you have to have fat, you know...grease or fat. People used to save fat from butchering or even bacon fat [for making soap], because soap was a scarce item until they came up with all these store brands.

[To make soap], you have to have [the fat] boiling and then you put your lye in. You'd buy [the lye] in a can. [You cooked the soap] out-side in a big iron pot. Some people stirred it with a sassafras stick or root, and that gave it a little better smell than ordinarily. Then you leave it set overnight and cut it in big oblong bars or squares, then separate [the squares] so the air will dry it. *-Bessie Moser vonGunten*

## Washday Every Monday

[My mother] used to do Doctor Campbell's wash. And they had so much wash, Doctor Campbell did, that Mother and Mrs. Thornton divided it between the two. They called it the "fine wash" and the other part. And they washed sheets and everything, too.

We never made that lye soap. [My mother] was kind of afraid of lye. But she would use soda. She would put this big boiler on the stove and fill it full of water. Then, while we were eating and doing, this would be heating. If [the clothes] were soiled, you put them in there, too...put them on top [of the stove] in cold water and let it come to a boil very slow.

She had to heat the water on the stove, but we had a well right there, so we didn't have to worry about water. One of my brothers was a little bit afflicted and he would always bring the water and change the water and be around to empty the tubs and things...that was a help. But she washed on the washboard, Mama, a long time before she had a washing machine.

I can see my mother's yard now! -- those great big lines outside, you know. It'd be just like snow...the whitest clothes you ever saw in your life! -*Minnie Clark Hebron*

Our first washing machine had a handle on it [that you turned] and a big tub with a paddle in the middle of it. Later on, we got a little gasoline motor that we put on to turn it. -*Mary Robinson Sprinkle*

## Ironing Every Tuesday

Tuesday was usually ironing day. At our house, my grandmother ironed everything, all the way down to the dust-cloths.

Just about everything was starched, and not a spray starch, either. It was a starch you had to boil on the stove. Starched all the pillow-cases and aprons and dresses and everything. They all had to be dampened and ironed, and in the summer time it was a hot job!

There were two different type irons. One had a permanently attached handle. On the other there were three different sized bases, and the one handle would fit them all. They would heat the bases on the stove [and then clamp on the handle to pick them up.]

It seemed that by the time you got set up and got the clothes on the board -- and, of course, everything had to be dampened because of this heavy starch -- once you started to tackle these wrinkles, which were really terrible, it was time to get another iron because the first one was cold. So you spent most of your time back and forth from the ironing board to the stove.

It seems a little unfair that when you didn't have convenient instruments, everything had to be ironed and now, when you have lightweight irons and electricity and all, most of the clothes are wash-and-wear. -*Margaret Bowers*

My mother was a small woman -- I don't know how she did it! How she could do those sheets and all like that...iron them...iron them with a sad-iron! Tablecloths from here to there. And the napkins would be that big!

And these people had a lot of shirts...shirts with starch in them. He was a doctor, Doctor Campbell, and his shirts had starch and plenty of tucks in them and then the collar went around with the edges turned over. *-Minnie Clark Hebron*

[My mother] had a cloth that had wax in it -- when she ran the hot iron over that, you'd see the steam come up. Then that iron would slide right over your clothes. *-Joseph Brown*

CHAPTER 2

What We Did For Fun

*Like many other aspects of life at the turn of the century, our entertainment was home-centered. Money was scarce, transportation was still primitive, and, to a large extent, public recreational facilities simply did not exist. And yet there is plenty of reason to envy the "home-grown" pleasures our narrators describe.*

-/-/-/-

## Pop Corn and Home-made Contraptions

John would say to me, "Let's have a game." I didn't care about checkers, but I would play with him and that was no fun because I didn't care which way I moved. Mom and Pop and some of the others played dominoes. [We would] pop corn and roast chestnuts. I'd eat mine raw, but my brothers would put them right on top of the stove until they popped. *-Dorothy King*

The dolls they have today look almost real, but the ones we had, if you look at them now, they weren't very pretty. [Their bodies] were made out of cloth and I don't know what the heads were made of, but if water got on them they would sort of dissolve.

I remember when I was about eight years old, I was just on the verge of believing in Santa Claus and not believing. We [children] had gone to bed and [our parents] were getting our things ready for Christmas. My mother was bringing [the presents] downstairs and on the way, the doll cried "Mama!" I'll never forget that. *-Elsie Durham*

Oh, we had toys, but most were things we made ourselves. We had some of the darndest contraptions you've ever seen -- wagons with four different wheels and a broomstick with a rope around it for the steering wheel. *-John Kellar*

## Making Mischief

We'd dam the creek up to make a swimming pool and then the storm would come along and wash the dam out and Mr. Trout's fence would go with it. Every time we'd go down to go swimming, Mr. Trout would catch us. We used to call him "Yellow Pants" because he'd always run us out.

We made a cave down in the woods one time -- made a great square hole about eight foot deep and then put an old truck chassis across it, put boards over it and old linoleum on it and built a tunnel to go into it. Old man Waggoner up there at the end of [Kingsley] road used to raise a lot of bees. He had bee-hives and we used to go down and pick up the top of the hive and reach in there and get a pound of honey, the bees after us. We'd roll on the ground to get rid of the bees and then go down in the cave and eat it.

[One time] we was playing down in the woods and we were teasing this old bull. We lassoed him with a rope and tied him to the fence. Old man Graef who owned the farm saw us and got after us. We left the bull tied to the fence and ran down through the woods and got in the cave. Mr. Graef run down through the woods after us and he jumped up and down on top of the cave and his feet come through. We come out the tunnel and left him in there with his feet hanging down in the cave and we took off up through the woods. That was me and Loki Bitzer and my brother, Walter, and Buck Pobletts who used live near us. -*James L. Bowers*

One time a friend said to [my brother] Frank and I, "How about hooking school?" I said, "Frank, it's not a good idea. 'Cause if Pap finds out, you know what we'll get!"

We hooked school anyhow. Went down along the railroad and the stream and walked around and sat around and ate our lunches.

We would have got away with it if someone hadn't of told. I think it was one of the Millers. When my father came home from the church that night, he said, "You two go to school today?" We kind of hesitated. He asked us a second time, "Did you go to school?"

"No."

He said, "Well, that's all I want to know."

I can still see him getting up from the table and going into the woods and getting himself a switch. I want to tell you, he really threw it into us. And he wasn't satisfied with that. He said, "I want you to hook up the horse and buggy." Then he took us up to school and he said to Mattie Hipsley, "My two boys hooked school. Give them a fair share of the vestibules [to clean]." So we had to clean them. -*Elmer Hobart Schaefer*

Chinquapins were sure to disrupt a classroom when they were shot at the blackboard, the ceiling, the doors. Of course, it was quite accidental if one hit an unsuspecting girl. If a girl's long braids happened to fall on a boy's desk, it was only "right and proper" for him to soak the ends of them in his inkwell. -*E. Bennett Bowen*

One time me and Phil Knatz and the boy that worked on the farm down at Painter's and I forget who all stole the tollgate keeper's buggy -- pretty buggy...red wheels. We took it up to the top of [Pleasant Hill]. The boy that worked at Painter's was going to run in front and hold the shafts up and we were going to ride down the hill in it.

We got about halfway down, and he was taking steps as long as that front door. Finally he says, "I can't hold it!" Phil says, "Let it go!" and he let it go and it ran over top of him. The thing turned around, broke one of the shafts and the buggy upset all in a heap.

The tollgate keeper was coming up the hill with a blacksnake whip. Everybody got up and ran but Studie [Stuart Knatz], and he was still struggling to get out of there. The old man got close to him and took a cut at him with that whip and he actually took a little piece out of his leg. Then he went and got old man Knatz.

[The rest of us] stayed up there [in the woods] for I don't know how long. We finally came down and got in that culvert under Reisterstown Road. Must have been an hour in there...seemed like all day. Finally, somebody says, "Let's get out of here." Phil says, "Don't you go yet, you let me look see where the old man is." He went out to the end of the culvert and looked around and old man Knatz hit him right between the eyes with the butt end of his cane. Knocked him out cold. That old man whipped every one of us.

I was six months getting mine. His daughter [Frances Knatz] had invited me over there for something and I was in the kitchen and he came in and says, "Hi there, Boy! I been looking for you." And I said, "Yeah!" and I got up and was going out the back door. He had one of these canes with a crook on the end of it; he hooked me in the leg with it and let me have it right there. He bought...Lockard a new buggy, but he whipped every boy that was in the bunch. *-Joseph Simonds*

Around the neighborhood, we had nicknames for everyone -- mine was "Pimple." Morris Richardson, they used to call him "Mutt" and still do. Rowe Hipsley we called "Hippo."

We had a lot of fun. We made our own amusements. We used to go back in the woods, dig dams, make swimming holes.

We used to get in a little mischief once in a while. Rowe was one of the most fantastic rock-throwers I've ever seen! He could take a rock and do things with it most of us couldn't do with a slingshot. I think poor Mr. Hipsley had replaced the best part of the windows in Owings Mills school because of Rowe. Every once in a while you would see Mr. Hipsley going up the hill with a ladder over his shoulder and a pane of glass in his arms, a putty knife in his pocket. Next thing you know, you'd hear Rowe over there yelling "Ow! Ow! Ow!" and you'd know what had happened to him! *-John Kellar*

### Sunday Tea and Home-Style Parties

Mr. Cradock always went for Sunday tea with my great-grandmother. Every once in a while, he could get Mrs. Cradock to come. But he'd always have a terrible time getting her to go home. He'd say, "Come on, Sally, it's time to go home now." He'd go get the wagon and bring it up to the door, and she'd still be in there talking. He'd holler, "Sally! Come on for heaven's sake! I had a hell of a time getting you here, and now I can't get you home!" *-Frances Benthall Marshall*

I know several times I walked from where we lived [on Pleasant Hill Road] way over to Garrison Road. Somebody would have oranges or apples...nothing but a few apples in their box for a little surprise party. You didn't think nothing of it! *-Lee Fox*

Sometimes people would go visit at each other's houses. But until people got done with the washing and the cooking and the sewing and this and that and the other, they didn't have too much time. Later on, they had card-parties and different things at the new school, although they never had anything like that that I know of at the old one. *-Bessie Moser vonGunten*

If you went to visit somebody, you'd take a lantern or something like that, you know. Some would play cards, but we never did...they wouldn't allow you to play cards. But other people played cards and danced and things like that. Where there were boys in the family they'd come along to different places. But mostly the girls would just stay around [the house]. Sew, knit, things like that. *-Minnie Clark Hebron*

My older sisters would go to different houses for parties and dances. Carlisle's was one place they always went to because they had a large front room and they had a player piano. Mr. and Mrs. Carlisle themselves were good dancers. They had a lot of fun down there. *-Lillian Demmitt Moser*

We used to go up to Shorty Tillman's Store on Park Heights Avenue. They had these square dances up there every Saturday night. *-Mary Robinson Sprinkle*

The Dolfields had a log cabin back there [in Soldiers Delight] that they called "Red Dog Lodge". I remember one night somebody [in our crowd] got a watermelon and I think we also had mint juleps. About six of us were all spread out on the grass -- boys and girls, all having a grand time -- when this big old car drove in. In those days, if a license plate had five numbers on it, it was a city car; if it had six numbers, it was a county car. I noticed this one had five numbers. This big old man got out and stood there and looked for a long time...saw that it was a bunch of kids having a good time. He wandered over and I, for some reason, selected myself as speaker for the gang. I said, "I don't know what your name is, Sir, but you knew how to get in here, now you turn around and get out. This is private property." I went on -- I guess it was the mint julep talking -- "You city guys seem to think you can just roam around out here and disturb people like us...." I didn't get very far before this man says, "My name is Dolfield and I own this place." *-William D. Groff, Jr.*

Well, we got moonshine back on Nicodemus Road in square quart jars from Shulteis and back on the other side of the Humane Society from old man Stricker who had one leg. I went back there one night and rapped on the door and asked for a quart of whiskey and the old man says, "Hey, Ma! Git Jim a jug -- I got my leg off and I can't get out of bed!"

Took it down to Park Heights airport and had a party down there. It was Wilson Richardson, Hap Moser and Jimmy Quant -- he owned an airplane down there. We went down and had the party in the hangar. We used to take the gals down there and have a party. Wasn't no grass growing on me, I'll tell you that! *-James L. Bowers*

Red Dog Lodge

Red Dog Lodge in Soldiers Delight was the rustic get-away for the Dolfield and Sherwood families and their guests. Front row, left to right: Roy Muller, William F. Stone, Frederick A. Dolfield. Back row, left to right: Mrs. Thomas, Mrs. Muller, Mrs. Frederick A. Dolfield, Mrs. William Stone. Photo courtesy of William S. Stone.

Us boys would get together, but I never fooled around with anybody and git into mischief...I never did. Once up at Twelve-Mile House they got me in a card game -- I loved to play cards just for fun. So much up and so much go bank and I just cleaned up. And I says no more cards for me!

One time I left my uncle's store once -- Hipsley's store on the corner [of Park Heights and Walnut Avenues]...Tillman ran that store for a while -- and there was a whole bunch [of guys] down along the branch shooting craps. I would have to get in the game! They came out with a pair of dice and it don't make no difference if I rolled eight, it'd come right back. I don't know how many pair of dice were throwed in the branch! I wouldn't bet, but the ones betting me on the side

141

broke the game. And I've never picked up another pair of dice to this day! *-Henry Hipsley*

Years ago, when any family was in dire need in the community a party was organized. Such parties were held in the first floor room of the Groff Hall [at Ritters Lane and Reisterstown Road]. [One type of entertainment] was provided by a costumed group that masqueraded as local persons, historical figures or state and local officials. Each member of the group made a small speech that was supposed to give a clue as to what character he or she represented. Those who were not identified by the audience received prizes.

At other times, the entertainment might be violin music or an elocutionist. There is a dim recollection of one speaker who talked about "Customs in the Chinese Empire."

The net proceeds of these parties was used to buy food, clothing or medicine.

At one of the last benevolent parties to be held at the Groff Hall, something went on behind the scenes. The master of ceremonies had charge of awarding the prizes. These were rather comical prizes, such as "Strongest Man Present" ... "Most Humorous Person Present" ... "Prettiest Girl Present," et cetera, and they were awarded by popular vote. The last prize on this particular night was to be for "Ugliest Man Present." Someone persuaded the master of ceremonies to award this prize to a particular guest...not the one who had received the most votes in this category.

When the winner of the fake prize was announced, he arose from his seat and stepped into the aisle, ready to go up to the stage and accept the prize. But his wife grabbed him by the coat tail. "You fool!" she snapped. "Can't you see everyone is laughing at you?"

That started an uproar! In fact, it continued for years, whenever the man and his wife heard any reference to that prize.

That was among the last of the gatherings at the Groff Hall, although it was not the cause of the hall's end. The building stood on a very small plot of ground and there was little room for hitching posts. Since the trolley tracks were on the east side of the road, buggies and wagons couldn't be parked there, either. The hall was later remodeled into apartments. A few years later it was destroyed by a fire which many in the community labeled arson. *-E. Bennett Bowen*

My cousin and all were having this big party. So I had this Model A Ford and I had a pet skunk, so I put the skunk in the rumble seat and took him up to the party. So about eleven o'clock they were all drinking and having a good time, and I went out and got the skunk out of the rumble seat and brought him in. The skunk walked across the floor and they all went out that door at the same time, one on top of the other. Everybody was gone except me and I laid there on the sofa and laughed. *-James Bowers*

## The Yodeling Hillbilly of Owings Mills

Eighty years ago, Miss Bell Scott taught piano. Later Miss Minnie Koerner and Miss Lillian Demmitt gave lessons. Professor Louis Susemihl [who lived on Pleasant Hill Road] gave both piano and organ instruction. A Mr. Wilson and his son, who lived in Owings Mills, were the community fiddlers. They sometimes walked five or six miles carrying the cases containing their fiddles.

An elderly lady instructed some of the young people and showed them how to perform the dances. The lady clapped her hands to teach the steps. One dance was called "My New Shoes."

Don't you see my new shoes?
Don't you see?
Won't you see my new shoes?
Don't they fit nice?
Don't they fit?
Don't they fit nice and buckle, too?

Another dance was called "Clapping Jupiter." First everyone clapped in rhythm and the men would make their boot heels click on the bare floor in rhythm with the clapping.

The jig was always popular as was square dancing. The Virginia Reel was looked upon as everyone's dance, and refreshements usually followed the reel. *-E. Bennett Bowen*

My Uncle Bill was blind...he went blind at sixteen. If we had a party or anything, he'd play his violin. Uncle Bill used to play at parties all throughout Soldiers Delight and he would pay my brother, Rezin, a quarter to lead him through the paths to Sherwood Road or Church Road or Cherry Hill. They had these big square dances. The first ones who got there would move all the furniture outside [so there was room to dance]. My brother said he remembered that sometimes when they left the parties he would look back over his shoulder and the sun would be coming up.

My mother used to always make apple-butter in a big kettle like everybody else did. The young people said, "Let's have a party...let's make the apple-butter at night instead of day-time." I was selected to get the twelve o'clock dinner, but it turned out that the older women had to do all the work because my uncle was playing the violin and all the young people were dancing. I know they made lemon pie and a big chicken dinner and we had everything -- corn and lima beans -- and we ate at twelve o'clock. The young people kind of got wild and carrying on and my uncle got mad and he said, "I'm not going to play for them...I can't hear my own fiddle." *-Eva Triplett Boyd*

Arthur Cradock used to go with Maggie Painter and he had a beautiful voice and so did she. They both sang in the choir. He used to come and visit her once a week. Sunday evening. She'd play the piano and they would sing with the windows open and you know, through the summer, boy! -- everything stopped around here when that happened. *-Joseph Simonds*

We were the best of friends -- Gertie and Elsie [Marshall] and myself. They had a piano and I'd go up there and we'd all sing. And we'd play the organ over at church. We sang and we played and we did all kinds of things, Gertie and Elsie and I. -*Nettie Clements Frank*

My mother sang good...hymns and things. She'd be humming all the time...rocking and humming when she wasn't [busy].

I played the piano and my sisters sang. We sang at our own church [Pleasant Hill Methodist] and other churches, too. When I got to Mr. Shaver's room at school, I played the piano for them. I also played at Sunday School and church.

That was all by ear. When I was about thirteen, we had an old piano and I'd go in there and try to make the chords. I could tell by sound if it was right or not.

Later on, I took lessons from Evelyn Brooks. The kind of music Miss Brooks taught was called "Winn" and it was played by chords in the left hand. I also took from Mrs. Tracey in Reisterstown for a while -- she lived right across from the high school. Later on, I gave lessons to a few around. -*Lillian Demmitt Moser*

We had a wind-up Victrola at home. Then we got a radio. The first [radio] we got was an Atwater Kent. I guess I was about eight or nine years old and I was born in 1916, [so that would have been about 1924]. -*James L. Bowers*

There was a Victrola which had some old records, including several of Caruso's. -*Waiva Dean Reese*

My husband [Jim Hooper] was interested in the organ. He had this expensive organ installed in our house. It had over 1,000 pipes and a harp and a chimes to it. It was quite beautiful. It was made in Providence, Rhode Island, and it took three men five weeks to install it. He played every evening -- mostly hymns. He belonged to the Organ Guild and different ones would come out and play. Sometimes they would bring a couple of singers -- Dorothy Ditmar, who was quite prominent around Baltimore [was one who came]. The organ is now in a Catholic church up near Rochester [New York]. -*Elsie Marshall Hooper*

As far as I remember, we always had radios...crystal sets we'd fool with and get a station now and then. The programs were better than they are now. Amos and Andy. Things like that were funny or educational. And you'd see their pictures in the paper and you'd know what they looked like. [Lowell Thomas] was on about six or seven [o'clock]. Never missed him. Then there was a program of four women -- I've forgot the name of it. They were always in trouble or getting out of trouble. But it wasn't any of this sexy stuff you have now! -*Sarah Cox Hewitt*

We had a wonderful, wonderful chorus [at Owings Mills Elementary School]! We got red capes for them and everybody around the community wanted Mrs. Turnbaugh to bring that chorus and sing. Mr.

144

Burkholder, who was president of the PTA at one time, wanted them to sing at the Lions' Club. They also sang at churches around the community. -*William C. Hull*

I used to be able to sing -- my aunts started me out real young. They had me sing up at Pleasant Hill Church with my uncle Roland Fox when I was only about four years old.

My aunt Frances [Demmitt] was the one got me started playing the guitar. Next thing you know, they got me going down to "Uncle George's Kiddie Klub" [at the Hippodrome Theater in Baltimore]. I was known as "Jackie Kellar, the Yodeling Hillbilly of Owings Mills." Got so I couldn't go anywheres without taking the darned guitar or singing or yodeling and carrying on. When I got about thirteen or fourteen years old, my voice changed so I couldn't do any more yodeling. When I was in the service, I mashed the fingers on my left hand, so I couldn't play the guitar. So that ended that. I've still got the guitar. -*John Kellar*

## Ice Skates and Double-Deckers

The only skates I ever had were the kind you had to screw onto your shoes. They were off more than they were on, so I never made out very good at skating. -*Elsie Durham*

You could [sled ride] from Pleasant Hill all the way down to the Mills. Not only once, but two or three times we'd go up and down there. If I had to walk back up that [hill] now! -*Lee Fox*

When we'd go on a double-decker [sled], they'd open the tollgate. Mom would say, "so many rides". They'd start at Pleasant Hill. Now that would be like Mr. [Clarence] Berryman at the controls. The Berrymans were builders and they always had a nice double-decker. It was like two sleds, a sled in the front and another in the back. [People built their own] and then they'd go to the blacks-smith shop for the runners. -*Dorothy King*

My mother, Bertha King Berryman, always told a story that the sleds were the prize possessions of Clarence [Berryman] and his brother, Jasper. She also said that "When Jasper let me guide his sled, I knew he trusted me and loved me." They were married December 4th, 1909. -*Genevieve Berryman Kelley*

They had a picture in the paper where they skated all the way from Owings Mills down to City Hall in Baltimore. Eb Disney and some others, it was. They were in it. -*Helen Carpenter*

[My sister] Grace [Demmitt] and some of the Carlisles went down to Clemmons's to skate on their ice-pond. It was in back of their barn. [My sister] Glean and I were called "the little ones" and we didn't get a chance to go out ice-skating or on the sleds. But [my older sisters] would start out with ten on one double-decker and go all

the way from our house to the bottom of the hill. Right down the middle of the highway. One person would guide it and the others would just hug around each other. Sometimes they'd upset or have an accident -- never anything serious. Then they'd come running into the house to get warm and go out again. They really had good times then!
*-Lillian Demmitt Moser*

Men on Sled
Riding a "Double-decker" sled down Reistertown Road was winter sport for both children and adults. Photo courtesy of Lee Fox.

Lots of times when it would be icy we'd take old dish-pans and sit in them and go down over the hill! Oh, that was grand! *-Grace Bowen Pape*

Henry Hoff built a double-decker and me -- tomboy! -- I used to wrap them ropes around my hand and steer that thing! Biggest tomboy in the country! My mother and Mr. Hoff used to get out there on it once in a great while. On Belt's Hill. From Saint Thomas Lane we

146

would go halfway up to Rosewood Lane. We used to have lots of fun! *-Virginia Clark Hoff*

We used to ride down Pleasant Hill on a double-decker. Ten or twelve people on it. We'd come down Pleasant Hill and all thru that bottom and run almost up to the top of Owings Mills hill up by the fire engine house, turn around there, get back on it, then we'd go clear up to about where the old tollgate was. Oh, yeah, we were flying! We cut old man Hoff's gas tank right off at the ground one night. *-Joseph Simonds*

I wasn't supposed to go on the road, but boy! -- it looked so tempting, so I got my little sled out and down I went! But then I got bumped into. Winnie Wineholt had a double-decker and Wilfred and Gerbrick and the big boys around there were on it. I was on this little sled by myself and they ran right into me. Boy! -- they were scared and so was I! *-Gladys Carpenter Grimes*

We would sometimes sled ride on Barney Clabber Hill. It would be families and everybody on that hill...a couple of hundred people some nights. We used to stay out there sometimes all night long. When the crust was good, we'd come down across that hill behind Owings Mills, jump over on Gwynns Falls on the ice, and go almost down to McDonogh pond. You'd only make that trip two or three times a night and you'd had it.

Reisterstown Road was the same way -- we'd sled ride down it and sometimes they'd have a train backed up across the road at Garner's store and we'd go right under the train. *-John Kellar*

I bought a big sleigh at some auction and we used to go sleigh-riding. Two horses and bells and blankets. A soapstone heated in the oven to warm our feet. *-Waiva Dean Reese*

[After sleighing parties,] various households provided refreshments. There was usually a large glass punch bowl filled with fruit juices and ginger ale which invariably tempted some rascal to "spike the punch." This was sure to happen if the hostess was a well-known teetotaler who would be shocked when she sampled the punch. Some aver that one such hostess always took a second sample "just to be sure she was right" before she began to express her outrage. *-E. Bennett Bowen*

## The Ole Swimming Hole

[There was a swimming hole] where the old train tracks went back past the lumber yard...the old tracks that go past Baltimore County Supply Company [at grade-level] now. They had a sort of dam back in there that was made by the hill for the railroad. There was a culvert there, they would all sit on top of this culvert and dive in the hole. *-Lee Fox*

147

In summer time you'd walk all the way back there in the Hook Farm to go swimming. Yeah, way back there, because that was the biggest hole. But mostly we were working, I tell you. *-Carl vonGunten*

A dam has been made near the upper crossing in the swamp. The grandchildren spend much time there when the weather is hot. Waiva is building a boat for Bill as a reward for swimming across the dam, a distance of fully ten feet. She is very handy with saw and hammer and can drive a nail as good as anyone -- in fact, better than many people I have seen. The boat is to be named "Bill" -- great ceremony will attend the launching. I suggested to Waiva that it would be much easier to build the boat with flat bottom and rectangular sides, but that would not be "artistic" enough for her. The bow is pointed, the stern square, but she had to make the bottom flat. The cracks are to be caulked with oakum, but if the boat leaks no great harm would result as the water is not very deep and the passengers go practically naked, no clothes on to get wet. -from a letter by *Francis David Reese* to his son, John Campbell Reese, August 2, 1933

I remember Hoffman Knatz used to have a tub and he'd wheel it down there to the Knatz's pond in a baby carriage and we'd all watch him paddle around in it. *-Elsie Marshall Hooper*

Right over here in the [Gwynns] falls, we used to have row boats on there. Swimming, fishing and everything was good. *-Joseph Simonds*

During the summer we fished for sunfish in Gwynns Falls, played in the Groff's mill on rainy days, took walks to Soldiers Delight to visit the chrome mines and built tree houses and forts in the woods. We swam in the Easter's pool and in the pool on the neighboring Bolton place. We played tennis on the Natwick and Campbell courts. -from a letter to the author from *Somerset R. Waters*, October 7, 1981

[At Lone Hickory Farm,] there was a tennis court that was built by Uncle Louis when he was an engineering student at Lehigh. In summertime, everybody played tennis.
We also had picnics in the woods and took walks. And everybody rode horseback. They made trips to the water-spout and to Soldiers Delight. *-Waiva Dean Reese*

In summer time, my aunts would come down from Frederick...camp meeting time. We'd take our lunch and go up there to Emory Grove. *-Lillian Demmitt Moser*

**Baseball at Lowe's Field**

About 1900, baseball became the popular sport. A local team arranged a slate of games with nearby teams. The Owings Mills team played on Lowe's field west of Church Road near Delight Road. Since the teams played on Sundays, the game aroused the ire of supporters of the Blue Laws. But the games went on. Refreshments were sold.

There was homemade ice-cream, or sherbet, cakes and other goods whose sale helped raise money for the support of the team. After many seasons, near-by ice-cream makers came in and shared their profits with the team. *-E. Bennett Bowen*

The Lowes had a ball team and [Mr. Bitzer] took a whole load of us somewhere back at Deer Park to a game. At a diamond back there. Lowes had their name on the team's shirts and who did they play? -- it must have been Oakland. *-Grace Bowen Pape*

They played baseball at Lowe's on Sunday afternoons -- that was about the only time the men would be free. We all went back to watch the games...cheer them on. My father played and he got hit with a ball and his nose was broken. *-Elsie Marshall Hooper*

My brother was president of the baseball club called "North Branch". They used to hold the meetings at our house. *-Eva Triplett Boyd*


## Church Festivals and Entertainments

At Gill's Church they'd have festivals sometimes on Saturday nights and we'd go to those. A whole bunch of us. They had games and they used to play the game where they run around and say, "Choose your wife"...I don't know what that was called. But I do know the one called "Drop The Handkerchief" -- somebody would run around the circle and they'd drop it behind somebody and then they'd pick it up and run and try to catch the other one before they got to their place. And they had stuff to eat -- ice-cream and stuff like that. *-Mary Kendig Gettierre*

[At Pleasant Hill Church], they'd hold oyster suppers and all those things. And oh, my, the strawberry festivals! That would be served on the lawn...in the summertime. You'd get ice-cream and cake if you wanted -- the cake was extra. Mrs. So-and-so would have a candy table. Bertha Berryman. Annie Hewes. They were tops. *-Grace Bowen Pape*

We used to go to Gwynn Oak [Amusement Park] on Sunday School picnics. They always chartered a streetcar and took us down. Mother used to pack lunch. We used to save up our money so we could ride on the amusements. The ride I liked best was the merry-go-round. *-Elsie Marshall Hooper*


## Holidays and Special Occasions

New Years' parties were home celebrations and often lasted well into the morning hours. It was a New Year's custom to discard the old and welcome the new. Housewives replaced their old tinware, and the old pots and pans were clanged and drummed at midnight to welcome in the New Year.

It was also widely believed that what you did on New Year's Day, you'd do for the entire year. Some families saved part of the children's Christmas presents to give to them on New Year's Day, thus ensuring that they would have new things throughout the year. -E. Bennett Bowen

[On Shrove Tuesday] everybody baked fat cakes. That was Fat Cake Day. "Fastnachts" was another name for them. You made them like you do donuts and there were raised ones and the other type, too. Frank Parker [still] makes them every year and brings them around. -Bessie Moser vonCunten

At Easter time, most families attended church services. Easter dinner usually included roast lamb or roast ham. The meal was not as elaborate as the Christmas dinner because the food stored in the previous season was getting low. Eggs, however, were plentiful. For many years, onion skins were used to dye the eggs. -E. Bennett Bowen.

At Easter we dyed eggs and had egg hunts. We tried to see how many eggs we could crack by hitting each other's eggs on end. It was wonderful if we had one new thing to wear to church. -Genevieve Berryman Kelley

On the Fourth of July, we'd go to the neighbors and we'd all have fireworks and we'd all set them off and have a big time and have some refreshments. -Mary Kendig Gettierre

Farmers who had watched their wheat fields ripen and dry feared the sparks from Fourth of July fireworks. All day long, there were booming and cracklng noises from small shooting crackers. Boys who lived along the Reisterstown Turnpike placed their fire crackers in spaces along the streetcar tracks. The loud reports always shocked the exasperated passengers. Sometimes an accident occurred when a large firecracker -- called a "torpedo" -- exploded in someone's hand.

At night, fireworks from Rosewood illuminated the evening sky. [We ooh-ed and ah-ed as] sky-rockets arched a red path into the sky then exploded in a diffusion of fiery streamers. -E. Bennett Bowen

Fourth of July we'd have lots of good things to eat. We'd get a five-gallon tub of ice-cream from Mr. Louis Knight and put it under the big grape-arbor in the back. We'd put it out there, and we'd eat ice-cream all day long. -Virginia Clark Hoff

On the Fourth of July, we had fire works -- sparklers, spit-devils you set off with the heel of your shoe. We had a picnic on the lawn, and, of course, the flag had to be put up. -Genevieve Berryman Kelley

Halloween was one of the more boisterous [holidays]. Some of the pranks were: building fences across roadways, opening gates to let

150

cattle roam, upsetting chicken coops, cutting ropes on dinner bells and upsetting empty milk cans. A farmer looked for his milk wagon one November 1st [and found it] astride the ridge of his barn roof. *-E. Bennett Bowen*

One time we went over to Painters farm on Halloween and took about fifty pumpkins out of a shed and put them in a big circle. Another time we went up there to the bottom of Pleasant Hill and somebody got hold of a wire gate and put it about twenty feet up a telephone pole. *-George B. P. Ward*

My older brother, Rubin, had a Christmas party. I was a little kid and I was slipping around trying to see and hear everything. [At that time,] I still believed in Santa Claus. One of the fellows picked up a little table I had gotten [for Christmas]. He said, "Rubin, is this your patent?" [The table] had legs from a chair...they had been cut off to make perfect table legs. I got to thinking, "Well, we had some chairs like that...." That was the end of my Santa Claus. *-Eva Triplett Boyd*

At Christmas, very few things were purchased from a store -- we made things by hand and goodies to eat for gifts. Embroidery, aprons, doll dresses, crocheted and knitted items, things from wood. There was love there.

We decorated the tree and the house inside, but I do not recall too many outside decorations. We visited families and there was always refreshments at each place. [We hung] our stockings and in them we always found an apple, an orange, some nuts, a little hard candy and - if you were lucky - a penny or a nickel. *-Genevieve Berryman Kelley*

At Christmas, if we got just one toy, we were lucky. All the neighbors would come in. My mother used to keep baking cakes. Back then they didn't have all these soft drinks -- she served them lemonade or coffee or homemade root beer. *-Mary Robinson Sprinkle*

Although many children rode to the Christmas parties at St. Thomas Church in carriages, others walked great distances for their annual Christmas treat. Miss Katie Craddock and Mrs Samuel M. Shoemaker would greet all comers with cups of hot cocoa and special crackers that they had brought out from the Hooper, McGraw store in Baltimore. At the party in 1906, two Schaefer boys were present, as well as Herschel MacCubbin, Walter and Henry Simmons. Among the girls were Margaret Clark, Clara, Blanche and Fannie MacCubbin. The children had a great party and everyone received presents. Since most homes still used coal oil lights, the children were enchanted to see the tinseled Christmas tree glittering with electric lights.

When the party was over, Miss Katie looked over the waiting drivers and picked the ones who looked most accommodating and secured rides back home for all the walkers. *-E. Bennett Bowen*

Our Christmas presents were usually clothes. We had a large tree in our front room. We'd leave it there up almost to Easter time. We hated to take it down. We had one of those round stoves you put chunks in and we never kept that room real hot. We used to sit around and someone would say they saw a certain color Christmas ball and the rest would have to guess which it was. *-Lillian Demmitt Moser*

Christmas dinners were the most sumptuous of the year. Most families hoped to have a roasted turkey, although a few opted for Christmas goose as English ancestors had done for centuries. Chestnuts were abundant and often flavored the dressing.

The dining room table groaned under a huge display of dishes -- steaming mounds of mashed potatoes, "boats" of brown gravy to swim the vegetables in, corn and string beans from the summer canning, large tureens of sauerkraut, sweet potatoes, choice apples, home-grown carrots, a variety of sweet and sour pickles, cranberries and -- a special treat if the wrapped green tomatoes in the cellar had ripened -- a large platter of red, ripe tomatoes.

The finest jellies were set out -- tart currant... dark, velvety wild fox grape...light red quince...the fine jelly made from tiny wild huckleberries. Mrs. Frank D. Reese of Gwynnbrook always treated her guests to a slice of delicious hickory nut bread that made one wish the task of shelling hickory nuts might be less tedious.

Dessert was a variety of pies and cakes. First place was given to mince pie, well seasoned with rum or whiskey. Second place favorite was pumpkin. A special Christmas pie was coconut custard. Layer cakes were baked a few days before Christmas -- big, round cakes with plenty of icing between the layers, around the sides, and over the top. Chocolate, sugar white frosting flavored with lemon, coconut layers heaped high to resemble and igloo, icing dotted with English Walnuts, jelly rolls with tart jelly inside and powdered sugar snowed across the top.

Beverages varied from home to home -- sweet cider, hard cider, wine, bought spirits. But the staple in all homes was plenty of strong, black coffee slightly diluted with rich cream from the family dairy.
*-E. Bennett Bowen*


**He Would A-Courtin' Go...**

I used to go to church and pick up the girls, take them home if they had a distance to walk. I'd take one home one time, another home another time. So when I got to going with my [future] wife, I just cut them all out -- nobody but my wife.

I went with my wife three years before I married her...I was courting with her. Mr. Stewart came and he said, "Joe, I want you to take Mr. Gill's place as farm manager."

I said, "Mr. Stewart, that won't suit me...takes a married man for farm manager [because] he's got to live on the place."

"Now, see here," Mr. Stewart said, "where are you going to find another girl better than the one you're going with?"

I said, "Well, I don't know...."

He said, "Well, I do -- you aint' going to find one any better!"

So I saw [the girl] I was going with and she said, "Well, what's wrong with getting married?"

So we got married and I took the job. We got married on 28 Feb. 1920 - if it had been the next day, it would have been Leap Year. So I went with her, and she worked hard all her life. *-Joseph Brown*

Soldiers Delight was a place we could go and know we could be pretty much alone. We'd get a fire going, cook a meal, have a few drinks. And then the girls and the boys would...well, we might do a little hugging, and we had a good time back there.

I always remember the remark Louisa Ghee made to my mother after I got home from the war and started running around with the young neighbor who is now my wife. She said, "I and Isaac was sitting on the side of the bed and I said, 'You know, Mister Billy is going to get married. He's gonna marry that girl.'" I and Isaac! *-William D. Groff, Jr.*

[The Demmitt sisters] were six beautiful girls, no question about that! People said that Frances was the most beautiful one, but I still think Louise was. *-Lee Fox*

It was a choice between Lee and Dave Disney! *-Louise Demmitt Fox*

My husband, Elmer Frank, was a conductor on the Emory Grove line. I met him riding up and down on the streetcars. *-Nettie Clements Frank*

There used to be an ice-cream parlor on Reisterstown Road in Garrison -- Broccato sold ice-cream there. A crowd of us went over one night and that's where I met [my husband]. *-Mary Robinson Sprinkle*

I met Francis Sidney Reese in Washington where he was at George Washington law school. We used to drive over to [Lone Hickory Farm] in his Model-T Ford. *-Waiva Dean Reese*

A matron who considered herself a "match maker" often arranged a Valentine's Day party and invited all the known lovers and those upon whom she hoped to work her charm. Kissing games were often the main amusement. It was considered bad luck for a girl to attend more than three such parties and not secure a husband.

In earlier times, neighbors most often intermarried. A bride from a distance of five miles was usually regarded as a "foreigner." *-E. Bennett Bowen*

That's how I got my wife. She was going around with somebody from town and I invited him out to help cut corn. He lasted about half a day and then he went back to town. That's when I won! *-George B. P. Ward*

Where I ran into him, he was agent at Glyndon Station. We shipped milk, and I took the milk out to the station. He was being very diplomatic, of course -- he'd come down and unload the milk on the platform for me. *-Sarah Cox Hewitt*

Henry and I had always been chummy since we were kids at school. So then we got married. *-Margaret Clark Hoff*

The most special friend I met in high school was my husband. We met in September of 1925. He was outstanding in all athletics, which impressed me. We were married in August, 1936. *-Genevieve Berryman Kelley*

[Clarence Herbert Reese] was a son of Charles Reese. He was a minister. He had a church in Philadelphia. When he came down here to visit, he'd always come to see us, and we'd write and let him know if there were children to be christened. He married my husband and I -- it was on Thanksgiving Day, the 24th of November in 1932. *-Helen Kendig Bowers*


## "Pickin' Up Posies, Put 'em In Your Pocket..."

Oh, I used to go every spring and pick wild flowers. We walked all around the country to get them. Back in Foster's Woods, they had the most beautiful trailing arbutus! This woods up here used to be filled with the little spring flowers -- bloodroots and hepaticas...they were tiny purple flowers, the wind-flowers or anemones, and myrtle that grew along the banks. We still have a lot of Jack-in-the-pulpits. *-Helen Kendig Bowers*

In May, city relatives and friends often came out to pick the blossoms and enjoy the sunshine. Blossoms were abundant, not only dogwood, but long-stemmed violets that ranged from pale purple to the deep shades of the large, coveted "velvet" variety. Blood-root stained the hands and pink honeysuckle grew in profusion on the wooded hillsides. *-E. Bennett Bowen*

Along the Cow Lane [Featherbed Lane] you'd see wild honeysuckle or wild azaleas. You don't see that any more. Or trailing arbutus. I think people just pulled it up.
We used to get ferns [and sell them] and we'd get -- I don't know, it wasn't a penny apiece. After a while, you didn't see them any more. And partridge berries and trailing crowsfoot and standing crowsfoot. *-Dorothy King*

We'd find velvet violets, arbutus and lady's slipper. Then there was bloodroot and mountain laurel...a lot of pretty flowers. We also broke off the honeysuckle blooms and some people ate the honeysuckle apples, too. *-Bessie Moser vonGunten*


## The Magic In Books

I had a real high bed and it was right near the window and I got up real early in the morning to read -- *The Five Little Peppers and How*

*They Grew...Rebecca of Sunnybrook Farm...Huck...when* I was older,
*On the Trail of the Lonesome Pine.* And the *Elsie [Dinsmore]* books.

The stories [I read] would say things like, "Fie on you!" Or there
would be a picture of a man asleep under the hay when he should be
making hay and that would be a lesson for you. Another would read:
"See the kitten on the wall, Playing with the leaves that fall. One,
two and three. Falling off the linden tree." Linden trees -- that was
something my grandfather had in his yard. Grandpap liked nature.

I did like to read. Vinton, my oldest brother, he'd take books away
from me. Horatio Alger books, he'd take those books away. That's
older brothers! *-Dorothy King*

### Hopalong Cassidy and All

At Rosewood, they used to have movies for the inmates. We'd go
over there and sit in the balcony. Hoppalong Cassidy and all. *-Joseph
Simonds*

The movie we went to was at [the former Children's Rehabilitation
Institute] on Westminster Pike. It used to be a Jewish Sanitarium and
my father worked for them when we lived in Reisterstown. They had
movies for the patients. The ones who were able to get out would go
out and sit on the lawn; they'd have these movies...old silent movies.
Old Charlie Chaplin things, most of them were. *-Elsie Durham*

They had the moving picture parlor up in Reisterstown. You'd go to
the movies for a nickel. A woman played the piano while the show
was going on. You had to read everything on the screen. Silent
movies. *-James L. Bowers*

There was a movie in Reisterstown which was in a building next to
Elines. Goodwin's Hall. Up over top of that. Folding chairs to sit
on. No music, of course. Black and white. The film would break
every now and then, and everybody would start stomping until they got
it going again. *-Genevieve Berryman Kelley*

Some people went to the movies, but not many. I remember going
to the movies in Reisterstown where that Acme [Market] was -- right
around in there was the movie place and under it a garage or something. There was Christhilf's bowling alley and there was Doctor
Michael's drug-store where you could go and get ice-cream late at
night. The same way at the bowling alley -- they had a soda-fountain
upstairs there. At the Hobbs Hotel there was a soda-fountain and
across the road was the ice-cream place. And years ago we used to
go up on Westminster Pike where the plumber [John Shaneybrook] is
now to get ice-cream. *-Bessie Moser vonGunten*

Once in a while we would go [into Baltimore]...fall of the year, if
we had any money. We'd go down on Eutaw Street and there was a
restaurant there across from the Hippodrome [Theater], and we'd get a
mess of oysters. Then we'd go to the Hippodrome. Vaudeville.

Mostly "Boots" [Marion] Moser and Raymond [Moser] and I would go.
*-Carl A. vonGunten*

The first movie theater I ever went to was up in Reisterstown. Every Saturday us boys would get there at two o'clock when it opened. There were always westerns on Saturday and they had these serials we followed. We'd watch the same movie over four or five times. *-John Kellar*

## Cristhilf's Bowling Alley

There was a bowling alley in Reisterstown -- Cristhilf owned it. Before the fire, it was originally, I think, next to Michael's drugstore, although I wouldn't swear to that. Later it came down to the Masonic Temple. My brother used to go there and set up pins. *-Genevieve Berryman Kelley*

## Footlights in Therapia's Barn

My grandmother had a boarding house down near Belvedere. Some of her boarders were actors and actresses. I used to go there and watch them and then I'd come home and play and sing those same things. I had a friend in Baltimore who used to come out to visit me. I'd give a play and we'd sing and act and do everything. We both planned to go to Hollywood. But my mother and father thought it was a disgrace to even talk about such stuff. Her father didn't [approve] either, but she was an only child and she went to Hollywood. *-Nettie Clements Frank*

We were looking all around for a place [to build a theater]. My sister Lynn actually found it -- it was the old Knatz farm in Owings Mills. [We paid] $50,000 for ten acres and a great big barn and a lot of little outbuildings and a small tenant house. But no theater. Then the question came up : How do you build a theater when you have no money? I went to five banks until finally one of them came up and said, 'We know it will cost you $60,000 to build the building and we can lend you $40,000 *if* you'll suborn your first-born to the mortgage and if the people from whom you're buying the place will go along with it."

We started to build that thing and it took five weeks and two days to build a 10,000 foot building seating 399. The actors all arrived and there's a building with no roof on it, no floor on the stage, and we were to have dress rehearsal Sunday night. Saturday, at about five in the afternoon, four men came by and said they were floor-layers. They stayed up all night and laid the whole floor. We opened only an hour and a half late. The [Reisterstown] Kiwanis Club [who were sponsoring the first show] didn't like it much, but it was one of those things we couldn't help.

We called it the "New Hilltop Theater." Governor McKeldin showed up for the opening. We had some very, very good houses. In fact, we

were only supposed to seat 399 but nobody said anything about putting extra chairs in the aisles, which we did.
We used very few local actors and we didn't have any "name" stars at Owings Mills. [The actors lived on the premises.] We finally ended up with seven houses at the Knatz Farm and we had the little calf barn, and we used the place they used to dip the cows in for a swimming pool -- it was very nice. We had a little art gallery in what we called the rehearsal hall. Then we had an enormous barn for scenery and costumes.
The theater had one bad facility -- it wasn't air-conditioned...at all. Sometimes it got quite warm, but if you turned on the fan, which was about eight feet across, you couldn't hear anything.
We were there two years and then, unfortunately, I hadn't paid the mortgage. I had a little talk with the bank. Ten acres, remember, and a great big 16-room house -- the Knatzes had lived well -- and we had fixed it up and it was in pretty good shape. I wanted them to give me another $10,000 since they said the property was worth $115,000 and I only owed them $40,000. I thought that was reasonable.
The [bank officer] asked me how we'd made out [financially]. Well, the first year we lost a few thousand dollars and the second year we broke even. After talking to their lawyers, the bank said no...I had to pay it all off. About four months later, the bank held an auction and, by the strangest coincidence, nobody bid more than $39,000, so the bank bought it back for $40,000. Six months later they sold it to a lady for $56,000 and she, after adding three acres to it, sold it to a builder for $186,000. When it was sold, I figured I'd lost $115,000 in about 45 minutes...which is not bad.
After the foreclosure another producer took it over for one year and changed the name to "Straw Hat Theater." I don't think it was too successful. After that, it was abandoned as a theater.
Then, of course, they opened the big tent theater out there at Owings Mills. Painters Mill [Music Fair]. I remember I was there when it *rained* like you wouldn't believe! They had to hold the tent down from the outside to get rid of the water that collected. But I give them credit -- that [theater] was a very fine thing. As long as they stayed in the tent. As soon as they invested two million dollars in a building it went to hell.
The original [Strawhat] theater is still standing there. [The developer who bought the property] divided [the theater building] into three separate rooms and built a pool next to it and 400 or 600 apartments around it. He thanked Danny Cedrone, who built the theater, for giving him a beautiful recreational building. Very nice neighborhood. It's called Morningside Heights. -*S. Donovan Swann*


**Trips and Excursions**

The bay steamer, *Louise*, carried many people to Betterton, Tolchester or Chesapeake Beach. Some took longer excursions to Luray Caverns, while still others had vacations at the Pen Mar Hotel, or spent two weeks at the Traymore in Atlantic City.

157

Some people [from Owings Mills] traveled to the 1892 Chicago World Fair. Children who accompanied their parents told their friends of the amazing exhibit which pictured real Eskimos seated on blocks of ice. -*E. Bennett Bowen*

We used to go down to Bay Shore. Tolchester. That was quite an event. We'd go down on the boat, get off, stay there a while and go in the water or something and then get back on the boat to come home. And at night time, too. I've forgotten what that was called, the boat we went down on at night. The ride lasted two or three hours. Didn't go too far...not all the way to Tolchester. They had a band on, and you danced and then turned around and came back. -*Genevieve B. Kelley*

## To Timonium Fair By Horse and Buggy

I remember one time, before we had a car, we went to Timonium Fair. We went on the streetcar to Reisterstown and rented this horse and I guess you'd call it a carriage because it had a roof on it. We got almost [to Timonium] and this awful storm came up. We had to get out of the carriage and go into somebody's little spring house. And then we went on to Timonium in the horse and buggy. Took a long while to get there. -*Genevieve Berryman Kelley*

We used to go to Timonium Fair in a horse and buggy. We'd go down there in September. We'd have practically all the corn cut and shocked and we'd get down there and going down [to Timonium] there'd be frost all along the road. We'd have blankets to cover ourselves up, it was that cold.

My mother, she'd always try to have a good chicken cooked and she'd have coffee or tea -- a big jug of that. Cake and stuff like that.

We'd tie the horse and then we'd go watch the races. Down at Timonium Fair one time a colored fellow came around and says, "Say, Boss -- lend me two dollars." I said, "No, I ain't got two dollars." Fellow says, "If you ain't gonna let me have the money, you bet on [these horses]." He named what races and what horses. So I set there and watched the races and five out of [the five horses he'd picked] won. I could have taken fifteen dollars and made all kinds of money. -*Joseph Brown*

We used to get up four o'clock in the morning and go over to Timonium so we'd get over there by seven or eight o'clock. To get a place to park up against the rail where you could see the races. -*Grace Bowen Pape*

We used to go to Timonium Fair one day every year in this old horse and wagon. Pack our lunch. Fried chicken. What I liked was the horse-racing. I never bet...I just like to watch them. -*Mary Robinson Sprinkle*

We always went over to the fair every year in our surrey. Took our dinner and away we'd go to Timonium. Things have changed, haven't they? -*Nettie Clements Frank*

## Jousting Tournaments

In his youth, Mr. Caleb Hobbs was often the champion at the jousting tournaments. A champion had the honor of crowning the "Queen of Love and Beauty." The couple then opened the dance of the evening by being the first couple upon the dance floor. -*E. Bennett Bowen*

The jousters came from all over -- a lot of them from over around Liberty Road. They'd have a spear and they'd ride along and try to spear the rings. The last tournament I went to at Owings Mills, my cousin Minnie Griswold and I were crowned. I think they had a dance that night. -*Elsie Marshall Hooper*

## Cockfighting: The Secret Sport

Summer time they'd have [cock fights] out in a meadow under a big shade tree. In winter time they'd have them in a barn. Fights started at Christmas and went to the Fourth of July. They didn't fight in the summer because the chickens were molting.

They'd have them one Saturday night at one place, and next week they'd have them about forty miles away. So the cops couldn't catch up with them and the busy blue-noses wouldn't know that something was going on.

Cock fighting is a Democratic sport. You don't find many Republicans there -- they've gone to church and Sunday school. While they're doing that, the other fellow picks up his game chickens, figures this is a good time to go out and fight because the blue-noses won't know about it.

I was never at a fight that got raided, but I was at one one time where they took a long time getting started...nine-thirty or ten. Finally, a kid jumped into the pen and whispered to a fellow. The guy turned around with his eyes as big as silver dollars and he says, "Boys, we gotta get out of here!" So everybody grabbed their chickens and ran out, and they fought about ten miles away.

I think a lot of these fellows had a deal on with the cops. I know one cop who used to go when he wasn't in uniform. Then, when [Spiro] Agnew got in there as [Baltimore County] Executive, he wanted to make a big play with the ladies. He wasn't in there very long -- the seat was hardly warm -- till they made a raid on the cockfights. I suspicioned that guy even before he got to be county executive. Like Fitzpatrick said one time when Tom Dewey was running for president; "You've got to know him to despise him!"

Betting at a fight is a gentleman's deal. A fellow setting up in the stands will holler across at another fellow -- "I'll bet you five dollars on the chicken down in this corner." And the other fellow says, "Okay." Then, when the fight's over, the fellows exchange money.

You practically never see a fight over a fellow not paying after he's made a bet.

There was a fellow I used to go to fights with when we were young. I was talking to him just the other day and he said, "Bob, the people who go to the fights today are really trash and riff-raff." I said, "That's right, but I reckon that when we went to the fights forty, fifty years ago, people thought we were riff-raff, too!" It just depends on where you're standing. *-Narrator requested that he remain anonymous.*

Cock fighting goes way, way back. Even the blue-bloods are involved in cock-fighting -- so-and so and so-and-so over in the valley...they all used to come. People used to come from all over the country. It was an all-night affair, you know. They'd start on a Saturday night and they wouldn't get home till Sunday morning some time. They'd have coffee and sandwiches, sodas and like that.

They have what they call derbies -- a five-stag derby, a seven-stag derby or a five-cock derby. The old birds -- last year's birds -- they're called cocks. The young chicks they raised this summer, they call stags. They [always] fight stags against stags, cocks against cocks. They're all weighed in and they match [the birds] up as close as they can...within three ounces. *-Mike Woolford*

You train [the game rooster] same as a boxer. You run him up and down a board like an ironing-board so many times and you flip him so many times. That gives him the wind. You got to feed them a certain way. You give them a hot meal ever so often-- oatmeal and stuff like that. After they get so old, you have to separate them, or they'll kill one another. Fight till one's dead.

When they fight, they put metal spurs on them... they use inch and a quarter around here. The pit's about eight feet [square]. You get cater-cornered to pit them, and they run across there and meet in the center. A bird has got to be hooked up -- have a spur in the other -- before the trainer can grab him and unhook him. Then the trainer takes him and rubs him down the back and neck and blows in his mouth. They put the [bird's] head in their mouth and suck the blood off his eyes. Old Frank Watts out here, he was the slickest pitter. He won religious! He could pump up a dead chicken and make it win one more time!

Me and Fritz [vonGunten] and Dutch [vonGunten] fought them. We won fourteen fights without losing with one bunch I called "The New York Blues." Them suckers was tame -- we could pick them up pretty near any time, but when they got in the pit, they was wicked! First one to fight wasn't very old. Harry Kellar had an old one there, and he said, "I'll lay you 30 to 1 I can beat that stag!" I said, "Okay." I got little Joe Woolford to pit him. They went together a little bit and they tore loose and flew around like pigeons. [Mine] landed on the other's back, shuffled into him Pop!...killed him. Mr. Strauss that owned [the Totalizator Company] was there and he was the only one to bet on that rooster of mine and he won.

They had [the fights] back at Gibson's on Deer Park Ioad. In Soldiers Delight. They raided that. It was a Sunday afternoon and Charlie

160

came running in there and told them the raiders were coming. Everybody just took off.

They've gotten pretty tight on them now. They raided W......'s barn over in Pleasant Hill Park. That's why he quit. That was about 1950.

*-Albert ("Hap") Moser*

In the early thirties when I was about twenty-one, twenty-two, I went to where quite wealthy people had private cock-fights. They had people who worked for them who didn't do anything but raise [fighting] chickens. Once I bet for two dollars with [one of the wealthy] men, and I won a couple of times. Finally, it came to another fight and I told him I was betting five dollars. He says, "No, I can't bet you."

He said, "When you're betting two dollars you're sporting, when you're betting five dollars with the money you've got, you're gambling."

I was at one of these places when a man had a heart-attack and died. They moved the chickens into the back room and laid the man who died down on the floor in the pit with the chicken feathers and all. The police and the hearse came and took the body out and they went back to fighting chickens. No questions asked. *-Samuel vonGunten*

### Skunks, Minks, Muskrats and Possums

When we were kids, all the money that we could spare we bought traps. Because we could go out and catch a skunk, and if it was a black one, we would probably get six dollars for him. Weasels [also] brought a lot of money.

When we went to school, not only did we buy all our clothing and all our spending money and everything [with the money we made from trapping], but quite often we helped support the family. I'll tell you how good it was -- we did good enough so that when we brought [the trapped animals] home, we would pay either our father or somebody else's father a quarter a piece to skin them.

We didn't have a good muskrat swamp, but they did around the ice-pond over at Moser's. But to trap muskrats, you should look at your traps four times a day. Because muskrats come out in the daytime to play...they have sliding boards and everything.

The other animals come out mostly at night. On a damp foggy evening, you could walk across the fields with a flashlight and pick skunks up. But when you pick them up, you make sure all their feet come off the ground. More than once I got sent home from school because I had skunk on me.

One time we got a couple of foxes in their den. About ten of us worked three days to dig those two foxes out. Finally we got them. I think we got about forty dollars whereas a man went out and worked all day for two dollars. We figured we'd made pretty good wages.
*-Samuel vonGunten*

Most of the time we'd find skunks around a barrack or a barn or chicken-houses where they'd be hunting eggs. I'll never forget the night we went out, and there was four of us. All of them had three skunks, and I didn't have none yet. I saw this big black one running and going through the fence, and I knew where the hole on the other side of the fence was, and I grabbed him by the tail. I didn't get him quick enough, and I got it [the skunk's scent] in my face. I couldn't see, and they had to lead me down to wash my face in the branch so I could see to get home. I didn't let him go! I couldn't see, but I still stayed with him.

I used to go to school and the old principal would say, "James! You been playing with them cats?" And I'd say, "Yessir." He'd say, "Well, get your books and get on the back step." I sat out on the steps many a time from fooling with the [pole]cats.

We used to skin them and sell the hides. Brought anywhere from five cents up to a dollar and a half. They'd grade them according to the stripe, or if they was all black you'd get $5.50 for him. We caught one red one...red as a fox. Never saw an all red one before in my life. We'd have hides there, as many as twenty-eight to thirty in a pen in the back yard at one time. We used to set as high as fifty to seventy-five traps.

We [hunted] up where Cedarmere is now. And we went on Trout's Farm where Richmar is built. Then we used to catch rabbits and possums. I caught one mink back near the Humane Society where old Mrs. Clark's farm used to be. Never did catch no foxes in the steel traps -- they were too smart. *-James L. Bowers*

Ed [Fleagle] built me a box-trap for rabbits. I set it in the cow lane down below the hog pen and watched it every morning for a while. Since nothing happened, I got discouraged and quit looking at it. Then one day Ed looked at it, and found a poor dead possum that had starved to death in the trap. This weighed heavily on my mind for years.

From age about twelve to eighteen, I trapped skunks, muskrats, and an occasional possum. [I caught] one mink which brought five dollars. [My brother] Lewis was my partner in this for a time. We sold the furs to old Johnny Uhler who lived in a cabin back on Chestnut Ridge and always smelled of skunk. He cheated us badly, but we had no other outlet.

Skunks and groundhogs are still plentiful. We have continued to trap muskrats because they bore holes in the icepond and fish pond. Rabbits are still plentiful, but due to fear of tularemia, we seldom eat any. Gray squirrels are still plentiful in the woods.

Last year I set a box trap for my Number One grandson, George Worthley. He tended it faithfully and got one rabbit. *-from* "Lone Hickory Farm Notes" October 16, 1955 by *Francis Sydney Reese*

[Mr. Kellar] brought a trap over there so I could catch [the coons] alive, and then he'd turn them out someplace else. I caught one old he-coon that had a scar down across his head where a dog had caught him one time and tore him or else somebody shot him with a rifle. Mr. Kellar took him over on the other side of Loch Raven [reservoir] and turned him loose. About two weeks afterward, we caught the same coon. He said, "It won't be back this time -- I'll take it over to the other side of Pretty Boy [Dam] and turn it loose...that's a good place up there for coons." So he took it up there, and in about two weeks I caught that coon again. I said, "That's the third time I've caught that coon -- it ain't going away from here no more." So I shot him with my rifle. -*Joseph Brown*

Dad used to have a home-made wooden rabbit trap. He would set that and put an apple or a carrot in the back of it and had a rope hooked to the door. There was a piece hooked in the back so that, when the rabbit got in, the door would fall down. A lot of times he'd catch a possum instead of a rabbit. But [the rabbits] were good because they hadn't been shot or anything -- they were really delicious. Mom used to boil them and then she'd fry them and make a gravy. I used to like squirrels, too -- they were good! -*Helen Kendig Bowers*

To tan hides, we just cut them off [the animal] and put them on a board. You had to be very careful you didn't cut the hide, because if you did, there was no value to it. An old fellow used to come around once a year in a horse and buggy -- really a hard-looking character -- and he'd buy the hides from us. We caught possum, fox, once in a while rabbits and muskrats. I caught one mink in the stream below Painter's .

One time over in back of Painter's farm I caught a jet-black polecat. That cat was worth five dollars. My brother, Charles, was with me, and while I was getting a stick to pick [the skunk] up with, Charles got to shooting the polecat with a BB gun. As I came back up the hill, he says, "I got him! I got him!" He started toward the polecat, and I ran after him. That bird got up, and we both got it! You talk about two sick boys! That ended our school-going for about a month. We'd gotten used to [the smell], but we'd go to school and as soon as the [class-room] started heating up....boy! I was in Miss Roach's class at the time. She says, "You're not right yet, Jack...go home!" -*John Kellar*

**Never Shot No Bears!**

We used to go coon-hunting, but we never raised coon dogs, so we went with other people. The first person I went coon-hunting with was Ted Easter. He had two very good coon dogs.

A coon dog's a hound. He's not too big...smaller than a conventional fox-hound, but bigger than a beagle. They come in "black-and-tan", "blue tick", and "red dog". Different people trained them differently. Some trained them so they bark a good bit and some train them so they don't bark so much...only bark now and then.

When the dog trees a coon, he stays there and continues to bark. Most people knew their dog's [bark] - they could tell by the howl where they were. Some coon dogs would howl differently if they treed a coon [than if] they treed a possum. Years back, it wasn't nothing for a good coon dog to bring a thousand dollars. -*Samuel vonGunten*

We used to go out there to the hunting lodge -- ["Red Dog Lodge"] -- that [Fred Dolfield and Watson Sherwood] built in Soldiers Delight.

We went there to go coon-hunting. We used to have a lot of fun that way. You know when we used to take those coon hunts, each one had to have a lantern because you were afraid of falling down into those open mine wells. In those coon hunts old Fred Dolfield would yell, "Hey! Hey! Hold that bush there -- you done knocked my eye out with the other one!"

The first time we went, we hit the coon's trail right after we left -- half an hour or so. And that little coon was tricky. He'd run up a tree for a short distance and then jump off and the dogs would stop and bark at the tree. Everytime [the dogs] would stop and bark at a tree, we'd stop and have a little bonfire and the guys would pull out the bottles. Some of us didn't drink anything, and we kept going. We trailed him until finally they got him up in the top of a tall tree. We had a fellow along with us who was a tree-climber in Druid Hill Park...he did the climbing for us. He said, "Here's that old S.B.! Get under the tree!" So we got around in a circle holding the dogs. And the poor old coon came down, and he hit the ground and bounded up right into the mouth of the biggest dog. He grabbed the coon by the neck, and oh, it was awful! Creeps! He killed the poor thing. -*William F. Stone*

We kept count of [how many] we killed and what we treed [that year] -- thirty-two coons. The next year we got about twenty or twenty-two and the third year we only got eight or ten. Mr. Kellar took them. I believe he ate some of them and gave some to colored people. -*Joseph Brown*

Boys regarded their first successful squirrel hunt as a big step toward manhood. Squirrel season opened in September and was no doubt a factor in the high rate of truancy at the local schools during that month.

Every farmer kept and trained several rabbit dogs. The men and the dogs spread out over the already-harvested fields and the dogs sought out the rabbit's scent. When a rabbit was "jumped," a gun roared and the rabbit was usually somebody's dinner.

For many years, there were shooting matches [with] live birds [as the targets]. In later years, clay "pigeons" were substituted. Prizes were awarded for the best marksmanship. Some matches were held at the Lowe farm. -*E. Bennett Bowen*

I had a 12-guage shotgun. I never shot no deer. Never shot no bears. Just hunted squirrels and rabbits, that's all I ever shot. -*Frank Schaefer*

## Eel Fishing and Frog Gigging

People used to fish in the Red Run and the Gwynns Falls. Food fish were plentiful in the streams and four or five fish made a meal for a family. Eels were also abundant and turtles were often taken from the streams and fattened before being made into turtle soup.

A good night's gigging often yielded 30 or 40 bullfrogs. The gig was a sharp three-pronged gadget fastened to a wooden handle. Only the frog-legs were eaten. *-E. Bennett Bowen*

At night in the Spring, Ed Fleagle took me eel-fishing in Kendig's dam. One time he pulled out a big eel which landed in a big skunk cabbage near where I was sitting. Its thrashing around scared me badly. -from "Hickory Farm Notes" October 16, 1955 by *Francis Sydney Reese*

## Yoicks! and Away!

There were so many foxes they would tear the sugar-corn up. Guys there in the valley didn't want you to kill foxes. They were fox-hunting, you see. We didn't know what to do. The foxes got so bad I couldn't raise nothing in the corn field. *-Joseph Brown*

Mr. Thomas Cockey had a promising horse which he could not race, as he did not belong to an organized club.. George and Robert North Elder, two noted horsemen and ardent fox hunters, decided to organize a club. Their father, Robert North Elder, Sr., was a grumpy man and he would not allow them to hold the meeting in his home so the first meeting was held in 1892 in the home of their sister, Ellin North White.

The neighbors, who had hounds of their own, gathered at "The Knoll" to organize the Green Spring Valley Hunt. Mint julips were served in abundance. A young fox hunter, Redmond Stewart, was made Master.

The kennels were first at Cliffholm -- Redmond Stewart's home -- and later they leased the Ten Mile House and the hounds were kenneled there. The lovely old house was suitable for gatherings, with a stable of fifteen horses.

By 1896, the membership had increased to over 140, [and it was decided to] buy a clubhouse and grounds. The board bought ten acres near the Carrison Station of the Green Spring Branch Railroad from Robert North Elder. The clubhouse was opened in the Fall of 1897. In 1909 a bungalow of nine rooms was built for members who wished to spend their summers in the valley. *-Susan White Whitman*

My father was one of the organizers of the Green Spring Valley hounds. [The Ten Mile House] was our clubhouse. He was interested in fox hunting, but not about anything to do with the club. He had a horse that was a perfect jumper, but very wild and I was scared to death of it. *-George B. P. Ward*

The fox, the hounds and the riders often came over the horizon with yelps and barks. The riders wore bright red coats that could be seen from afar. The horses' sleek coats shone in the sunshine. The fox picked the course, which usually led to the entrance of his den. Many chases led across two or three farms. The farmers became irate when the turf of their future hay fields flew into the air. Still worse, were the balls of mud that were flung up containing the seed of winter wheat. Such destruction was beyond endurance and all the farmers were happy when the kennels moved miles away to the Worthington Valley. -*E. Bennett Bowen*

I remember when they used to ride from the Green Spring Valley Hunt Club and they'd just ride right on up through your garden and over the fences and everything. With all those horses! You'd look, and here they'd come, they had the garden all chewed up just right where they rode. They went straight over anybody. Supposed to be fox-hunting, so I understood. -*Viola Clark Nesbitt*

The only fox-hunting I have ever done was on board an impetuous, tough-mouthed, fore-and-aft horse that had emotional insanity. This horse, as soon as the pack broke into full cry, climbed over a fence that had wrought-iron briers on it, lit in a cornfield, stabbed his hindleg through a sere and yellow pumpkin, which he wore the rest of the day, and, with seven yards of pumpkin-vine streaming out behind, away we dashed 'cross country.

I remained mounted because I hated to get off in sections. If I can't get off a horse's back as a whole I would rather adhere to the horse.

We did not see the fox, but we saw almost everything else. I remember, among other things, riding through a hothouse. A morning scamper through a conservatory when the syringas and jonquils and Jack roses lie cuddled up together in their little beds is a thing to remember and look back to and pay for. To stand knee-deep in glass and gladioli... to smell the mashed and mussed-up mignonette... the last fragrant sigh of the scrunched heliotrope beneath the hoof of your horse, while far away the deep-mouthed baying of the hounds calls on the gorgeously caparisoned hills to give back their merry music, is joy to the huntsman's heart. -Excerpt from *Old Bay Line Bulletin*, 1910, Author Anonymous

Hunters And Hounds

In the early years of this century, fox-hunting was a popular sport in the Greenspring Valley and surrounding countryside; the hunters, their mounts and the dogs such as this group gathered at Cliffholme eagerly anticipate the chase over hill and dale, across fields and meadows. Photo courtesy of the C. Rieman McIntosh Collection, Baltimore County Public Library.

1st O. M. Elementary School, before 1900

John Reese donated land for this frame school-house, the first public elementary school in Owings Mills. Photo courtesy of E. Bennett Bowen.

# CHAPTER 3

## School Days

*Free public education is a right we pretty much take for granted. But it was not always so. Even though the Maryland legislature passed laws providing for the education of children in the 1700s and early 1800s, it wasn't until after the Civil War that sufficient general interest was aroused to make public schools a reality for people living in Owings Mills. Until then, many children were taught at home. Others attended the small private or church-affiliated schools that were established in the area.*

*By the 1860s, a number of one- or two-room public schools had been established in the Owings Mills area.* A report of the Board of School Commissioners for Baltimore County published in the The Union News *of December 25, 1869 reveals that the average yearly cost to maintain each school was $777.18, of which $145.31 was allotted for books and stationery. The average yearly cost per pupil was $15.35. The maximum salary for teachers was $600 per year, the minimum $400.*

*In Owings Mills, a log building in the Pleasant Hill churchyard served as a school house. It was replaced by a three-room frame school built on land donated by John Reese. Later, this school was replaced by a three-room brick school and, even later, the elementary school was relocated to its present site, approximately 1,000 yards north of the old one.*

*Few children born around the turn of the century enjoyed the privilege of education beyond the seventh grade; many did not even get that far. Those who did continue on attended Franklin High School in Reisterstown.*

*Two schools in the Owings Mills area provided a private education -- Garrison Forest, an exclusive girls' school that was an outgrowth of an earlier school conducted at St. Thomas Church, and McDonogh, originally founded as a "farm school" for poor city boys, later becoming a military academy and, even more recently, a co-ed preparatory school.*

*-/-/-/-*

**Deportment: 100; Neatness: 98; Dictation: 99-6/17**

They didn't go by grades [at St. Thomas Parish School]. It all went by readers. You got out of the first reader and you went on up to the twelfth reader. I don't know -- you learned more in those days in a year than you do now in two or three. History, geography, reading, spelling, arithmetic, penmanship, drawing. And catechism. You learned the church from bottom to top. These people going to church now, they have to look in the book to see what they're going to say; I knew all that by heart and I still know it today. *-Margaret Clark Hoff*

I was born in '97, so I must have started school in '03...I would have been six years old then. My mother said that my father would have me out in the field plowing before I was old enough to go to school, so she started me. I went to Miss Barbara Walter's school up here on the corner of Gwynnbrook Lane [and Reisterstown Road]. Miss Barbara was crippled. She rode around in a wheelchair. The school was one room. It cost you fifty cents a week. *-Lee Fox*

Mom went to Miss Barbara Walter's School and Mr. [William D.] Groff, Sr. and Mr. [Goucher] Tase went there - he was a nephew to Miss Barbara. A lot of people would just teach their children at home. I know the Owings family that lived there at Delight got their education at home.

I was four when I started school. I went to school right across the road from where we live. Right there at Gwynnbrook Lane. At Miss Barbara Walter's. I went there right along, but they didn't have grades or anything. I had a slate and I supplied my own books.

I came home [from school] for lunch. If you did carry your lunch it was in a bucket. You would have a piece of fruit and I guess a jelly sandwich or like a roll or a biscuit.

Sometimes [Miss Walter] would take us in the yard. We'd play "I Spy" and like that. I guess she was getting a rest from teaching.

The last day of school was special. Outside, we'd have cookies and lozenges - mints - they'd give you. And you had a little card at the end of the week that said "Good", and you didn't get anything if you weren't good. I didn't get too many. *-Dorothy King*

My father only had about third or fourth grade. They lived on the farm back on Garrison Forest Road and Miss Alverta Gore had a school there at the little house that sat where [Baltimore County Police Station at Garrison] is now. He walked there from back of Rosewood. He paid seventy-five cents - I guess it was that much per quarter. It wasn't a public school then. *-Sarah Cox Hewitt*

By the mid-1800s, there were not enough children at Harrisonville to guarantee the daily average of 13 children required for a public school. Mrs. George W. Bower [nee Isabella Peck] went to Baltimore and hired an instructor to come to her home and instruct her three younger children and several neighbors' children.

The school began with Harriett Bower, Grace Bower, Herbert Bower, Anna Stanfield and Katherine Stanfield. The teacher's name was Nancy and the rear second-story bedroom became the classroom.

By the time the school was three years old, a school was opened for the community's children in the Harrisonville Hall. Finally, a public school was built at the intersection of Deer Park and Liberty Roads. *-E. Bennett Bowen*

My two older sisters went to school at the neighbor's farmhouse - Mrs. Charles Reese taught school there. That was called Millbank School. They went through seven grades there. *-Helen Kendig Bowers*

This is my father's [Frances Sydney Reese's] report card from the Millbank School. December 31, 1901. I want you to know he got 100 in deportment, 98 in neatness and 99-6/17 in dictation. The teacher was Aunt Agnes Reese. They lived on what is now Friedel's farm. *-Jean Reese Worthley*

### And So I Learnt

My father went to Powell's Run Academy. That was probably the oldest public school of the 1848 variety. We [children] went to the little one-room school-house [at the corner of Deer Park and Liberty Roads] that later became a Maryland State Police sub-station. *-Wilson Herera*

When I wasn't working in the [chrome] mines, I went to Frog Pond School [Tyler School - #6]. That's at Deer Park and Oakland Road. I got there by foot power. Rain, shine, hail or blow, we were in school! We went through Zeiglers and hit Deer Park Road. In good weather, we cut off at Wards Chapel Road and went out across Mineral Hill right past the old mine. But in bad weather, we stayed on the highway. *-A. Franklin Parker*

I went to Frog Pond School. Frank Parker went there, too, and his teacher was my teacher - Miss Nellie Gore. *-Mabel Triplett Hunt*

I went to Randallstown to school. We had to walk over there to Millers's house on Lyons Mill Road to catch the school bus. It was a horse bus. Old man Clagett ran it. It was a covered wagon like...an old market wagon with a bench on each side. It held 15 or 20 kids.

Randallstown School was that same gray stone building that's over there now [on Liberty Road near the intersection of McDonogh Road]. Nice school. Susie McClure was principal. She was one hell of a teacher...only one I ever learned anything from. *-Carl A. vonGunten*

[Gill's School] had no electricity and no water. There was a pump outside. The old well was hand-dug and it always had plenty of really great water. They brought water in a bucket and it sat on a bench and when you wanted a drink you drank out of the dipper everybody else drank out of. [It was the job of some of the boys] to carry in the water and to carry wood for the stove.

One teacher was Miss Roach. There were two [Hipsley sisters] who taught - Mary and Mattie. Mattie was the one who taught [at Gills].

The desks were wooden with iron work at the bottom. Your seat was fastened to the next one behind you. They were quite heavy and they were screwed to the floor so you didn't move them all around. They were double; you sat with someone else and shared the desk. They had little places underneath the top where you put your books and things. [Each desk had] an inkwell. [You used a pen-holder] that you stuck a point in. It was a wooden holder and it didn't seem you ever got a point that worked well. Ink always dripped and made blots on your paper. Never had fountain pens when I went to school up until I don't know what year. It was so wonderful when you got a fountain pen! *-Elsie Durham*

Gills. That was an old mud-hole in them days when I first started, you know. [Garrison Forest Road] had ruts in it about a foot deep.

Mattie Hipsley. She was the teacher. But that was quite a time in them days, you know, when it was snow and winter time. There was only three of us got there one time and the snow was up to our knees the last mile and a quarter. Walked all the way. But you know that school-teacher got there, too, and she lived over there off of Park Heights Avenue...over there in the bottom. She walked, too. And she never missed a day.

I think she had about 37 [students] in that one room. She'd teach anywhere from the first grade to the seventh grade.

I took my lunch to school in a paper bag. Sometimes somebody would swipe it and then you didn't have any.

They kept the school warm with an old wood-stove. One of them round ones.... It had some kind of shield on the outside of it. Burned wood in it and that's what heated the building. *-Frank Schaefer*

I went to a two-room schoolhouse on Broadway Road at Greenspring Avenue. I had for teachers Miss Eliza Burton and Miss Hale. *-Mary Robinson Sprinkle*

I went to North Branch school. They had two teachers. Most of the boys were farmers and they didn't go to school a whole year at a time. They had to stay home most of the time [to work]. They were real men and they were still in school. *-Eva Triplett Boyd*

We only went to school two months in the winter time. When spring opened up, we'd have to stay home and help with the work. There wasn't no law then that you had to go to school.

I went to school and I was ashamed to go - sixteen years old and only in the fifth grade. [But] I could spell. All I had to do was say the word and it come in my mind and I could spell it. We had a spelling bee and I stayed in there till the next-to-last one. [I missed, finally] on "chrysanthemum" - I still can't spell it...never could.

[At Butler School], Walter Turnbaugh was the teacher and they had an assistant teacher named Erlou England. She was a nice woman.

My first day at that school, she came back and sat beside me and showed what my lessons were going to be. She kept easing over, getting over against me, so I took my arm and put it on the back of the seat that-a-way. She didn't say nothing...just let my arm stay there, you know. Then she turned around and said, "Joseph, take your arm away. You want to put your arm around me, wait till after school." [I was] sixteen years old at the time. She was I guess twenty-five. She fell for me right way. And she'd come back and tell me my lesson and show me how to do it and all. So I learnt. -*Joseph Brown*

**The Same Books My Mother Had**

The first colored school was at Mount Pleasant A.M.E....behind the church. The old log building had served as the church before Emancipation and perhaps for a few years afterward. The old building never looked like a school. The windows were small and the roof low. There was hardly any place for the children to play except in the woods, the graveyard or on the road.

That was my first contact with school when I was a youngster. My cousin and I went up there and lay on the ground and listened to the colored children recite their lessons. As I remember it, it certainly showed the need for equality of education. Because they had nothing! Just the least they could have. The books and maps were brought from other schools. Slates and pencils and, later, pens and ink, arrived new, but it was seldom that anything else arrived that was not second-handed.

The old building and the old books didn't discourage Miss Alverta Norris who lived next door and taught the Mt. Pleasant children for many years.

Children [from the Figgs family] who lived just west of Watts Road walked to the Mount Pleasant School. The Breckinridge children who lived opposite Painters Lane on the turnpike also walked to school.

Finally, in the early 1920s, the old building was so dilapidated that the school moved to the lodge hall [Golden Guild Hall] on Featherbed Lane next to where Mrs. Louisa Ghee lives. Attendance declined and the school was consolidated with the Reisterstown School on Bond Avenue. -*E. Bennett Bowen*

Of course when I went to school, it was just a frame school. My Mama said it was a log school and that frame was put over top, but it was still a log school. Of course she went there herself. It went way back. I had some of the same books she had. The first little school book she had in school.

Alverta Norris. She was a lovely person. She taught me. She taught for years and years and years. Way late in life she married and she went to Virginia to live and she still taught school down there. Laura Thornton's daughter, Edith Tucker, also taught school. -*Minnie Clark Hebron*

My grandmother was going to church down there many a day before we ever went to school there. We used to have like a huge telephone pole out there with a great big bell. When it was time for school they used to ring that bell. -*Viola Clark Nesbitt*

## I'll Whale You While I Can Hold You!

The first [established public school in Owings Mills] stood in [what is now] Pleasant Hill Church graveyard. It was a log school and it stood on piers. When a new school was needed and the county was slow in giving it, the youth of the community used fence-rails and upset the school on Halloween night.

Then, [some time after the Civil War] Mr. [John] Reese gave a small piece of ground in the 10700 block of Reisterstown Road and they built a frame school which served until 1900 and was torn down. The red three-story house [north of Pleasant Hill Church] was used as an annex while the new school was being built, so you can see how small the school was in 1900. Mr. Charles Marshall built the three-room brick school which still stands on the bank and is now used as a residence. -*E. Bennett Bowen*

At the close of the Civil War, a two-room building of board and batten was erected on the west side of the Pike, halfway up the hill toward Pleasant Hill. This school was one of the 102 school in [Baltimore] County in operation by 1864.

A paling fence along the hill in front of the school kept the youngsters from falling into the Pike when too engrossed in a game of tag to see where they were going. There was a platform entrance to a vestibule lined with hooks for the coats and hats and a shelf for the dinner pails. In the upper grade room, the boys sat on one side and the girls on the other. -*Helen Carpenter*

I went to the old Owings Mills School. It had up-and-down boards. They tore that down. You know that house that sits next to Marguerite Berryman's bungalow? Well, that's where we went to school while the new school was built.

Amos Frank was up there with us [as Principal]. He was an ornery thing! Don't look crossways or you'd get a crack on the back. I got one one time. With a ruler. And then there was a woods in the back there and he'd send boys down there to cut a switch and then he'd beat them with it. Oh, he'd cut them around their legs! He cut Horace Drummond's fingernail right off. You know he went out West from that brick school. The rumor was he was going out somewhere to teach Indians and all the kids said, "I hope they kill him!" Oh, I heard that a thousand times.

The old school [the wooden one] only had a stove [for heat]. I doubt if it even had a basement. In the new brick school they had a furnace and heat came up through the floor - each room had a register.

Miss Sarah Marriott was the teacher who came after Amos Frank. Then Miss Weller came - she lived at Randallstown. And Miss Grace Lyle. I started in Miss Weller's room and from there went into the principal's class - Charlie Wineholt.

Some days Mr. Wineholt was strict. He used to beat the kids. Oh, he used to drink a lot. That's what it was. Some days he was nasty. The school-rooms weren't very big. They had three rows of desks...about twenty to a room. In those days you learned your ABCs and the multiplication tables. That was something very, very important. If he'd ask you what twelve and twelve was, you'd want to be able to answer it. [Nowadays] you say, "What's six nines?" and nine-tenths of the high-school kids would have to take a pad and pencil to give you an answer. I don't remember what school books we used, but you'd better know it when you went next day or you'd get a crack with a ruler.

[We wrote with] a slate and a slate pencil. There was an ink-well on every desk and a pen there. [You had] pen points that you stuck in your pen-holder. [It was a big thing] when you started to use ink.

Nine-tenths or more of the children lived so far there'd be no sense going home for lunch. You carried your lunch in a little lunch box. No paper bags in those days - a lunch box or a lunch pail. They were red. A little red square. With a handle over. [Mother would give us] anything for a sandwich. Piece of cake. I remember she used to give us a hard-boiled egg, a little salt and pepper. We always had plenty of apples, but bananas and oranges, there was nowhere in those days to get them.

[At recess time] we'd play "Heavy-Heavy hangs over thy head...What will the answer be?" and you'd guess what's over you - real thrilling, you know! "King William was King James's son...Upon the royal race he run" - you'd sing it and then you'd change hands or something to the next one. We could have fun with nothing. -*Grace Bowen Pape*

You carried water for the school from the spring down there just on the other side of the little stream. Many a time I went down there and got a bucket of water. And every kid put a dipper in that bucket and all drank out of the same dipper and the same bucket of water. Set the dipper down and the next kid comes along, he takes it and drinks. Talk about healthy or unhealthy! -*Lee Fox*

Pleasant Hill School, a three-room brick building on Reisterstown Road, was located on top of a steep bank. It had the narrow, unpaved road in front and an abandoned stone quarry was in the rear. Several tall oak trees grew close by [the school]. Running around the outside oi the building was a 4-inch brick ledge which extended to about three feet above ground level. The outsides of the windows were covered with gratings. Mr. Shaver, the principal, used to walk around that building and peep in the windows to catch the kids.

When you went down the back, you went way down-hill to a stream; on the other side of the stream was a fairly deep woods.

There were no indoor plumbing facilities. Outhouses on either side of the building - one for girls, the other for boys - accommodated both teachers and pupils. In the front yard there was a pump.

Classrooms were large and well-ventilated with windows in the back and side walls. A hallway extended the length of the building with shelves for stowing books and supplies and hooks for the children's coats and caps. In a vestibule inside the front door, a bench held buckets of water and dippers. Here there were more shelves and hooks for coats as well as the rope which dangled from the bell-tower on the roof.

The building was lighted with electricity and heated with a furnace in the cellar. In cold weather the principal kept the fire burning.

Since there was no transportation, children walked to school in all kinds of weather - no snow days! - no matter how far away they lived. Teachers rode the street car.

The school day began at nine in the morning; at 8:45, the principal rang the tower bell as a warning and at nine the bell rang for classes to start. The first fifteen minutes were for opening exercises. In each room, the Lord's Prayer and the Pledge to the Flag were repeated, after which the teacher read from the Bible and a few songs were sung. Then lessons until ten-fifteen, a fifteen-minute recess for getting drinks, sharpening pencils, going to the yard, and so forth, and then lessons again until noon.

Lunch period was from noon until 1 P.M. Children living near the school went home. After eating their lunch, everyone went out to the school-yard to play if the weather was fine. There being no equipment, the big boys brought balls and bats from home and played ball. Some played marbles, others played games and jumped rope. They played group games such as "I Spy", "Run Sheep, Run", "Red Rover" "Farmer in the Dell", and "Drop the Handkerchief."

When the bell rang at 1:00, it was lessons again until 2:15, then another fifteen-minute recess. The first graders then went home, but the rest of us went back to work until dismissed at 3:30.

Usually the day went along with very little trouble from most of the children. The younger ones thought the teacher was someone special and were well behaved. I can't say the same for some of the older boys. Punishments were having play time taken away, staying in at recesses and being kept after school to write numerous words and sentences or to learn poetry. [Mr. Shaver] asked one boy, "Kenny! - do you have a knife?" "Yessir!" "Will you go down to the woods and cut me a switch?" "Yessir!" So Kenny marched himself down and cut a switch and then Mr. Shaver used it on him! When someone was punished, he or she didn't tell it at home for fear of getting extra [punishment] from a parent.

My first-grade teacher was Miss Carrie Stocksdale. She had first and second grades. Miss Clara B. Hill had third and fourth. Mrs. Preston B. Shaver had fifth, sixth and seventh. The [classroom] teacher had to do everything - she was a mother, she was a nurse, she was a doctor and she was a teacher. There were no special teachers. When I was in Mr. Shaver's class, my mother used to volunteer to play the piano and teach the kids singing.

Mrs. Mehring, who was a patron, organized the original PTA at Owings Mills School - they called it "The Mothers' Club" and they met in the afternoon. Later, through the efforts of the Mothers' Club, the school purchased a tall white bubble fountain which was placed in the hall. Good-bye to buckets, dippers and collapsible drinking cups! However, the fountain still had to be filled from the pump in the yard.

176

Principal, Preston Shaver, and Students – 1915

Principal, Preston Shaver, and students from his fifth, sixth, and seventh grade classes. Photo courtesy of Helen Carpenter.

177

I also remember the supervisor coming once in a while. I think it was Lida Lee Tall. I have a little history about her. She was engaged to my mother's brother at one time. I think he was about 21 and he was taken with pneumonia and died. I didn't know Miss Tall then, but she told my grandfather that she would never marry and she never did. Later, she came to be principal of Maryland State Normal School [now Towson State University].

First graders listened to stories, memorized some poems and the ABCs, learned to read, write and do simple arithmetic. Grades two, three and four had more advanced reading, arithmetic, spelling and English. In grades five, six and seven, basic subjects were still more advanced with history, geography and physiology added.

Teaching was mostly by the book. Grades given were "E" for Excellent, "VG," "G," "M" and "F" for "Very Good," "Good," "Moderate," and "Failing." Children were also graded in effort, attendance and deportment. At the close of the year in June, each child's report card had written on it "Promoted" or "Not Promoted." Those who failed sometimes had to repeat the grade.

The seventh-grade girls had to go to Franklin to take cooking lessons once a week and the boys went to take manual training. We went on the street-car and the car-fare was three cents and I think that was supplied for us.

Mr. Shaver would come over to my father's barber shop while he was waiting ior the street-car to go home and he and my father got to be quite friendly. Mr. Shaver needed a janitor and asked my father if he would do it. He said Yes, he would, so he took care of the school. There was a iurnace down in the cellar and Mr. Shaver kept the fire going during the daytime and my father managed it at night...banked it so it would be all right for the next day. *-Helen C. Carpenter*

"I'll whale you while I can hold you!" Pres Shaver used to say. He always kept an 18-inch ruler in the chalk tray at the board and he knew right where that was, too. Do you remember Charles Lutz? He was a big boy. Pres Shaver was trying to beat him one day and Charles Lutz was resisting and Pres was all out of breath...had all he could do to beat him. Another one was Loki Bitzer. Loki used to get it! *-James Carpenter*

I walked from Lehnert's [at intersection of Pleasant Hill and Dolfield Roads] out across the fields to join my cousin, Isabel Disney, through the Easter's woods to Nellie Disney's and out the road [approximately three miles in all].

I started in April 1901. There were three grade levels, but only two teachers. The older boys were George Hunt, Ollie Cook, Ollie Disney - my cousin...he's eleven years older than I am and he was still in elementary school - and Edna Marshall who was the first person from Owings Mills to graduate from Franklin. And the Kings were there - Sally and Bertha and Anna. And the Hunts - Howard and Wayne Hunt. They seemed like men to me. Some of the Lockards - Elmer Shoemaker's wife, Lillie Lockard, Mary Lockard, Alice Lockard, Arthur Lockard. The Lockard's lived on Mr. Knatz's place.

To keep the average [attendance] up, we started school in April when the big boys went out [remained at home to help with farm work]. They had to have an average of 42 [students] to keep two teachers. Owings Mills was always a little short of having three [teachers.] When I was in second or third grade they got three teachers because they kept the average up for a while. Then they lost them and they were back to two teachers. When I started high-school in 1909, they were back to two teachers.

First we were in the "Chart Class." Reading instruction began from the pages of a large chart. The group was taken to a corner of the room several times a day and the chart was read to us. We were shown such words as "mamma" and told to see that the word was all "m's" and "a's". then we went back to our seats. Someone in the room wrote the word on each slate, then the beginner from the chart class was supposed to fill the slate with the word of the day. Those who mastered that chore were praised.

I'm left-handed and they made me write with my right hand. I hurt my right hand when I was little and it wasn't set right, and that made it much harder for me, but nonetheless, I had to write with that hand. I remember when this [left] hand got hit for holding a pencil. *-E. Bennett Bowen*

The school was about three miles from where we lived. It was quite a walk in winter. We'd cut across through Disney's and come out at Easter's woods. It was bad when it was snowing but it was the shortest way. We would hit up there on top of Old Tollgate Road at that house where the Joneses live now and walk down the hill from there and up the bank into the back of the school.

Edna Marquess, the Constantines, the Helmrichs, Bill Simmons and Mildred Yox all went there. Pres Shaver was the Principal. The teachers were Miss Roach, Miss Owings, Pres Shaver and Mrs. Carpenter.

We played in the stone quarry [behind the school]. That's where we had our games. I went to Patterson Park [for the county athletic meets]. I won badges for all those kids out there. For throwing the ball and maybe broad-jump. Because I could throw real good, you know. Oh, yes, that was a big event to go to Patterson Park! We rode in on the streetcars and you could push the seat so that you would face each other and that was the way we would ride. You'd come back sun-burned and sore and tired, I'm telling you! There was never a dull moment. That was really a day! *-Bessie Moser vonGunten*

At the old Owings Mills School [there was no cafeteria]. Some of the seventh grade girls would make soup or cocoa. Right in the vestibule. We got out fifteen minutes early to fix it, so that was really something. One day it was Elsie Constantine's turn and my turn to do this. So we were making the cocoa and we had salt and sugar in brown paper bags, and I dumped what I thought was sugar into the cocoa, and it turned out to be salt.

We didn't know what to do - you couldn't drink the stuff. I had to go tell Mr. Shaver. I knocked on his door and said, "Mr. Shaver, the

179

sugar we put in the cocoa turned to salt!" That got the kids laughing and we got off the hook. *-Gladys C. Grimes*

### The School Built on a Mud-Hole

In 1926, the new Owings Mills Elementary School was built several hundred Yards north of the older building which was sold at public auction. *-Helen C. Carpenter*

I recall seeing that piece of ground before the school was built. It was gullied. The area where the school sits was sort of bellied out and always wet. That was a mud-hole...a swamp. That school was built on pilings. *-James Carpenter*

When they built [the old section of the present] Owings Mills school, they didn't dig 30 feet before they ran into water and sort of like quicksand. They drove pilings for weeks up there. This pile-driver went CHUCK! ... CHUCK! ... CHUCK! ... CHUCK! till it would get the weight way up and then cut it off - BOOM!
Somerset Waters, I remember, had this big geography book and he would pretend to be the pile driver and Bobby Natwick pretended to be the engine. Bobby Natwick would run this thing and Somerset would take that book and bring it down, BOOM! Mr. Shaver caught them, and for one week after school they had to run that pile driver. We'd all stand there and watch those two sitting in there while we were playing. CHUCK! ... CHUCK! ... CHUCK! ... BOOM! "Boy!" Somerset Waters said, "if I never see another pile driver!" *-William D. Groff, Jr.*

When I first came to Owings Mills School as principal it was mostly a rural area. It was a six-teacher school, but the building had eleven classrooms and an auditorium.
I was there as principal at Owings Mills School for 18 years. It grew very slowly. We had around 260 pupils when I went there and I never had fewer than 50 pupils in my classroom. [At that time], in every school in Baltimore County the principal had to teach at least one grade. Mr. Cooper [the Baltimore County Superintendent of Schools] didn't want them to forget how to teach.
Hardly any of the classroom teachers had fewer than forty pupils. Miss Roach had fifth and part of the sixth grade. Mis Turnbaugh taught fourth grade and Miss Owings had the second and third grades. Miss Elsie Hanna was the only one that had a single grade, because she had the first-graders. But she had a large class - over forty children. Mr. Cooper would come around and he'd say, "We can stick some more in your room."
We had five vacant rooms. It shouldn't have been that way. If you had the room, you ought to have been able to cut the class size down to thirty or thirty-five.
Mr. Cooper was so tight with money! He said I had one of the highest-priced schools in the county - $35 per child a year.

9-Rm. Elem School, 1932

In 1926, this nine-room brick school replaced the three-room elementary school. Its location in a swampy area made construction particularly difficult – pilings had to be sunk under the entire structure – and also created many problems later on. Photo courtesy of Helen Carpenter.

Faculty at 9-Rm School, 1936
Principal William C. Hull poses with his staff of teachers. Left to right: Miss Parker, Miss Elsie Hanna, Miss Edith Roach, Mr. Hull, Miss Beryl Owings, Miss Eleanor Bruell (Turnbaugh). Photo courtesy of William C. Hull.

You had to be so, so watchful with paper and everything. We didn't get a school secretary until the last year I was there. We got Mrs. Evelyn Peeling, and we had to use the seventh-grade cloak-room for her office.

We didn't get a phone until two years before that. It was strictly rural, and Mr. Cooper thought we didn't need phones. We couldn't leave, so we just didn't make phone calls. When the phone was installed, I put it upstairs where there was a vacant room so it wouldn't bother me. Miss Roach, who was the vice-principal, she'd answer it and send a child down to me.

When we had real heavy rains, the basement filled up. One time it was so deep you couldn't see the furnace. We had a pump, a great big pump. When that would go on, it would almost shake the building. Then we had a septic tank, a hole dug out in the ground that was so big you could put a house down there. Every year it had to be pumped out two or three times. The people who lived [behind the school] on Ritters Lane had small septic tanks, and every time there was a heavy rain, all that stuff from their septic tanks came down across our school-ground. Today's sanitation wouldn't permit it.

Teachers had to buy many of their own supplies, such as poster paper. The school board supplied straight pens and pencils and paper. We got newsprint quality paper for most work, lined better quality paper for important assignments. The board furnished black tablets to which water was added to make ink. There were ink wells in each desk. Students hated the straight pens and teachers also disliked them. Kids would break the pen-points deliberately and then make impressions in the desk with the remaining part.

Those days, you had to have a standard [of academic achievement] to match the whole county, because you were rated. "Why isn't this child up?" you'd be asked and you had to have good reasons why a child was failing. You also had to have an open plan book; the superintendent, Miss Jennie Jessop, came around once a month to each teacher in the building. Each teacher felt she had to get her own ratings up so she wouldn't be counted a poor teacher.

They were all dedicated teachers in those days – they took an interest in their students, and they'd stay late in the evening, come early in the morning. Miss Elsie Hanna was a marvelous person! You could hear a pin drop any time you went into her room. Miss Roach, she was something. It was a pleasure to work with those people – they never complained.

Mr. Cooper was a Columbia man and he made all of us, especially the principals, go to Columbia University. I spent eight summers up there. I went to Towson two years and I got my degree up at Columbia. So we were right up there with the men who wrote the books on education for all the other colleges. If you went to summer school in Maryland – at Hopkins or University of Maryland or Western Maryland – they gave you $25 toward your expenses. If you went to Columbia, they gave you $50. It cost you every summer anywhere from $200 to $300. The first year I taught, my salary was $1400 a year.

Everybody had to teach their own music. Miss Turnbaugh was a very good fourth-grade teacher and was very good with music. So I taught arithmetic for her while she taught music to my class.

When Walter Damrosch would be on the radio conducting symphonies, we'd take the classes up to the library to listen. They had a guide book and teachers were supposed to tell the children what to listen for.

And then they had finger-painting. We had an art supervisor, Miss Jobe, who'd come and she could make the most beautiful drawings. She could put four or five children up along the blackboard and she'd say, "You do this and you do this." I never had art training before, so I was learning at the same time.

The PTA paid for a man from the Public Athletic League in Baltimore to come to the school to teach athletics. We had one of the best there was – Fred Crosby, who later became one of the supervisors. He loved to get the kids doing all kinds of games and tap-dancing. He came out one day a week. I think he went to Franklin, too. Fred had to earn his own money. He'd put on a show to raise his salary. But he was just as happy about doing that!

We had athletic meets and we'd got to Patterson Park for track and field games. I mean to tell you, we always had a good soft-ball team there. And girls volley-ball and softball. They were country girls and they really played hard! They were strong. And those boys back there in Pleasant Hill Park – the Stierhoffs. Athletic! – they could knock a home-run anytime! We had athletics, I'm telling you!

We always had a fall festival. Carl vonGunten would go up some-place and pick up apples and he'd come down to school and get a couple of boys to help him and they'd take it to the cider mill and make cider. That was one of the big things they sold.

In the spring, we had a bird-house contest. The state sent out these red-backed books and we'd have a certain thing about birds to teach each month. One of the things was how to make bird-houses. You could take just a rotten tree with a hole in it and saw it off and put a top and bottom on it, and the bird would just hop right in. We had to put up tables all around the auditorium to hold all the bird-houses the children made. People who didn't even have kids would come to see those bird-houses.

Bird-House Contest, 1935

The bird-house contests held each spring at Owings Mills school allowed stu-dents – with considerable help from parents – to demonstrate their design skills. Prizes were awarded for the most original and appropriate designs from each grade level. Photo courtesy of William C. Hull.

And I loved dancing. We always had a good Victrola, so when it was raining, I had them doing square-dances out there in the auditorium. They learned to fox-trot and waltz and all those things, the sixth and seventh grades, especially. Some of the girls could really dance. The boys though.... I'll never forget one boy named Yox: "He wasn't putting his arm around no girl!" But one thing they did get from me was love of dancing because I loved it.

Every year we'd take a school trip to Mount Vernon. We'd spend part of the day in Washington and then we'd go down to Mount Vernon and have lunch. One time a couple of the girls found some land-turtles. I said, "You shouldn't carry them back on the the bus with you - you don't know what those turtles are going to do on the way back." But they insisted on bringing them along, and didn't they get their dresses messed up! We had to stop the bus and throw the turtles out. The odor was awful!

When we sent PTA notices or other bulletins home, we didn't have a typist or a mimeograph machine or anything like that. Instead, we'd write a letter and give it to the teacher and each teacher would write to the parents. In the upper grades, the teachers would put it on the board and the children would copy it and take it home.

Owings Mills PTA was always generous in supplying the school's needs, although at other schools, PTAs argued against having to furnish [such things as] chairs [for the auditorium]. Our parents would back you to the full. The PTA at Owings Mills bought the assembly-hall chairs and stage curtains and famous pictures for the class-rooms. They also bought the dodgeballs and basketballs for athletics and the basketball backboards and baskets which Mr. Carpenter installed.

We only had one bus. Mr. Hoff was our bus-driver. He made two trips. He was a wonderful bus driver and a very nice man. First it was a county-owned bus, a White. Then, when it wore out, Mr. Cooper said, "You can buy your own bus, and we'll pay you for it." But when Mr. Hoff got to be sixty years old, Mr. Cooper says, "You're too old, we'll have to get somebody else to drive the bus." I felt so sorry for Mr Hoff! - there didn't seem to be anything wrong with him, but Mr. Cooper thought sixty was old enough. Why he was that old himself!

St. Thomas Lane was the dividing line between Garrison School and Owings Mills at first. The people on the right-hand side going toward Garrison couldn't ride the bus, but the ones on the left-hand side could. They were always battling. There was one family there, and the mother said, "My son's going to ride that bus and I'm going to put him on there!" She finally got the whole street, both sides, so they could ride the bus.

There was a crossing guard, Mr. Eli Hewitt at the school. If somebody came down Reisterstown Road real fast, Mr. Hewitt would get in his own car and chase after them and stop them even though he had no right to do that. Yes, he would! I had a nice Ford coupe, a beautiful car, and he would give his eye-teeth to drive that car! For him to drive my coupe and have that uniform on and go up around Reisterstown, I'm telling you right now, that was something!

Mrs. Hewitt later ran the cafeteria at the school. Sometimes Mrs. Hewitt would have sandwiches, but at first it was just soup and milk. But she sold her own milk, which wasn't pasteurized. The law said we had to have pasteurized milk. Finally, I said we would have to get someone else. We got Mrs. Owings who lived in Garrison. She was wonderful - we were fortunate to get her.

We had to have one fire-drill a month. We had a bell right in back of the principal's desk. We'd push so many bells and they'd all march out to the playground. I remember one of the mothers thought I was too strict because I wouldn't give the first-graders time to get their clothes on. Oh, my! "You'll give them pneumonia!" she said.

I was a right strict principal. I really was. And most of the parents appreciated that. They sent their children to school to learn, and I was right with them. I said, "If you want them to loaf, okay, but they're not going to loaf in my room. I have too many in here, and everybody's going to work." I never had much trouble. *-Wm. C. Hull*

## Higher Education

Then I graduated to the 8th grade which would have put me in high-school. But my father wouldn't pay a nickel for me to ride the damn street-car to Reisterstown and back. So that ended that. *-Frank Schaefer*

We walked from this house up to the track, from the track to Owings Mills, caught the trolley, then went to Franklin. *-Joseph Simonds*

Professor Zacharias Ebaugh was Principal of Franklin High School, Reisterstown, Maryland, when I attended there in 1903-1904. He was a mighty man, feared and respected by all. I once saw him grab Bill Kellar by the back of his coat collar, haul him up over the railing at the top of the stairs and take him into the office, whence loud wails then issued. Bill had been poking the boy in front of him coming down the stairs.

Professor Ebaugh was a mathmatical wizard and made geometry and trigonometry very plain to me. He criticized my work on the blackboard as "turkey tracks", but he passed me. His daughter, Harriet, teacher of algebra, pulled me through that subject. She was not much older than I was, but knew her stuff.

Professor Ebaugh's bust is at the top of the front steps of Franklin High School today, and I see it when I go up there to see events in which my son, Andy Reese participates. -from "Lone Hickory Farm Notes", October 16, 1955 by *Francis Sydney Reese*

[It was unusual] for children to go to high school. When you had an invitation to graduation, there'd only be three or four names on the program. When Gertrude Marshall graduated, I think there were only eight then. And that doesn't seem all that long ago. *-Dorothy King*

When we got to high school, we weren't allowed to ride on the school wagon. High school children weren't furnished transportation. When we weren't busy at home, I rode my horse. Down behind [Randallstown High School] were some people by the name of Cowan who had a stable. We would rent a stall from them, and once a year my father would go with the wagon and horses and haul grain and hay down. I would ride my horse down, take the bridle off of him, feed him, go to school. When I came out in the evening, I'd get on my horse and ride home. By that time they had an old Model-T truck they'd made into a bus and they were hauling the [elementary] kids on that. When I was riding home on my horse, I'd always pass the bus.

In winter, if there was something going on at school [at night], I'd ride my horse to school, and coming home, if it was cold, he'd be in a dead run and I'd lean down to warm my ears on the side of his neck. If he felt I was leaning to that side, he'd come over to that side of the road to make sure I didn't fall off. Prince. He was probably the best horse anybody ever had. *-Samuel vonGunten*

I graduated from Franklin [High School] in 1927. I'd get a ride part of the time with neighbors and then again I'd walk. Walk out to Reisterstown Road which was a mile and a half or two miles and went to school on the street-car. Then in the evening I'd come back home on the street-car and walk back to Gwynbrook Avenue.

The graduation was over at Emory Grove. We didn't have an auditorium in the school at that time. Every graduation usually there was a thunder-storm, and then there was plenty of mud! We had quite a time.

We all made our own dresses for graduation. We made them in school so everybody would have the same quality dress. Because then, you know, some dressed a lot better than others. Mine was made out of silk. We didn't have to have any particular color then. So mine was blue. *-Helen Kendig Bowers*

At Franklin commencements there were two special nights. The first was "Class Night", with a prophecy, a "class will", a band and much singing. The four high school classes and the seventh grade were all seated on stage to help with the singing.

Commencement was held on Thursday night. There were speeches by the graduates, and a long address by an invited guest speaker. Winners of scholarships were also announced on this night.

On Friday night, the graduates were introduced as "the alumni." One year, there were only five graduates. Another year there were eleven, later fifteen, and then, in June of 1911, a large class of twenty-seven. During his remarks, Mr. A. S. Cook, Baltimore County Superintendent of Schools, announced that "This is the largest class to be graduated in Baltimore County." *-E. Bennett Bowen*

When I went to high school, it wasn't like junior and senior high then - it was all just high school. First, second, third, fourth year of high school - period. Our original high school building is not there anymore. It's where the [Franklin] Middle School building now is.

We rode the streetcar [to Franklin High School in Reisterstown]. It came at twenty minutes of nine. The regular streetcar came along at 8:30. If you missed that, you caught "The Tripper" that came at twenty minutes of nine. "The Tripper" was always jammed with kids from Pikesville - evidently that was the reason it was put on...to bring them up and get them there in time for school. Usually it was a wild crowd. The boys would take the handle [that opened the doors] and we couldn't get out. We up here tried to avoid that Tripper if we could.

My favorite teacher at Franklin was Miss Mollie Saffell who taught the commercial course. She always had a smile for you and was very kind. Miss Ethel Parsons taught English and Music and had charge of the library. I helped her with library after school. Most students didn't like her, but I saw a side of her they didn't.

Another favorite teacher was Helen Tovell Reese - we became good friends after my boys were in high school. I still correspond with Miss Helen Huttenhauer who also taught me English. After leaving

187

Franklin she worked at the school board office writing books to be used in the school curriculum. I have visited her at Penick Home in North Carolina and, for Christmas, I received the book she wrote, *Young Southern Pines.*

We had three nights of celebration for graduation. One was baccalaureate, the other was graduation and I can't remember what the third night was. But there were three nights for which we had to have a different dress. The one, we had to make ourselves. And I couldn't sew...I made the worst mess out of sewing! I got so upset because I was going to have to wear one of those dresses.

Graduation night at Emory Grove we would have quite a big parade in. The lower classmen would walk in with flags over their shoulders and then they crossed the flags and we walked underneath them. Everything was all decorated with flowers. Somebody from the school board would come and give us our diploma. *-Genevieve B. Kelley*

I went to Franklin High School. There used to be a store across [Reisterstown] road [from the school]. In those days you could get a little pie for five cents or something like that. My mother would give me five cents to buy a pie when she didn't pack my lunch. Along with dozens of other kids from the high school, I'd go over there. A man that worked there was called "Boob" Berryman [and he had some sort of speech defect]. "Boob, what kind of pies you got today?" [I'd ask him]. "Oh, I don't know - I got feach, fineapple, fumpkin, foconut fustard...." *-Laura Wimsett Redifer*

I went to Harvard. I didn't want to go - I didn't want to go out of town - but my family insisted on it. I had an uncle who died about two years before I graduated from [Johns Hopkins University] and he left me a little bit of money. My father and my mother insisted that I go to law school at Harvard. So I did. I stayed in by the skin of my teeth and got through and went back to the 50th anniversary last Spring. First time. *-George B. P. Ward*

**The Butler Did It!**

Hobart Smith [Rector of St. Thomas] was getting old and they just couldn't carry on the [St. Thomas parish] school any more so it was closed down. The teacher we had up here - Miss Mary Livingston - opened and started Garrison Forest School. *-Margaret Clark Hoff*

Around 1927 Garrison Forest school started to landslide. It is said the headmaster or headmistress makes a school, and sometimes the reins must change hands. Miss Livingston hung on. Sadly, after many years, the school reached the point where a new driver must take over.

In 1929, the trustees approached Dorothy Hall, an excellent teacher who had served under Miss Livingston. She declined the offer. The next prospect was Jean Marshall, a teacher at Roland Park Country School. She requested that her best friend and associate [Nancy Offutt] join her. When Miss Marshall and Miss Offutt took over the

188

school in 1929, the buildings were in need of repairs, equipment was in need of overhauling.

I decided to ride my young horse, Ace, over to the school one day. Nancy and Jean were sitting on the porch steps. They told me the condition of the school, that there were few pupils left in the wake of Miss Livingston's leaving. Laughingly, I said, "Let me get into this racket – Monk Clark says 'Get yourself a horse and you can ride into any parlor!' I'll start riding and fox-hunting [as part of the school curriculum]."

I was really joking in a sense, but my boys and my little girl were in school, I was on the loose and had to have a project. I took over what was called the Riding Department. It consisted of one nag at the school, two nice horses, my Ace, and three ponies given to me by the A. Felix du Ponts of Wilmington. I got a horse, you got a horse, we go a-fox hunting in God's country! –*Susan White Whitman*

When Jean [Marshall] and I came to the school [as co-headmistresses] in 1929, we had 28 students. Most of them were local, but we had a few from New York and a few from Pittsburgh.

Miss Livingston [continued to live] at the school during our first year. She had a nice big room in Manor House overlooking the whole campus, so she could see all the goings in and the comings out. The morning after our first senior dance, she was told by a friend that the whole road was littered with whiskey bottles and that there had been a terrible drunken brawl. Miss L. sent for us, and we went up to see her and told her there had only been one pint whiskey bottle someone had turned in and [just one young man who had become "bombed" and tried to sit in the History instructor's lap], and that we thought it was kind of funny. But she didn't think it was funny at all.

As you can well imagine, it was not the happiest situation for her...to see two young women who didn't know which end was up coming in there to take over. After that first year she went to live with her sister and brother-in-law [the Hobart Smiths] and later moved to the Ten Mile House where she spent the remainder of her liie.

I taught all the English through the upper school. I was also secretary the first year – we won't go into that! If you'd ever see my typing you'd understand – the letters I wrote would never induce anyone to send a child to school there!

My partner, Jean Marshall, who was a very, very fine athlete – she had been head of the athletic department at Roland Park School – took care of the sports and also taught History.

We had someone named Mary Moore who taught math and we had a very fine French teacher, named Madame Gille who had certain hang-ups. She felt it was too menial a task to lock the door of Moncrief when she went to dinner at night, so she refused. She also refused to see that the windows were closed because that was *too* degrading. She also had a lot of things she couldn't eat, so that she was very apt to say, "That ees bad for my leev-air!" But she was a very colorful and interesting person and a very fine teacher.

[Later], we had an English teacher who was just a genius. I would rather talk to Alice Taylor sitting in this room than anyone I can think of, she was so great. But she didn't get along with the students. She

189

was a purist herself, and she wouldn't accept anything but perfection. So at recess there'd be a line outside my door. "Children, what are you waiting for?"

"We want to talk to you about Miss Taylor." "She failed me, because I didn't put in a comma." "Miss Offutt, that's not fair!"

She was there two years – that was about all any school could stand of her!

For a while, I took care of the food, too. It was hard because there weren't that many people. The original staff consisted of four. A butler if you please! Oh, he was a very fine butler! He served food and directed the tweeny outside to wash the dishes because we didn't have a dish-washing machine at the time. If guests came he went to the door – he was really a very fine butler.

Unfortunately, he happened also to be a thief! We were told that he was taking things, so Jean and I went upstairs to the third floor of Moncrief where he was living. Under the bed we saw his suitcase packed and ready to go. We didn't open it -- we decided that was not nice. But we would watch him when he left. So that evening in the Ford we stationed ourselves. Turner came out along the road to get got on the bus with his suitcase. We followed him and said, "Stop!"

Turner threw the suitcase off as he got on the bus. The suitcase flew open, and all the bacon and things fell out in the road. The bus went rolling down the road, and we pursued it, and finally it stopped, and there was just a great tumult. So that was the end of Turner. But we did not prosecute him, because he had worked there for some time and his son worked there, too, although he wasn't very good. But we found out that Turner was trying to take care of two families at once, and he really was a nice guy at heart.

[And there was] Mary Purdy who started out as a maid in the kitchen. She came from the corn-fields of Virginia. When she was sixteen years old. Mary was an absolutely irreplaceable person and she took care of so many things. She directed the staff and supervised the dining room and the cleaning. She was supervisor of the whole thing when she left. I always think of what she said one day when things were just so bleak and it seemed that everything bad that could happen had happened: I said, "Mary, how are we going to get through this?" She looked at me for a while and then she said, "Miss Offutt, we just got to tough it out."

That first year, we had taken care of the books ourselves. We went into a meeting of the school's board of trustees at the B & O building. Mr. Shriver, Mr. Sawyer Wilson, my brother Tom Offutt, Jean's brother Benny Marshall and Mr. Ben Williams were there. They asked were we ready with the report and we said "yes". Then I said, 'We seem to have lost roughly ten thousand dollars."

Mr. Shriver, who had a habit of going, "Ahh-hmmmm!" when he didn't quite know what to say, said, "Ahhh-hmmmm! Well, I suppose that's partly due to the debts you couldn't collect?"

We said, "Yes...but most of it we lost because we spent it and didn't have it."

After this meeting, Mr. Shriver arranged for our accounts to be kept with some professional help. He went with us to the Mercantile [Bank

190

and Trust] and went on our note so we could pay off all our debts. That's the kind of guy he was.

In '41, we decided we had to have a new gym. We told Mr. Shriver about that and he said, "Ahh-hmmm! Ahhh-hmmm! - and where would you like to have it?"

We said, "Come with us!" So we went up to see the spot [we'd picked out] for the gym and Jean told him the specifications [for the building] - she really knew all those things very, very well. And then we repaired back to our house. Tip Shriver, Mr. Shiver's daughter, was with us. She always accompanied her father and we knew why she did: to keep Papa from just simply giving away everything he had. So Tip was with us and we had a drink of some kind and he said, all right, we could go ahead.

So we went ahead - promptly! First thing you know, we had this big hole dug. Then the vice-president [of the school's board of directors] came along and he was a little outraged. We called Mr. Shriver and said, "Mr. Wilson doesn't think this is a good idea. Do you think we'd better fill up that hole?"

Mr. Shriver said, "No...no...no. I'll talk with him." So, with that, he calmly bought out all the stock of Mr. Wilson. So Mr. Wilson was happy and pacified and the building was built. You can see it to this day - we still call it "the new gym".

We were very, very happy that before Mr. Shriver died, the school was able to pay back most of the money he had advanced...to take up his notes. He didn't lose a lot. I'm so grateful for that.

Jean and I allowed our students to do things that were considered very *avant garde* at the time. We let them play hockey without long, black stockings. People said, "Their legs will get chilblains!" We said, "Oh, chilblains - bosh!" Before we came, the faculty were not allowed to smoke, so naturally they went outside on the fire-escape and smoked. We said they could smoke and that the seniors could smoke if they had permission. Oh, my! Chick-a-lick, the sky is falling!

We had very few rules. One of them was 'You cannot smoke without permission' and another was 'You must not leave the campus without permission.' So that settled that. The other rule was that if you were cheating you were due for suspension and if you did it again you would be expelled. We didn't want rules - we felt we could rule by the rule of love...that people were always willing to learn. As Socrates said: *No one who knows the best can choose the less.*

But we soon had to make some rules. One night we were aroused about one o'clock in the morning - I guess this was one of those gruesome Maryland Hunt Cup weekends...everything seemed to happen then - [by a phone call saying] that two of the girls were in the police station down at Pikesville and would we come get them out. [It turned out that the girls] had been driving [back to school] with two boys -- whom they'd never seen before that afternoon -- and the boys had beer and had run into a parking meter. That was right before commencement and both girls had to be expelled. That was very, very sad. The parents of one child understood very well, but the father of the other child -- oh, boy did he let me have it!...all guns on the battleship! He said that he knew the commandant of the Naval Academy and he had

191

asked him what he would do when a thing like this happened. The commandant said, "Well, I would simply put him on bounds for so long." And I said, "Look, we can't do that. We're not the Naval Academy and this is our rule." He said, "You're ruining this child's life!" I said, "No, I don't think so."

Riding was always a feature [of Garrison Forest]. [In the early days], many of the children rode their ponies over and tied them to the hitching post outside the stables. [For commuters], the train would stop at the little village down there at Garrison. Apparently a surrey used to go meet the train.

Horse shows were always big events. Our commencement horse-show was big. Mrs. Whitman knew a lot of people who had horses. We couldn't afford them, but she would get them for us - people would lend them and heaven knows what - so we really had a very good stable. Maude Jones taught riding and she was also a very, very fine person for dramatics. We did an awful lot with dramatics. "I Remember Mama" - that was really just professional, it was so good.

[At the time the school was founded], what they called a "finishing school" was very popular, but Garrison Forest was never really a finishing school. I know we sent our first student to college -- which happened to be Vassar and which we were very proud of -- in 1933. From then on we did send them pretty much to college. Not to the great variety of universities that people go to today, but to colleges mostly along the East Coast.

Through the years, we kept wanting to have a chapel so badly. That was Jean's dream - she was a very spiritual person. We didn't have one until just before we left - that was in 1960. I think one of the most important things to both of us was when we were able to have our first services in the chapel. -*Nancy Offutt*


### Walnut Day and Thinning Corn

I marched up the road [to McDonogh School] in August of 1915 and I walked into a revolution. Although it wasn't obvious to me that I was in a revolution.

By 1915, McDonogh was quite satisfied with itself. I can prove this with a song we were required to learn:

All hail to our McDonogh
With some garb of labor on her
She is threshing out the vicious from the
true.
She is heaping up her treasure
She will overflow her measure
When she renders to the Lord what is His due.

If that isn't straight Puritan ethic, I've never heard it!

You see, students at that time were aged 10 to 15. They were getting up at 5:15, making their beds, having prayers, having discussions of newspapers, all before they ever got any breakfast. Classes began as early as 7:15 and went on until 2:00 pm. Then work began.

Everybody around the school had a job, depending on the seasons. In summertimes, you would get up earlier. I've gotten up as early as 4:30 here to thin corn. It was either you get up and get that corn thinned or you're going to be awfully hot doing it at 3 in the afternoon. In the summer you stayed here and worked as a way to earn your keep. We couldn't earn more than fourteen days summer vacation. They allowed you fourteen days, and then they started subtracting. If you didn't stay proper in your studies, or if you earned too many demerits, you lost vacation days. There were some poor dogs who ended up minus days.

The military structure was used from the very beginning. I think Colonel Allen began it for two reasons: It was an excellent way to use leftover cloth from the Civil War which was still around in the inventory of some of these Southern mills, and he could get it at a good price. More important, the colonel had been aide-de-camp to Robert E. Lee.

The school, being of the kind it was, had no use for mothers. Mothers were allowed to come two days a year: October, when they had "Walnut Day" and sometime in April. Otherwise, no mothers around. They were afraid of coddling.

[The way Walnut Day worked was], [the students] all formed a circle and, at the shooting of a gun, you ran for a walnut tree. The first one to arrive [at a particular tree], picked up walnuts - at least three - and put them at the base of the tree. That was your tree. That was respected. You went around and inspected the walnuts beforehand because, if you know anything about walnuts, there are a lot of "floaters", nuts that look beautiful, but have nothing in them. The best walnut tree was over in back of the chapel. Later on when the walnuts were ripe we shook them or picked them up with the hulls on and dried them and sold them or took them down to your "bunk".

The "bunks" [were crude houses the students were allowed to build] down in the woods. Some were very elaborate - we even had a two-story building. We had cooking there. We made caramels, for instance. We also sometimes had chicken because a neighboring farmer's chicken had strayed too close to the fence.

They [also] had land customs. The boys, for the time they were in school, owned areas of land. For example, down here where the back road is now was a swamp...that was very important... muskrat areas were very important. Many of us used to trap muskrats. I myself caught a mink one time. At that time furs were valuable and we sold them.

You had a monetary system - a credit was worth two cents. You could write a note and say, "I, Paul Carre, transfer ten credits to Wilson, here, for something" and turn it in and the record was kept. You could form partnerships and seek out a person just for your money's sake. That was all developed through the students' initiative.

Reading, writing, Arithmetic, Music and The Bible - I'd say that was a pretty good education. It was a basically clerical education. They asked the [incoming] students to spell ten words and to write a composition. Those two things were revealing enough to classify the students when they started out.

Mary Purdy, 1983
According to Headmistress, Nancy Offutt, Mary Purdy came to work at Garrison Forest School "fresh from the cornfields of Virginia." Mrs. Purdy
remained at the school until her retirement, highly valued by students and
staff alike for the thoroughness with which she performed her housekeeping
duties. Photo courtesy of the author.

McDonogh School Rifle Team

Military maneuvers as well as farm labor were all part of the McDonogh School students' training in the early days of the academy. Photo courtesy of the Jacques Kelly Collection, Baltimore County Public Library.

With that sort of thing, McDonogh seemed very satisfied with itself. And yet there were a couple of trustees who doubted it. So they required an educational survey from the Russell Sage Foundation. That, along with another survey, really tore the school to pieces.

We had to change headmasters. The new headmaster brought reforms. At that time they began to pay more attention to the academics. I was required to take both courses, the Commercial and the Academic. When I graduated, I was able to type 60 words a minute and take Gregg shorthand at 110.

The schedule was changed to something that was more human - we didn't get up until 6:15.

[The headmaster's] wife began social dancing. [Before that,] we'd never had any social dances here. It's true that the chaperones had rulers, and they may have measured spaces [between the dancers], but it was over and above what we had known before.

We had a very dark basement in the Allen building and one of the changes was to put white doorknobs around through that basement.

Outside, the military formation took place in the quadrangle, and that was basically red clay. They got some cracked stones and put on it. At this time, we were now allowed to plant a class tree on campus. All these types of things. This was the first time McDonogh got things other private schools had. The student body at this time was 150 - all boys. All foundation students.

The faculty up to this time had been strongly Southern. Now these were Southern gentlemen and they were fine, but they were innocent of any methods of teaching. Changes began to come, and we got a more cosmopolitan faculty.

As we came into the '20s, the emphasis shifted to the academic. In the 1930s, when Dr. Lambert came we put in dairy and animal husbandry and shops and all that kind of thing. Auto driving - we were one of the first schools in the United States to have a driving course. Now students and parents want nothing but straight academics. No book-keeping, no shop, nothing.

The school took pay students gradually. They had big fights about all the changes, because the old alumni were very conservative. They loved this place. This was just after World War I, and the school had suffered greatly from inflation. So at that time, we not only took pay students, but we brought alumni into the life of the school more.

The fire was a crisis. Eighty-five percent of the floor space of the school was gone. Everyone wanted to close up the school except Doctor Lambert. He saw it as an opportunity. One of the alumni at Consolidated Engineering brought his entire work force; they had wooden bunks built in the gymnasium for kids to sleep in by that night.

The trustees were careful when it came to co-education. They knew that there were 400 families in the student body that had potential [students] in the form of girls. We surveyed and searched out the situation before we ever moved. Amazingly, we expected 60 girls the first year, we got 90. Every year they've increased and now the problem comes: what's going to be the relationship of girls to boys in the student population. An even larger problem is, the girls and the girls' families are demanding boarding. The trustees are wrestling with that now. -*Paul Carre*

# CHAPTER 4

## Church Bells, Oyster Suppers And Sunday School

*For many community residents in the early 1900s the church was many things: a place of worship, a social center, a place to ex-change information, a source of comfort in times of sorrow and ad-versity. Church affiliation was much stronger in those days and church attendance was mandatory in the majority of households. A number of churches served Owings Mills and its surrounding area. Most persons worshipped at the church with which they were affiliated, but on social occasions they were decidedly less denominational.*

-/-/-/-

### The Church at Pleasant Hill

At Pleasant Hill Church, this one-room, brown clapboard dilapidated building with a great big pot-bellied stove right in the middle was the Sunday school. In the back was Miss Annie [Disney Cox's] class. She taught me when I was small enough that my brother carried me.

They had a chart and each Sunday there was a lesson. It was a pic-ture and she had a long stick and she'd tell you all this, explain it all. Then, each Sunday when she was finished, a child got that chart to take home. Mine was [a picture of] a little girl kneeling by her bed saying her prayers. Mama framed it.

That was in the back room. It was all open, no doors or anything. As you got older, you went to Miss So-and-so's class.

They'd hold oyster suppers and all those things in that [same] room. The women cooked it and they served it family style. They cooked them in the back [where there was] a chimney. Most of the people donated. The oyster suppers were something to look forward to. *-Grace Bowen Pape*

Where we went to Sunday School, it was something like a log cabin, all one big room. And it wasn't connected to the church. You had to go outside to get into the Sunday School. *-Lillian Demmitt Moser*

When they [dug the foundations for] the water tank behind Pleasant Hill Church, they found many, many bones. They think they were from

197

colored people [who had been buried there], because they were not on Pleasant Hill Church property, but adjoining. There was no identification whatsoever and [the bodies] were not [contained] in anything -- they were just buried there. -*Catherine Dimmling Morris*

I started going here to Sunday school in 1916, when I was four years old and have been a church member for sixty-three years. The present sanctuary was built in 1871. Originally it was called Morrow Chapel in honor of John Morrow, my great-grandfather, who made the bricks for it at his home [now 11106 Reisterstown Road].

Up to 1925, the church was on a circuit, sharing a minister with others and our service was in the afternoon. I walked to Sunday School. It was held in a slab building that stood next to the sanctuary. Beginners department was behind the stage, this room was also used as a kitchen. The rest of the building was just one large room, all the other classes were there. No dividers - [the classes] just formed groups with chairs.

This large room was also where we held socials and plays. The young adults were very active with plays and minstrel shows, charging admission. At the socials, we had games and refreshments. The most popular games were "Musical Chairs," taking a title like "George Washington's Birthday" and seeing how many words you could make out of it in a given time, relays [that involved] dropping a stick in a bottle or carrying corn on a knife, [guessing] at advertisements that showed the slogan but not the name of the [product].

Originally, a long shed-roof, closed in on three sides, [stood] at the edge of the church property beside what is now called East Pleasant Hill Road, and was used for the horses. The driveway at that time came past the shed and made a semi-circle in front of the church. There was also a black iron fence in front [of the church]

In 1926, a Sunday School building was added on the north side of the sanctuary. In 1961, another building was added on the south side - the Wesleyan Wing.

When I was teaching in the Beginners and Primary departments, I would have a picnic for these children at Lutz's meadow on Pleasant Hill Road in spring or summer. We met at the church then walked to Lutz's meadow, carrying our lunch which was usually hot dogs, marshmallows, etc. At the meadow we went wading and played ball. ...a couple of times the whole Sunday School went there for a picnic.

The whole Sunday School also had yearly picnics, sometimes at Druid Hill Park, sometimes at a place in Union Mills where they had a swimming pool.

We had festivals, bake sales and suppers to raise money [and these were carried out] by the women of the church.

The first organ that I remember had quite a display of pipes, but air had to be pumped to make it play. There was a large wheel on the side that the young boys took turns turning by hand. The organist, Mrs. Isabelle Disney Cooper, kept a long stick handy, so that when the boy turning went to sleep during the sermon, she could poke him and wake him up before she played the next hymn.

The organ was not electrified until 1936. I was to be married and was afraid it would stop during my procession, so I made the trustees a proposition - I would pay $50 toward the cost [of electrifying the organ].

My mother told the story that someone once varnished the choir chairs, thought they were dry enough for Sunday service. The choir members sat on them, but when they stood for the first hymn, everyone stuck and all you could hear was Ri-i-ip! Ri-i-ip! Mother had on a taffeta print dress and a print of the chair remained on the back of it. *-Genevieve Berryman Kelley*

## St. Thomas: The Oldest Church

We walked from here to Saint Thomas Church and thought nothing about it. Reverend Hobart Smith was then preacher. He and Miss Katie Cradock and Miss Katie Cradock's sister used to teach [Sunday School]. *-Laura Wimsett Redifer*

I was confirmed at age twelve. When I was young, I went to Sunday School at ten o'clock. I went to church at eleven o'clock. During Lent, I went to Saturday afternoon services. As soon as I got declared a little independence, I just stopped altogether for a considerable time. I go now, but not as often as I should.

Philip James Jensen [came to Saint Thomas as rector] after World War I. He was about six feet four inches tall and very thin and bald. He [had been] a captain in the Black Watch Scottish regiment and was very severely wounded. One of the stories that I heard, was that he was wounded and lay out in no-man's-land for a considerable period of time, like over a couple of days. During that time, he made up his mind that if he ever got out of there he was going to be a preacher. *-George B. P. Ward*

When I was a boy, I helped my father cut the grass [at St. Thomas Church] with a push-mower. Cut it all. Trim it with a pair of hedge-shears, down on your hands and knees around them stones [in the churchyard]. All they had in them days was a wheel-barrow and a shovel.

Ruth Jean Gufe and I were married at St. Thomas Church in Garrison Forest by Reverend Philip Jensen at 4 p.m. on April 18, 1936. When we came back from our honeymoon, we lived with my father for about a year. That's when Dr. Jensen and my father got together and said that I could come live at St. Thomas's rectory. [Some time later,] I came to work with my father as a helper.

[A sexton] has almost as many things to do as a housewife -- you have inside work to do and outside work to do. You have windows to wash, you have grounds to take care of, in summer rake the grass to get out the old sticks so you can cut the grass proper. You have to do a lot of trimming.

You always have to be there on Sundays. St. Thomas always has church at eight and eleven, so you have to ring the 7:45 bell and the 8:00 bell and the same with the 10:45 bell and the 11 o'clock bell. Sometimes you have five days to work and sometimes six and a half.

Towards the last, I said something to Dr. Jensen and he said, "Well, Pete," - most of the time he called me Pete...a lot of people call me Pete - he said, "I think it's time for you to take a little time off." I think I took about a week off and finally I took two weeks off each year.

[After my father retired], I did it all myself. I worked from eight o'clock in the morning till five at night. Sometimes I came home and ate my supper and went back, especially in the summertime. There was a lot of grass to cut. We had push mowers. And that was awful, of course, [but] then you didn't mind because that was all you had.

I think the first [power] mower we bought was when General Crane was a church warden. Rotary mower. Then finally I got a helper. Ralph Wolfe, from Rosewood State Hospital. He was a faithful worker, you tell him to do something and he'd do it right. Then, later on, my brother, Frank, came into the picture. He worked for me until Ralph Wolfe died.

Digging graves and foundations were my extra money. $175 to dig a grave by hand. It's all hand dug and that's what I did and what my father did.

At weddings I'd park the cars and look out for the bridal party. Also, after the ushers went up and got the runner straight, then I would straighten out the bride's dress. Then after the service I would go down and ring the bell. I loved it. People probably thought the Church was on fire.

Dr. Jensen and I always worked together and we never had any ups and downs. He died May 5, 1956. And he died with his boots on - he was still a minister here. He was here till the good Lord came and took him. I worked until 1975. *-Elmer Hobart Schafer*

When they remodeled St. Thomas Church, Elmer Schaefer gave so many bricks in the walk in remembrance of his father who was the church custodian. *-Laura Wimsett Redifer*

### Mount Pleasant A.M.E. Church

I found this receipt where the Mount Pleasant A.M.E. Church paid rent to Mr. John Reese for the church. My grandmother, Miss Laura Thornton, Mr. Figgs, all of them - they rented that building, I imagine, and had church in there. Then they bought the property from John Reese. They got the new church built in 1884.

[I've helped with the church] all my life. I lived in New York City for nine years, but I never did stop contributing to this church.

[Some of the older church people I remember when I was growing up were] Louis Gray, Willie Gray's father. He had a large family...eight or ten of them.

The Figgses. The old people were named Henry and Emma Figgs. THey lived somewhere back near Raymond Moser ... where the stream of water crosses Dolfield Road ... [about one-quarter mile west of Pleasant Hill Road]. I remember their house was always chalk-white ... how you white-wash things with white paint. He had all kinds of fruit trees around there. A beautiful place when you got up in there.

Emma Figgs was the mother and her maiden name was Smith. He was Henry Figgs and I always remembered him because he came to church in a horse and a surrey with a fringe on top ... always came in that. Brought his wife and maybe one or two children. Laura Thornton lived down there by the church. And Elias Norris and Alberta Norris. Alberta Norris was a Sunday School teacher and a teacher for the public school.

Next to her - in the house where Happy Ghee used to live - was named Josephine Fax. She was a Sunday School teacher for a long time. She remained single for years and years and she finally married and she was Josephine Bell. Mr. Bell was once married to my great-aunt, Julia Davis, and then she passed and he married Josephine Fax.

Then there were the Ghees - Isaac Ghee and Louise Ghee ... Clarence's grandparents. The Ghees lived not in the house that's there now, but in a little log cabin that's gone. Isaac Ghee was Sunday School superintendent once. And before him, my grandfather - James Alexander Branson - was superintendent. My grandfather had long braids. Years ago, men used to wear their hair like that. His wife was Nancy Branson. Before that, my great-grandparents were out there. Their names were Nicholas and Louise Davis.

There was a Reverend Murray I can remember when I was small. We were on a circuit then - we were connected with a church on Liberty Road in Randallstown and one in Pikesville. There was [another preacher] named Nelson.

[Even] before we were going to school down there, my grandmother was going to church there many a day. *-Viola Clark Nesbitt*

[At Pleasant Hill A. M. E. Church] we had a regular choir. I used to play for the Sunday School. And this Miss Thornton who lived there by the church, her daughter was a music teacher, too. Miss Edith Tucker. She taught me my first music lessons. And she taught people around.

They'd have choir rehearsal. And Children's Day. The first Sunday in June. There'd be a lot of children there. They'd be behind my father's house in this big field - just a field of daisies - and they'd get these daisies and make a big daisy chain, decorate the church all around. It'd just be lovely! And the little children with their white dresses on - it'd just be something!

I'd always have a little piece to say. I can remember the first recitation I was ever in and the little plays I was in.

[My mother] was an active lady [in the church]. She gave the first donation to it, I think, the first twenty-five dollars. In those days, twenty-five dollars was a lot of money. When they built the church, they had a little back part to it that they named after my mother -- Rachel E. Clark. *-Minnie Clark Hebron*

The Reverend Henry Bell was a colored circuit rider. He was a very old man when I was little. He lived on the road that led from Mr. vonGunten's through to Randallstown. *-E. Bennett Bowen*

201

Some of Louise Ghee's daughters come to see me when they want a donation for the church. I give them respect for trying to keep the church going. I'm always glad to give. *-Sarah Cox Hewitt*

Portrait of Rachel Clark
Rachel Clark was a faithful supporter of Mount Pleasant A. M. E. Church and a wing of the building is now named in her honor. Photo courtesy of Minnie Clark Hebron.

## A Chicken for the Preacher

I'd take and I'd walk clear over to Sater's [Baptist Church on Chestnut Ridge] to meeting Sunday. Just to hear them recite at Christmas or Children's Day. It was a bunch of us and we all walked...all get together...the Raver boys. Anything going on at Hunt's, we'd walk down to Hunt's...walk to the Ridge Church...walk down to Stevenson...walk across here to Pleasant Hill Church. *-Henry Clay Hipsley*

The early churches were St. Thomas, Sater's, Mount Paran and Stone Chapel. *-E. Bennett Bowen*

[I first went to church] over at Holbrook. At the Episcopal Church. Then they closed it up and sold it and they've made a house out of it. Then the next one I went to - [the Presbyterian Church in Owings Mills] - they turned into a lamp shop. *-A. Franklin Parker*

Dr. William H. H. Campbell gave the land for the Presbyterian Church. It was part of the parcel where he had his house that burned down. He was a leader in building that church. *-E. Bennett Bowen*

We went to the Presbyterian Church at Owings Mills. At one time, when Doctor Cummings was there, that church was packed. I was sixteen or seventeen years old, so that was in about 1925. Mrs. [William H. H.] Campbell went there and Mrs. Rose. And old Mr. [Edward G.] Knatz. The Helmrichs who lived next door. And Mrs. Simmons. The Warrens came some and Mr. Garner. *-Bessie Moser vonGunten*

The only church in the [Soldiers Delight] area in the early days was Mt. Paran Presbyterian. We attended services at a house on Berryman's Lane. The owner donated the use of it for the Church of the Brethren. Harry Lau was minister.

A lot of us worked to build the present church. Last year, on my 85th birthday, the congregation threw a surprise party for me. They invited all my family. When all my family began pouring in from Maryland, Virginia and West Virginia, even the ones who were planning the surprise party were astonished at how many there were. *-Valley R. Shipe*

[The preacher who served Gill's Church had a circuit...more than one church.] In those days, anybody who had a buggy and a horse would go pick up the preacher and bring him here and then afterwards take him on to his next assignment. I can remember him being at our house lots of times for dinner, and then my father would take him on to his next appointment, or somebody would take him home if he was finished.

He got very little salary. Give him a big slice of meat, maybe, or a chicken to take home. *-Elsie Durham*

203

[In the afternoon,] we went to Carroll's Church - the old one that they tore down. In the morning, I'd get up and walk from Broadway [and Greenspring Ave.] over to Sater's Church. *-Mary R. Sprinkle*

I got married in 1920 and I've been going to Gill's Church since 1915. The old church burned and a new one was built. It was only built a short time when it burned down...it was set on fire during the night. [I was told that] a woman that worked there by the name of Mrs. Mertz fell out with some of them boys and told them to stay away from that church...she didn't want to see them any more. They got noisy or something or other, I guess.

Then they had to build [another] new church. They didn't have any money to build it, so my wife's mother and father - they were the Gills, and they lived in that house where George Mahoney lives now - they held suppers in that house to get money to build the church. They held suppers and meetings and one thing and another and when they got enough money together they started building.

It was finished in 1915. I went there when they dedicated it and put the corner-stone in. The church was crowded and the hall was crowded, with everybody standing up. So I stood outside on the steps. When they came out and put the cornerstone in, they put all of the names of people who belonged to the church and each one of them put in a little bit of money...their change. *-Joseph Brown*

204

# CHAPTER 5

## Quite a Bit of Land

*It is not unusual to hear older persons in our community reminisce that, when traveling Reisterstown Road, there was once nothing but farmland to be seen from Owings Mills north to Reisterstown and from Owings Mills south to Pikesville. Most of the land in the area remained in fairly large family-owned tracts until the mid-1950s. Blessed with some of the richest, most fertile soil in Baltimore County, Owings Mills farmers and their families pursued a way of life that had remained relatively unchanged for over two centuries.*

-/-/-/-

**Some Local Farmers**

I saw him many a time...old John Reese. Damn right. The one that had the farm where all of Tollgate is now, built up in houses. *-Frank Nelson Schaefer*

I was born on the Reese farm. My father worked on the place. I remember old Mr. Reese – the father. He was a little old man with a cane, and I remember as well as if it was today how he came to our house this one day when it was hot. He came and sat on the step, and he said, "Gracie, will you go down to the spring and get me a fresh drink of water? If you do, the first penny I find with your name on, I'm going to give it to you." And, don't you know, I thought I was going to get a cent!

The Reeses had everything in the way of wagons and stock. The very best cows and horses and things like that. It was a very well equipped place. Pete and Irvin Moran ran the farm. *-Grace B. Pape*

My grandmother, Florence Owings Waters, was a direct descendant of the first Samuel Owings. I was born in 1914 on the Reese farm. My grandfather rented the Reese residence in about 1910, and my family lived there until the farm was sold in about 1945.

John B. Reese lived with us and spent much of his time caring for about twenty hives of bees and entertaining my brothers and me by reading to us, teaching us the art of gardening, the setting of rabbit traps and where to find wild strawberries, chinquapins and other nuts and berries.

When I was growing up on the Reese farm, it was a 200-acre, self-sufficient operation. There were two barns, a stable, an ice house, smoke house, two tenant houses, a blacksmith shop, spring house, various small buildings for pigs and chickens. An old sorghum mill was used for our garage and to stable my pony, "Bobby," and the pony cart. -from a letter to the author from *Somerset R. Waters* October 7, 1981

I got a job working for Jim Barnes on Reese's farm and there I made one dollar a day. I was making good money then. *-James Bowers*

[My grandfather] Snowden James Disney came out here about 1845 and built a four-room house. He had peach orchards and Andre Disney told me they were the best peaches he ever saw. And Philip Pape, who was in his nineties when he died, said that many times he had gone into that orchard and filled himself up. [My grandfather] used to haul [the peaches] to Baltimore with a horse and wagon and sold them.
Grandfather [originally] lived down near Park Circle. He bought this land and was farming it before he built his house. He would walk out here to work and walk back.
[His house, which is still standing next door to mine on Pleasant Hill Road] was just two rooms down, two rooms up. There was no stairway - in the cupboard, there's a ladder you went up to the second floor. It had an open fireplace that was in the kitchen that they cooked with. [And the ceilings were] very low. It was a log house and it's been weatherboarded and fixed up. *-Sarah Cox Hewitt*

The Lowe place was called "Food Aplenty." You see, that land was in the Lowe family all along. It was a grant from the king of England. They owned quite a bit of land. It came out as far as Delight. That's what Uncle Gene [Lowe] said. Now sometimes he could be a little colorful - not about the property, but about other things. You'd say to him, "Uncle Gene, so-and-so doesn't drink, do they?" He'd say, "Don't let them get the bottle first!" *-Dorothy King*

My father bought his place from Mr. Lowe. All that place around there [belonged to the Lowes]. They used to bury back in there. Lived in this l-o-o-o-ng house. We'd like to look at that, too. We children were curious, you know. Peep at them. "Here he comes! Here he comes!" The [Lowe's] house was old then...I guess it fell down. *-Minnie Clark Hebron*

George Washington Aler, grandson of an immigrant from Germany, was born at the Fourteen Mile House on Reisterstown Road. He bought the 146-acre tract previously known as "The Lowe Homestead" from his uncle, John Lowe. Aler married Elizabeth Triplett, daughter of Edward and Catherine Ware Triplett. His grandson, George Washington Aler Lockard, was born on the home farm where the family still resides. *-Wilson Herera*

Daniel W. Lutz, a native of Chestnut Ridge, and his wife, Mary Burk Lutz, bought the David Slade farm and moved to Owings Mills in the 1880s. He was a very capable farmer. Two of the Lutz's sons, Albert and Arthur, continued to carry on the family dairy farm after their parents died. *-E. Bennett Bowen*

Mr. Schnavely moved away and the farm [on Bonita Avenue] was sold to Mr. Charles Reese. *-Helen Kendig Bowers*

"Lone Hickory Farm", Gingrich Switch, on Western Maryland Railroad was our original address. The farm was called "Lone Hickory" because when the land was cleared one hickory tree was left standing on the hill where the house was built.

My father, Francis David Reese, was close to six feet, a good man. He had a bad case of scarlet fever as a youth, and as a result was quite deaf. He chewed "fine cut" tobacco very moderately. Once when he sent me down to the store for a pack I tasted it on the way back but did not like it. He also smoked a pipe moderately and, occasionally, a cigar.

Dad was sent first to the grade school at Owings Mills, Maryland, built on land donated by Grandpa Reese. Later [he attended] a private school in Westminster, Maryland. He was well read, intelligent and could discuss any subject.

[My father married] Clemmis Ida Pfoutz. Their first two children, Sydney and Elizabeth were born at the house of Grandpa Reese at Owings Mills. [The others, born at Lone Hickory Farm] were: Lewis Rhinehart Pfoutz Reese, John Campbell Reese, Clement Milton Reese, Dorothy Reese, and Donald Reese.

Lewis, John, Clement and Donald were born downstairs in our parents' bedroom. Dorothy was born upstairs in the front room over the parlor, Lydia Circle presiding. Donald was born on a fine sunny day in early Spring. I remember that Lewis, John and I were in the yard when Dad came out with a smile on his face and told us we had a new brother. I said, "Dad, can we go fishing?" Since he could not well refuse, we made the first fishing expedition of the year, up to Kendig's dam. *-from "Lone Hickory Farm Notes" October 16, 1955 by Francis Sydney Reese*

My father bought back the old Owings place on Liberty Road in 1916. The old cabin, which we assume was built sometime near the time of the original land grant in 1720, had a fireplace that would reach from here to that wall. You could walk right in without lowering yourself.

Mr. Peck, the previous owner, had added to the stone cabin...doubled the height and length of it. But it had no plumbing. A good old Indian spring was down at the bottom of that hill. There was a pump they put in, but it was too slow for my mother. She'd walk down to the bottom of the hill. *-Wilson Herera*

My father worked on the [George P.] Mahoney farm [on Garrison Forest Road]. It was the Kempers [who owned it] at that time.  -*Elsie Durham*

[Dolfield's] farm was a pretty good one and [the Mosers] farmed the Rose place too. I guess Bill Rose didn't like farming much and the grandsons didn't like it, either, so they ran a little store downtown. But when old Mrs. Rose was living, they were really truck farming...really making money. Tom Offutt only paid a little over $2,000 during the Depression for the Rose place and that was over 100 acres.

[The farm where Tom Offutt] lives was the Hook farm. The Hooks must have been people with a little means, too. -*Carl A. vonGunten*

Trouts owned the big field behind our house. One year they'd plant corn in it and the next year wheat. And always threshed over the Fourth of July.

The Trouts were bachelors - Norman and Milton - and their mother was always there when we went down there for eggs or milk. They used to come up Kingsley Road with their horse and wagon and they could also go out [by way of] Gwynnbrook Lane.

Brandt bought that farm after it changed hands a couple of times and [later] they sold it to Richmar Apartments. -*Genevieve B. Kelley*

The Fritz farm [on Academy Avenue] was a pretty good-sized farm...it went from Timber Grove down to Kendig's Mill Road. The house was built right where it's standing. Before the Fritzes lived there, there were people named Rose. Now people named Weiss have it.

The Wyatt place [on Timber Grove Road] seemed huge, but of course it was 200 and some acres. It probably goes all the way out to the Western Maryland Railroad and down Timber Grove Road.

My grandfather came up from St. Mary's County with Mr. Wyatt. [Grandfather] lived in a house over there on what they called the Fleagle's place, which ended up being Robinson's place.

[The Wyatts] had what they called a spring house and a big dairy there, a stone house. They had two wells on the place, one up by the house and one farther down that they pumped water from with a gasoline engine...used to pump it up to a big tank. They had plumbing and everything...a bathroom. There were plenty of fruit trees and they used to raise grain and all that. -*Viola Clark Nesbitt*

## Raising The Barn

My father up on the farm there he had a barn-raising. They had a big dinner for them and all the farmers would come and help raise the logs up. They built a scaffold to get them up there, and three or four men would get hold of them with long poles, and they'd hold them up that way. There'd be one up at the top to drive these pegs in that hold [the logs] together. Back in those days, one would help the other if they could. -*Joseph Brown*

I helped with two barn-raisings. One wasn't exactly a barn, it was a big barrack* back at Sherwood's. I helped raise that. And then when Gore's burnt out, I helped raise that barn. In fact, I helped saw some of the lumber for it. *-A. Franklin Parker*

* "Barrack" refers to a hay storage building, usually with an open middle section and enclosed hay-mows on either side.

## Kicked by Mules Many a Time

My father used to buy four young mules every year. We'd raise them up and break them to work and then we'd sell them. You had to watch a mule or he'd kick you before you knowed it. Me and [my brother] John been kicked by mules many a time.

The young mules, we'd catch them and trim the mane and ears and tail. Sometimes when us boys wanted to have some fun, we'd hold one of these young mules and one would help another up on it. No bridle or nothing. John and I, our legs were just long enough [so] we could reach down and hook our heels underneath them. He could buck and carry on and he couldn't get you off, because you were tight there on him. We'd stay on that mule till he quit trying to buck us off, until you could get on him and ride him around the barnyard. *-Joseph Brown*

Clements' Receipt for Shoe Boils on Horses: Clodion and Castor Oil in equal parts. Lance boil and apply mixture twice a day until cured. -from *Joseph Simonds* ledger for Painters Mill - 1913

[When a farmer bought a horse or a mule] he was taking a chance just like you are today [when you buy an automobile]. Some of those fellows were pretty smart about horses. Sometimes you could have them on trial, like if you wanted a horse that could do a certain thing. *-Carl A. vonGunten*

Farmers had standards they used in selection of horses, mules, cows and other livestock. There was a saying about colts: "Four white feet and a white nose - lop off the head and feed it to the crows." *-E. Bennett Bowen*

## Three Horses and a Furrow Plow

When I was eleven years old I was plowing with three horses and a furrow plow. The plow sometimes used to hit me upside the head and knock me clear down on the ground. I'd have to run to get hold of the plow handles and straighten it up and go on.

Three horses and a spring-tooth harrow - go out in the morning early and walk behind that harrow from morning to night. I [even] used to go back out [and harrow some more] after supper. Some times I'd be so tired I'd sit down and couldn't hardly get up. Dirty! Dust all over you, so you'd have to take a bath in a great big wash-tub. *-Joseph Brown*

## Stacking the Sheaves

You couldn't plant [winter] wheat before October 15th, because if you did it would grow too high. At the same time that you planted wheat you [also planted] timothy and clover seed -- that was on the front of the grain drill in a little box.

The wheat was ready to be reaped towards the end of June. We used to get Ed Shoemaker and his son, Elmer, who lived back of Painters Lane just past Meadows Road, to come cut it. They had a binder, and Elmer would ride one of the four horses that pulled it, and his father would sit up there and make sure that the sheaves of wheat were tied when they kicked off. We would follow along and pick up the sheaves and stack them. *-George B. P. Ward*

Before the reaper was invented, all grain was cut by hand. The workers used a cradle, similar to a mowing scythe, but it had an additional frame of fingers that caught the cut stems. Mr. Joshua Griffin was said to be the best hand that could be hired to cradle grain. [Even after the invention of the reaper], many farmers continued to cradle paths around their fields so that the binders would not ruin the grain on their first pass. *-E. Bennett Bowen*

When we'd cut wheat with a wheat binder, we'd have to cradle all the way around the field. I've cradled around twenty acres many a time. [Your back got sore] and your arms and shoulders -- you had to get used to it. *-Joseph Brown*

## Scared to Death of the Threshing Machine

Oh, boy! I was scared of those things! When I'd hear the threshing machines coming up that back road, coming up by Coleman's, I was scared to death. They couldn't possibly hurt you, but that noise was just so different. I guess about once or twice a summer they'd come up there - to Andrew Disney's and a couple of those places. Charley Yox and Horace Strevig had machines. They'd send you word that they'd be there to thresh tomorrow. You had to feed them. *-Grace Bowen Pape*

The greatest event for the children was the arrival of the threshing machines each fall. When the great steam engine arrived, pulling a train of machines including the thresher, the baler and the water wagon, all of the children followed the parade up the dirt road from Reisterstown Road to the barnyard. When the threshing machine left, there was an immense mountain of straw for us to use as a sliding board, and a barn full of baled hay useful for building forts and houses with secret entrances through tunnels. *-from a letter to the author from Somerset R. Waters, October 7, 1981*

210

I started the hard way. My Daddy died when I wasn't but nine years old. I started firing a steam engine at eleven. It was Charley Yox's. [He threshed] all over the country. The farthest I was ever with him was around over by Gwynnbrook and up through Glyndon and all around through Deer Park. It took him pretty near a year by the time he went his rounds.

[His crew was] three men. He paid two men and himself. The farmer had to furnish the rest. We didn't do anything [except] just [run] the machine. Feed the machine. The biggest thing was to keep the steam up out there in the engine. They had to haul water with a barrel and a horse from a creek or something. That was usually a kid's job on the farm.

At thirteen I was feeding the threshing machine. Big old table up there and they'd throw it up there and one man would cut the bands and you'd push it over into the cylinders. The wheat would come to you in a bundle and you'd take your hands under it and just flip it and that would loosen it all up.

I've worked under the wind-stackers, too. Oh, that's a dirty job. All threshing is dirty.

The place that stands out in my mind [as having the best food for the threshers] was over at Charley Cockey's. Right above Stevenson Station, on top of the hill. We worked there Thanksgiving day. So he come out at ten minutes of twelve and told Mr. Henry, "You fellows will have to run a little longer - dinner ain't quite ready yet." By the time we got in the house it was after one o'clock. And he had a turkey there that was a monster! [Mr. Cockey] told Henry Adams, he says, ""Listen! - I'll never work you fellows overtime again!"

[When we went to places that were some distance from home], we'd sleep out under an apple tree or anyplace. Get a whole pile of wheat bags - granite bags - and use them for a pillow. Wait till everybody went to bed and go out to the engine and get a bucket of hot water and go down to the horse trough and take a bath. -*A. Franklin Parker*

The threshers in the neighborhood were Strewig, who lived at the corner of Bitzer's Lane and Reisterstown Road and Klohr, who lived back at Painters Lane and Lyons Mill Road. -*George B. P. Ward*

Walter Geiss had [a threshing machine] and Dick Tillman had one here at Park Heights. Most of the farmers would cut the wheat and put it in the barn in the mow. When you put wheat in the barn it would get warm and go through a sweat. Then the threshers would come in and thresh it.

Sometimes the threshing machine would come right to the field. You'd have to come around with a pitch-fork and fork the shocks of wheat on a wagon. Have one person up on top of the wagon loading.

The steam engine set way back - about forty feet from the thresher. [They were connected with a long belt.] They had a place on the back of the thresher where there was a cylinder with spikes on it and a platform where you threw in the wheat.

They wanted small kids to haul water for the engines. Haul water to make steam for the steam engine. We had a two-wheel car with shafts on it and a barrel on it. You'd fill the barrel with water and

211

take it up to the engine and they'd draw this water out with the engine. They drawed it out of the barrel with the steam.

The thresher had a blower on it to blow the straw out into the barnyard. You'd have to have somebody out there to shake it around and rick it. Many a time I've ricked it. That was a dirty job! All that dust and stuff!

The wheat [kernels] came out on the side of the thresher. You hooked a bag on [the chute]. There was a thing on the thresher that held a half-bushel and it would dump itself. That came down into the bag, so if you wanted two bushels in a bag, it would have to be dumped four times.

Later on, they had the balers, and you could be threshing and baling at the same time. *-Joseph Brown*

That was a big day when the threshing machine came around! I always had to be on the wagon and help load. My father would jump into me if I didn't get it packed right. There were times when we just made it to the barn and [the load] slipped off. That was ten times worse than if it slipped off outside. *-Wilson Herera*

When the threshing machine was going to be on the Fritz place or say the Graef place on Timber Grove road - if it was engaged for the Reeses or whatever - he'd try to go to all the farms in the area. *-Viola Clark Nesbitt*

The farmers from around close by had sort of an alliance - they would help each other thresh. A whole gang of them would come. They'd be threshing all day long. Aunt Minnie and Cristie, the cook, would fix a big meal for them. They'd bake bread and pies and cakes and cook potatoes and sauerkraut and vegetables of all kinds.

The threshers didn't waste any time. They came up to the back steps where the towels and soap and buckets of water and the wash basins were. They washed quick and came in and sat down at the table. They ate silently and constantly until they were filled. When they wanted something, they didn't ask to have it passed, they just stood up and reached over with their fork and got whatever it was. When they were finished, they left. *-Waiva Dean Reese*

We always had Adam Klohr. Later Josh Crooks took over from Adam Klohr - he was his son-in-law. Strevig was another thresher and we may have had him at first.

They'd thresh soon after the Fourth of July. You really had to cook a lot because there would be at least twelve men to feed. You had a small table for the colored [men] and a big table for the white ones. All the men sat down and the women did the work.

Mom made pies and cooked off a ham and they'd have string-beans and, of course, potatoes. I don't remember about frying chickens, but chances are that for one meal - either dinner or supper - it would be chicken. Yellow apples were the first thing in and she always made pies with them. And you would wash off a piece [of ice from the icehouse] and put it in a bucket or crock of tea and take it out to the field. *-Bessie Moser vonGunten*

Josh Crooks used to come thresh. Us kids would have to haul the water for the engine. We'd get to fooling around down in the branch and the whistle would blow and we'd have to get a barrel of water real fast.

When it was threshed, the wheat was hauled right down to Groff's [mill]. -*Sarah Cox Hewitt*

**Flailing The Rye**

[Ed Fleagle] told us [stories] while he was flailing our rye, of which we raised one acre each year. [The rye grew] six feet high and was stored in the loft above the barn floor [to be] flailed out by Ed during snowy days in winter. He bound the straw with two straw bands, nice and straight, in bundles about a foot thick. [This resulted in] one big load of rye straw which we sold to a doctor in Baltimore who preferred rye straw to bed down his horses. -from "Lone Hickory Farm Notes" October 16, 1955 by *Francis Sydney Reese*

**Five Grains of Corn to a Hill**

My father dropped corn for ten cents a day and a dinner of stale bread and tough salted meat. Five grains of corn were dropped into each hill and covered. [There was] a little ditty about the number of grains:

One for the blackbird,
Two for the crow
Three for the cutworm
And Four and Five to grow!
-*E. Bennett Bowen*

They planted corn around Decoration Day with a horse-drawn planter. That was checked - you had a wire with knots in it that ran across the field. As you went along, this thing on the planter would hit a knot and drop a couple of kernels of corn. You'd move it over each time you finished a row. Consequently, when you got the field done, it was what you called cross-checked and could be cultivated both ways - up and down and across the rows.

We worked [cultivated] the corn about three times. The corn worker had big iron shovels and you could actually steer the wheels so that you could keep them right in the rows.

Right after Labor Day the job was cutting corn. They went through the field and made "horses", which meant you took four stalks from four different hills and pulled them together and wrapped them around each other. That gave you your base. Then you cut the fodder and laid it up against that.

To cut corn, you take an old coat sleeve and tie it over your arm with a hole that your thumb would go through. String would go around your neck and you wore an old cap pulled down over your ears. You had a glove on one hand and a corn knife in the other.

Then came the husking. I was never any good at husking. It seemed to me like a very slow thing. You'd throw the shock over and sit on it with a husking pin, breaking the ears off. I never liked that.
–*George B. P. Ward*

My father always checkered the field corn. When you planted, you had a reel with an overhead arm on it. In later years, we had hybrid corn that didn't grow quite so tall so you planted much closer.

A Mr. William Black always husked our corn. Then we'd come along and pick it up. Only trouble was, rats and mice would get into the corn piles. The dogs would have a great time chasing them.
–*Wilson Herera*

You see, there's two rows of corn here like this. You get a stalk or two stalks from that hill and get two over here and bring it in and hold [them all together] and twist one of them stalks around it. If the stalk breaks you can use string to tie it. [That's called a "buck".] Then, you see, you can set your corn around them. [That's called a "shock".] Then when you want to [husk] the corn, you cut these four corners and you can push [the shock] right over.

You put a husking peg [on your hand] for husking out the corn. It had straps on it that went across your hand and it came out and caught the ear of corn. You take it that-a-way and get hold of the ear and rip back the husk. I used to have my hands all tore up. Mostly you wore gloves if you could. We'd have gloves that had the fingers out...wouldn't have any fingers in them. It was a cold job, sitting out there in the cold. I've husked a many of it. –*Joseph Brown*

The corn was often cut by a neighboring family. A man, his wife and two children would come. Often they cut on moonlight nights and they would sing as they stacked it. They came back later and husked it.

They would throw the ears into piles and tie the fodder into bundles and then tie them into a great big "shock" – ten or twelve bundles made a shock. The shocks were tied around with binder twine and were fed to the cows during the winter. A wagon and horses went out and picked up all the piles and put the husked ears in the corn crib. They were fed to the horses in winter and some were ground up for cow feed.

Later, we hired various huskers. One pair would work until they had two or three dollars, and then they went and celebrated. Came back when they needed more money. –*Waiva Dean Reese*

We'd have a corn-cutting time if it was real moonlight. We might go out there - a whole bunch gathered together - and cut corn one night. Have a little cider...little refreshments. –*Carl A. vonGunten*

## Hay in Windrows

[My grandfather] used to cut [hay] with a scythe. And then he had another thing called a cradle. A scythe is just one blade. [The cradle had a blade and] two or three racks. When he cut [with] that, he could do two or three cuts and pile it up at the same time. With a scythe, you can do very little piling. [Grandfather] used to get a tree branch that was forked like prongs and we'd use that for helping him gather up his hay. -*Viola Clark Nesbitt*

If one man had a lot of hay down and it looked like it was going to come a rain, the others would come help him get it in. -*Sarah Cox Hewitt*

Women helped some [with making hay]. In those days they cut it down and raked it up in windrows, and you had to go along and put it in piles for when they came with the wagon to pick it up. -*Bessie Moser vonGunten*

The prize job in making hay was to be up on the wagon and tromp the hay down as it was thrown up. I'll tell you something - you've never lived until you've had a long-handled pitch-fork and just turned over a pile of hay and here comes a black snake! -*George B. P. Ward*

The hay was brought up to the barn where there was a big, two-pronged fork hanging from the ceiling. That was operated by a rope that ran on pulleys and was pulled by a horse. The fork was pulled down to the wagon load of hay, stuck firmly in the hay and fastened with little clamps on [either] side. Some child would drive or ride the horse [out away from the barn] until the fork load of hay reached the roof of the barn. Then they tripped a little lever, and the load of hay fell into the haymow. -*Waiva Dean Reese*

You had a hay fork and a system of pulleys. You pulled [the hay] up until it went across a track and over into the mow*. Then you pulled a ring and tripped it. We had good times on those hay ropes! -*Wilson Herera*

* "Mow" (pronounced to rhyme with "how") refers to a hay storage area. Most local barns were bank barns, with an upper story reached by a dirt ramp. Usually this upper area had mows on either side of the central barn floor.

Salt helps to keep the hay sweet. You sprinkle it on as you put it in the barn. Cattle will eat it twice as good. -*A. Franklin Parker*

## Frosty Mornings In the Meadow

We'd turn the cows out at night and when we'd go out into the pasture to get them, there'd be frost on the grass some places and we'd be bare-footed.   Where an old cow had slept on the ground all night, you'd step on it...and get your feet warm.   *-Joseph Brown*

When I worked for Lev Bowen, they used to have about 40 head of cows.   I used to have to get up at four o'clock in the morning, get out there and find them in the pasture.   [That was] back down there by that place that had all them plays in it [Painters Mill Music Fair].

One morning I went to round up a cow back in there and this damn bull, he laid for me.   He was a Guernsey.   'Course, I could run in them days.   I couldn't go through that barb-wire fence, so I rolled under the gate, and when he came, he hit the gate with his head.   He didn't get me.   I told the man to get rid of him, or I was going to kill him.   So he got rid of him.

I'd get up four o'clock in the morning, go find them cows, and work all day out there on the farm, come in at six o'clock and then had to clean the dairy.   I could set down and go to sleep, half the time, with a knife and fork in my hand and pretty near kept my face in my food.   I got ten dollars a week.   Yep.   Ten dollars a week.   I only got one day off a month.

[At first] we milked by hand and then they got milkers.   They bottled it up, you know, and had a route around here, just like that one over on Pleasant Hill Road that they called Silver-something-or-other. [Silverbrook Dairy run by Albert Lutz].   Used to bottle it and sell it and some of it they shipped.

And then they made ice-cream out of it.   [Had a] mixer...it was run by electric.   Bowen used to serve that little stand out there across from Roach's Lane with ice-cream.   And on this side - where Lyon Brothers is - the Bowens had a little shanty house where they sold ice-cream, candy, stuff like that.   *-Frank Nelson Schaefer*

My father had twenty-five cows and you had to hand milk.   In the summer time when they were harvesting, my sister and I would get the cows in, milk them, and then turn them back out.   My father was very smart, because he would tell us how much we helped him and how much he appreciated that.   I'm telling you, we just felt real big!

Andrew Disney was a dairy farmer.   He retailed.   A Bowen who was Grace Pape's brother used to deliver the milk around for him with a horse and wagon.   I remember when Lutzes delivered, too.   [The milk] wasn't pasteurized.

[People like Raymond Moser who shipped their milk] got paid according to the butterfat.   In them days, they had Jersey cows and the milk was better.   The Holstein's milk is the worst.   *-Sarah Cox Hewitt*

We milked at 5 am and at 5 pm.   At quarter to 5 am, Dad would yell up the stairs - "Get up boys, it's late!"   (It was *always* late!) He would then add a direct order to me as the oldest - "Sydney, get them up."   Since this probably flattered me, I took an inhuman delight in rolling out my poor sleepy brothers.   -from "Lone Hickory Farm Notes" October 16, 1955 by *Francis Sydney Reese*

216

[After the men brought the buckets of milk up from the barn,] first we strained it. You had a big [funnel-shaped] strainer with a little disc you put in the bottom. You sat the strainer on top of a milk can and poured the milk through it. Then the milk was poured into the cooler. The cooler [was an upright metal device] that had a lot of coils with water running through them. The water came from a pump that was in the dairy...the pump ran off of gasoline power. Before we had the gasoline engine we used to pump by hand. We poured the milk into a container at the top of the cooler and it ran down over the coils and into a sort of trough at the bottom and from there into a milk can. Then we put the cans into a big trough filled with water that was built right into one corner of the dairy. In summer, we would put ice from the ice-house in there to keep it colder.

To clean up the milk buckets and cans and the strainer and the cooler parts, we washed everything with hot, soapy water and then there was a regular chlorine solution we used to rinse them. *-Elsie Moser Bates*

There were two Trout brothers who lived down there [on Gwynnbrook Lane]. We used to go down there and get milk - twenty cents a gallon. They used to raise cattle and ship milk. *-James L. Bowers*

One of my earliest memories is watching Dad and Ed Fleagle treat "Wolf" in cows' tails. A cow would get sick, off her feed, feeble and failing in milk. They would take a pocket knife, cut a slit in the skin of the cow's tail about eight inches long, put a lot of salt in it, then bind up the tail with string. The cow would act very lively, switching her tail, shuffling her feet, and would be thought to show improvement.

Some years later, after the practice had been abandoned, I asked my father about it. He admitted, with a rather shamed look, that he knew now that this had been only a baseless superstition, an example of some old practice he had learned from his father. My own opinion now is that the cow probably had tuberculosis or some other malady. -from "Lone Hickory Notes" October 16, 1955 by *Francis Sydney Reese*

When you were milking, you'd squirt the milk and the cats would catch it right in their mouth. *-Paul Englar*

Raymond [Moser] would take his milk out to the train. Then, later, when the train quit taking it, they took it out and put it on the milk stand [by Gwynns Falls stream on Reisterstown Road.] He was always late getting his milk out to the train. That old horse would go out that road! I mean that was a driving horse...that sucker could go! *-Carl A. vonGunten*

We had Guernsey and some Jersey [cows] because we wanted cream. Cream was kept in the dairy in a little concrete trough my father made. We set those big ten-gallon cans right in the spring. My mother said a coconut made the best cup for dipping up cream - lasted twenty years or more.

We had ten or eleven cows. Even as late as World War II, there were many farms with eight to twelve cows. Now, I suppose, fifty is the least you can get by with. *-Wilson Herera*

Mr. Chester Reter, who lived across from us [on Walnut Avenue] had a big dairy farm. *-Catherine Dimmling Morris*

We shipped milk. We put it through a cooler in the dairy, then lowered the tub into the ice-house. Somebody down there would have a big old ladder and a big old pulley. *-Jean Reese Worthley*

That [little brick] building at the corner of Bonita Avenue and Gwynnbrook was a spring house. There is a huge spring there where they cooled their milk. It is really old. *-Helen Kendig Bowers*


### Running the Egg Route

My mother would set a chicken hen on about a dozen eggs. They would take three weeks and one day to hatch out. We usually raised Barred Rocks and sometimes Rhode Island Reds. We'd use the roosters for fryers and keep the hens for layers. We'd take the eggs to Garner's store and trade them for groceries. *-Elsie Moser Bates*

Our place was called "Egypt Farms" and at one time it was a large chicken business. They were in egg production. The eggs went mostly to New York. They'd take them down to Owings Mills station and ship them. *-Elsie Marshall Hooper*

We had a route where we delivered and sold most of our eggs. That way you got more money than if you wholesaled them. We had between four and five thousand laying. That was a lot of laying hens for a little space.

My husband died in '57 and later my son died and after that, I raised chickens for Bauman and didn't do the eggs [any more]. I raised 20,000 chickens a year - two batches a year. Of course, you didn't make a whole lot - I made about $5,000 a year. But that was better than nothing and I liked it, too. I'm sorry that I'm not doing it now, because I think it did me good...kept me going. *-Sarah Cox Hewitt*


### Eat a Lot of Cherries!

There were many varieties of winter apples grown in in farm orchards - "Seek-Me-Farther", "Paradise", "York Imperial", "MacIntosh", "Black Astrican", and "Ben Davis", which was not well-liked. Summer varieties included the "Maiden's Blush", "Summer Rambo" and, in September, "Smokehouse."

The largest local orchard had, perhaps, five hundred apple trees. Peaches were grown in smaller quantities.

Nearly every home had a plum tree. The Bartlett and the Seckle pear were the general favorites. Quinces were grown and used for making delicious preserves and jellies.

Cherry trees grew in nearly every yard. Black cherries, wax cherries and sour cherries all flourished in our area. They were usually canned and preserved for winter and appeared on the table as a favorite dessert - cherry pie.

Diseases were a problem in the orchards. Black rot killed many plum trees and various forms of scale affected other fruit trees. *-E. Bennett Bowen*

We had a grape arbor and we made wine which we could drink only at Thanksgiving and Christmas as my parents were rather tee-totalers.

I think my father tried everything a little bit - he had a plum tree, he had a damson, he had cherry trees. The cherry trees were planted right along Rosewood Lane and my father had a very easy method of protecting them - he just let the poison oak grow up around them. I remember one occasion when three boys climbed up in the cherry trees on a very hot day. They were from Pimlico and had ridden out on bicycles. My father went out and said to them, "Do you know what that green stuff is?"

"Nossir."

He said, "Eat a lot of cherries!"

Kieffer pears are, to my mind, an abomination because they're as hard as rocks and then they all get ripe at once and rot within three or four days. The seckel pears were delicious. The only trouble with them was that when they fell off the tree they would start to rot and all the yellow-jackets in the world would gather around. When you went out there in your bare feet, that was murder! *-George B. P. Ward*

## Filling The Ice-House

Dad [Frank Reese] and [our hired man] Ed Fleagle built the ice pond with plow and horse scoop. Before that, we got ice from Kendig's dam, and then for a few years from Phillips' ice pond on the farm now owned by George Mahoney, the perpetual candidate for Senator, et cetera. Dad laid out the ice pond and made a good job of it. He borrowed a level from Dave Kendig, the miller. By driving two stakes in the ground, laying a board on them and the level on top of that, he sighted [from] where he proposed to put the lower bank to a spot on the stream that came down from the springs. He determined that if he put the intake at that spot, the pond would always be full but the water would not overflow the banks.

However, Ed Fleagle argued that it did not look right, that it looked as though if the intake was put at that spot the pond would not fill to the top. So Dad agreed to move the intake spot farther upstream. This proved to be an error, and had to be dug up and moved down to the spot he had originally determined.

The pond was a success, still exists, and for many years we filled our icehouse from it. [The icehouse] is a hole sixteen feet square and sixteen feet deep, under the truck garage. It took sixteen four-horse loads of ice to fill it. -from "Lone Hickory Farm Notes" October 16, 1955 by *Francis Sydney Reese*

Down here where the Crown [gas] station is, [east side of Reisterstown Road, north of Tollgate Road intersection] that was an old ice-pond. The Lockards who lived on the Knatz farm had a big ice pond there.

Winter time, that was our main source of a little bit of revenue -- cutting ice. We used to cut it off of Easter's pond. [Many people had ice-houses.] Clements had one, Susemihl had one and Doctor Warner up there also. The [John] Reeses also had an ice-house. I remember that because my uncle died of typhoid back there in 1904, and I went down to Reese's with my father...down to the old ice house...to get a piece of ice to put on his head. -*Lee Fox*

[I've cut] many a ton of ice...many a ton! Mostly [you'd] have a big saw and then you'd break it up into blocks and put it out a chute onto a pile, let it freeze-dry. Then you pushed it up on the wagon. If it was cold enough, you pushed it right up on the wagon and it would be dry before you got to the house...before you'd [have to] pick it up to handle it. The wagon would be gone while you'd push out blocks for the next load. I've gone home many a time soaking wet...soaking wet from my arms down both sides. Where that water'd run down your arms, you know. -*A. Franklin Parker*

Ice was hauled up on the sled by horses. They brought it up and dumped it in the ice-house with loads of straw in between. We used it to cool the milk and for making ice-cream and cooling watermelons. -*Waiva Dean Reese*

The [John] Reese farm had two ice-ponds. The finest pond was the large Easter pond which became a lake. The Groff/Knatz pond [on Reisterstown Road opposite the present Tollgate Road] was the one most available for winter sports.

Ice-cutting had to be done in the bitterest cold weather. It began as soon as the ice was three inches thick. The men wore heavy gloves. A large pile of dry guana [or "gunny"] sacks helped them in lifting and loading the ice.

Ice was cut by chopping a hole through the surface, then sawing a long slit in the ice. The next cut was made parallel to the first, then the long slab was cut in pieces that could be easily handled. Sometimes a special chute was built into the bank of the pond. The chunks of ice [were floated into position] then pushed up the chute and onto a wagon. The wagons were pulled by four horses that had been "rough shod" for hard pulling over slippery terrain.

The ice-houses were really pits in the earth that were lined with notched logs. A roof was built over the pit. The floor was covered with straw or sawdust.

When the wagon reached the ice-house, a chute was ready for unloading. The straw or sawdust at the bottom of the pit kept the ice from shattering as it fell. When the wagon was unloaded, the men climbed down into the pit to push more straw against the sides and to stack the ice in an even layer. Each successive load was carefully packed with plenty of straw or sawdust between layers. When the ice house was full, more straw was thrust in and packed by tamping or stomping feet. Finally, a layer of loose straw was added and the ice house was ready for summer use. Ice usually kept well. The best proof of an ice-house's efficiency was when an unmelted chunk was found when the ice house was readied for a fresh crop of ice a year later.

Of course, straw and sawdust adhered to the ice and it had to be thoroughly washed before using it to cool summer drinks. But on remote farms with no electric refrigeration and often no commercial ice deliveries available, that was a small price to pay. Of course the greatest advantage to having stored ice was that during the summer months it was available for making home-made ice-cream...a treat every farm boy and girl remembers with pleasure. *-E. Bennett Bowen*

Ice houses were [like a pit]...built like a well. There was one right here at Clements and Burnses had one, too. That's how Honey Triplett - Mabel Hunt would have been his sister - that's how he lost his life. I guess he was going down on the rope when he was about fifteen years old and he was alone. We figured that he fell. The rope was around his neck. *-Dorothy King*

They would never let us skate on the pond until they had finished cutting the ice. *-George B. P. Ward*

## To Market, To Market

My father stood in Lexington Market on Tuesdays for over sixty years. He always backed his wagon into the street right in front of C. D. Kenney's store.

He took live chickens to market in a crate. He had a lot of Jewish customers who liked them that way. I remember once there was this chicken with the most mixed-up colors and I thought it was *so* beautiful! When I saw he had that rooster in the crate, I yelled, "You can't sell that!" A little later, he said, "Don't you want to go get an ice-cream cone?" When I came back, the rooster was gone.

We sold butter and smearkaese [cottage cheese]. He made a nice tin box for the cream and butter. My father got a big, heavy steel drum and Gilbey Randall cut that off and made a rack for it and he sold milk from that. Sometime in the 1920s, Baltimore City became conscious of health qualities of milk, [so he had to stop selling it].

I remember the old two-horse market wagon...pulling in on a rainy night right to the kitchen door and unloading. He always brought us little rectangular cookies somewhat like ginger snaps. *-Wilson Herera*

[When I first came to Lone Hickory], Clement Reese was running the farm. He raised chickens and had a poultry, egg and vegetable route in Baltimore. He went in once a week with farm produce to sell.

221

He sold apples, peaches, raspberries, blackberries, cider, whatever there was to sell. *-Waiva Dean Reese*

We had fifty acres where we just trucked, you know. [My father had a produce route.] He used to sell to all the stores down on Falls Road. We had all kinds of fruit - every kind of apple you could think of. He'd put acres of sugar-corn in and put a thousand tomato plants and cabbage - we'd go out there and cut a whole load of cabbage for the wholesale market. In winter he'd take a load of potatoes and sell them. *-Henry Clay Hipsley*

## Cross-cut Saws and Splitting Axes

During the winter months, trees were cut while the "sap was down" to make firewood. Firewood was cut, ranked, sawed and split, then taken to the woodshed and packed for later use in wet weather. Stacks of split wood were placed beside the shed, some of slow-burning green wood, others of knotty wood and a special pile for kindling wood. *-E. Bennett Bowen*

When us boys came home from school, my mother'd have a sandwich for us, and then she'd say, "Now you boys go out and saw wood." Saw wood and cut wood - had to do it all by hand with a cross-cut saw [and an axe]. A couple of us would be sawing and one would split it and a couple little ones would be carrying in wood. We had a big wood-box we'd fill every evening.

We didn't have [many trees] on that farm, so my father went down to [Chestnut] Ridge and bought ten cords of wood. Us boys hauled it home and started cutting it up with a cross-cut, working it up that way. Joe Kessler, who lived down at Butler - the one who had the canning house - he said to us, "Look, don't tell your father, but if you boys bring a pair of horses next Saturday and haul my gasoline saw down, I'll come saw it up for you." I said, "Well, what will you charge?" He said, "I ain't going to charge you nothing, but you can pay me a little bit for the gasoline you use." Joe Kessler stayed down and sawed up wood all that day. Oh, we had an awful big pile! So we didn't have to cut no wood that winter - all we had to do was split it up and carry it in. *-Joseph Brown*

## Keeping Things in Working Order

[When a wagon broke down] we repaired it mostly. Pull the old wheel off and take it down to Hoff's blacksmith shop, and get them to put a new spoke in it or put a new rim on. Or you'd break a wagon tongue out, you'd get a new tongue put in.

I used to haul cinders and I got hung up back on Bonita Avenue - used to be nothing but a mud-hole there where you go into the Colt training ground. I broke a tongue out and came home with four horses and left the wagon sitting in the middle [of the road]. Paw had to take a tongue out of another one and go with me to get the other one and haul it home. *-Lee Fox*

When anything broke [on the Moser farm], Bob [Moser] would fix it with tar rope and binder twine. He did many a thing with tar rope and binder twine. *-Carl A. vonGunten*

During the winter months or on wet days, machinery and plows were repaired, painted and made ready for spring and summer use. If a spare day came with clear weather, the whole "outside force" jumped in and painted weather-beaten buildings or any machinery that was rusting. In winter, pig pens were readied for new occupants and chicken coops made ready for the coming broods. *-E. Bennett Bowen*

## Split-Rail Fences

Our earliest fences were built by placing rails at angles one above the other, then securing them with tilted stakes. This was called a "snake fence."

Next came the familiar "post and rail" fences. The split logs were flattened with an adz so that each post had two flat sides. Augurs were used to bore holes. The rails were sharpened at each end so they would fit snugly into the posts.

Mr. William Zeigler of Pleasant Hill Road was an expert fencer. Some of his fences were made 3 three rails each, others had 4 rails.

My great-grandfather, Snowden Disney, who lived in Arlington, was the rail-splitter for the farmers of the Owings Mills area. Even after he was 80 years old, he walked from Arlington to Owings Mills to cut trees and split logs into posts and rails. One of his great-grandsons recalled that the old gentleman delivered him the best switching he ever had because he cut his axe into the ground. This treatment of an axe was a real sin in the eyes of a rail-splitter.

When the Western Maryland Railroad condemned a right-of-way through his property, Snowden Disney built fences across it. The fences did not stop the railroad, but when Snowden lost the battle, he vowed never to ride on a train. *-E. Bennett Bowen*

## Salty Hailstones and Thousands of Locusts

They had this hail-storm and the fields and everything were beautiful before that. When that hail-storm got through stripping them down, all you saw was corn-stalks. We went out there and picked up shovelfuls and bucketfuls of these big hailstones and watched them melt down. Picked them up and tasted them and they were salty.

I think that same year was a locust year. I've never seen so many locusts in my life. Where there was a log house right in the corner of Kendigs Mill [Road] and Academy Avenue, my grandfather Branson had a field of barley. It was full of locusts. We went out there and picked them all and put them in bushel baskets. Dumped those baskets and watched these things wiggle down there. *-Viola Clark Nesbitt*

223

**Carroll County Stage**

In the early 1900s, the Greenmount stage transported passengers traveling north from Owings Mills into Carroll County. Photo courtesy of Jacques Kelly.

## CHAPTER 6

## Dirt Roads, Streetcar Tracks, and Railway Lines

*In an era when practically every adult – and many teen-agers – owns his or her own car, it's hard to visualize the travel difficulties our predecessors encountered. Although railroad transportation was available to our community well before the time of the Civil War, public roads and highways were ill-maintained and often impassible in bad weather. For many, foot travel and the faithful family horse remained the most important means of transportation until well into the present century.*

*Beginning in 1895, a streetcar line provided service to both Baltimore on the south and Reisterstown and Glyndon on the north. However, it was well after the turn of the century when the private automobile appeared as an alternative to public transportation. It is in those early years of the public's newfound mobility that we find also the predecessors of the modern-day Howard Johnson's and Holiday Inn – the roadside inn.*

*From the very beginnings of the automotive age, motorcycles offered a daredevil image some found it impossible to resist. Even more daring was that amazing new contraption, the airplane.*

-/-/-/-

### Sleighbells, Tassels and Fringes

[Sometimes it was people from the Greenspring Valley] you would see ride past, but sometimes when they had a horse or a buggy or carriage they would let their servants [use them to] go visiting. They'd ride around like that. They used to have a marvelous time!

They'd have the horses fixed up so pretty and once in a while they'd have a couple of bells on the horse. They had that hooked in their harness. You could always hear them coming. Especially when the snow was on the ground and they'd come through with their sleighs.

Then they had brass – all this pretty brass on there – everything polished and shined and just beautiful. Some of them had in the summertime what they called a net ... that looked almost like a fish-net with all these little fringes on the bottom of it all around. When the horse would be going along that would keep the flies off.

225

Then they had these little tassels on their horses – oh, they had them fixed up so pretty! They really loved those horses ... just knew them so well. *–Viola Clark Nesbitt*

The quarries, the breweries, the bakeries and all of them – they used to really decorate their horses. There were big leather things called "housings" that fit over the hames and had [the company] names [on them]. *–Lee Fox*

My Daddy remembered the stage-coaches that ran on Reisterstown Road and would stop at the different mile houses that were inns and stop-overs. He remembered when they had the six-horse teams. He said it was interesting to watch the drivers because the drivers were very professional. They had a hand full of reins in the left hand and a hand full of reins in the right hand to control these horses. *–John King*

Only way you'd ever get to Baltimore would be with a team of horses when there was a load of hay to take in. John and I used to haul loads of hay into Baltimore when we were fifteen, sixteen with a team of six horses. Sometimes the load of hay would weigh five tons. Loose hay, as wide as this room. Have to load it and tie it so it wouldn't slip off.

The wagon's brake was on the back. When you came down a grade too steep for the wheel-horses to hold back, someone would get off and walk to draw the brake. The brake was a couple of blocks set in front of the hind wheels and when you drawed it, those would come up and drag against the wheels. We used to take an old shoe-sole and nail it onto the block. [That] would last longer than the brake.

One time we had on 150 bushels of wheat. We got to one farm that had a steep hill on it. A fellow came out and he said, "You fellows wait before you go up that steep hill – I'll go get another pair of horses and hook onto you." John, he was driving. John looked and him and says, "We ain't hung up yet!" Just that way! Well, we made it and the next time we come along that way [the man] come out there and said he never saw a team of horses pull like they did. *–Joseph Brown*

My dad was an expert loader and built a tremendous square load of loose hay on the wagon bed. Ed Fleagle would then hitch up the four-horse team and pull it out to the [Reisterstown] Pike that evening. About 5 the next morning, he would take the horses out there and pull the load to the hayscales in Baltimore, get it weighed, and deliver it to a customer. He got home with the empty wagon about 7 to 9 pm, a 30-mile round trip. After supper, he counted out the money for the hay to my father on the table-cloth, a very exciting thing to us children. –from "Lone Hickory Farm Notes" October 16, 1955 by *Francis Sydney Reese*

## Bill Bitzer's Moving Vans and Livery Stable

Where Bitzer's house is now on Kingsley Road, used to be a big livery stable there. You could rent horses, or a team of horses, or a horse and buggy, and go over to Timonium Fair if you wanted to. –*James L. Bowers*

Mr. William Bitzer carried on the moving and hauling business for may years from his home and barns which were located on the northeast corner of the Reisterstown Road and Kingsley Road. The moving vans were horse-drawn covered wagons. Longer and wider than most other wagons on the road. Four or six horses pulled a van loaded with heavy furniture. Some hauls were made from Baltimore to Emory Grove summer cottages.

Household goods and furniture were carefully handled, and the large cooking and heating stoves were set up in the new location before Mr. Bitzer accepted his pay. The prices seemed high then, and people dreaded paying $35 to have their furniture hauled to a new location. –*E. Bennett Bowen*

When we were kids going to Saint Thomas Sunday School, [Mr. Bitzer] drive the bus. [It was a] coach ... a horse-drawn coach. It had seats down both sides and a seat across the back. It would hold eight or nine [people]. I know he picked up the Carpenter kids and the Hopkins kids. At Saint Thomas lane, he picked up people who had come out on the streetcar. –*Helen Carpenter*

My friend, Wilson Waggoner, said that when Mr. Bitzer was nothing but a kid his father would give him a pair of horses and he'd go down there with a coach that would hold about six people and wait for the streetcar to go up. Then he'd take them up to Saint Thomas church and bring them back afterwards.

He'd take you along if you wanted to go to Timonium fair, and it cost so much. I think a dollar and a half. He also did furniture moving with his horses.

The coach was closed and you entered it from the back. It had steps to go in the back and seats on both sides of it. That's the same way with the big coaches that you went to Timonium in. They probably held twenty. –*Grace Bowen Pape*

Bill Bitzer used two coaches if it was Christmas or sometime like that. [There were seats down each side] and then the step was in the back. When it was slippery and we'd slide, Miss Lizzie Belt would holler so, and oh, the kids would like that, you know! –*Dorothy King*

Only licking I ever got [was] for not getting on [Bitzer's] bus and going [to church]. Pat Hoff and I were building a water wheel in that little stream that comes down there by the Hoff's. The rest of them came home from church and said they didn't see me. [My father] soon found out where [I'd been]. Did he ever flail me! –*Joseph Simonds*

### Burning the Tollgate

Oh, definitely I remember the tollgate! Mr. Lockard [was the tollgate keeper]. He was a tall, lean fellow. [He'd] come out of their house on the side-porch, cross a little bridge over the stream and open the tollgate. *-Grace Bowen Pape*

There was a tollgate at Owings Mills next to where the storage booths are now. The toll varied from five cents to forty-two cents.

In June of 1912, the Democratic convention nominated Woodrow Wilson for president of the United States. Mr. Wilson left the Fifth Regiment Armory in Baltimore in a car. Another car went ahead and told the tollgate keepers [along the route] to throw up their gates when they saw the car coming with the flag on its hood.

Mr. James A. Lockard was the tollgate keeper at Owings Mills. He did not put his gate up. He told the driver, "I want the ten cent toll to keep, for it will be a souvenir from the next president of the United States. He received the ten cents from the driver, raised the gate and pocketed the dime. *-E. Bennett Bowen*

To get through the tollgate if you were hauling a little produce into the city, at two or three o'clock in the morning, Mr. Lockard down there at the tollgate, he'd come out in his undies to let you through and collect your nickel. And you didn't get through that tollgate until you paid your fee! *-Lee Fox*

I've heard tell about fellows riding up the streetcar tracks in a buggy to get around paying at the toll gate. *-Wilson Herera*

What the streetcar motormen would do when they were intending to go into the carbarn was to pull the trolley down off the wires and go down that hill like a bat out of hell. They'd go almost up to where the fire house now is and then drift back down and go into the yard. This one night the streetcar came down the hill ripping and roaring and no lights on at the same time this fellow was trying to cut around the toll gate. The driver got out of it alive, but his horse was killed and the buggy demolished. *-George B. P. Ward*

We used to ride down Pleasant Hill on four wheels ... buggy wheels. That old man would see us coming and he'd have the tollgate up and he'd run out there and slap it down. We ran into it one day and broke it in half. Boogered up a couple of kids, too.
[When they took the tollgate down,] they had a big to-do in that meadow right there, as you go past Hoff's shop and turn the corner. Baseball game. I remember a little girl with a baby in a baby carriage and somebody hit a foul ball ... hit her right in the head. She grew up to be a professor in college, so it must not have hurt her too bad. Maybe even did her some good. *-Joseph Simonds*

The old tollgate was burned the 31st of May in 1915. They had a big barbecue back there in Reese's meadow, right behind the old blacksmith shop. [My daughter] Esther was an infant and the nurse I had said to me, "Are you going to sit [home] here in sack-cloth and ashes for the next month? Get out of here! Put this baby on a pillow and we'll put her in the machine and we're going to the barbecue!" Off we went to the barbecue and that was the 31st of May, 1915. *-Virginia Clark Hoff*

I went with Annie Kendig when they gave the tollgate celebration and had a bull roast. The men were playing ball. Helen Crouse was a baby and she was in the baby carriage and the ball hit her. I remember Mrs. Crouse going to pieces about it. I don't think she was hurt, but that's how I remember her age. *-Dorothy King*

## Rolling Down the Reisterstown Turnpike

Just plain country road. And they used to bring the hay wagons down. We used to come sometimes out to the road and watch them. They'd come down at certain times, all of them sort of together. They'd have four and six horses. [The brasses on the horses polished] and everything shining. Now you can't realize how that would be. *-Minnie Clark Hebron*

They'd haul hay down [Reisterstown Road] in six-mule teams. My wife, Louise, [Louise Demmitt Fox] will tell you herself how she used to hang on the back of the old hay carriages from the school house down here to the old [Demmitt] home. Right on top of this hill – Louise saw this – one of the Carlisle boys ran behind one of these big hay teams and an auto ran right over him and killed him.

We always said that if we had a good walking team we could make it in three hours from here to what is now Liberty Heights and Reisterstown Road. Of course, that wasn't a trotting team and it was pulling a wagon. Where Mondawmin Shopping Center is now, was known as Brown's Hill ... that belonged to Alexander Brown who was a big broker or something.

On the corner of Clifton Avenue and Pennsylvania Avenue, there was a man named Hebble who ran a little store. He had feed troughs there and a big old wooden pump that stood right out at the street. We'd go in there and pump water and water the horses and buy a peck of corn or whatever we needed to feed the horses. He always had horse troughs to feed them from and then we'd start on back home. *-Lee Fox*

It must be difficult for people born since the Great Depression to imagine the Reisterstown Turnpike when more than 99% of the traffic was horse-drawn. Traction engines, a few bicycles and, in summer, one or two automobiles a month made up the other percent.

At that time, the road was owned by the turnpike company which had its headquarters in Westminster. The president of the turnpike company was a Doctor Billingsley. The Emory Grove streetcars came up the road on the east side.

The traffic was all horse-drawn wagons or drawn by mules. There were all sorts of wagons - hay wagons, market wagons, vegetable wagons, covered wagons and there was a light variety of wagon. People traveled in their dayton wagons, their buggies and their sur-

reys. The speed was three, five, six miles an hour – that was fast.
The hazards were mud, dirt, fog and, in winter time, ice.

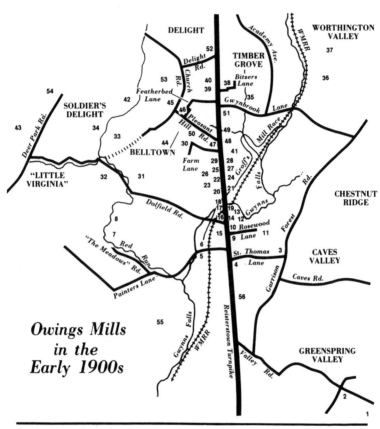

*Owings Mills in the Early 1900s*

| | | |
|---|---|---|
| 1 Garrison Fort | 12 "Windswept Hill"/ 3rd Dr. Campbell Home | 22 Reisterstown Turnpike Tollgate #3 |
| 2 "Greenspring Punch" (Original Owings Home) | 13 United Railway Powerhouse, Trouble Station & Carbarn | 23 John Reese Farm |
| 3 St. Thomas Church | | 24 "Therapia"-Grupy/ Fangmyer/Knatz Farm |
| 4 "Red Lantern" Tavern | 14 Original WMRR Station/ 2nd Garner's Store | 25 1st & 2nd Public Elementary Schools |
| 5 Lower Mill | 15 "Sunshine", 2nd Dr. Campbell Home | 26 Bihy Quarry |
| 6 "Ulm", Samuel Owings/ Milton Painter Home | 16 Owings Mills Presbyterian Church | 27 Terry Florist |
| 7 "The Meadows"/ Thomas Owings Home | 17 Harmon Home & Store | 28 Wheat Barn |
| 8 Thomas Owing's Mills | 18 Original Garner's Store | 29 Wheat Tavern |
| 9 Watson Sherwood Home | 19 "12 Mile House/ Fitch-Clark Tavern | 30 Ritter Farm |
| 10 "Twin Oaks"/ Ward Home | 20 Cooper Shop | 31 Oliver Disney Farm |
| 11 Rosewood State Institution | 21 Upper Mill-"Eureka"/ Groff's Mill | 32 "Alyedo"-Dolfield/ Moser Farm |

There were hill-boys stationed in Owings Mills and Garrison with extra horses to help the loads of hay up or down over the hills. [The hill-boys] hitched extra horses to the wagons and earned a few dollars for spending money.

The stretch of pike which extended from Delight to Tobins [Garrison] was quite rural with herds of dairy cows grazing in the meadow lands along both sides of the road.

The Western Maryland Railroad crossed [Reisterstown Turnpike] just in front of where the Baltimore County Supply Company is today. The Owings Mills [railroad] station was there, a quite spacious building for the rural area it served. Passengers who waited at the station had a splendid view of "Windswept Hill", the home of Doctor William H. H. Campbell.

Opposite the station was Mrs. Harmon's house, which had been an old mill. It stood where the coal chute is today. There was a lumber yard in the rear of it, back beyond where the present railroad station is. The post-office was in the house south of the railroad and was run by Mrs. William Scott. On the opposite side, there was a house where the McCubbin family lived.

Mr. Garner's store was on the west side of the road at that time ... where the abutment is today. On the east side was Fitch's Tavern, an attractive roadhouse with wide porches and lacy grill work that sat among a cluster of willow trees. The Hoff blacksmith shop was opposite, where the glue factory [Baltimore Adhesive Company] is today.

Beside Mr. Hoff's shop there were three houses. The houses were all built close to the road and they seemed to me to be old then, but I don't think they were. North of the Gwynns Falls stream, stood the old Cooper Shop where Mrs. Fleigh could often be seen tending her garden.

Neat osage orange hedges enclosed the gardens and lawn of the Groff house on the opposite side of the road. A large ice-pond occupied the spot where the Crown gas station now sits.

Farther north, the old schoolhouse stood on the west side of the road while Mr. Edward G. Knatz's large home towered on the opposite bank. A well-edged driveway circled past the Knatz's front door; there was always an attractive bed of flowers at the center of the circle.

North of the Knatz home was the florist shop and greenhouse operated by Mrs. William Terry and next to that the home of Mr. Milton C. Paine, a real-estate dealer.

Opposite the florist shop was the home of Mrs. Luella D. Cleveland, daughter of Mr. A. Y. Dolfield, who owned a number of land tracts in the area, including land on Bonita Avenue and Dolfield Road. The house, hexagonal in shape, had originally belonged to Captain Edward Wheat and had once served as a tavern. There was a large windmill near the house and two barns, one on either side of Reisterstown Road. The larger barn, on the west side, collapsed one fall afternoon just as school children were walking toward Pleasant Hill.

Groff's Hall stood at the southwest corner of the Ritter's farm lane. Farther north stood Mr. Charles Marshall's home with its abundant orchards of plums, apples and quince. The yard of Mr. Henry Nelson's home was noted for its fine cherry trees.

Farther up the road - near where the Colonial Inn stands today - the McCloskey home stood amid sweeping evergreens and the Cedarmere house was opposite. *-E. Bennett Bowen*

Them days, you know, this road wasn't like this. It had breakers and you'd go up and you'd go down. I had a bicycle and I'd get on my bicycle, and ride down these breakers and up these breakers. *-Nettie Clements Frank*

Before Reisterstown Road was paved, [there was] quite a [high] bank through here. The road was steeper and narrower. There were cedar trees [growing] on the bank [in front of] Grandfather Nelson's house, and they were covered when they [filled in to level the road]. Not too many automobiles [went] past. You'd know who they were. *-Dorothy King*

There was a high bank in front of our house and we sat out on the front steps and watched them cement the road. It was just dirt before that. When they built the road, they moved a lot of dirt and filled in a lot of places. Before that, it was a right high hill between our house and Pleasant Hill. Deeper than it is now. *-Lillian Demmitt Moser*

Before the road was paved, it wasn't actually a dirt road ... it had white stone all in it. It was hard on the horses feet. And when people were walking and passing a wagon, the wagon would hit one of those [stones] and throw it up against your leg.

When they first modernized this road, they made it out of concrete. A company by the name of Fisher and Crozier laid the concrete. Now this was told to me and I don't know how authentic it is, but they said that if the last load of concrete [for the day arrived on the job late], the road men wouldn't bother to lay it. [So] from Pleasant Hill on up the road, the people's cellars [all got] cemented. Just backed the truck up, you know and pour it in, and [the homeowners] would spread it themselves. I don't think [the concrete road] lasted more than two years before it all cracked up. That was because it wasn't properly laid ... it didn't have the foundation. So tbey took it up and put down a macadam road. Bill Hooper would gather that concrete up and take it back [to the houses he was building on Ritters Lane]. Half those houses back there have foundations that were laid from what he picked up off the road here. *-Laura Wimsett Redifer*

I remember when they paved [Reisterstown Road] because my father was going to Lexington Market. We had to go down through the valley and down Park Heights because they were paving the road. *-Sarah Cox Hewitt*

Reisterstown Road changed to cement - two lanes - around 1916 or 1917. When they were putting down the paving, Josh and Gertie Gorsuch were getting married. I was their flower girl and they carried me across so I didn't get any of the wet cement on my shoes. *-Genevieve Berryman Kelley*

**Featherbed Lane and The Switch Road**

All the roads around here were rough in those days. Sometimes we'd start out for Owings Mills with a load of wood for somebody and if it was a little soft, we'd have to put two extra horses in to get out the road. *-Frank Parker*

Oh, the roads were sometimes closed, and you'd have to get around by somebody's field. Didn't have no way to open them up then except by shovel ... had to go by hand and shovel them out. *-Joseph Brown*

When I was quite young, coming back Pleasant Hill Road with horses and mules, the sassafras bushes would hit you almost on both sides of your face, the road was so bad. Mr. James Easter moved out here in the late 1800s, and after he got here he had quite a bit of work done on the road and it was much better.
Dolfield Road did not [originally] go in between [the railroad and] Hoff's [blacksmith] shop. It was moved from its original location [approximately opposite the Owings Mills firehouse] on account of the railroad ... because it was so dangerous for horses and wagons going up over that steep [railroad embankment]. My cousin, Wade Walters, and I took horses and carts and went down there and we worked on that road for the county. I was driving the cart to haul the dirt [used] to fill in. I must have been - well, I was old enough to drive a cart, so I must have been about ten, eleven years old. *-Lee Fox*

[Ritters Lane] was named for the Ritters who lived on the corner of it. We used to say "Bitzer's Lane" [for Kingsley Road], but the Kings were there - Jess King was there a long time. We called [the road that connects Reisterstown Road and Pleasant Hill] the "Featherbed

Lane". But it's a cow lane ... there's only room for a cow to go up. *-Dorothy King*

You know, it was my father [Henry Clark] named that Featherbed Road. There was so many stones and rocks and things that my father started calling it Featherbed Lane and then everybody around started calling it that. *-Minnie Clark Hebron*

[Garrison Forest Road and Gwynnbrook Lane] were narrow dirt roads when we first went there. You got around with horses and buggies – you never even saw a car then. And you couldn't come down Pleasant Hill past Easter's. The stumps had to be blown out and the road made after Lehnerts moved there. They had to dynamite all along there to get those stumps out, because they didn't have all this big equipment to do the work. Dolfield Road was just a dirt road. At one time it came up past where Wesley Mack lived and went on through Rose's place. *-Bessie Moser vonCunten*

Fred [Dolfield] said that the road they called Dolfield Road was cut in during his father's time. They liked it a whole lot better than going all the way up to Pleasant Hill. Those roads weren't too good. *-William F. Stone*

The roads around our home were in dreadful condition with ruts sometimes over two feet deep. Doctor Martin would drive to the end of Shipe Lane and leave his car, then put on high boots and walk back to the houses. *-Valley R. Shipe*

There was a road that came from Gingrich's Switch and ran alongside our farm to Mr. [George] Mahoney's. It went over to Garrison Forest Road and it was called "The Switch Road." *-Jean Reese Worthley*

Lyons Mill Road was once a link in the route that went to Frederick, before the straight versions of Liberty Pike were laid out. *-John McGrain*

At one time Lyons Mill Road came all the way out to Reisterstown Road ... I guess where McDonogh Lane is now. The Wheats lived on the corner of Lyons Mill and Deer Park Roads. Parsley lived next to them. There was an old house on the corner of Lathe Road and then past that is where Camp Springs Road came in [to Lyons Mill Road]. *-Carl A. vonGunten*

At one time, the intersection of Dolfield Road and Reisterstown Road was about where the Kimmel Tire is. It was there until about 1907 when the railroad blocked it. Later, when Dolfield Road was laid out to parallel to the new railroad track, across the Reese meadow, that stretch was jokingly dubbed "Park Heights Avenue". This referred to the portion of Park Heights Avenue above Cold Spring Lane which was in the county and had a reputation for mud holes.

234

Red Hill on the Caves Road and Barney Clabber [Baughnaugh-claughbaugh] Hill on Tollgate Road were always referred to as "death traps" for men and teams.

There were few bridges spanning any streams. In 1901, the timbers of the bridge across Red Run on Dolfield Road snapped and let a traction engine right down into the water. Several months passed before it was rebuilt.

In summer, trotting horses stirred up clouds of dust. Can you imagine what automobiles did? Early drivers, such as James Easter and John Sherwood always protected their clothing with linen dusters.

After 1905, Bonita Avenue and Gwynnbrook Avenue were kept open by the men who worked at the Gwynnbrook Distillery. There were long periods of time in which the wash-outs on Academy Avenue prevented through traffic. Painters Lane was always known to flood near the mill.

There was great danger crossing Soldiers Delight after winter thaws when melting snow and ice flooded the roads, especially if a skittish horse gave a sudden lurch toward one of the open pits that had been left by the miners. One such pit was not more than three feet from the edge of the road.

Another road that no longer exists would, if it were re-opened today, pass through the office complex of the Owings Mills Elementary School, pass south of Ritters Lane, bend toward the Junior-Senior High School, then cross Ritters Lane before intersecting with Tollgate Road. This was called the "Slope Road" and it was so muddy that it was often impassable.

At that time, Ritters Lane was a private road leading to George Ritter's farm and it stopped at his barn. School children began using the "Ritter's Lane", even though Mrs. Ritter's ill-tempered black-and-tan dog, "Min," often chased them ... especially when they helped themselves to apples from the Ritter's trees. Later, Mr. Oliver Disney, who owned land on the northwest side of the pathway deeded the county a strip of land three feet wide for a legal pathway.

However, the squabbling over the right of way continued. Mr. Thomas Bowers once boarded up the entrance to the Slope Road and traffic was forced to use the Ritter's private lane. A few years later Mr. Ritter bought the Groff Hall which stood on the southwest corner of the lane at Reisterstown Road and then he controlled access to both ends of the lane. After the hall burned, Mr. Ritter built a cottage that almost blocked the old farm lane.

Finally Mr. J. M. Disney gave the county enough land to create an entrance from Tollgate Road to Ritters Lane and the road was no longer in danger of being closed. After the narrow, sharply-angled farm lane became a county road, the Ritters profited from the change by selling building lots along both sides. -*E. Bennett Bowen.*

My grandfather and old A. Y. Dolfield who lived back Dolfield Road opened Bonita Avenue. Mr. Dolfield planned to develop it all back in there. Never lived to do it. The Groffs opened the road [for another reason] - to get trade in from the Worthington Valley with wheat [to be ground at the Groff's mill]. -*William D. Groff, Jr.*

235

When Gwynnbrook Store was built, two new roads were cut through the area, Gwynnbrook Avenue and Bonita Avenue, intersecting near the store. I can remember when Bonita Avenue was being built by pick-and-shovel gangs. One day my father took me down back of the lime-kiln which then stood on our place to watch them work. The foreman was a man with a beard, a veteran of the Civil War. He told us of his adventures in the war and exhibited a metal whisky flask which he took from his shirt pocket. It had a dent which he said was made by a rebel bullet and declared that this [flask], being over his heart, had saved his life. I do not recall whether he drew any moral conclusion from this. -from "Lone Hickory Farm Notes" October 16, 1955 by *Francis Sydney Reese*

## The Village Smithy

Before 1900 Hoff's Garage was a wheelwright shop and a blacksmith shop and a horse-shoeing shop. And also, a wonderful painting shop. Grandfather Hoff put out some paint jobs that you could paint your nose in they were that beautiful. They would be surreys with fringe around the top, you know, and they were really gorgeous. He'd put varnish on there and pumice it down one time after another until he'd get it so you could just see your face in it.

It was all under one roof, but the horse-shoeing place was under a shed on the outside. Those old lazy horses! - I can see them yet. They'd lean right on Henry. He was taken out of there one day and rushed to the hospital with appendicitis, and they said it was the weight of those horses that did it.

And wouldn't you know, they were spoilt! [Henry] had a pouch of tobacco he'd put in his hip-pocket, and that old horse would reach around there and get that tobacco out and chew that tobacco while he was being shod. Can you imagine! Old Mr. Andrew Disney - his horse was one of the rotten spoilt ones.

Then, after that, Grandfather Hoff got into - I think it was the first of 1900 - he was the first Chevrolet man in the state of Maryland. The showroom was built right onto the front of the wheelwright shop because the wheelwright business had more or less dwindled down. And then, that just kept going until the fire came along and wiped it all out. -*Margaret Clark Hoff*

[At Hoff's blacksmith shop] they shoed horses and put tires on wagon wheels. Farmers would bring their wagons in and they'd put the metal bands around the wooden wheels. We lived next to the shop and behind that, Mr. Hoff had a tremendous building with all kinds of lumber in it for repairing wagons. -*Laura Wimsett Redifer*

My great uncle, Charles Rumstein, leased the blacksmith shop off Reisterstown Road from the Cradocks. When I was a child, Tolley Gill rented Hoff's blacksmith shop. -*Borden Simonds*

Charlie Long had a blacksmith shop in the shed behind Hoff's Garage as late as the 1930s. -*George B. P. Ward*

[North of Cradock Lane] there were two stone houses on the road and a blacksmith shop was there, too. *-Laura Wimsett Redifer*

[There was a] blacksmith shop at Gwynnbrook ... right on the corner of Gwynnbrook, across the railroad tracks. *-Mary Kendig Gettierre*

Bill Keller was a blacksmith at Buchman's, on Garrison Forest Road, south of St. Thomas Lane. Most horses he shod were from people in Greenspring Valley. And they used to make buggies, all kinds of wagons, stuff like that. *-Elmer Hobart Schaefer*

[Buchman's blacksmith shop] did a tremendous business. In those days they had horse-shoeing shops and buggy shops, painting and repairing, all that sort of thing. *-Lee Fox*

My grandfather King was a blacksmith. He had a place right there at Delight where the funeral place [Eckhardt's] is. *-Dorothy King*

I worked at a blacksmith shop when I was a kid. [It was owned by] a fellow name of Thomas. Up on Berrymans's Lane. I helped build wheels ... wagon bodies. Then I was with a [blacksmith] named Cassidy on Liberty Road and I learned to shoe horses. I liked wheel work but I didn't like them horses' feet! I told Joe Cassidy one time - "Mr. Cassidy , the first one kicks me I'm going home!" One of them kicked me out into the middle of the road one day, and I quit. I said, "I can learn something better than this, anyhow!" *-A. Franklin Parker*


**One Hell of an Automobile!**

[When the first cars went up the road] you'd go out and watch. Clevelands had this old Ford, you know, with open sides, a two-seated one. The first car Fred Dolfield had was a 1904 Cadillac. He told about taking his mother to Reisterstown and he had a flat tire. People were running that store where Caltrider was and he got some rope there to put around it so he could get home with a flat tire.
[The first car I ever had] was a Model-T roadster. A 1926. One of the last ones. You could have the Model T in any color you wanted as long as it was black. Then, in '28, after a long delay, they finally came out with the Model A. But the Model A's did have color.
In the Model T, sometimes people would back up steep hills if they were low on gas. The gas would go to the back of the tank going uphill and it wouldn't draw it all out.
They had three pedals there and a hand throttle. When you were going along, you didn't have to touch a pedal. You were in high gear - you had high and low and that's all. When you got to a hill, you'd have to push this thing in and hold it and give her the gas - you were in low then. If you wanted to back up, you had to push in the other pedal. That was the reverse.
It was a lousy car! Oh, it had helluva tires. Now mine had a little better tires on it, but Raymond [Moser's] had these little old skinny

tires. Old high-pressure ties. You had to patch them all the time. If we made it to Baltimore and back we were lucky ... really lucky! *-Carl A. vonGunten*

I bought my first car making one dollar a day. Paid twenty-five dollars for it. Bought it from Vernon Brown down on Gwynnbrook Avenue - 1925 Chevrolet. *-James L. Bowers*

The thing that I was attracted to very much about Miss Margaret Painter was that she had a Dodge automobile. Do you remember the days when any color was good as long as it was black? [The car] didn't have a separate starter and generator - it had a combination. After the motor started, it acted as the generator.

[Miss Painter] had a guy named Oscar Makowski who was the chauffeur. Anyhow, I was called upon to drive my mother and Miss Margaret Painter to the garden club meetings, which of course - oh, boy! I was 17 and ready! *-George B. P. Ward*

There were no automobiles then, except for Mr. Knatz's. He and the Terrys who had the florist shop. Then Clara McCubbin got a Chevrolet. She used to take the kids around. *-Helen Carpenter*

Mr. Terry had an old automobile and they didn't have any tow wagons in those days, so he got me and I hooked two horses onto it and dragged it into town. *-Lee Fox*

[My first car] was a Model-T Ford. [I got it in] '24. I think I had the first 4-door Ford sedan that went up and down this road.

My gosh, that was something! You ran out of gas, you had to take the front seat out ... the tank was underneath the seat. Then, when the next [model] came out, the tank was up under the hood. If you went down to the valley - down Dick's Hill, any of those places - you might start up there [all right], but she'd stop halfway up on you. You'd have to pull back down and back up the hill. When you backed up, the gas would go to the front. I backed up Greenspring Avenue many a time. *-Henry Clay Hipsley*

In 1938 I had a small, two-seater Ford and would go over to Mr. Burkholder's and buy fifty cents worth of gasoline, which would take me to Baltimore and back. *-Catherine Dimmling Morris*

I bought my first automobile at Hoff's Garage in '19. Then the Chevrolet people wanted him to put up a show-room, and him being a typical Dutchman, they weren't going to tell him what to do. He wouldn't do it and I think they took the agency away from him. *-Lee Fox*

[When Hoff's Garage burned], Mr. Hoff, Sr. was aging by this time, and Henry Hoff took over the business, rebuilding [on the same site] with a block building and becoming a Chevrolet agency. He was a poor businessman. Later on, he sold Durands. [His brother], "Bun" [Bernard Hoff] held the mortgage on the property. When the business failed, he foreclosed and the property, including the two houses north of the garage, were auctioned off. "Bun" bought it in and the family split. -*George B. P. Ward*

Hoff's Garage sold Rocknes. I think quite a few of the local people bought them, in fact, I got my driver's license on Helen Carpenter's Rockne. She had a nice little car and it had a "hill hold" on it and boy, that helped me, because Westminster had a place up there where I think they tried to fail you giving you your license. -*Morris G. Richardson*

After we got a car, car trips were very popular. We'd go to Pen Mar, Antietam, Hagerstown, Cumberland. Four or five cars would go together, almost like a caravan. They'd all get together and we'd transfer children back and forth, more or less of a family day trip.

The first car my father had was a two-door. In the back, the seat was only big enough for one person because in back of the driver there was a thing like a box, with maybe two feet from the top of the box to the ceiling of the car. We took other children who didn't have a car and we would have three and four children back there, somebody sitting on the box, others crowded on the seat. You didn't go out for a trip like that unless the car was full. -*Genevieve Berryman Kelley*

I couldn't afford to buy a new car. I could patch them up, you know. You had to. Wasn't many places around to get them fixed and you didn't have the money to fix it. -*Frank Schaefer*

Clyde Richardson was two years older than me and he was a wizard of a mechanic. Clyde had an old Model-T Ford. We were working on the Ford one day and had the gear-shift all apart. Clyde put it back together and got the gears all mixed up -- you had to put it in reverse to go forward.

We had pushed the car back behind the greenhouses and got it in the garage when Mr. Richardson came running out of the house with a bouquet of flowers in his arm. He went around there and grabbed Clyde's car - I guess he wanted to save a dollar ... work off of Clyde's gas instead of his delivery truck. He put the Ford in reverse to back it out of the garage, but instead of going out he went forward through the front of the garage.

At one time, Old Clyde, he got that car fixed up with the fenders mounted on springs. [From the looks of it,] you'd think that car couldn't do two miles an hour, but that thing could really roll! He'd go out on Reisterstown Road and wait for some big car to come down the road [and challenge him to race]. And he'd go along, smoking his pipe and all the fenders would be flapping up and down and you'd think it was going to fly to pieces. -*John Kellar*

## A Motorcycle Fanatic

Herb Gorsuch, Doctor Koerner and my brother, Arnold Bowen -- they were the ones mostly traveled on motorcycles. They'd get out in our back yard, the three of them starting them up and working on them, and the motorcycles would POP! POP! POP! My father used to get so aggravated with them making all that racket! *-Grace Bowen Pape*

Wilson Richardson was really a motorcycle fanatic! And he could really ride that motorcycle! Him and Sergeant Blizzard! Wilson would set up in front of the florist waiting for Blizzard to come along -- Blizzard was a state policeman. [Soon as Blizzard came past], old Wilson would take off and down the hill he'd go, Blizzard after him. Wilson would lay that motorcycle of his over on one side far enough - like at Pleasant Hill Road, he'd duck in there, and Blizzard couldn't do it because his kick-stand on both sides would hold him up.

Wilson would go back through the fields ... run down through somebody's cornfield. Blizzard couldn't give him a ticket unless he caught him on the road. That was Wilson's game - give him a merry chase and be back in front of Richardson's Florist again and be sitting there gunning his motor next time Blizzard came by. *-John Kellar*

### The Men Who Built the Roads

There were a lot of jokes about the county roads supervisors. The local farmers said that the best supervisor spotted a mud hole, threw in a few stones, and covered the stones with leaves which the first wind blew away. The poorest supervisor filled up one mud hole and created two. *-E. Bennett Bowen*

For the first part of my tenure, I was in charge of [road] construction in Baltimore and Harford County. Then they took me in the Baltimore office against my will. Which was still a good move, as it turned out. Then I was assistant to the Chief Engineer, Dave Fisher, I couldn't tell you how many years. Put me on easy street.

When I was out here, I took little Bill Leon as an inspector, and do you know where he is now? - he's chief engineer. He went the same road that I did, night school to get his degree. Slade Caltrider went the same way, he's chairman of [the State Roads] Commission. Arnold Gardner, he's assistant chief engineer - lived right next door to me.

That little Harris boy - Norman Harris ... George Gorsuch. All of them were my gang. All of them. You can pick practically every district engineer out of the state and he was in my gang when I had charge of construction of Baltimore and Harford counties. I hired 'em. *-Joseph Simonds*

### Taking the Train

In 1905, railroad officials decided to make the Western Maryland Railroad a double track and eliminate the dangerous curves and crossings from the roadbed. The [grade-level] crossing at Owings Mills was a particularly dangerous one [and it was proposed to run the tracks along the west side of the Turnpike to Reisterstown].

240

There was so much protest by the Reisterstown people about the proposed route that the railroad had to alter its intended course. That's why the rail line now crosses [to the east side of] the road in Owings Mills. The creation of the new right-of-way was a long and hard-fought series of deals with property owners. When the deals were finally closed, Owings Mills almost became a ghost town. The new tracks [were destined to] pass right through Mr. Garner's general store, the Fitch Tavern, the trouble station owned by the United Railway Streetcar Company, and the lumberyard at the rear of Garner's store. Several houses were moved or destroyed and "Therapia Farm", the property of Mr. Edward G. Knatz, was cut in two.

An embankment was built across the Groff meadow on the east side of Reisterstown Road and across Dolfield Road on the west side. Trestles were erected across the lower sections of Groff's meadow, an engineering mistake which Mr. E. G. Knatz recognized, saying it would "eventually wash away." His prediction came true [some seventy years later] in 1971 when the storm "Agnes" caused the waters of the Gwynns Falls to burst through the embankment, devastating the center of Owings Mills.

Mr. William Fitzell, born in Ireland, served for a time as foreman for the contractor building the railroad. His family later located permanently in the Twelfth District of Baltimore County, where his descendants still live today.

A steam shovel was brought in to do the digging and a string of little cars hauled the red earth out on the trestles and dropped it on the meadow land beneath. A "dinky" engine hauled small loads of dirt out from behind the Knatz house and barn. The digging went on for more than a year. Workers were housed in the empty houses and in derailed boxcars along the right of way.

There was much furor when the public learned that a pylon with a concrete base was to be placed directly in the center of Reisterstown Road to support the overhead span. "A death-trap!" cried the foresighted Mr. E. G. Knatz. Nobody supported him and we got the pylon – it's still there and has caused a number of accidents as he forecast.
-*E. Bennett Bowen*

I took the train in to college for four years from Gwynnbrook. But I had to flag it down every morning. Sometimes my father was with me. He'd bring a big pile of newspapers and set them on fire when he heard the train blow its whistle. Set this big bonfire ... especially on winter mornings when it was still dark. -*Jean Reese Worthley*

My father's brother was a great roustabout ... a party man. They used to stop [the train] here at Bonita Avenue and let him off. He'd have on his white tie and tails. "Guy Groff is on here ... let him off," they'd say. A "Rummy Stop", they called it. -*William D. Groff, Jr.*

Shaver, the principal [at Owings Mills Elementary School], used to travel on the train. He lived at Upperco and he'd take the train from Upperco to Glyndon and then take the streetcar to Pleasant Hill. -*Grace Bowen Pape*

241

## Chattolanee Train Station

In 1886, this group of commuters gathered at the Chattolanee station to await the train. As the sign next to the stationmaster's window indicates, the Adams Express transported debarking passengers who wished to continue their journey. Photo courtesy of the Baltimore County Public Library; A. H. Brinkmann, photographer.

My father was a stationary engineer in Sudbrook. To get to work, he would go to Owings Mills and get on the train there. *-Dorothy King*

When the trains went by [Gwynnbrook Station], they had the mail-crane that would grab the mail-bags as they went by. That was rather interesting to see them grab the mail-bags off the hooks. They had one [train] that went down that picked up the mail and one that went up and picked up the mail.

[Farmers] shipped milk from there. There were two platforms, one on each side of the railroad tracks. They loaded the milk in the morning to take down [to Baltimore] on the right-hand side of the tracks from the milk stand. On the opposite side of the track, they had a stand where they dropped off the empty milk cans in the evening and the farmers would get them the next morning when they brought their milk down. Some of the farmers were Mr. Frank Reese, Mr. Frank Price, Mr. Milton Trout and Mr. Gardner and Mr. Friedel.

They also had warehouses on both sides of the track where they stored the feed that Mr. Davis sold [in his store]. Later, they built a warehouse up the track farther at Gingrich's Switch. The trains came in and unloaded the feed and coal - they had a coal-yard there, and hauled the feed and the coal from there. *-Helen Kendig Bowers*

I never rode the train. I never got on that for some reason. I'd have liked to get on it. But it sure went up and down this track many a time. *-Frank Schaefer*

## Accidents on the Line

In the spring of 1892, my grandfather was run over by a railroad train. He was pretty nearly stone deaf, and he walked out of the Owings Mills station. *-George B. P. Ward*

Mr. Lynn Painter, the lawyer, was walking on the railroad tracks -- he always walked from his house up to get the mail ... walked the tracks. He was thinking, I suppose, about what he was going to do, and he didn't get off the tracks in time. *-E. Bennett Bowen*

Somebody said [Mr. Lynn Painter] was killed on the railroad track. Somebody said purposely, but I don't know about that ... you know how rumors fly. Seemed like his life was kind of sad ... I think the lady-friend passed or something. I don't know. *-Viola Clark Nesbitt*

I had heard that [Lynn Painter] was walking his dog. He would walk over to Owings Mills and get his mail and come back, and very likely he was reading and they had changed the schedule or something on the tracks. That's how my mother's nephew, Pete Grimstead, got killed. He was walking the track and his trick was up. *-Laura W. Redifer*

[My sister, Emma (Kendig), was killed by a train] in 1921. We used to get our Sunday paper at the [Davis] store and she went that morning to get the paper. There was a double track then, and she stepped into the path of a passenger train. She was killed right close to the house here. *-Helen Kendig Bowers*

## The Pikesville to Emory Grove Line

The streetcar line to Owings Mills began to operate in 1895, and continued until 1932.

The Emory Grove streetcars came up [Reisterstown] Road on the east side. At Woodley Avenue in Reisterstown, they gradually reached the center of the road, then swung to the left at Hobbs's Hotel [opposite Cockeysmill Road]. They made the trip up the Reisterstown and Hanover Roads to Neal's Curve and continued on over the elevated span that crossed the Western Maryland Railroad [on Butler Road].

About an hour and a half was needed to make the trip [from Baltimore to Emory Grove]. At night, the cars ran once each hour. In morning or evening hours, they ran every fifteen or twenty minutes. There were marked stops where the cars picked up or dropped riders. The motormen and conductors knew the riders and often waited a few seconds for a passenger who was in sight. Fares were collected by hand, the conductor ringing each fare up on the indicator that was placed at mid-point in the front of the car.

The streetcars ran in the days before the A&P and the Acme stores moved into the suburban areas. Housewives used the cars to reach Lexington Market and the front platform was often piled high with their baskets.

Some Franklin High School students at that time drove horses from Randallstown to the Ten Mile House and, from there, took the streetcar to school. Elizabeth Ruff Harker, her brother Seymour Ruff, the Klohr girls, Catherine Stanfield Wolf and Esther Black Mowbray were some who reached school in this manner. *-E. Bennett Bowen*

When they started building that United Railway [streetcar line], my grandmother kept the old [Fitch's] inn going. She used to have the men who couldn't connect with their run stay there ... more or lass as roomers. And she had two of the head ones of United. Her specialty was making custard pies. This one they called Colonel Jemison -- I don't know what the title was for -- he insisted on bringing his daughter there to taste those custard pies. I was a tiny infant at the time and he gave me a silver dessert spoon. It had '95 on it, so I gave it to my great-grandchild who's named for me, little Margaret Elizabeth Quinn. *-Margaret Clark Hoff*

The streetcar company had cut [the road-bed] down considerably and filled so that their tracks were much more level than the road surface. *-George B. P. Ward*

Reisterstown Road is wider because the street-car took up two tracks. When they modernized it, the road still kept its same contours and hills and valleys - ups and downs. The route [went from Pikesville through Owings Mills] then through Reisterstown to Butler Road where the vehicle bridge is now. Alongside [that bridge] was an old wooden trestle for the streetcars and that's how they got across the Western Maryland Railroad tracks. They went down to Waugh Avenue and that was the end of the street-car line, right near Emory Grove campground.

The speed of the cars was from eight to sixty miles-per-hour. They were heated and lighted by electricity.

The first cars equipped with air-brakes were built in 1905. Part of them were assigned to the Baltimore-Pikesville-Owings Mills line. Everything before that was a handle the poor old motorman had to crank up to stop the car. *-George Nixon*, Curator, Baltimore Streetcar Museum

Mr. [Anthony] Lehman [who was a motorman on the streetcars] lived right across [Reisterstown Road] from us. When he came near, he'd ring his bell and we'd all run to the windows to see him.

When we were kids and it would snow, they had a snowplow on one of the streetcars. At any time during the night – two, three, four o'clock – you could hear them going up and down. *-Lillian Demmitt Moser*

## Riding the Electric Cars

From Baltimore to Emory Grove where we had camp meeting in the summer, they had those electric cars. They didn't run every 2 or 3 minutes, but we had them. Every time you changed a zone it was another nickel. If you got off right at the top of Pleasant Hill – right at Pleasant Hill lane before [the streetcar] started down over the hill to Gwynnbrook Lane – you saved another fare. *-Minnie Clark Hebron*

I walked to Pleasant Hill to save a fare. Then after a while they moved [the fare zone] up to Delight. We had three fares to pay [between Owings Mills and Baltimore]. Sometimes when it wasn't one of the old conductors, they'd hand me two cents back. Because I wasn't big for my age. *-Dorothy King*

My mother died in '06. And they put her on the streetcar and took her into University Hospital to be operated on and she came home on the streetcar. *-Lee Fox*

That funeral car was named "Dolores", which in Spanish means "sorrow". It was built by the United Railways in 1900 especially for funerals. It had a special compartment for the casket and a secluded area for the immediate family as well as conventional seating for the other mourners.

The funeral car was first used to transport Civil War veterans' bodies from Pikesville Confederate Soldiers' Home to Loudon Park Cemetery. It did a tremendous business – so many of those old fellows died off. Later, Dolores was made available for general public use. The fee for use was twenty dollars inside the city limits and twenty-five dollars over the line. Dolores ran until March 1927, after which she was placed in storage. *-George Nixon*

Streetcar at Pleasant Hill, about 1910

Streetcar meets early automobile at the crest of Pleasant Hill, perhaps foreshadowing the time when the streetcar would be supplanted by private vehicles. Photo courtesy of Lee Fox.

Funeral Car "Dolores", about 1920

A special streetcar, "Dolores", was run for the accomdation of funeral parties. It contained a special glass-enclosed compartment for the casket and seats for the mourners. Photo courtesy of the Baltimore Streetcar Museum.

Our grandmother was taken to Loudon Park [Cemetery] on the funeral car. We lived up at Bond Avenue then. *-Helen Carpenter*

I used to get awful sick. You ever get streetcar sick? Oh, boy! - you think it's your last! Mama and I used to go to Lawrey's [Department Store] on Gay Street. [We went] in on the Emory Grove car and you had to walk from City Hall over to Gay Street where the store was. I was always crazy about watermelons and when we got off the car, Mama would buy me some at Belair Market. They'd put it on these big blocks of ice to get it cold and then they'd sell it in slices. Five cents a slice. *-Grace Bowen Pape*

My aunt came out from Annapolis to visit. Our driveway makes a complete loop off of Reisterstown Road and our house was about 400 yards from the streetcar stop. My aunt was quite an old lady and she had a big suitcase. Mr. Hipsley, who was the conductor, got off at the lower road, carried her suitcase up to the house, saw that she got in the house and walked out the upper entrance some thousand feet up the road and hopped back on the streetcar. *-William D. Groff, Jr.*

My husband [Samuel Morris] would ride his horse from the farm out on Bonita Avenue, put the horse in Mr. Groff's barn and take the streetcar to Reisterstown where he attended the Franklin Academy. The main transportation was the streetcar - people even went places in their evening clothes on the streetcar. *-Catherine Dimmling Morris*

You could always tell when a streetcar was coming. You could hear the bell clanging at the top of Pleasant Hill. *-Helen Carpenter*

### Carbarn, Powerhouse and Trouble Station

My grandfather, Jessie Livingston King, worked at the United Railway [streetcar company] car-barn at night. That was behind Garner's store. He went to work in the evening while it was still light and came home early the next morning by streetcar. After we got a car, we'd go down there to visit him every now and then and take him a special dessert. That was quite a treat to go down and see "Pap-Pap." When we'd go, he'd be so excited to see us.

I was interested in what you'd call turbines ... real large wheels. I remember two turbines ... there could have been more. And he was constantly excusing himself to go around and check them, and then he'd come back and talk to us.

It was always so hot in the power-house. We never saw [my grandfather] undressed - he always had long-sleeved blue shirts on. But when we went down there to see him, he just had his undershirt on. *-Genevieve Berryman Kelley*

Inside the power-house were three bright red generators with gold decoration on them. One of them was a great big thing that had to be recessed way down into the floor. Otherwise it would have been up as high as the ceiling. *-George B. P. Ward*

Exterior Powerhouse, about 1918

Exterior of the United Railway powerhouse at Owings Mills. The power-house, carbarn, and trouble station were located on the east side of Reis-terstown Road on the site later occupied by the Park and Tilford Distillery. Photo courtesy of the Baltimore Streetcar Museum.

The United Railway Trouble Station, about 1918
Photo courtesy of the Baltimore Streetcar Museum.

The powerhouse there at Owings Mills is a very interesting thing. It was a steam plant; they generated electricity to run the streetcars. Their fuel was coal and the siding into there is still in the street [Reisterstown Road] just east of the Western Maryland overhead bridge. The side track off the Western Maryland [Railroad] crossed the Reisterstown Road and took coal cars and dumped them in the power-house bins. Then the next day or so, they took the empties out and brought full ones in. -*George Nixon*

The main power-house was here in Owings Mills. That furnished all the current. We'd have somebody stationed here in Owings Mills and they wouldn't let but two street-cars go up Pleasant Hill at the same time because it'd blow a breaker in the power-house when two were pulling that heavy grade. They'd [also] have somebody stationed at Sacred Heart Lane, and one streetcar had to get back to Emory Grove before they'd let the next one in. They'd run for Emory Grove and they'd allow about a ten-minute headway.

They also had a big barn here for all the street-cars to pull in. And in the building that faces toward the front, they had two horses right there at all times. They could press a button and let the harness right down on them. If a line was torn down, you'd see these two horses and the wagon coming to fix it. -*Henry Clay Hipsley*

My uncle, he had this wagon with two great big black horses and one of those extension ladders that you push up ... that you wind up, you know? And Will King was his assistant. Those two used to take care of the [streetcar] line.

I remember one time they had a real ice-storm and those poor kids never got in for three days. People along the road fed them hot coffee and food. That was the time my uncle had his eyes what they call "flashed." He never did have side sight after that. It was from a flash they got off the wires ... an electric thing. Oh, it used to just lightning and carry on like a storm, [especially] in the ice storms. -*Helen Clark Hoff*

**Smoking Down Ten Mile Hill**

Mr. Hand was a conductor, a very nice, gentle little man and he was the brunt of many tricks that we [high school] students played on the streetcar. For instance, somebody would reach out the back window and pull the trolley down then let it go. Of course, they'd lose power on the streetcar and Mr. Hand would have to get off and see what was wrong. When he'd step off - say like up at Roach's Lane - it wasn't like there was a landing or anything, and the darn step would be up to here on him when he tried to crawl back in. As soon as he'd get off and get the trolley back on the line, some guy would reach up and pull the string and go Ding! Ding! with the bell. That meant for the motorman way up at the other end to go ahead and turn the current on. So there'd be Mr. Hand out there standing in the middle of the track! And he'd usually have his lunch sitting there in the streetcar, and as soon as he went out they'd steal it.

Finally, they put an enforcer on there -- Henry Hipsley. The first morning, Donald Horsey and some other guy from down in Sudbrook stole his lunch. Henry Hipsley came back and combed that streetcar till he found his lunch and he took those two kids and banged their heads together - Wham! And I'll tell you, the pranks just stopped ... just like that! *-William D. Groff, Jr.*

I conducted on the United Railway Streetcar line when it was three cents half fare and five cents full fare. I started going up and down here way back in 1915 as a conductor. Eighteen years.

They'd catch me smoking out here behind the breaker at Ten Mile House. I'd be holding the trolley coming down Ten Mile Hill and they'd have somebody standing behind the bank to catch me if I wasn't holding that trolley rope. You had to have that rope in your hand going down those hills like Tobins Hill and places like that because the trolley'd jump off if you wasn't holding it and before you'd get the car stopped it would tear the whole line down. They'd mark me up and I'd have to go in and see the superintendent.

[Back then, conductors] were only getting eighteen cents an hour. I'd go out across country and husk corn, twenty cents a barrel, or I'd go back to Scott's in cherry-picking time - all them big trees where Caves Road comes off of Greenspring - I'd go back there because I could make three times as much picking cherries. I'd come back to work and the superintendent would say, "Hipsley! Where you been?" I'd say, "I been home sick ... didn't have to see no doctor or nothing." He'd get me to hang up his old derby hat and he says, "Look, Hipsley - you just get sick whenever you want to and that's just got to be cut out!" So I'd be looking out the window there on Fulton Avenue and Druid Hill, and he'd give me the devil, and then he'd come out and pat me on the back and say, "Hipsley, how *is* everything back there on the farm?" I says, "Fine." *-Henry Hipsley*

Henry Hipsley was some tough man! But when they switched from streetcars to buses, he wasn't too well suited to the mechanism ... he just threw the thing in gear. This one time we were all on the bus coming from Pikesville, and there was nobody in sight as we came over the hill at Cradock's Lane [and Reisterstown Road]. There was a man on there that said, "Okay, Henry - what will she do?"

So Henry opened her up, and we came down through that hollow and up the top of the hill and down through Tobins [Garrison], the throttle laying wide open. As we went over the top of the hill, there was this perfectly awful noise. We're all standing up front right behind him. We looked way out through the back of the bus and here's these great big pieces of engine all over the road. The whole engine fell out of that bus, the transmission and everything!

We got down to the bottom of Tobin's Hill, and that's where the bus stopped. We had a string of metal all the way down the hill. Hipsley's sitting there saying, "What in the world have we done?" They were rough on buses, those men! *-William D. Groff, Jr.*

A number of local men worked on the streetcars: Walter Barnhart, William Flater, Albert Chenowith, Clayton Hann, Bernard Hoff,

Thomas O'Neil, Martin Smith, Nelson Bowen, Charles Bosley, John King, Elmer Frank and many others. The last Emory Grove streetcar man I remember died in 1985 at the age of 91; he was Henry Hipsley. *-E. Bennett Bowen*

Elmer Frank of Owings Mills, Number One man with the Baltimore Transit Company, is due to retire after 49 years. He started in 1907 as a conductor with the United Railway and Electric Company. Mr. Frank says traffic problems were worse in the horse-drawn era. Said Mr. Frank, "Quite often the wheels of a coal cart or fruit wagon would get caught on the tracks. The streetcar would have to follow the wagon until it could maneuver out of the tracks."
Mr. Frank started at $10 per week as a conductor. For many years he alternately froze and sweltered on the open streetcars' rear platforms. In 1932, he started driving buses and has done so ever since, except for a short period of driving trackless trolleys. Two years ago, his seniority with the company entitled him to the Number One badge. -Article in *Baltimore Sun*, August, 1956

My father started to work for United Railway on the track parts. Putting in cross-ties. He got twelve cents an hour and got paid every ten days. Then he went to motor-man, and when he got rid of the streetcars, he went to driving buses. Then they retired him. He had thirty-one years there. *-James L. Bowers*

## Mr. Fitch's Tavern

On the east side [of Reisterstown Road] where the [railroad] abuttment is, was the Fitch tavern [also known as 12-Mile House]. I think the last proprietor was named Clark. He was Mrs. Henry Hoff's father.
The house had wide porches on at least two sides. The front porch was supported by iron grillwork that extended from both the first and second floors. Virginia Creeper and ivy interlaced the grillwork past the second floor, creating cool shade for anyone who wished to enjoy the view from the porches.
Travelers drove into the large yard on the northeast side of the hotel. The driveway separated the barn and the stables from the house. There was a huge colony house for bee martins that fed in the nearby meadow lands and kept the mosquitoes in check. The southern side of the barn was partly covered by a pigeon house that must have been home for a hundred strutting, cooing pigeons. *-E. Bennett Bowen*

My step-grandfather was Henry S. Fitch. He was the owner of that ... what-you-call-it ... roadhouse ... something. [Later,] my father was there with Mr. Fitch in that roadhouse business. They had a general store hooked up with it.
The grounds of [the Fitch Tavern] were closed in with lattice-work fences and they had several gates. Over all those gates they had these rambling roses, and they were beautiful. All that yard was full of weeping willow trees. There was this big courtyard and this big pond in the middle.

They had watering troughs all around where [the teamsters] got water. Right under that [railroad] abuttment on the east side [of Reisterstown Road] is where the pump was. A great big pump - it was one of those hewed out of a log. From that pump they had a stream that went into the courtyard and the pigeons would get out there of a morning and take a bath. Cutest sight you've ever seen!

In the back - toward Reisterstown - they had a high porch for the ladies to get on the horse without climbing up. My grandmother used to go out there - my uncle had the dearest old horse, Dixie - she used to get on him of a night and ride around ... get on there sideways and ride around that court of a night on this horse, mind you!

They had a bar there, and old Captain Carey Wilson used to get off the train up there and get a drink before he went home. But you know, with all that, there wasn't the carryings-on you have today. They'd get a drink and go on home, and that would be it. *-Virginia Clark Hoff*

You know where the power-house was? That was like an inn or something there. Pop said Virginia Hoff's mother, Mrs. Clark, was small and she was a barmaid or whatever they'd call it, and he'd kid her. Because she'd be on tippy-toes to wait on him. *-Dorothy King*

I loved to play cards just for fun, and once at Twelve Mile House they got me in a card game ... so much up and so much go bank. I just cleaned up. And I says, "No more cards for me!" *-Henry Clay Hipsley*

## The Ten Mile House

There were three boys that ran the Ten Mile House. They rented [the inn] from the Cradocks, but you'd think they owned the place. When their mother passed away her chair and her wrap stayed just the way [they'd always been]. And Cradocks, you see, that would go with them ... that was to their taste.

You know, John L. Sullivan [the boxer] stayed at the Ten Mile House. He sweated it out there under the manure. I guess to lose weight. *-Dorothy King*

My father always used to see that we had a good bottle of whiskey in the cupboard. He used to get it from down here at the Ten Mile House ... from the Myrley brothers. They were close friends. I was never in the bar of the Ten Mile House, but they said it was very elaborate for those days. *-Virginia Clark Hoff*

Ten Mile House was vacant for a long, long, time. I don't remember anybody being there until Thompson. He had the restaurant and rooms there, too. Miss Mary Livingston lived there for a couple of years before she died. The place caught fire once, and we had to carry her out over the roof. *-George B. P. Ward*

The people who owned [Ten Mile House] were named Thompson. I used to go there because the Rotary Club met there, and my husband was a member.

It was a very gracious house. It had wide, thick stone walls so that it had very wide window sills. It had an entrance hall with a stairway going up out of it. On the right was a living room, and all the furniture in there was so antique - the little settees and the chairs.

You didn't just sit down and look at a menu - you had your drink in the living room and ordered there.... Then, when dinner was ready and the first course was on the table, you'd be escorted into the dining room. The tables were set with candles. Just beautifully done.

They always had hot bread, hot biscuits. As I remember, their fried chicken was out of this world, a specialty of theirs. And at Thanksgiving time they always had what I called Hattie Thompson's cranberries - she chopped up raw cranberries and oranges and lemon and sugar. Hattie gave me the recipe for it - I still make it. All the foods were out of this world ... delicious.

The waiters were black men in white coats and very gracious. They knew everybody that came in and they were so very polite. All the people Hattie had working there had been there a long time. The cook in the kitchen had been there for 25 years ... like that, you know.

They had a small bar in a room with wood tables and chairs. Old also ... maple tables and chairs. A very charming place.

The upstairs was where the Thompson family lived and they had lovely rooms. Many antiques around the place. Hattie and Harry Thompson were old people, up in their seventies when I first knew them. When both Thompsons died, their sons tried to make a go of running it for a while, but they just couldn't do it like Hattie and Harry did. Then they sold it and it was torn down. It was terrible to me to see them destroy a beautiful old stone building. The inn was a little north of the shopping center they built there. They didn't build on the exact spot, so I don't see why they tore it down. -Dorothy Smullen

Owings Mills Elementary School occupies the site of the former tavern run by Captain Edward Wheat. The tavern was a large brick building with a hexagonal front and two wings that stretched westward. There were large porches on the south side of the building. The stable and hay barns were located on the opposite [east] side of the Reisterstown Turnpike. After being unused for many years, the roof collapsed and the barn fell down.

The building that houses Colonial Inn today was built by Mr. John Marshall about a century ago. It was the residence of the Lilly family, the David McLeans and the Thompson family.

Mr. and Mrs. David Slade moved from their Pleasant Hill Road farm and lived in the brick house that once stood where Captain Harvey conducts his restaurant today. -E. Bennett Bowen

## Summer Boarding Houses

Many city residents fled from the city's heat and disease epidemics each summer to boarding houses in the country. The father usually commuted to work by the trolley or the Western Maryland Railroad passenger trains.

Accepting boarders meant extra cooking and housekeeping and usually the hiring of extra help. The success of the house depended upon it's reputation for providing a "good table."

Mrs. Winfield Lockard of "Therapia" farm [now the site of Morningside Apartments] was one local woman who took in boarders for the summer. That house had twenty-two rooms, so she always had a slew of boarders.

Mr. and Mrs. Boggs kept a large summer boarding house on the east side of Reisterstown Road, opposite Old Tollgate Road. Mr. Boggs was a semi-retired Methodist Episcopal minister. Although unable to deliver sermons because of a throat and speech difficulty, he did much work among the poor families and visited newcomers to the area.

Each summer the Boggs house overflowed with boarders. Those who couldn't secure rooms on the premises roomed at neighboring homes. The house had a large dining room built to accommodate the crowd. Mrs. Boggs was assisted in running the house by her sister Elizabeth Broyshow and a full-time cook.

The enterprise came to an abrupt end when Miss Broyshow died. The house was sold to the Shipleys and was later inherited by the Shipley's daughter, Mrs. Orten Dorsey. *-E. Bennett Bowen*

## The Monster In the Sky

An old farmer of our area was walking across one of his fields when he spotted the first airplane he had ever seen. At first he tried to knock it out of the sky with stones. After many stones and a few profanities failed to bring it down, he fell down on his knees and prayed to be spared from the monster in the skies above him. *-E. Bennett Bowen*

Arthur Wyatt was stationed at Aberdeen. He flew down to Lone Hickory Farm from up there. He landed in the field back of the barn and misjudged a little rise and bent his propellor. The next morning the take-off was exceptional. I still don't know how he got up in the air between the field and Bonita Avenue ... going down through this field on grass! *-Paul Englar*

[After the war], my husband [James Hooper] belonged to the National Guard and every Saturday they'd go down to Logan Field and fly. He entertained the officers one Saturday [at our place], and they all landed in Lutz's field. *-Elsie Marshall Hooper*

# CHAPTER 7

## Stick Candy and Kerosene

*If there was a central gathering place in the Owings Mills community, it was in the general stores which provided not only a public forum but a source for everything from dynamite for removing stumps to a length of calico for a farm wife's apron. For the more isolated farms in the area, as well as for housewives in general, door-to-door peddlers supplied many essential items of merchandise.*

$$-/-/-/-$$

### Mr. Garner's Straw Hat

A store on the west side of the turnpike was operated first by the Harmons, then by Mr. Kephardt Pfieffer and then by two brothers, Jesse and Alva C. Garner. The two-story frame building with a long line of hitching posts in front of it stood about where the present-day [railroad] abuttment is located. It was razed in 1906 to make way for the double-track Western Maryland Railroad.

Mr. Alva Garner remained in the neighborhood. For a time he occupied a two-room building that had been the office for the lumber yard in the rear. This building stood close to the present-day railroad switch. He had a small stock of goods left from the old store and he took orders and obliged his former customers in many ways.

[Some time later,] Mr. Garner announced that he had bought the building [on the east side of the turnpike] that had formerly been used as the railroad station, and was planning to make it into a first-class general store.

A local builder, Mr. Samuel B. Marshall, remodeled the old building. He removed the waiting room partitions, built a long balcony above the counters and turned the alcove that had been used for the telegraph and ticket office into a semi-private office for the bookkeeper. The freight warehouse [in the rear] became the store-house for bulkier products. Also in the rear, a frame house was built for one of the clerks and a stable for the horses and delivery wagons.

Alva Garner was a unique character. He wore a straw hat all winter and would not sell cigarettes. He knew his customers -- their history, family problems and approximate income. He was careful not to overextend credit, but his liberality in dealing with the ill, the aged or the indigent was known throughout the neighborhood. *-E. Bennett Bowen*

Mr. Garner was something else. He'd go around all summer with a felt hat on. As soon as it got to be about October, he'd put on a straw hat and he wore the straw hat all winter. *-George B. P. Ward*

[At first], Garners kept the store along about where the coal chute is now ... to your right going [south] on Reisterstown Road. Bill Russell was the clerk and he lived there over top of the store. I used to go down and take the store order. It was all torn down and [Garner's] moved across the road to where the Baltimore County Supply Company is now. *-Grace Bowen Pape*

I worked at Garner's store when I was about twelve. In the afternoon and evening and on Saturday. Because I had to have money to go to high school.

There wasn't any electricity out here then. Gas lights illuminated the store. Mr. Garner made the gas himself. There was a great big tub [down in the cellar] – I don't know the capacity. They would put the carbide in there and then, if I remember correctly, they poured water over that. It would bubble up and carry on and make gas. Right quick they'd close the gas up. It was all piped up and the lights in the store were all run from this acid down in the basement.

They had a big furnace in the cellar and [on the main floor] there was a radiator that stood about three feet off the floor. The heat came up and was dispersed out of that. Beside the radiator was a box filled with sand – the men all used that as a cuspidor and they could spit across the store.

Mrs. Shoemaker [who lived] next to the old school used to bring eggs down to trade for merchandise. On the day she'd bring them down, there'd be a man from Garrison who would come in with a big market basket and buy all the eggs. Because they were nice and fresh.

There was a man named Roop who ran a big truck [that went into Baltimore] to market – he would bring out oranges and things like that, and Mr. Garner would buy from him. Cantaloupes – he'd buy two or three baskets of cantaloupes.

[There was no refrigeration in the store.] Mr. Garner would buy maybe fifteen or eighteen pounds of smoked sausage, and he would hang them up in the window.

[Farmers] came from miles around to buy dynamite from Mr. Garner. He had it way in back of the store in one of those buildings. He also built a home behind the store, and one of his men lived in that. Later, Harry Glover lived there. Shoemaker also lived there.

Mr. Garner ran a [delivery] wagon down almost as far as Pikesville. The driver would change occasionally – George Bange ... John Eaton. *-Laura Wimsett Redifer*

The building had originally been the train station and the railroad clock was still in the store. Mr. Garner and the four people in our family lived on the fourth floor. Mr. Garner had separate quarters, but

258

he took his meals with us. When my father and mother moved there in 1905, there were only six rooms. When we children came along, Mr. Garner added four rooms on the back. Then he built an upstairs back porch and another room for himself. The back porch faced the railroad tracks, and my mother used it for drying the family wash. There was no heat in the upstairs except for wood stoves, and the bathroom would sometimes freeze in winter.

In addition to my father, some of the people who worked there at various times were George Banges, John Eaton, John Jones, Thelma Shoemaker, Bertha Disney, Charlie Roemer, Julia Lockard, Laura Wimsett and myself.

On the main floor, there were all the canned vegetables and smoked meats - no fresh meats - and butter. He had a little tiny icebox he kept the butter in. Everything else was out. Patent medicines, loose buckwheat, cornmeal, beans of all sorts. Cookies in boxes with the front that opened up, and you weighed them out by the pound. Penny candy. Children always wanted my father [Bill King] to wait on them for candy because they got more for their money.

There was a large case with a huge round of cheese in it and a cleaver to cut it with. People called it "rat cheese", "store cheese", or "box cheese".

He had tobacco, and I remember my father cutting that. And also cutting glass, because people could come in and get a window pane cut to any measurement. He also carried all kinds of stockings and cotton to sew with.

Besides the main room on the first floor, there were two rooms in the back. In back there were oranges and lemons and barrels of mackerel and pickles and smoked meats and a barrel of peanuts. He kept walnuts and all kinds of nuts back there in barrels and boxes.

The work clothes and shoes were on the balcony. The buildings behind the store held feed, flour, straw and building supplies.

They had rubbers and boots in the basement and syrup in big barrels. The overshoes, galoshes, lamps, lanterns and [glass] lampshades were down there, too.

Some of the regular customers were the Painters, the Easters, the Wards, the Campbells, the Mosers, the Knatzes, the Carpenters, the Dolfields, the Sherwoods, the Shoemakers, Frank Price and the Simonds family. Mary Mack came out to the store almost every morning - she rode out with Raymond Moser [when he brought his milk to the train]. Mrs. Douglas Campbell used to come in and perch on the heater that was in the middle of the floor. There was a captain's chair with the rungs worn completely down where the men would come in and talk and prop their feet.

Mr. Garner was from Union Bridge. He went home on weekends and returned Sunday morning [to attend services at the] Presbyterian Church which was on the opposite side of Reisterstown Road [north of the grade-level railroad crossing]. -*Anna King Swem*

Mr. Garner was short, on the heavy side and had a real "whiny-like" voice. There was a little alcove office on the right side of the store [about halfway to the rear], and this was where you usually saw Mr. Garner.

To the right as you entered the store, there was a beautiful beveled glass candy case. All penny candy, some one cent each, some two for a penny or five for a penny. When I went to visit, I always had five cents for candy, but made sure Uncle Will [King] waited on me. He gave me three times as much as I was suppose to get. Mr. Garner gave you what you paid for. *-Genevieve Berryman Kelley*

Garner and Bill King and Bertha Disney - I'll never forget them! You could get whatever you wanted - take a big old jug over there and he'd go down and draw it full of molasses for you. Kerosene. Big containers they had out there on the porch, and they'd pump you kerosene. *-A. Franklin Parker*

Oh, you just can't imagine all the kinds of stuff that were there at one time! *-Bessie Moser vonGunten*

They sold everything in that store from horse-collars to single-trees. Those days, you went there and bought one-cent candies, two cents a piece and five cents a piece. And you'd go up there with a quarter and come home with a pocket full of this and that. But now-a-days, you just may as well forget about the quarter because that's gone down the drain.
But Mr. Garner was a fine man. I can see him yet. He would use a pencil about as big as my little finger [to write orders]. I often wondered if he was gonna get a big one, but he always wrote it down, and he always got everything right. *-Elmer Hobart Schaefer*

I can still remember Mr. Garner and all the old farmers sitting around in there and spitting into the box of sand or something they had. *-Frank Schaefer*

## The Store at Gwynnbrook Crossing

When I was about six years old [about 1890), Gwynnbrook Station was established, a stone three-story building containing grocery store, railroad ticket office, express and freight office, and postoffice, all operated by one man. The [proprietors] were, successively, MacElroy, Jones, George French, and George Davis. During Jones's regime, we heard the first talking machine, an Edison cylinder affair, which gave out with "Uncle Josh" records - "Uncle Josh at the Dentist," "All Bound Round With Woolen String," and others which we natives thought were very amusing, as we sat round the stove with our mouths hanging open. -from "Lone Hickory Farm Notes", October 16, 1955 by *Francis Sydney Reese*

Davis owned the big store here. It was right where you crossed the railroad tracks [on Gwynnbrook Avenue.] A big old country store -- you could get anything there you liked. You got food there and men got stuff to fix their wagons and their harnesses. Then you bought peanut butter and syrup in gallon buckets. *-Elsie Durham*

Store at Gwynnbrook, about 1918
This substantial building on Gwynnbrook Lane at Bonita Ave. housed a large general store, a post-office, and a train station. The owners occupied the spacious apartment on the second and third floors. Photo courtesy of Jean Reese Worthley.

Back in 1888 when Dad and Mom were married, they had a store down there at Gwynnbrook. It was a big, three-story place, a lovely building.

There were quite a few [different] store-keepers. I remember her talking about a Mr. James and a Mr. Staub and Mr. Specht who had it. When I was old enough to remember, Mr. George Davis was running the store. He had a family of six children. He ran it for some time.

There were warehouses on both sides of the tracks where they stored the feed that Mr. Davis sold. They had a coal-yard farther up the track at Gingrich's Switch. He had trucks and two or three men working for him and they delivered feed and coal. They hauled to Glyndon and through Owings Mills. He had a big business there.

I worked in the store. I was there for six years. I waited on the store and the gas tanks and I used to go over to the warehouse and get the feed for the different people who came. [That's where I met my husband.] He worked there. He delivered the feed and coal ... drove one of the trucks. John Clark worked there, too, and he delivered feed.

So then, in 1928, Mr. Davis died and Mr. Hilberg took over the store in 1929. Mr. Hilberg ran the store until about 1934 or 1935 and then the state took over the building, and they had apartments made there. Later, it was demolished. *-Helen Kendig Bowers*


**Keeping Store**

People by the name of Bell lived on Pleasant Hill Road [opposite Tollgate Road]. The Bells kept store there and then my mother and father bought it and my mother kept store. General store. There weren't any supermarkets or places to buy fresh meats like there are now. In fact, they didn't eat then like they do now. Now you can get anything at any time. [Then] it was just dry groceries - sugar ... salt ... no fresh meats. *-Grace Bowen Pape*

When [railroad construction] closed the Harmon Store, Mr. Charles Roemer began to sell goods from his quarters in the old Fitch Hotel. But that building was also scheduled for destruction. A Mr. McCloskey owned some unoccupied land on the west side of the turnpike [north of the Western Maryland Railroad overpass]. He built a store for Mr. Roemer, who was joined in his venture by Mr. Charles Wineholt, the local school principal.

For a time, the store also housed the post office, but there were some objections and Mr. Roemer moved the post office to the house next-door.

Mr. Wineholt resigned his school position and took over management of the store, which was known as "Charles Roemer & Company, General Merchandise." Mr. Wineholt died in 1914, shortly after he sold the business. From then on, the store had a number of proprietors, including William Reter who later located in Clyndon. The last owner was James Wisner, who sold the building to a liquor store and built a new grocery store adjacent to it. [This building is the present-day Sweetwater Pool Store].

In the early years of this century, Mr. Sylvester Marshall built a store room at the end of his house on the northwest corner of Pleasant Hill and Reisterstown Roads. After a year or two, Mr. Marshall sold the store and later, the entire building was destroyed by fire. Mr. Goucher Tase, owner of the land, built the brick building that still stands. For some years, this was operated as a store by William Hooper and, later, by other storekeepers.

The Doll family built a small store near the new Owings Mills School. This store was bought and enlarged by Mr. Abraham Burkholder and later operated by his son, Frank Burkholder.

Over eighty years ago, the Parsley family opened the store known as "Maple Heights" on the west side of Reisterstown Road approximately halfway between Pleasant Hill Road and Gwynnbrook Lane. Various grocers operated there until about 1949.

On the site where the Niemeyer home now stands at the corner of Delight and Reisterstown Roads, Mr. John French operated a store from 1893 to 1913. Opposite, on the site of what is now the Eckhardt Funeral Home, a Mr. Ford operated the Delight postoffice and also sold candies, cakes and a few groceries. Both original buildings were destroyed by fire.

On the southwest corner of Timber Grove Road and Reisterstown Road, Mr. William Brown operated a grocery business.

The Cullison brothers built a large frame store in Garrison [then known as "Tobins"] about 1915. Mr. Linwood Sullivan purchased this property and his family operated a successful grocery business there for many years. The building now houses the Garrison postoffice.

Mr. Kephart Pfeiffer, who operated the Harmon store for a time, opened a store in Garrison which he leased in 1905 to a Mr. Gott. Later, the store became Angor Food Market. Opposite, Mr. John Bell, a butcher, slaughtered and sold meats at his shop. This building and the adjoining residence, later the Basler home, has now disappeared.

When the Soldiers Delight mines were in full swing, the former Daniel W. Lutz house was a store and a tavern. This building was also destroyed by fire.

Mr. Walter O'Dell operated a grocery store at the corner of Deer Park and Liberty Roads for a number of years and the Harker family operated a grocery store and tavern at the corner of Liberty and Wards Chapel Roads for a couple of generations.

On the east side of Owings Mills, the Hipsley family had a thriving store at Park Heights and Walnut Avenues. This was later operated by "Shorty" Tillman and has, since his death, changed hands several times.

The Hoffman store at the corner of Greenspring Avenue and Dover Road was bought by William J. Harris in about 1900, and he continued to operate a small store there until about 1920. *-E. Bennett Bowen*

In the *Community Times*, I saw a reference to my grandfather, George French and his store at Gwynnbrook. I don't know very much about him except that he kept store there. My father helped him in the store, and, as a young man, opened his own store at Delight - where William Neimeyer now has his home. I have some ledgers of charged purchases from 1900 to 1908. They give names of people who lived near and the article and the price charged. -From a letter to the author by *Helen French Barnhart*

Up where John French had his store, they'd have watermelons down in the ice-house for chilling. When Mom would send [my brother] John to the store and she'd say, "a half-pound of this, or a pound of that," John would mix it all up ... he'd say it all the opposite. When we'd go there for coal-oil, John would say, "You ask for it." I would have to go along and ask for the coal-oil. *-Dorothy King*

Shorty Tillman's was [another] an old country store. He had everything. *-Elsie Durham*

Pop Warren, who had one leg and walked with crutches, had a little store next to the post-office where he sold soda pop. That was another gathering place. *-Morris G. Richardson*

At the top of Pleasant Hill was Gettierre's. Harry Cooper had that store at one time, also. And Mr. Weber was there - Mr. Gettierre's brother-in-law. He moved from there down to Garrison and opened a store down there. Mr. Burley Myers sold ice-cream at that store. He brought cans of ice-cream and sold them out on the porch. *-Helen Carpenter*

Before they opened [the Gwynnbrook] store, we had to go out to Delight. That was the only store and it was run by John French. I used to go with Pop to the store every Saturday night. We went out there and he'd get a bag of candy - about a pound of hard candy and a pound of cakes - and that would last us all week. And that didn't cost very much ... things were very cheap then.

I don't remember who had [the store at Maple Heights, on the west side of Reisterstown Road south of Gwynnbrook Lane] before the Loves, but Schaeffer had it afterwards. Lawson's had it after Schaeffer and then they closed up. *-Mary Kendig Gettierre*

Strevigs started out with a fruit-stand [on Reisterstown Road opposite Kingsley Road]. They used to sell farm stuff along the road. Then he built the little store and he sold ice-cream and sodas and candy and bread. *-James L. Bowers*

To many of their customers in isolated parts of Soldiers Delight, Harker's delivery was the chief contact with the outside world. The store's list of supplies ... was an index to the changing times: coal oil, tar rope, horse collars, hames strings, plug tobacco. Today's supermarket clerk would not recognize many of them.

Harker's installed one of the first gasoline pumps between Baltimore and Frederick. The store performed many local services for its customers: paid tax bills, picked up special items, and provided telephone service with the first telephone in the area. *-Wilson Herera* from an article in *The Randallstown Times*, February 7, 1974

When we happened to go out Liberty Road way, we'd go to Berry's. Sugar and coffee were about all we bought. And a little salt. -*A. Franklin Parker*

Another store was Perry Wade's at Randallstown. It was a large country store where one could buy tobacco, groceries, dry goods and building supplies. -*Valley R. Shipe*

## Ice-Cream on Saturday Nights

The Knetzers used to bring ice-cream to the store that Jim Wisner moved. They only did it in the summer time ... made ice-cream and brought it out. I used to walk out Pleasant Hill road and all the way down there to get a pint of ice-cream. -*Grace Bowen Pape*

And then the Knetzers on Saturday night used to bring ice-cream out to Garner's store and sell it. Right out there on the porch on Saturday nights. -*Margaret Clark Hoff*

A man by the name of Naylor and also a man named Knight who lived over in Glyndon would come around on the Fourth of July with a horse and wagon and a gallon of ice-cream packed. You had to order it.

The small shop [behind the house at the southwest corner of Pleasant Hill and Reisterstown Roads] was where Burley Myers ran his ice-cream place around '20.

[Also] a man by the name of Knetzer lived back of Painters Lane. He'd make ice-cream on Saturday night and bring it out to the store that Jim Wisner later ran. I think it was about fifteen cents a pint. I'd walk down to Owings Mills and get a pint of ice-cream on Saturday night - you really got something. -*Lee Fox*

## Sewing Needles, Fresh Fish and Tin Cups

Old Charlie Williams went to huckstering after he left my father. I can see him so plain up there on that wagon. He'd stop at houses, you know, with cantaloupes or anything that a huckster would have. Elias Norris, who lived near the Mount Pleasant A. M. E. church, used to huckster, too.

Plenty of [peddlers] came through. Tin-cups, tin pans ... all that. They could get more stuff in one basket than anybody ever dreamed of. We used to have women ... women peddlers. I still have a ricer that I bought from a woman peddling.

And do you know where we got our bananas? - from old John with a basket on his shoulder. He was an Italian. He probably came from Baltimore. He had one of those great big wicker baskets filled with bananas. That's the only bananas [you ever had]. Where else would you get them? -*Grace Bowen Pape*

265

One old black man who was very well thought of used to stop at our place at Owings Mills. Henry Hawkins. He used to come down with these great big fat chickens, and my grandmother used to go out there and get a couple if she wanted big fat chickens for soup or something.

Then there was another wagon came down. A Mister Zepp. He used to have a covered wagon. Of course that was way back at the beginning of the 1900s.

There were [also] a couple of women who used to come through here with baskets. They would have just about everything -- little trinkets, kitchen things, maybe dish-cloths, towels. They used to have these huge, great baskets. I wondered how they toted them sometimes.
*-Margaret Clark Hoff*

Tin peddlers! I used to love that because they'd get them all out on the floor - dippers, tea-strainers and so on.

A fish peddler came around with a wicker basket, an Italian man. He'd sell fish and oysters and then there was a colored man that used to come with fish and oysters. *-Dorothy King*

Years ago, we had the peddlers coming up and down the railroad tracks. We had one organ grinder man who had a little monkey and he would sharpen your scissors. You would ask them in and then they'd play with music, you know. They had this little handle and they'd turn that and make music; the little monkey would dance. It was funny!

There was another one who mended your umbrellas. And the fruit man. He was from down in Pikesville. He walked and carried a big woven basket that had fruit in ... different varieties of fruit. Then, later, he started a fruit store down in Pikesville. His name was Broccato. *-Helen Kendig Bowers*

For years, Owings Mills housewives bought their meat from butchers' wagons. Mr. John C. Bell came with his wagon from Garrison, and Mr. Leonidas Gies came from Reisterstown. Mr. Bell sold various cuts of beef, smoked sausage and bologna.

Later, a Mr. Shearer came from Carroll County with pork products. He only came in winter, and only served customers living near the turnpike. Mr. Joseph Merryman from Pleasant Hill Road also sold meat in the neighborhood at a later time.

The butcher wagon was equipped so that large pieces of meat could be hung from the sides. There was a hard-wood cutting block at the rear of the wagon. Narrow slots on each side of the wagon held the knives, saws and cleavers. *-E. Bennett Bowen*

I can still see the crab man with a big, old, white apron! He'd carry the fish in baskets with ice on it all the way from in town. You'd hear him holler, "Oysters! Great big oysters! Big as the palm of your hand." *-Minnie Clark Hebron*

These [hucksters] would have butter and eggs and whatever they could find in their covered wagons. And that was a long haul for them down to Owings Mills. They changed horses there and went on to Baltimore. They would sell flowers ... wild flowers ... flowers that they cultivated ... anything that they could to make a dollar.  Then they would buy groceries and things that they didn't have up there in the country, and take them up there to sell.  *-Laura Wimsett Redifer*

I remember the A-rabs.  They'd have peaches or some kind of fruit.  They'd drive a wagon and holler.  You could hear them when they were back of Ritters Lane.  *-Sarah Cox Hewitt*

We had a butcher who came by and he'd ring his butcher bell.  John made up a rhyme about him.  It had Hell in it, and Mom punished him and sent him up to his room.  It was a warm day, so he drew a picture on the calcimined wall of a barbed wire fence and a boy sitting there eating ice-cream.  You see, it was hot, and I guess he was thinking about ice-cream.  *-Dorothy King*

I think some of them used to drive around with a covered wagon.  They'd have odds and ends that people didn't get out to buy.  Stuff like you used to get in the ten-cent store.

The McNess man carried liniments, pie-fillings, vanilla, all kinds of things.  People mostly knew about when they would come - a couple of times a year.  Some of the stuff they had was really good - the extracts and things.  *-Bessie Moser vonGunten*

Oh, yes!  He had all kinds of things in there - needles and pins and snaps and buttons and hooks and eyes and ribbons.  He'd have laces like you'd sew on your skirt or slip and rick-rack.  Different colors.  I remember that because I used to think they were so pretty.  And collars.  Those days men used to wear those stiff collars, and they fastened them with a sort of brass-looking button and then it laid open, the collar laid open on each side.

And hatpins.  Women used to wear those long hatpins.  And hairpins and bone combs - women used to set these combs in their hair.  Some of them we used to call "chair-backs" - they had long teeth and they put them in their hair like the Spanish people did.

Sometimes the peddler had shawls and fans - sometimes they were painted, pretty hand-painted fans.  Buttons.  And hair ribbons.

People were a little bit afraid of [one of the peddlers], because he'd get angry if they didn't buy from him.  Oh, he used to get furious!  I remember my mother closing the door ... rather than arguing with him, she just closed the door.  Because she didn't have the money to buy things from him.  *-Viola Clark Nesbitt*

Peddlers came around fairly regularly.  With packs on their backs.  When they opened the packs, they had an incredible number of things inside - pins, needles, safety pins, ribbon, elastic, crochet needles and hooks.  They would come in the kitchen and spread out the bundle - you picked out what you wanted and paid for it on the spot.

Tramps came around quite regularly, too.  They traveled up and down the railroad tracks.  I've always heard that they marked the places where they were welcome.  They would come up the hill here and knock on the door and the cook would tell them to split some wood.  They would go and split some wood and then she'd give them their supper on the back steps. Grandfather would ask them to give him their matches, which they did, and then they would sleep in the barn overnight. Next morning they got up early and split some more wood without being told, then got their breakfast and they'd be on their way. Some of the same ones came back year after year. *-Waiva Dean Reese*

I remember the gypsies on Reisterstown Road. If my mother knew they were coming, boy! - she'd gather us up in a hurry, take us in the house. She always said that the gypsies would steal little children.

They always had a big crowd in their open wagons. Their skin was always dark, and I wonder if it was because they were dirty or because they just had dark skin. They were dressed in these wild-looking clothes - long, flowing, all different colors. Nothing matched. And my father always said they wore those big, flowing clothes so they could steal stuff and stick it up underneath.

I know my mother would never have gone to the door if they tried to sell her anything. It was just like you hid, and you were quiet and didn't let anybody know you were around. *-Genevieve Berryman Kelley*

Just mention the word "gypsies" and I was scared to death. They claimed there'd been several children kidnapped by them. And they'd steal lightning! They'd come to your house and scare you to death till you gave them what they wanted. [Say they were going to] put a spell on you. They used to come sometimes in their wagons and camp in the stone quarry back of the school. "Oh," they would say, "the gypsies are in!" We used to go stand and look down at them. *-Grace Bowen Pape*

# CHAPTER 8

## Whitewash Brushes and Paper Cups

*Throughout the years, Owings Mills residents have earned their living in a variety of trades and professions. For women of the community, there has been a gradual transition from home to employment, although even in earlier times there were a few women who pioneered their way into the business world. Children's chores were also an important contribution to the family.*

*-/-/-/*

### Twenty-five Cents for a Haircut, Fifteen Cents for a Shave

My father [Henry Clark] was a barber. Cut your hair. Right there at Owings Mills. Down there where Dolfield Road turns in at the [railroad] bridge, between there and the Tollgate. [North of Hoff's] blacksmith shop. His barber shop was part on the bank and part over the water [of the Gwynns Falls]. Like pilings underneath. He cut the children's hair. On Saturday afternoons, all the children be lined up. I guess he charged fifteen cents. *-Minnie Clark Hebron*

A good many of the world's affairs were settled right there [in my father's barber shop]. I remember as a kid going down to the shop and listening to all those World War I veterans talking - Henry Hipsley, Henry Simmons, several others.

I remember a lot of the old gentlemen who came in in those days. Tobacco chewers! My father had an old stove over in the corner with a bucket in front to catch the ashes. Those guys - boy, they were great spitters! They'd sit back there and chew their tobacco and spit over there in that bucket.

You'd see the same customers in there every Saturday morning - Raymond Moser, Bob Moser, Mr. Bowen, Mr. Guy Harden, old Mr. Chris vonGunten, Mr. Dave Disney.

On Thursday nights, most every week, Mr. Knatz - E. G., they called him - would come over. He had a beard and the ordeal of trimming that beard would take nearly an hour. Mr. Knatz brought along his own gown to put around himself, and he'd hold a mirror the whole time he was being worked on so he could tell my father exactly which hair to cut. Very particular about that beard ... had to be just right!

269

Johnny Reese was another one who came to get his hair cut and he always paid with honey. Another one who used to bring honey up here was Guy Harden. Somebody down at Garrison brought Pop apples. We would find a bag of apples or a bag of potatoes on the back porch.

Pop didn't have running water in the shop, just a dry sink and a little can that he sat on the stove to heat the water for shaves. I still have a pair of the hand-clippers he used for cutting hair.

Pop never kept any records or anything. He charged 25 cents for a haircut, 15 cents for a shave, and if anybody didn't have any money, they'd write what they owed him on the wall. I don't think there was ever a kid came in there to get his hair cut that didn't get a nickel back. Then they'd head up to Doll's store [later Burkholders, now the site of the Sunoco service station] to spend it on penny candy.

But it got so people were coming from Pikesville, Reisterstown, all over to get their hair cut at those prices, and they were working him to death. So before I went in the service, I made a sign and increased his prices to 50 cents for a haircut and 25 for a shave. I don't know whether he abided by the [new] prices or not, though. *-James M. Carpenter*

## From Hobby to Thriving Florist Business

Mr. William Terry, an electrician, was brought here from Pittsburgh to supervise the overhead work for the generation of current from the streetcar power station. The family took up residence here, and Mrs. Terry decided to pursue her hobby of raising plants on a larger scale. She soon had a greenhouse in her backyard, and gave away many of the plants and flowers.

Later, she started to sell them. As her business grew, she added more greenhouses. Her "hobby" became a family business when Mr. Terry left his job and became a florist, although he still worked as an electrician for local builders. When the three-room brick school house was built, it was he who did the wiring.

The Terry family did not have good luck. Their oldest son, Scott, died - from eating raw chestnuts, it was said, although it was later learned the real cause of his death was a ruptured appendix. In the early 1920s, the Terry family sold their property and business to Mr. Calvin E. Richardson from Perry Hall. *-E. Bennett Bowen*

The florist business was bought by my father in 1924 from people named Terry. I remember the date so well, because I was three the day after we moved there.

It had the house and five greenhouses. Most of the old greenhouses needed patching all the time - I remember that quite well. The house, itself, had been a bungalow, and they had raised it on stilts someone told me, and nailed boards around the bottom and made it a two-story house. I look at the house now and I don't know how we all slept in that place, because there were quite a few of us at the time. I'm the youngest of thirteen.

We had a shop in the back. We had a very nice business there ... my father was well known. Everybody liked him, I think.

Richardson Delivery Truck

The Richardson Florists, now operated by the third generation of the same family, once delivered its arrangements in this early truck. Photo courtesy of Morris G. Richardson.

When I came out of service, I went into business with him, and I was working as a florist when Mr. French retired and I was asked about being post master, since I had worked [at the postoffice] before. Then, I was both florist and postmaster from about '48 to '55.

We got too busy [at the post-office for me to hold both jobs] after Mr. Chew built all the houses [Tollgate development] up on the old Reese farm and we established city delivery. Then the place just went like wild-fire.

My nephew [Calvin Richardson] is running [the florist business] now, in the same house. -*Morris G. Richardson*

### The Men Who Built Our Homes

Two generations of the Tase family were builders. Mr. Si (possibly "Josias" or "Joseph") Tase built some substantial homes that still stand in the community. His brother, Andrew, kept a beautiful team of horses with which he did hauling, grading and all the jobs that are done today with earth-moving equipment. Another brother was also a builder and carpenter. His son, Mr. Goucher Tase, became a large contractor. He built office buildings, schools, banks and churches. His grandson, Henry Lewis, continues as a successful building contractor.

John Turner married Mary E. Tase, daughter of Andrew Tase and Emma Bowen Tase. The Turner's son, Robert L. Turner, became a contractor and builder.

The Marshalls - originally from Virginia - were another family that produced a number of builders. Many homes in Owings Mills, particularly along Reisterstown and Pleasant Hill Roads were constructed by them as well as a number of homes in Reisterstown and Glyndon. Charles Marshall built the three-room brick school which still stands on the bank [on Reisterstown Road south of the present elementary school]. It is now used as a residence. -*E. Bennett Bowen*

Mr. Hopkins was a stone mason. For every dollar he made, he gave a tenth of it to the church, and he was never without work. -*Laura Wimsett Redifer*

Goucher Tase was quite a contractor in those days and built the Western Maryland warehouse down on Hillen Street. I helped carry many a piece of lumber for that house Doctor Rider built [on Church Road, north of Pleasant Hill Road]. He would send a postal card saying that he was sending out so much lumber or so much plaster or something down to the Owings Mills station for us to pick up and take out to his place. -*Lee Fox*

Fred Dolfield asked me to design a small house for speculation. He wanted to be able to sell this house and make some money out of it. This lot [on Reisterstown Road south of Pleasant Hill Road] belonged to the estate of his father [Alex Y. Dolfield]. So I designed it and Sylvester Marshall, he built it ... and went broke. I had a bond so the bonding company finished the job although it wasn't too much to finish. The Clevelands lived in it, Fred Dolfield's sister and her family. -*William F. Stone*

In about '32, I went with a construction company. Stayed with them seven years. Right across from the Pimlico Race track, at Pimlico Road and Park Heights, we built all that up. They used to have the circus there, on the old carbarn lot. The last year it was there they tied some of the tents to our fence. That's where I was working when I burnt out [when the old Parker home on Sherwood Road burned].

I didn't do anything for a couple of years until I re-built the house and got things straightened out. Then I was with Bob Turner for five years. They I went to work over the other side of Catonsville, but I didn't like it much because it was an awful drive and a rough darn drinking bunch.

I had talked to Walter Crismer before, and one evening coming home from work I went to see Mr. Walter. He said, "Where you been? Can you go to work?" I says, "What time do you go to work tomorrow morning?" He says, "Seven-thirty." I says, "Okay."

I stayed with him for nineteen years. Then, I didn't quit him or leave him. He quit me. His son-in-law was starting some houses over on Winans road, so he sent me over there to help him get started. I stayed with him until I was 72 or 73. -*A. Franklin Parker*


### Mr. Venus's Lumber Yard

Mr. Venus had a lumber yard right there alongside the railroad tracks [on the west side of Reisterstown Road]. About where the coal yard is now. -*Lee Fox*


### Pleasant Hill B & L Directors

Oct. 23, 1908: Messers. Shipley, Bowen, Ritter, Tase, Sherwood, Hooper, and Rutter met in the room adjoining Mr. Hooper's Store and formed an association to be known as the Pleasant Hill Permanent Building & Loan Assn.

Nov. 21, 1908: The following officers were elected: J. Frank Shipley, Pres.; J. George Ritter, vice Pres.; Frank C. Rutter, Sect.; Goucher Tase, Treas.; Watson E. Sherwood, solicitor. It was decided to increase the number of Directors to Eleven: Messers. Edward Shoemaker, W. H. Buck, H. L. ----, and Dr. W. H. H. Campbell were elected directors.

Aug. 23, 1909: Moved and seconded that Secty. be instructed to draw check in favor of Mr. Hugo L. A. Schmidt for $600.00, amount secured by mortgage on property located on Gwynnbrook Avenue.

June 24, 1912: Committee reported sale of property on west side of pike to Upton I. Berryman for $1200.00 and recommended that a new mortgage be taken up for $300. Five Dollars accepted on acct. of Mtge. Moved to adjourn. -*from the minutes of the Pleasant Hill Permanent Bldg. & Loan Assn.*

P. H. Bldg. and Loan

The Pleasant Hill Building and Loan, founded in 1908, continued in operation until the 1970s. During this time, it provided funding for many local
home-owners and businesses. In 1955, its board of directors consisted of
(seated, l. to r.) Frank Rutter, Frank Burkholder, Samuel Morris, and
(standing l. to r.) Morris Richardson, George B. P. Ward, David Nichol, John
Hopkins, William D. Brown, and James Wisner. Photo courtesy of William
D. Brown.

## Springs, Wells and Wooden Pumps

Springs were the first source of water supply for the early houses in the community. Often the spring water which was thought to be pure was polluted by run-off from the house and barnyard. Shallow wells allowed the use of a lift pump, but often they, too, became polluted. Invention of force pumps allowed deeper wells.

The digging and maintenance of deep wells created a number of problems. In loose soil, landslides were frequent. Large underground rocks often required blasting with dynamite to dislodge them. The ignition of the fuse attached to the dynamite left only seconds for the worker to return to the surface.

Carbon dioxide sometimes collected in the well pits as they were dug and could cause suffocation. Well diggers tested for foul air by lowering a caged pigeon or other bird into the well. If the bird died, the well had to be abandoned. Wells were also known to cave in, sometimes with fatal results. Few people wanted to take the risk of going down into a very deep well.

During unusually dry seasons, the underground steam that supplied the well often stopped flowing, and water had to be hauled from another well, or the well had to be deepened. One well was deepened several times until it reached a depth of 144 feet.

Wells were walled with stones or bricks. The well platforms had to fit snugly to prevent drainage from contaminating the water below. People were advised to keep animals away from their well platforms. When cement became available, concrete slabs were poured for platforms with a trap-door for access to the well. -*E. Bennett Bowen*

[Mr. Shray] made pumps. Out of tree-trunks. Did you ever see those big wooden pumps? They'd kill you! An iron handle and usually there'd be a knob on the end of the handle. Reeses had one on their porch. [And] they had one up there at Si Disney's. -*Grace B. Pape*

[For making pumps,] they took the poplar trees because they were the truest and straightest. They bored them out and then the rod went through all the way to the bottom of the well. At the end of the rod there was what they called a "bucket" - it had flappers on. It went down and when it came up, it gathered water and that would come out the wooden spout.

We had some colored people who worked for my father and they had twin boys. They had to carry water from our house to their house up at the edge of the woods. One of them came down in the winter time and - why, I don't know - he stuck his tongue on the iron pump handle. It pulled all the skin off. The other twin wanted to see what his brother had done and he went and did the same thing. -*Lee Fox*

## Blowed Up With Dynamite

Bihys quarried a little stone in there [behind the old elementary school.] It's a sort of soapstone, used mostly for foundations. -*Lee Fox*

I have heard that the flagstone for the Cradock houses came from the Miller place off Lyons Mill Road. -*Carl A. vonGunten*

After my grandfather, John Brown, got out of the Civil War, he got married and had a family. He was in his forties or fifties when he got blowed up with dynamite in a stone quarry.

He was working at Bollinger's on Stringtown Road, and he drilled a hole and was going to put a heavy load in it, so he drilled deep. He had an eight-foot drill, and he had a hames-string tied on it to go deeper.

I think he put a half-gallon of powder in the hole and three or four sticks of dynamite. He put a fuse on it, packed clay around it and ran a dirt pipe down the hole to make the explosion down below.

So it didn't go off. He had a drill swab he was spooning it out with, and he got down too low and hit the cap. It went off and blowed him up - blowed one arm off and blowed both eyes out. The explosion also threw my uncle [whose name was also John Brown] up over a bank about twenty feet. They said that when it went off, Uncle John looked and saw his father up I don't know how high.

[My grandfather] was in awful shape. Holes all over his body like you'd take a pen and put ink in them. They took him to the hospital in a horse and wagon. The doctor tried to save his arm but gangrene started and they took his arm off. He lived eight years after that, but he never saw again. -*Joseph Brown*

## Painters and Paperhangers

In the early 1900s, Mr. Walter Robey was the chief house painter in the area. He lived next to the Terry/Richardson Florist on Reisterstown Road. Mr. Howard Paul, who married Miss Goldie Zeigler of Pleasant Hill Road, was soon recognized as a good worker and painter. There were a number of other local house-painters: Harry C. Rutter was both a house-painter and paper-hanger, as was Harry Waggoner, who married Nellie Bitzer of Kingsley Road. -*E. Bennett Bowen*

My husband, [Philip Pape], was a painter all his life. He did all of Garrison Forest School and all of Hannah More Academy. -*Grace Bowen Pape*

## Whitewashing the School House

The Figgses lived where [Dolfield] Road went across that little branch [Red Run]. Their father, [Henry Figgs,] was a calciminer, as they called it. He would paint everybody's house in spring and fall and all like that. Yellow and green ... he was good on that. -*Minnie Clark Hebron*

Recipe for Whitewash: One-half bushel of lime. Slack [slake] with warm water. See that lime is kept covered during slacking. Add one package salt [and] three pounds ground rice made into a thin paste. (Use warm water.) One pound clear glue made to thin paste with boiling water, the glue and rice to be added to the lime while it is warm. Then add one-half pound Spanish whiting. Keep stirring all the while you are adding the ingredients. -From *Joseph Simonds* ledger for Painter's Mill

Spring cleaning included whitewashing on the inside walls of the house and cellar, the stable and the stalls. School-house walls were whitewashed before school began and re-washed after any epidemic.

Whitewash was made by slacking newly-burned caustic lime. The slacking was done in a large tub or barrel. Many buckets of water were required to keep the lime from burning and the mixture had to be stirred briskly. Glue in crystal form was mixed with the lime, and other ingredients were added to make the lime stick.

To secure the whitest white, a box of washing bluing was added to the mixture. Other colors were added for other tints. Ochre was used to take the glare off of white walls and a pale green or blue was often used for decorating a bedroom.

Many families did their own whitewashing, but all who could afford it employed Mr. Henry Figgs to come with his boys and a supply of brushes to complete the job in a few days. -*E. Bennett Bowen*


## Going...Going...Gone!

For at least two generations, Caleb S. Hobbs was the best known auctioneer, not only in the Owings Mills area but in Baltimore County and the adjoining counties as well. If a sale was scheduled "come rain, shine, snow or blow," the public knew that Mr. Hobbs would be chanting the auctioneer's well-known call for bids.

The Hobbs family lived near the intersection of Lyons Mill Road and Deer Park Road. There were two sons, Worthington and Rezin and - if memory serves - three daughters. Mrs. William L. Niemeyer of Delight is a granddaughter.

Public sales on farms were well advertised. Large sale bills were tacked to trees along the road, posted in the general stores and in the post offices. Mr. Hobbs employed "inside" clerks and "outside" clerks. The outside clerk noted buyers and amounts; terms of settlement were arranged by the inside clerk. -*E. Bennett Bowen*


## Re-Cycling Farm Animals

My father worked for Friedels on Bonita Avenue. Mr. Friedel would go around to all these farms and get dead cows and horses and stuff like that. [My father] used to skin them horses and cut that meat up in the slaughterhouse and grind it up for chicken feed.

Outside they had big iron pots on an iron stand. They would put cord-wood under [the pots] and build a fire. They'd have four or five pots going at one time. They'd take a pitchfork and take the meat out of these iron pots and lay it on long boards like an old barn-door to dry

277

out in the sun. Then they'd put it through the grinder. They had an old gasoline engine with a belt [that ran] to this grinder, and they'd grind it up into chicken feed.

After they took all the meat off the bones, they'd have a great big truckload of bones and they'd haul them off and sell them to the fertilizer houses ... grind them up and make fertilizer out of them. They sold the hides for making shoes. *-James L. Bowers*

## "Pappy" Tinkler's Garage

Across the street [from the post-office] was Pappy Tinkler's [garage] -- I believe it was Crown gasoline back then ... I remember it was a cheap gasoline at the time ... thirteen cents a gallon, eight for a dollar.

I have a lot of things I could say about Pappy Tinkler's! I know quite a few poker games went on there ... all day long. There again things are re-cycling - I guess it was our first pin-ball arcade. They had pin-ball machines in there, and a lot of money when through those pin-ball machines. I think Uncle Phil [Knatz] spent a lot of time there, and he used to feed them pretty well. Good, though - he knew how to make them hit.

Pappy Tinkler, himself, was a character. As were most of the people who went in there. I was too young and too broke and too tight to play poker at that time. *-Morris G. Richardson*

## Vanilla, Peach, Chocolate and a Little Pecan

I read in a book that the first ice-cream factory in the United States was owned by Milton Painter in Owings Mills. He iced the cream and hauled it to Baltimore to Fussell's store which was located on Eutaw Street. There was another ice-cream making place on Edell's which is now the Easter farm. Those two places were pioneers in the ice-cream business. *-E. Bennett Bowen*

I helped Lev Bowen make ice-cream. [They made] vanilla and peach and chocolate and a little pecan. It was run by electric - a mixer, you know, run by electric. They had a little shanty there [on Reisterstown Road near Painters Lane] where he sold ice-cream, candy, stuff like that. He used to serve that little stand out there across from Roach's Lane with ice-cream and then he had a place over there on Dogwood Road that the woman used to get ice-cream from him. He hauled it in a pick-up truck. In these containers, you know - a can with a lid on. *-Frank Schaefer*

## A Sticky Business

[In 1949], rather than go back in the distillery business, I decided I would start something of my own. When I was in the research department at Seagram's distillery, I did my research work on adhesives.

278

Since I had an in with the distilleries and had some idea about adhesives, I [decided to] start a small [adhesives] manufacturing plant.

The first year, we sold one barrel of adhesive and our gross was $24. No employees, practically nothing. When they shut down the Hunter-Wilson distillery in 1950, I asked Ralph Kelbaugh, who was working there, to come with me and help do the leg work. I took him around and showed him how to approach the people. In order to be an adhesive salesman, you have to know [your customer's] industry. If you're selling adhesive to a paper cup company, you have to know how that machine operates before you can make the adhesive. That worked out very well and Ralph Kelbaugh was here with me for twenty-nine years until he retired.

Since that time, we grew from $24 a year to in excess of one million dollars a year. We have seven employees, five of whom have been with the company for over twenty-five years. We sell adhesives for boxes, cups, bags, shoes, furniture - to anybody that manufactures something that wraps up. All the bindings, all the furniture, all the women's shoes, they're all put together with adhesive today.

About 25% of our business is in Maryland but we supply adhesives in all the Middle Atlantic states. *-Harry L. Shay*

## Maryland Cup Company

Mr. Joe Shapiro and his son-in-law, who is now Chairman of the Board [of Maryland Cup Company] came out here before they got the land [to build their Owings Mills plant]. Dr. Saffell [owned the land] and he couldn't get it zoned and he asked me if I would help him. So I went around, of course, and we had a lot of controversy about it. Mr. Groff didn't want it to come out here because it would kill the environment. Gordon Harden didn't want it here. All the people living up and down the road, I took them all over to Towson and we got it zoned.

Mr. Joe Shapiro owned the company and Mr. Sam Shapiro was his brother. Mr. Joe was the boss. He was a beautiful fellow. Whatever he told you he would do, he did.

I've been selling adhesive to Maryland Cup Company since 1950. I dealt with Mr. Shapiro and Mr. Paul Wixon, who engineered the first machines for Maryland Cup [in their old plant] on High Street in Baltimore. Mr. Wixon lived in Reisterstown and he just happened to come by and see my sign and stopped in. He was having trouble getting adhesive from the large manufacturers. So he asked me if I would work with him. The closeness allowed me a big advantage - I supplied them all their adhesive as long as Mr. Wixon was there. *-Harry L. Shay*

## Women At Work

My mother was a houseworker - that's all. She was busy taking care of the children, taking care of the house, cleaning the house, stuff like that. She, every once in a while, raised chickens. We raised hogs, and she never had to take care of the hogs. Every once in a while, she'd feed the chickens. *-Elmer Hobart Schaefer*

I was a Daddy's girl. I helped him outside and I loved that. My mother used to say, "You'd better stay in. You're going to wish you knew how to sew someday." But it didn't mean anything [to me]. So it upset me terribly when my father died, and I got married as sort of a rebound. *-Sarah Cox Hewitt*

I used to help Papa grease the wheels and throw the corn in the hoppers. I [also] used to help him out on the sawmill. When he was repairing things, I'd bring his tools. We'd help him do whatever we could. We only had girls. *-Mary Kendig Gettierre*

I worked [first] at the Price Company. It was a litho place. They'd litho and then they'd imprint, too -- letterheads and envelopes, all like that.

[My next job was] at H. Gamse. I was a job-pressman ... or presswoman. [At first], they composed type by hand and after that they used linotype and monotype. Mr. Johnson always said he'd let me compose, but we were always too busy.

I was at Arnold's for a couple of years - a small place. No girls worked where I did, just men. But it was war-time and that made a difference. Mr. Spencer said that the men were nicer with a female in there. Anyhow, it was sort of fun in a way, [although] sometimes the fellows would print things that weren't so nice. They'd call me "Toots," although not when the boss was around. Then it was sup-posed to be "Miss Dorothy."

Later, I quit there and went back to Gamse's. I worked ten hours [a day]. We used to work on Saturdays until four o'clock, then they changed it to noon and then to no Saturdays at all.

We went into receivership in the Depression at Gamse's. I know all about the Depression! When [my brother and I] would look for jobs, we'd say, "You work that side [of the street] and I'll work the other. And, you see, they'd take a man before they'd take me. And that would be no more than fair that they'd take a man that's out of work before they'd take me. But I did get a job! With a Mr. Creagar at the John Lucas Company. It was through my brother. [Mr. Creager] said, "Tell your sister to come see us." Then I stayed on there until one of the men came back. But it helped out. *-Dorothy King*

First I went in training for a nurse, but I couldn't stand blood ... I'd faint. I was in the infirmary more than I was in class and I almost cut my finger off. That was the end of my career. *-Laura W. Redifer*

Mrs. Isaac Ghee always felt that her ability to remain for long periods of time with the same employer was a good recommendation when she needed one. Her last place of employment was at the Silver Cross Home [now Bent Nursing Home] in Reisterstown. She was cook there until she passed the age of 85. She died in 1977, aged 101 years. *-E. Bennett Bowen*

[My mother, Annie Cox,] did an awful lot of dressmaking; she hired five or six women. You know, in those days, you couldn't buy ready-made clothes. She dress-made for people like the Shoemakers and the valley people. She said they'd go to New York and buy material and bring her clothes and material for her to make.

[One of her machines] was a Wilcox and Gibbs. It was a chain-stitch instead of a lock-stitch. Another was a Wheeler and Wilson. [Of course there was a lot of hand-sewing, too.] When you saw those dresses, you'd be amazed at the amount of hand-sewing. And all the seams were whipped ... no raw seams.

She made everything. She made my father's good suits. She tailored them and you couldn't tell it from a tailor. And she never had any lessons. -*Sarah Cox Hewitt*

My first job was at a pants factory. That was in '19 and my first pay was $5 [a week]. Eight o'clock in the morning until five o'clock at night, half day on Saturdays. We got half an hour for lunch. I worked there for a couple of years and then I worked at a moving picture parlor on North Avenue. I was usher and part-time cashier. I liked that - I didn't have to get up until two o'clock. I think I got $10 a week for that. And I [got to see a lot of movies]. Old Charlie Chaplin and the Little Rascals - all that bunch was "in" then.

After that, I went to work for Konthe Brothers [a sewing factory] in Hampden. I was a cutter. I worked there a couple of years -- to me it seemed like a century.

[Later, after I was married,] my sister, who lived in Pikesville, it struck her that she had to do something that she could do in her own home. The only thing she could think of was to sew. She didn't want to do it by herself, [so] she asked me if I didn't want to come down and help her. We started, and it was a success from the day we started.

I had a lot of people from over in the Valley [as clients]. I had one girl from Germany that mailed her fabric over here, and I made her dresses and mailed them back to Germany. The only thing that went wrong was when the length changed. I made her dresses too short. I gave her deep hems, so she was still okay.

I still sew for the former Mrs. Hopkins, Dee Hardy. She's a character! I have to give her credit -- she got me on the front page of the *Baltimore Sun* and just recently she got me on a national magazine. The [article] in the *Sun* was about this bathing suit I made for her little girl. The other was for "Home and Garden" and it was about this crazy little apron I made. She had the picture of the apron in the magazine.

[Around Owings Mills, my customers] were Mrs. Ashley, the Altmans, Margaret Beck, Mrs. Black, Mrs. Richard Blue, Mrs. Buck, Mrs. Milton Brown, Louise Buckheimer - I'm only in the 'Bs' ... do you want me to do the whole book? -*Belle S. Zepp*

Helen Barnhart's mother, Grace Nelson French, was employed before her marriage by Horace White of Greenspring Valley as a live-in dressmaker. She came home only on weekends. In later years, she was also seamstress for Garrison Forest School on a daily basis. *-Genevieve Berryman Kelley*

Clara McCubbin worked for USF&G [United States Fidelity and Guarantee in Baltimore]. At one time, she was one of the highest-salaried women in Maryland. She had a very responsible position. Fannie McCubbin was with the B&O [Railroad]. Blanche was a teacher. *-Helen Carpenter*

I went to Notre Dame and then to Bryn Mawr School from which I graduated in 1915. Then I went to Bryn Mawr College. [After] I came back home, I went to Hopkins and took some courses. [I wasn't preparing for any particular career.] People didn't think far ahead in those days.

I taught at the Roland Park School for five years, then at Bryn Mawr School for one year. In 1929 I came out to Garrison Forest School where I remained *in situ* until 1960. *-Nancy Offutt*

My sister, Emma, graduated from Franklin High School and she worked in the office at O'Neill's [department store] in Baltimore. *-Helen Kendig Bowers*

After [Burley Myers] moved out [of the shop behind the house on the southwest corner of Pleasant Hill and Reisterstown Roads], Catherine Hoff opened up a beauty shop there. *-Lee Fox*

Mrs. Fitch was the McCubbin girls' mother. She was the telegraph operator in Glyndon.

The Berrymans had one daughter, and she married a Zeigler. During the war, she used to flag the crossing back there at Bonita Avenue all by herself, all day long. *-Laura Wimsett Redifer*

I went to work for Eastman Kodak Company in June 1929 -- one day after graduating from Franklin High School. I applied for the bookkeeping division where I started as a file clerk and telephone operator. In September, I was put in bookkeeping where I remained until 1941 when I left to raise a family.

I rode the streetcar to work, got off at Lexington Market and walked to Park Avenue. The first day, my mother had to take me, because I didn't know how to get there.

The second day I was there, the regular telephone operator said as she was walking out, "You take over while I'm gone to lunch. Push this key here ... pull out here." I had no idea what she was talking about. The first call I did okay. The second call, I cut the *boss* off from a long distance call to Rochester. Wow! I didn't answer the phone for a while. *-Genevieve Berryman Kelley*

Not too many [women went out to work when I was young.] [When they did,] it was mostly the Gas and Electric Company, Hutzler's [Department store in Baltimore] or little stores around here. *-Nettie Clements Frank*

Painter's Mill

Photo courtesy of the E. P. Library.

[When my daughter, Sarah Hewitt Wilson, went to work,] she went with the telephone company right from the beginning. She worked at Pikesville and then down on Garrison Avenue and then she went to Belair. *-Sarah Cox Hewitt*

## Hardly Big Enough to Carry a Lantern

When children reached home in the afternoons, they changed their clothes and helped with the chores. Eggs had to be gathered, kindling wood had to be split, the wood-box filled, the pigs fed, the horses curried. Girls helped prepare the evening meal and, after supper, helped with the dishes. Often they also had to wash and scald the milk buckets and strainers used in the dairy.

Small boys hunted for eggs and fed the chickens. Both boys and girls went berrying for wild berries which they sold. Sometimes it was possible to carry water to someone's horse and receive a nickel or three pennies. Most parents believed that children must earn their spending money. *-E. Bennett Bowen*

There was little duties I would have [when school was out in the summer.] Because there were younger ones than myself, and I was supposed to look after them. They would come to Mom, and she would say, "Go to Da" - Dorothy was hard to say and they would say "Da." That's how it was. Even when they got older. But we were always very close in the family. *-Dorothy King*

Lone Hickory Farm is cursed with stones, a brown flint, in sizes from one to one hundred pounds. This side of the lower crossing was particularly stony, and when I was ten or twelve Dad made us a proposition to pick up stones on that knoll at one cent a pile. So [my brothers] Lewis, John, Clement and, I think, [my sister] Elizabeth, and I worked at it for days. We would mark out a square about 40 feet on a side, then put the stones in a pile in the center. I think we picked maybe two hundred piles or more. Then Ed Fleagle came with the four-horse team and stonebed and forked them up with a stonefork and hauled them on the county road [Bonita Avenue]. The wagonbed held two perch and my dad was paid fifty cents a perch for putting stones on the road. -from "Lone Hickory Farm Notes" October 16, 1955 by *Francis Sydney Reese*

I used to work up at the Wyatt's. They had a big house up in there [on Timber Grove Road] called "Walnut Hill." I wasn't hardly even big enough to carry a lantern when I used to go up there and set the tables for them ... about six or seven years old. I'd put the knives and forks and things on the table. *-Viola Clark Nesbitt*

# CHAPTER 9

## The Mills of Owings Mills

*Of Samuel Owings's three original mills, only the Upper Mill (now Groff's Mill) and the Lower Mill (Painter's Mill) survived into the 20th century, and only Groff's Mill is presently standing. But older residents have very vivid memories of the days when these mills and others along the Red Run and Gwynns Falls streams were productive.*

-/-/-/-

**The Cooper Shop**

The oldest landmark is gone. That was the house with the big chimneys ... the cooper shop for the Owings's mills.

Mrs. Sidney Owings said she heard her father-in-law say that when the Owingses first came, they built that house [the cooper shop] first. And while they were building the house on the hill, that was their residence ... that they built the brick house gradually as the bricks came in. *-E. Bennett Bowen*

[At the old cooper shop], they made the barrels for the mill. The Groffs bought the mill in 1848 and of course they were making barrels long before that ... in the 1700s. Old Mr. August Fleigh lived there. Daddy said he was a little man ... a very powerful little man. He had this contraption that he'd made for carrying the barrels. Big poles went out like that, and he'd suspend a barrel on either end. You'd see him walking down there carrying these two barrels. He walked the barrels down to the mill the Harmons owned - the Middle Mill - and then he'd walk them down to Painter's Mill.

Mrs. Fleigh, she had the right to all the manure that fell along the road from Bonita Avenue down to the old railroad tracks. Some other woman had the rights from there up. You could say it was the beginning of the compost pile. *-William D. Groff, Jr.*

Oh, yes! We knew Mrs. Fleigh! She was a nice old lady. She'd come and talk to everybody. If you went down to Owings Mills, on the way back you'd have to stop and talk, and it'd be about an hour and a half. Because she was lonesome, too. Mr. Fleigh worked for the Groffs. *-Minnie Clark Hebron*

[The Cooper shop] was a little, low white-washed house. My mother used to stop and talk [to Mrs. Fleigh] when we were driving down the pike. When I was going to Hannah More Academy to school, Mrs. Fleigh would always come out when the trolley car was going by and I'd wave to her out the window. *-Susan White Whitman*

## Lyon's Mill

I'm told by an old McDonogh alumnus that it's the Lyon mill that now lends its name to Olde Mill Estates off Lyons Mill Road. The new development over there goes right back to the ruin, which is alongside Gwynns Falls.

There's this huge stone structure in the middle of the woods west of the railroad that sets back into a bank. There is a mill race that can still be seen. Although it's wooded over and filled in to a great extent, there's still an impression you can trace for quite a ways. *-Robert Lyon*

My father told me that McDonogh Road was always called "Lyon's Mill Road" until the school really started to grow up. *-William D. Groff, Jr.*

## Painter's Mill

My mother's father ran Painter's Mill for years. His name was John Hood. He had long whiskers that covered all the front of him. A mouse got into them and chewed them while he was sleeping - his magnificent whiskers! *-Laura Wimsett Redifer*

Painter's Mill was still running. I went down there many a time -- old Mr. Simonds -- Joe Simonds's father -- ran the mill. He used to press cider. *-Lee Fox*

My father came [to Painter's Mill] as miller before he and my mother were married. He was head miller at Campbell's flour mill in Ellicott City. Then he came here and rented the mill from the Painter family.

I was born there. It used to be a flour mill and grind grist as well. [My father] kept on with the grist part of it, although the flour equipment was still there.

There was a mill race that took off at Owings Mills. The water [from the mill-race] came in [at the third floor level and into] a big pipe, probably two feet in diameter, that went from the third floor to a pit under the first floor. The mill wheel sat right at the bottom of that, and it was a turbine, but not very big ... probably about eighteen inches across. It was made of metal and had fins.

[My father] built the cider mill. When he was going there, he used to make about 3,000 barrels a year there. At a dollar a barrel, that was a good income in those days.

Just beyond the cider mill was a building. Just half of it was standing [when I was a boy], but it had been a two-story building at one time. It was an ice-cream factory. My father didn't have anything to do with that.

[The grist mill was very active then.] They had him down there some nights until ten or eleven o'clock. A lot of transaction going on. People would bring four-horse loads in and only want a certain amount of it done up. Some of it may have had to be shelled. That was a job I hated. Feeding that corn sheller. It ran by the mill, but you had to put them in there, two cobs at a time.

[When] the farmers brought their grain in, we'd take the stuff in on the second floor level where the crushers were. They ground it to whatever degree was wanted, and then we bagged it, and it went out the door into the wagon.

And he also made corn meal and hominy. That was taken care of on the first floor. He made some yellow corn meal, but most people didn't want yellow corn meal, [they wanted the white].

He used to ship the corn meal out all over the place. [Once he] shipped his glasses with it, and they shipped them back. He'd bought them in the ten-cent store in the first place. Cost them more to ship them back than he'd paid for them.

Garner got all his stuff from my father - cracked corn, cornmeal, bran, what-have-you. My father also sold Rosewood about twelve to fourteen barrels of vinegar a year.

[When my father was 77, he was still working in the mill.] One night I went down there to pick him up, bring him home. The mill was running, nothing going through it. He had had a stroke. He couldn't even tell me what happened. He died the next day.

He died in October, and I finished up teaching to the end of that year. I ran the mill for almost a year till I got it straightened out there. -*Joseph Simonds*

Joe Simonds was in my normal school class and taught four years. Then, when his father died, he took over the mill. But Miss Painter wouldn't clean out the mill race, and he just couldn't grind any more, so he had to give it up. Besides, the farms around there were being taken up [by developers], so there wasn't that much demand for a miller any more. -*William C. Hull*

### Groff's Mill

In Groff's mill, they made flour ... ground flour. An old fat fellow named Price lived up in the mill then. He was real jolly. Us kids used to go up and we'd get weighed. Maybe two, three or four of us would be going down to the store at Garner's for our parents, and we'd go up to the mill and get weighed. He'd weigh us all.

He was the miller. He'd be white with flour, his face and all. Just dripping with flour! -*Grace Bowen Pape*

My grandmother bought her wood and coal from these [Groff] boys' grandfather. He was a gentleman - a graduate of West Point. He

287

didn't tip his hat - he took it all the way off his head. When I was
working in Mr. Garner's and living down in Hoff's house, if I was any
place around and he saw me, off would come his hat. *-Laura Wimsett
Redifer*

## The Mill Race

The mill race ran back of Hoff's blacksmith shop -- back of those
buildings -- crossed under Dolfield Road and followed the railroad
down. It followed more or less around to the right of the railroad
tracks into the [painter's] mill. *-Lee Fox*

Even up to 1918 the mill race was still filled with water. It ran in
back of the Hoff house, the Hobbs house and the other house north of
Hoff's Garage. *-Bessie vonGunten*

## The Schnavely/Kendig Mill

Mr. Schnavely is the first one I remember who owned the mill. He
made flour and he ground feed for people's cattle. Then, in 1863, my
grandfather's family moved here and my grandfather ran the mill for
Mr. Schnavely.

Then my grandfather moved elsewhere and there were other millers
who came - maybe four or five of those were here from different
times. Then Mr. Schnavely moved away and the farm was sold to Mr.
Charles Reese.

My father's name was David Bowers. In 1888 he married my
mother, Laura Beeswanger. She was from Baltimore, and her folks
were all German. In 1889, they moved up here and then Dad ran the
mill for Mr. Reese. Then, in 1902, he bought eleven acres from Mr.
Reese. Dad lived here for the rest of his life and ran the mill.

Dad made flour part of the time, and then he discontinued that. He
ground feed for the farmers' cattle and made buckwheat, cornmeal and
hominy. Later the farmers had the hammer-mills, and then he just
ground cornmeal. The best cornmeal I've ever had! - very fine. My
father was very particular about the corn that he would grind for
cornmeal. He wouldn't make cornmeal out of anything except real dry
corn. He had an office, and he had two benches in there, one on each
side of the stove, and he kept the corn in there to dry.

Some of the men who brought feed to the mill paid for [the
grinding], and with the others Dad took out so much feed called a toll.
He had a certain little box that he measured the feed in as to how
much he was supposed to have. He called that a "toll dish."

He had a corn sheller, and he'd shell the corn. I used to love to
shell the corn and pick out the corn cobs. It was a double sheller that
you could put two ears in at a time.

Of course, he had the mill race where the water came from the dam,
and when it came time to clean that, you had to have help. If farmers
plowed the fields too close to the race it would wash in, and then he'd

have to clean that out. And that was a job! I helped him clean it one time. Um!

Then, in 1935, he had to give up the mill. He was in his 80s by then. In 1953, when he was 99 years old, he passed away. He had six daughters, and we lived here all our lives. The home we live in now [December, 1980], was built by Mr. Schnavely and it must be close to two hundred years old. *-Helen Kendig Bowers*

The building was a right good size wooden building. You'd go onto the mill porch, and then into the mill.

[There were] burrs that did the grinding. Dad had to take them apart, and he had hammers that he picked them with to make them rough. They had to be rough, and the corn would go between them and break it up. Where he made hominy and ground feed, he put the whole ear of corn in and ground the shocks for the cattle. He put different kinds of cogs in there when he ground hominy and corn-meal. I think there was a smooth burr it went through after the rough one ground it.

In winter, he'd cut the ice around the water wheel and let [the flow] come on down.

[My father] had a lot of customers and they didn't come from just close around but came from a ways. Back in the valley there were people who used to come. He ground for Mr. Frank Reese and Mr. Charles Reese and Mr. William Uhler and I guess he ground some for Mr. Charles Schwartz, too. When he got disabled, it just fell all down. *-Mary Kendig Gettierre*

## Hardy Green's Sawmill

An old house that was never painted stood on the corner of [Lathe Road and Lyons Mill Road]. Hardy Green was a bachelor and he rented that. He had a sawmill back in there. His main business was making "felloes" ... the wood rims for the the outsides of wagon wheels. For these rims, he sought out special trees - white oak, generally. They felled the trees without notching them, so as to save as much as possible of the butt ends of the trunks. They used a two-man saw to cut the trees down, and they had a band saw run by a steam engine that they used to rip out the felloes. They hauled the felloes down to Baltimore by wagon and sold them to wagon-makers.

Gus Bowers, who lived in the old Waters house on Lyons Mill Road, and Henry Zeigler, who lived on Deer Park Road, worked for Hardy Green. Gus Bowers ran the steam engine and fed the logs into the mill. Henry Zeigler was the "off bearer" ... he had the tough job of carrying the slabs and lumber from the mill. Hardy Green paid them about two dollars a day. *-Carl A. vonGunten*

My brother-in-law, Joseph Shipe, was the first of our family to move to Owings Mills from Powells Fort, Shenandoah County, Virginia. Work was scarce down there and he moved up here to take work in a sawmill. The sawmill was operating on the property where this house now stands [on Shipe Lane, west of the intersection of Dolfield and Deer Park Roads].

My husband and I moved here in about 1936. At that time, the place was mostly overgrown with woods. A huge sawdust pile towered higher than the tree-tops. Later on, one of my nephews hauled the sawdust by the truckload to florists. They used it for mulch. *-Valley R. Shipe*

Dad had a sawmill, too. He sawed lumber for all the farmers around here and he sold lumber for some of the houses that were built. He sawed boards and plastering laths and shingles and all the materials that were used in building houses. He sawed lumber for Mr. Fleagle's house and Mr. Michael's. He did it all by himself. *-Helen Kendig Bowers*

By then, the ice-cream factory was a sawmill. They would bring logs and [my father] would cut them into board lumber. He cut the stuff two inches thick, which most farmers wanted anyway. All he had in that line was an up-and-down saw, not a circular one. No fine cutting because it was getting to the end of the rope for that mill. *-Joseph Simonds*

Mr. Zimmerman, who was a barn-builder, had the wood sawed at Painters Mill for the Lycett barn and many others. *-Borden Simonds*

I helped Rezin Triplett [in the sawmill] ... worked with him nearly a year. You set up in one spot, cut out one woods. And then I helped Charlie Yox some ... anybody that would need a day or two, I'd help them out. I helped saw out three barns that there wasn't another stick of lumber hauled from anywhere but that woods - even the shingles. Then we sawed out the framing for two houses and all the sheathing and everything ... even the shingles and laths.

I've edged hundreds of shingles. You see, you cut your logs and you split them in quarters and then you put them in this saw and you sawed them off at a taper. Then they fall on a shelf and you bundle them up and these two big wheels go around. You put so many of them in there at a time and that's what straightened the edges up. The machine had gauges on it that you'd go by and that would just square up the edges of the shingles.

You could saw out everything [for a house]. If they wanted fancy siding, or so forth, they'd have to get that [elsewhere], but otherwise, everything could be sawed right out of the woods. *-A. Franklin Parker*

# CHAPTER 10

## The Soldiers Delight Chrome Mines

*Although once the largest single source of chrome in the world, by the turn of the century the mines in Soldiers Delight were no longer able to compete with other sources of the valuable ore. However, chrome continued to be extracted until well into the present century and a number of narrators recalled their involvement in the process.*

-/-/-/-

### Chrome from the Streams

Mr. Resin Triplett's family – originally from Virginia – operated the chrome mine for Mr. Jesse Tyson. There were three types of mines over there [in Soldiers Delight]. They had a placer mine where they washed [the chrome ore] out of the steam. There was also hydraulic mining. In addition, there were both open pit and underground mines.

The Choate mine, one of the underground mines, is on the east side of Deer Park Road, next to what is known as "The Fox Hunt Club". It has a great diagonally sunk shaft and great wooden piers to hold it up.

[Another underground mine,] the Ware Mine, is on the west side of Deer Park, about a thousand feet from the road, right near the Van Hessen lumber yard. Mr. Henry Ware says he has no idea why they called it the Ware mine – that they had nothing to do with it. But the Wares had the farm down over the hills from the mines and also operated the flint mill down under the hill. Flint is also found around the chrome area. The two Ware mines are just like hand-dug wells ... just perfectly straight down. There were once the remains of an old barbed wire fence, but it completely collapsed and I'd take some of [my students] back there and they'd like to throw a stone over and you'd hear it go, "WHOU-U-UMP!" ... way, deep, deep down.

Across the road from [the Ware mine] – toward Red Dog Lodge – you'll come across an open pit mine that was no longer than about fifteen feet and went down some 10 or 12 feet. There are a number of those open pit ones like that scattered over Soldiers Delight.

Triplett's Chrome Buddle, about 1929

Ore from the streams and mines in Soldiers Delight was refined at the buddle operated by the Triplett family. The chrome ore passed through a series of sluices which separated the heavier chrome from sand and soil. Photo courtesy of Eva Triplett Boyd.

The Triplett family also operated Triplett's buddle. When they opened the Choate mine again in World War I, they hauled the ore over to Triplett's buddle to run it through their sluice.

The whole Triplett family - two or three generations of them - operated the buddles. The last ore that was taken out was somewhere around 1928 or 1929. Miss Eva Triplett Boyd's brother, Mr. Rezin Triplett, who was 8 years older, told me that the last ore they knew of that was taken out, was taken by his father in 1929. They determined that he and Miss Annie, who was also a Triplett, had taken it out because, "We had built the new house out here on Liberty Road, so that would have been about such-and-such-a-time, and Pap went back there, and the day was so hot he took off his coat and the dog went with him, and the dog laid down on the coat, and when Pap came home, he came alone, and the dog didn't come with him. The dog stayed there all night. So that would have made it about 1929." But that was only for a minor hauling to some customer in Baltimore. -*Wilson Herera*

I was borned in 1894 back in Deer Park ... Berryman's Lane. My maiden name was Triplett. My father puddled the chrome ore. They had many troughs and they washed that ore. -*Mabel Triplett Hunt.*

My father was working at this chrome ore, and before I went to school, I used to help him. They made the dam, and then he had what they called a "head gate" that he would open up when he wanted it to come down over the ore to wash the sand out.

First they got the ore out of the branch. It just looked like sand they shoveled in. Two men would have this sieve and they'd have a barrel of water. They'd shovel the green ore and put it in and shake it around and get as much sand as possible out of it. Then they would put it in a pile, and then somebody would come pick it up and take it [to the buddle] to be washed.

The ore had to be washed three different times. When my father was washing it, he would tell me when to put in a stop ... when the water got up so high. [The sluice] was about a foot wide and the stops were pieces of wood you put across that. He had them set there for me. When he wanted me to put one in, he'd holler, "Stop!" and I'd put one in. So then I would put in this stop made of wood - I think we had about six of them through the whole process.

My father bought the mineral rights to these branches, and then he would work them. When he got so many barrels, he'd take it to Owings Mills and load it on the freight cars and ship it.

One man came out there [to the Choate mine] and said he had a machine that would clean the sand out of the ore. But it wouldn't work. So the man hauled all that ore he had down to my father's buddle.

We didn't do any of the paper work, my uncle Horace did all that. When they shipped the ore, they had all the papers and everything. My uncle had a better education than my father, and he could tend to that better.

293

Then we had another uncle who lived near us ... his wife was my father's sister. It was a sort of a family affair – he done the hauling. He had the wagon and the horses. That was Mr. Arnold Greis.

They had to have the wagon re-inforced to haul it, because a couple barrels of it weighed I couldn't tell how much. That chrome was so heavy nobody would believe you. If you had a little vial of it you had to lift up on it. One night a bunch of my brother's friends – they were all at our house and my brother was telling them how heavy this ore was. One of the fellows said, "Oh, it couldn't be that heavy!" My brother said, "There are very few people who have ever been able to up-end a barrel of it." So they broke up the meeting and got lanterns and all went up to the branch, and this fellow was going to show them that he could lift it. But he didn't. He couldn't lift it. That was the end of the argument.

My father had a boat load of chrome that was going to Belgium on the seas. When the first world war broke out, he was kind of worried about it, but it got there all right. They didn't work at it much after that. *-Eva Triplett Boyd*

Well, they worked a lot of those branches getting chrome. They went along the branches with tubs and sieves. They'd shovel this sand out of the branches and sieve it and then haul it to a buddle and wash it. That was a big old job – I've been soaking wet many a time shoveling that stuff out of the branch. I've hauled many a ton of it with an old mule and cart. That was my job when I was off from school. I hauled that stuff when I was only about eight, ten years old.

There was a buddle right back of Mann's old house ... [on Dolfield Road] right across from Watts Road. It was down in the bottom as you go up toward my house through the woods. Mr. Gore also had a buddle in the stream behind Elsie Bates's house.

The Tripletts had them over there, too, but I can't exactly tell you which branch they had them on. There were two or three of them around the country.

The [chrome ore] looked just like black sand. They washed all the other sand and dirt out of it, and then they barreled it up and shipped it – Baltimore or somewheres.

[The mines were closed at that time,] but they were open during World War I. In '17 and '18, they opened that one on Deer Park Road, the Choate mine. (Mineral Hill over on Ward's Chapel [had been] one of the main ones, but the water came in so bad they had to give up. That was before my time, that was when my grandfather worked in it.) Fellow by the name of Buckston was the superintendent of the mine. I think the Dolfields and the Sherwoods were connected with it.

Keeping water out of the mines was a big job. When we worked there at the Choate mine, we had big steam pumps. I worked with the engineer, mostly, oiling pumps and fixing pumps and adding pipe. Up in the upstairs on the machinery. I think I was making about two dollars an hour as an engineer, but I didn't work steady – only in the summer because of school.

At Mineral Hill, they [had] used buckets to haul the ore out, but in the Choate mine they had a car. I guess that track's still there. [The mine went] a little farther back than Deer Park Road. I guess it was a good hundred feet deep. It was dug out head high and you could walk around in there. At places it was dug out deeper than others. It was a big tunnel and they worked both sides. The trouble there was, that [the chrome] was too hard to get for the amount it would bring. You see, it runs in veins.

[After the chrome was mined], they hauled it over to Owings Mills and loaded it on [railroad] cars. They hauled some out with horses and some with trucks. Trucks were coming in about then. -*A. Franklin Parker*

## A Right Dismal Place to Be

The people who came in when the Soldiers Delight mines were operating were Germans, Irish and Polish. The Irish settled over toward Liberty Road – the Bradys and the Dwyers. Thomas Hanley came from Ireland and opened a store on Liberty Road. The Trepinskys and Sanduskys and Szymonskys all came from Poland to work in the mines. They were the beginning of the Holy Family Catholic Church. The Germans were the Klinglehofers, the Roses and the Zimmers, but I don't know whether they were connected with the mines. Other names associated with the area are McGowan, Cummings, Vogel, Bartholmey, Griswold and Noyse.

The miners lived in small houses dotted over Soldiers Delight. I remember a number of shanties dotted that area when the open pit mines were operating. When I was a kid, a lot of them were still standing. People who had no employment usually moved into one. [Many of the houses] gradually burned down or fell down.

The Cummings house showed the Victorian influence. The Campbell house stood beside Dolfield Road near the Deer Park Road. It was a T-shaped house that had once been well-painted. Mr. Campbell had consumption and after he died, nobody would live there anymore. His house burned about 1905.

[A number of] log cabins stood near the streams. Jesse Cook and his family narrowly escaped when one burned. The Figgs dwelling housed several generations of that family before it, too, burned. -*E. Bennett Bowen*

There was a nice house up here [off Dolfield Road just past Watts Road.] At one time, it was Crockett [who lived there] and then it was Bolgiano ... an Italian name. Jimmy Nolan owned it, Bolgiano just rented it. Jimmy Nolan ran a place down there on Monroe Street - Nolan's Cafe. He was a saloon keeper. That was a nice square house. There was another one up on the hill, but it wasn't so much.

Pete Smith, he was back there with the Tripletts ... back on the old Triplett farm. Out Wards Chapel Road and off to the left. There was a bunch of Tripletts out on Liberty Road, but back there was the old home place. Pete's wife was Bertha Triplett. *-Carl A. vonGunten*

All those houses [in Soldiers Delight] were so old! And they had those great big [mine] holes out there. Wasn't no lights or nothing back there then. The Figgs family lived where the road went across that little branch [Red Run]. THey had a regular log cabin. They had about 15 children, I believe. Wes Mack lived right across the road from them. There was another family of people around there named Campbell in later years ... they had a lovely house. *-Minnie Clark Hebron*

That property the [fellow] by the name of Mann owned had so many different ones in and out I can't think of all their names. One old fellow [who lived there] had both legs cut off on the railroad. He repaired shoes and all of us round there took our shoes to him, and we kept him in wood. The neighbors would gather it for him. *-A. Franklin Parker*

The people who didn't know Soldiers Delight before Dolfield Road was paved, don't know how completely different it was. Because the road just went anywhere. Paths went every which way.
Have you ever been lost in Soldiers Delight at night? It's a right dismal place to be. My father got lost in there one foggy night when he was moving somebody with his market wagon. He knew about Dr. Ward having fallen in a mine hole, so he stopped and was going to unhook his horses and camp for the night when he saw one of those dark cabins that were up there just a little beyond the von-Gunten place. When he saw that, it gave him his bearings. *-Wilson Herera*

# CHAPTER 11

## The Gwynnbrook Distillery

*For many years, the Gwynnbrook Distillery provided employment for a large number of local men and women while the by-products of the distilling process provided nourishment for local livestock.*

-/-/-/-

**Whiskey for the Soldiers, Slops for the Cows**

J. Frank Shipley was president of the Gwynnbrook Distilling Company. He was married to Mary Shipley of Randallstown and they had five children, J. Frank, Jr., Mathias, Edward, Marcella and Anna. The family lived on Reisterstown Road near Pleasant Hill Road. *-E. Bennett Bowen*

That place [the Gwynnbrook Distillery] crumbled down one time. The whole place caved in and the whiskey was running down the branch. They said the men were laying on the banks drinking it up like pigs! Clara McCubbin and I went out through the woods to see it, but I don't think we ever got there.

[And] somebody told me about men who held up the distillery during Prohibition and stole whiskey. I believe they shot a watchman. *-Margaret Clark Hoff*

Ella Whiten's husband and my father [Henry Clark], were working down at the distillery the time a man shot John Whiten. Some burglars that came up there to burglarize the distillery, they tied my father to a chair and he had to cross the railroad and walk up through the woods there to Hugo Schmidt's [house at the corner of Gwynnbrook opposite Academy Avenue] with the chair tied to his back.

I think there were three or four burglars. Some of them were watching and when John Whiten went to punch this clock – he had this big clock encased in leather that hung around his neck and he had this key that he had to do something to the clock and the key to the warehouse – they told him what to do, and he didn't do it. I think he struck one of them with this clock, and that's when they shot him. He had this big watch in his pocket that his wife had given him, and if the bullet hadn't hit the watch it might have killed him.

They told my father don't do anything, because if he did he'd be killed and remember he had children. Seems like these were big-time gangster-type people - they study the background of everybody and know where everything is. So he didn't make any effort to do anything, but they tied him to the chair.

[Later,] there was another robbery. I think somebody got shot that time. They made away with quite a lot of whiskey that night ... used trucks. I think they found one truck partly loaded in Featherbed Lane. They said gangsters were the instigators of it. -*Viola Clark Nesbitt*

[Over at the distillery during Prohibition] that boy, Lanin Winters, shot the watchman. -*Lee Fox*

They had a robbery at Gwynnbrook Distillery in '24 and Ed Blucher, the night watchman was shot. We moved back there in '26 when my husband took the job of watchman.

All the government men would come out on the streetcar every day ... walk back that road. They had to be there all the time, day and night. They had the keys to the [bonded warehouses] and they had to be there when anyone went in. -*Mabel Triplett Hunt*

The biggest industries [in Owings Mills] [during the time I was growing up] were the distilleries. Both distilleries were running - Park and Tilford, sometimes known as "Owings Mills Distillery", was open, and Hunter-Wilson on Bonita Avenue was running full-force. -*Morris G. Richardson*

Gwynnbrook Distillery did a heck of a business then. All the farmers back there had slop tanks and hauled this slop for their cows. Some of them had an old farm wagon with four or five hogsheads in it for hauling slop.

I knew all the fellows who worked there. And the fellows in the office used to ride with me on the streetcars. When I went home - back to the home place - I'd walk past [the distillery]. I could go in there and get whatever I wanted. Josephine Gillman and that whole bunch would be there bottling, and when the bottle come around, they'd pull it off [the conveyor] and hand it to me. I'd take a couple of swills out of it and put it back on the bottler again. Yeah! -*Henry Clay Hipsley*

Up back of the warehouses, they had big ponds and they pumped the slops up in there. All the farmers around had trucks and they would haul the slops and feed them to their cattle. They used to have their trucks lined up all the way up the road.

They also had a big swimming pool back there where they had dammed the stream. We used to have the most fun! All the kids from Pleasant Hill Park came there - the Hinkhouses, the Allenders, the Woolfords, the Stierhoffs. -*Viola Hunt Keller*

My husband's father, who was George Weed Morris, bought a farm on Garrison Forest Road and Crondall Lane. They had a lot of cattle and the mash from the distillery was piped back to the farm. -*Catherine Dimmling Morris*

298

Gwynnbrook Distillery

Photo courtesy of the Baltimore County Public Library.

Joseph E. Seagram's and Son purchased the Hunter-Wilson [Gwynnbrook] Distillery in the early forties. The old management operated it for approximately a year. They made whiskey until the second World War required all distilleries to close and make alcohol. This was a very small distillery and processed from 1,000 to 1,500 bushels of corn a day, which made five gallons of whiskey to the bushel of corn. That was converted to alcohol and distributed to the war effort. This was ethyl alcohol, which is necessary in the use and manufacturing of gun-powder.

In early 1945, they gave the distilleries one month to produce whiskey, because the [warehouses] were running out of whiskey and there was a high demand on whiskey for the soldiers as well. Not [just] American soldiers, but the allied soldiers.

This distillery produced whiskey only one month during the whole time the war was in progress, and that was in January of 1945, I believe, just prior to when I came here in March of '45.

Before I came here, I was production manager of the central office of all the distilleries, and [during the month we were allowed to produce whiskey] we made 8,000,500 gallons. All eighteen of our distilleries made all the whiskey that we could make, 24 hours a day.

The Hunter-Wilson distillery was the only distillery that was bottling whiskey. All the whiskey was bottled during the time I was manager, which was approximately two-and-a-half to three years.

All the whiskey we bottled was for overseas shipment. We didn't bottle any domestic whiskey as long as I was there, because we were bottling whiskey that had been made prior to the war and sending it to the various Army camps and various allied camps. The labels we used were Calvert and Seagram. They were both blended whiskeys.

The bi-product [of the distilling process] was what the farmers call "slop" - the distilling industry calls it "distillage." It was a spent material which was discharged from the bottom of the still. It had high protein and high fiber, which was fit for cattle feeding and cattle fattening. We would hold it in a holding tank and the farmers would line up for a half a mile and get it while it was hot to feed to their hogs and cattle. They would pay a small amount for it - maybe five cents a load or something like that. The portion the farmers couldn't use, we would have to haul and dump on somebody's property. A lot of it was put on top of this hill where houses are built now - Tollgate ... the Reese farm. Jacob vonGunten owned it at the time we were dumping.

We had about three- to four-hundred people working [at the distillery], including the bottling house and everything. We were running twenty-four hours a day. The bottling house, which employed probably 150 women from this area, ran only eight hours a day. It was very hard to get help because everybody was working on the farm and in the war industries. We had to run a bus into Baltimore to get people to come and work.

I left to go to New York in 1946 or 1947. I was replaced by a Mr. Hammer at Hunter-Wilson Distillery. He operated the distillery until the middle of the 1950s, at which time it closed down and was never reopened. It was still used as a warehouse until about 1955 when the distillery disposed of it to some real-estate people. -*Harry L. Shay*

# CHAPTER 12

"Barney Clabber Hill," "Little Virginia," and "Good Husband's Row"

*Like every community, Owings Mills has its distinctive place names and landmarks.*

-/-/-/-

The Lowe place was called "Food A-Plenty." Grandmother King's place at Delight was called "Idle Hour" ... in the late 1800s.
"Belt's Hill" was right there at St. Thomas Lane. THe Belt family had it for an inn at one time.
We kept horses back at what they called "Robbers' Roost" on the old Flint farm. The house was in the Bailey family long ago.
I had an acre out front and I called that "Golden Acre." That was the Old Morgan place where the log house was.
Mrs. Jones wanted to know from me why they called [that hill] "Barney Clabber", but Pop was gone. Pop, you know, liked to talk about things like that and he'd have known. *-Dorothy King*

B-A-U-G-H-N-A-U-G-H C-L-A-U-G-H-B-A-U-G-H – that's how my father taught me to spell "Barney Clabber Hill". *-Jean Reese Worthley*

"Belt's Hill" is the original old Sandalwood Knoll up here. [Where Sandalwood Apartments are.] That whole property belonged to the Randall Belts. *-Margaret Clark Hoff*

"Berry's Hill" is between the two mines. They always told me they hung a man there. I don't think we ever thought about it being haunted. I been out over them hills day and night and every kind of weather and I never seen anybody walking around up there. *-A. Franklin Parker*

The Garrison Forest Road near Gwynnbrook was once known as the "Newfoundland Road." The deed to a log house shown as Conrad Yox's in the 1877 Baltimore County Atlas proves this point. *-John McGrain*

"Five Oaks" was George Ward's father's place [at the corner of Reisterstown Road and Rosewood Lane]. "Windswept Hill" was Doctor Campbell's [home] ... later Mr. and Mrs. Keith Spayde's. My mother and grandmother's property on the Liberty Road was "Plains of Paran."

The section [of Reisterstown Road] in front of this house [10620] was known as "The Mud Flats" because two streams converged and over-ran the surface of the road. -*E. Bennett Bowen*

The Yox family owned "Sunnybrook Farm". The Sears house, "Cedarmere", was a big house located where the Twin Kiss and the adjoining car lot now stands. -*Irma Williams Crunkleton*

There was a little school there in "Belltown" right back of the [Mount Pleasant A. M. E.] church. Elias Norris lived near the church - he used to huckster. [Others] who lived near there were Chance Fax and Laura Thornton. -*Grace Bowen Pape*

Tobin had a store and saloon right on the north corner of Valley Road and Reisterstown Road. -*William D. Groff, Jr.*

Mr. Joshua Raver successfully farmed several farms on Chestnut Ridge before buying the "Palace Farm" on Greenspring Avenue. -*E. Bennett Bowen*

"Goldeisen Row" was also known as "Good Husband's Row." -*William D. Groff, Jr.*

Because the houses in "Goldeisen Row" sat below the level of the road, when you'd go by on the streetcar you could look right in the bedroom windows! -*Genevieve Berryman Kelley*

"Buzzard's Glory" was [a large field on the Moser farm] up above his meadow. -*Carl A. vonGunten*

"Therapia Farm" was originally owned by my grandfather's sister who married a Fangmeyer. -*Robert S. Knatz*

Watson [Sherwood's] summer bungalow ... that was "Persimmon Lodge." -*A. Franklin Parker*

Part of the land on which "Pleasant Hill Park" is located was originally owned by the Cooper family. Hugh Cooper was a coffee importer of the early 19th century and he bought the farm for his son and daughter-in-law, Hugh and Nellie Allen Cooper. Two of the Cooper's sons married into the Disney family.
Later, the Cooper property was owned by the Morris family. It was a Mr. Bihy who developed the land as "Pleasant Hill Park." -*E. Bennett Bowen*

"Betsy Clark Hill" is right there by Little Virginia. -*Wilson Herera*

People sometimes referred to this as "Shipetown" or "Little Virginia." Some even called it "Shantytown," but one thing sure - none of our people who came up here and built bit off more than they could chew. They bought and paid for what they got - they owned their homes free and clear." -*Valley R. Shipe*

# CHAPTER 13

## Keeping in Touch

*In a time when traveling to visit distant friends and relatives was not generally a viable option, letters were often the only means of staying in touch. In the late 18th and early 19th centuries, mail was often left at the inns to be picked up and carried to its destination by whoever might be traveling in that direction. The coming of the railroad made regular mail service a possibility. Later, the streetcar was employed to deliver mail to the various rural post-offices. And - difficult as it is to comprehend in our telephone-oriented present-day society - the century was one-fourth over before even the lucky few had heard the sound of a human voice transmitted over telephone wires.*

-/-/-/-

### Papa Was a Mail Carrier

The first post-office I remember was in the house just south of the [grade-level] railroad crossing. The post-office was kept by Mrs. William Scott. It was a one room office about seven feet by ten feet. At first, there was no parcel post and no Rural Free Delivery.

There was a small post office at Pleasant Hill and another at Delight. The mail sacks were dropped as a street-car passed near each office. Further inland, there was the Cronhart post office on Chestnut Ridge.

In 1901 or 1902, the first rural free delivery came to Owings Mills, and the Pleasant Hill and Delight offices were consolidated with Owings Mills.

The first carriers were Mr. Frank Fox and Mr. Clarence Engles. Mr. Fox drove up the Turnpike to Delight and worked eastward to Chestnut Ridge. Mr. Engles drove southward to Painters Lane and then west to the Liberty Road, followed Liberty Road to Wards Chapel Road, then turned homeward. He drove through Soldiers Delight to the Dolfield Road, then past the Lutz farm, up Barney Clabber Hill and returned to the post office. -*E. Bennett Bowen*

My uncle, Frank Fox, carried mail for a while. Horse and buggy. -*Grace Bowen Pape*

I've seen Clarence Engle when the snow was so bad he could only deliver the mail by horseback ... the letters only. *-Lee Fox*

Papa was a mail carrier. He would have to get up early and come up to the post-office and sort the mail and all. [At that time], we lived up on a little knoll in a house that's now part of Garrison Forest School. [Papa's] horses would hardly have time to eat [before he had to leave home in the morning], so Mr. Hoff asked him if he would like to rent his house [next to the post office]. We moved there ... so Papa and the horses would have more time.

There were three houses there. The post office was in the first one. There was a store there, too. A man by the name of Wineholt ran it. Later, Mrs. Wineholt married Roemer who was the postmaster. We lived next to the blacksmith shop. The mill race ran in back of our place.

[Mr. Hoff still had his blacksmith business], and in winter he would have to shoe the horses before Papa would take them out on the road. Papa would get so far -- Caves Road, there was a blacksmith shop there -- and he'd have to have the shoes sharpened up again so the horses wouldn't slip on the ice. The roads were nothing.

[The mail wagon] was very small ... not nearly as big as a truck, [and] it had to have <u>U. S. Mail</u> painted on it. [My father] used to get a man to come all the way from Baltimore to put those three words on it ... <u>U. S. Mail.</u> [One time,] Papa [decided] to paint it himself. He painted it with shellac, and the next morning when he went out to get in, it was white. From the dampness. We all had to get out and wash that off.

[When] my cousin was a child, sometimes Papa would take him [along on the mail route.] He'd put him in a mail bag to keep him warm. And that was illegal, you know!

In those days, you couldn't trust everybody - you had to deliver the mail and take it up to the house, [especially] if they thought there'd be a check in there or some money.

I don't know if it was compulsory or not, but you could buy stamps from the mailman. Everybody didn't have a horse and buggy or a car of any kind, [so] that would be the only way of getting their letters out. And I can see my father now, [how he would heft a package to judge its weight] - "Three and a half ounces!" He weighed it with his hand. I'm sure he didn't miss out far if any. *-Laura Wimsett Redifer*

[From Chestnut Ridge], we used to have to go out [to Gwynnbrook] to get the mail, you know, at little boxes. Had to come out there on horseback or else walk out there to get it. Till Wimsett started Rural Free Delivery with horse and buggy. *-Henry Clay Hipsley*

When the trains went by [the Gwynnbrook Station], the mail-crane would grab the mail-bags. That was rather interesting to see them grab the mail-bags off the hooks. They had one train that went down that picked up the mail and one train that went up and picked up the mail. *-Helen Kendig Bowers*

304

## In the Days of Three-Cent Stamps

My first memory of the Owings Mills post office was of the little house that was recently torn down to make way for the Northwest Expressway bridge [over Reisterstown Road] ... right next to the [grade-level] railroad track. I used to go there when I was a mere boy to buy stamps. It was just a cute little building, handy to the railroad station [with the post-office in a room] on the side.

Of course, at that time we had trains. There was a post-office at Gwynnbook and one at St. George's and one at Timber Grove also. They all followed the railroad because all the mail moved by train. When they discontinued the trains, we had to go to trucks. Now most everything goes by airplane.

I guess I really got close to it in 1933 when Mr. French, who had worked for Mr. Groff all his life, became post master at Owings Mills. He moved the post office to where the Baltimore Adhesive Company is now. I think he had to move because he ousted Mr. Roemer, and they had to find new quarters. So, I got very well acquainted with Mr. French, worked with him at Christmas time.

We had two railway post offices that went through Owings Mills every day. I got the job somewhere in the early thirties of meeting those trains. I met the two trains on my bicycle, and carried all the mail for Owings Mills on my handle-bars. Prior to that, when Mr. Roemer was post-master, his stepson, Arthur Wineholt, pushed the mail back and forth on a wheel-barrow.

Two of the trains didn't stop at that time ... they were through trains. They would only stop on a flag. They had a contraption over by the railroad tracks. You would hang the pouch [for out-going mail], bottom up, and you would have this strap in the center so the mail clerk [on the train] would catch it with a hook. And, as he caught it with the hook, he'd kick one [bag] off. It would roll ... sometimes it would roll almost all the way to Owings Mills, especially if it was full.

Sometimes we had to ship the empty sacks back. There was only one way - you had to put thirty in a bag because they would count a bag of sacks as thirty. If you had ten bags, you had three hundred sacks, and they got right heavy. You'd have to lift the bags up into this mail cart, but sometimes the train would miss that loading platform and go farther down [the track] and drop another foot [below the platform]. Many times the railway mail clerk would jump out of his car to help me throw the empty mail sacks up on the train.

If you recall, the old post-office building had a show window. It was a garage ... formerly Henry Hoff's garage. The post office, when I worked there for Mr. French, wasn't too busy. We opened at 7 in the morning and closed at 6. We had a big morris chair in the back where we'd lay down and take a nap during the day. If someone came in, they'd knock on the counter, and you'd wake up, or be reading a magazine. The "Saturday Evening Post" magazine used to come on Tuesday and you would always hold them for delivery on Saturday, so we could always have time to read the serials in the *Saturday Evening Post*. Had to be careful not to eat while you were doing it, so you didn't drop crumbs in the magazine.

Those were the days of three-cent postage cents for out-of-town, two cents local. For a penny, you had a drop-rate; if you mailed at a post office that had no delivery, you could mail for one cent. Garrison and Glyndon, for example, were post offices where you could mail a first-class letter for a penny. Then we had the penny post-card.

Mr. French sold the morning *Baltimore Sun* newpspaper in the post office for a nickel. People would walk in, buy a paper and read it [as they rode] the train into town. Things are re-cycling now, and it seems like we'll be able to do that again [on the Metro].

Those were some good days. The post office was a meeting place. Tidewater Express used to have a [milk] pick-up just up the street by what was then Bigger's store and was later bought by Bill Reter and even later by Jim and Marie Wisner. Raymond Moser used to bring the milk out from Alyedo farm. Frank Price used to come the other way with his big white horse and a little donkey cart ... just a two-wheeler with enough room on the back to put his milk on. Then Frank and Raymond would meet in the post office, Phil Knatz would come in for his paper, and we'd have a real session there every day. They'd read the paper and discuss the news - it was quite a time.

We had some funny stories in Owings Mills. I can remember Raymond Moser was nice to the kids. He'd always buy an ice-cream cone or a candy-bar for anybody ... give them a dime. One of the girls who lived next to the post-office was going to get married when she graduated from high school, so she was taking collection ... asking everybody for a dollar to buy her wedding dress ... trying to raise ten dollars. So she hit Raymond Moser up one morning for a dollar to help buy her wedding dress. He was a real character some times! He looked at her and said, "I'll buy you a wedding dress if you can say your ABCs." And you know, she couldn't!

[One day,] Mr. Price hauled his milk out, and I'm not sure whether he was sitting at the milk stand or where. A tractor-trailer came down [Reisterstown Road] and hit him ... hit the cart and put the horse on the front porch of the house next-door to the store. The truck came on up and pushed a couple of cars up to the post office and ran into Dorothy Hammer whose husband was, at that time, running the Hunter-Wilson Distillery back on Gwynnbrook Avenue.

After I was post master for a while, Harry Shay bought the building, and we had to find new quarters. Fyfe Symington and Tom Offutt had a building in the rear of what is now the Baltimore County Supply Company [formerly Garner's Store and, previous to that, the Western Maryland Railway Station]. That building became the post-office for a number of years. Then, during my term of office, we moved again and built a new post-office opposite the corner of Rosewood Lane and Reisterstown Road, right next to where the Pizza Hut is now located; the Owings Mills Transmission Company is now there.

I left there in 1966 and took a promotion. Since that, they've built the new place down on Dolfield Road.

[During my term as postmaster,] we had two RFD [Rural Free Delivery] routes. Route 2 was carried by John Gingrich for a number of years. It used to travel down through the [Greenspring] valley, come back to the post office, pick up another load, and go back through Painters Lane and Lyons Mill Road, all the way over to

306

Liberty [Road] and out to an area that is now underneath the Liberty Lake, back in [Old Oakland Mills road] about a mile and come back by way of Ward's Chapel [Road] to Owings Mills. A lot of people used to get confused about their address: they would tell someone they lived in Owings Mills and it looked like Randallstown.

Route 1 went on the east side, up Reisterstown Road, in Delight [Road], back to the Emory Michaels farm where Thoroughbred Lane now runs. It used to cut across his field, go down along a hedge row and come out at Bonita Avenue just above Jean [Reese] Worthley's house. Then it would go down and wind around through Cave's Road and end up at Greenspring Avenue and out Greenspring to Park Heights and up through the Foster Farm. It was quite an area.

Vernon Sullivan was postmaster down in Garrison - we were both appointed on the same day. He is still working [as of 1985]. I retired in 1977. -*Morris G. Richardson*

## Hanging On the Party Line

At first there were two telephone companies - the Maryland, and the Chesapeake and the Potomac. The wires were on opposite sides of the road and people who had one phone - say a Maryland phone - couldn't call Chesapeake and Potomac. Laundry wagons and other wagons had both phone numbers painted on back. Store advertisements or announcements [also carried both numbers]. Finally, the C&P bought out the Maryland phone.

[As Owings Mills was located halfway between Pikesville and Owings Mills,] many years passed during which Owings Mills residents could choose [to be connected to] either [the Reisterstown or the Pikesville] exchange. However, there was a toll charge if you had a Pikesville phone and wished to call someone with a Reisterstown number or vice versa.

Party lines were almost the only service available. "Listening in" was a general practice. It was widely rumored that a young gentleman in the neighborhood called his lady love and greeted her with a very endearing term. "Oh, be careful!" she exclaimed. "Mrs. ---- is sure to be listening." At that, a third voice came over the line, "Oh, I am not!" -*E. Bennett Bowen*

A telephone wasn't put in here till 1925. -*Waiva Dean Reese*

Mrs. McC--- on Chestnut Ridge had a telephone - one of those kind you had to crank ... grind it up. Everybody was on the same line, and she would listen in on all the conversations that went on. She knew everybody's business! -*Mary Robinson Sprinkle*

Telephone operators back then had to dress just right. You couldn't go without hose. In the beginning you had to wear a hat. I started working at the Forest exchange when I was sixteen. I made about $12.50 a week. I worked swing - something like nine to twelve and six to ten. Then, for two years at Pikesville, I worked all night - that was eleven to seven by yourself. I went out to Reisterstown for a time and helped Miss Kearns out there. At Reisterstown they had no more than five operators. At Pikesville we had thirty or forty.

At that time I was an operator – that was answering the calls and running the "B" board and the rural lines where you rang three rings for this one and two rings for that one.

As many as five people would be on a single rural line and each one had a certain number of rings. Their number would be like "753 ring 2." When someone turned the handle on their home set, little shutters would fall down on the switchboard and a number would show. We took a cord and plugged into the hole that was right beside it. We would say, "Operator", and they would tell us the number they wanted to call.

Operators had to handle all the calls ... people couldn't call directly to each other. They would tell us the number and we we had to ring it by hand. When you rang "1", 2, 3, 4 and 5 would come on the line. Everybody knew what was going on!

The local board was for incoming calls from customers only. I also worked the "B" board which was much different. That's for when say someone from Glen Burnie was putting a call in to Pikesville. The Glen Burnie operator would come on the line and say, "Calvert so-and-so" and give you the number and you'd have to ring the local customer for them. I can hear myself now, saying "Wait your turn, Calvert! Wait your turn!"

[The home phones looked different then, too.] On the rural lines, people had those boxes with the handle and mouthpiece coming out of it. Other phones were the tall ones with the receiver hanging on the side.

Sometimes you got to know the people personally. You didn't get a chance to talk too much because it was very busy. But you would know them when they came on the line. Sometimes they'd come on and ask you questions. The kids would come on and ask you questions for their homework.

Fires came in, and we'd have to ring the fire department. That was a problem – you had to find out [in which company's area] the fire was, and you were responsible for ringing the right one.

One time at Pikesville a car hit a telephone pole about three or four in the morning. Every light on the board lit up! And there I am by myself! But I had heard the noise, and before I knew what I was doing, I had the cord into the connection to the police.

Another time I was there by myself, and I heard this noise, and I looked up and there was a bat flying around the room. I didn't know what to do! Some men were working next door, so I called them and said, "Come over here quick – there's a bat!" They came over and gave me a rag to put on my head, and they swatted at the bat and it went back down in the basement. It came back the next day, and the girls called the fire department. I've had some experiences!

We made a ticket on every call unless it was a local call. You'd hand-write a ticket. Little yellow tickets. At Pikesville we had those fans that came down from the ceiling, and even when it got hot I wouldn't turn the fans on, because it would blow the tickets, and it would make a noise, and I couldn't hear.

With pay stations we had a collect-and-return button. You'd have to tell them how much money and watch the time and notify them. We had fun at the Belmont exchange with those boys from Johns Hopkins! They made a recording of quarters and nickels and dimes. We'd say "Deposit twenty-five cents, please" and they'd make it sound like twenty-five ... "Deposit ten" and they'd make it sound like a dime. I said to the girls, "We've got to [put a stop to] that. Change around and say it different ways. Tell them to deposit five cents and then a dime and then a quarter ... mix it around." We finally got them. And then they wired their telephones backwards so that when you collected, it would return their money! -*Ethel M. Gamber*

## O. M. Fire Truck

In 1923, the Owings Mills Volunteer Fire Company acquired its first truck, an American LaFrance Type 38 triple combination 600-gallon-per-minute pumper, shown here in front of the United Railway trouble station which served at that time as a fire station. The vehicle had solid tires on wood spoke wheels, nickel-plated headlights, and was powered by a chain drive engine. Photo courtesy of Gary Kadoff.

## CHAPTER 14

### Fires and Other Disasters

*For a rural community such as Owings Mills, fire protection was a critical need. Our dependence on wood and kerosene stoves for heating made house fires an ever-present danger. Few of our original barns survived the fires caused by the inflammable nature of hay and straw, the threat of summer lightning and the hazards of careless smoking. Until very recent times, the only fire protection was provided by community volunteers.*

*While other, more serious disasters seemed to by-pass our community, in 1972 the Gwynns Falls unleashed all the fury it had been storing up for centuries and demolished the center of Owings Mills.*

-/-/-/-

**A Good Time for Old Men To Get Up on the Porch**

The Owings Mills Volunteer Fire Department was organized on Friday, September 16th, 1921, when a group of residents who realized the need for adequate fire protection in the community met at John Hoff's blacksmith shop. They elected Douglas P. Campbell, district Engineer of the State Roads Commission as President, George Ward as Treasurer, and William E. (Bill) King as Captain. The first Secretary of the company was a woman.

This led to a formal organization meeting on September 21, 1921, at the main hall of Rosewood State Training School. This was the official meeting place for more than ten years.

After two years of growing pains, our American La France Type 38 triple combination 600 g.p.m. pumping engine arrived. It was equipped with right-hand drive, solid tires on wood spoke wheels, nickel-plated drum type headlights and spotlight, coal-oil lanterns, chain drive and a 35-gallon soda-acid tank. After several training periods - which consisted principally of water battles between two groups manning the two and one-half inch lines - it was put in service.

The station was the abandoned trouble station at the United Railways [streetcar company] carbarn. Fire calls were received by the trolley dispatcher (whose main job was counting nickels). He would answer the phone, push a button which rang a bell in the power-house

311

boiler room, the engineer would blow the steam whistle -- four blasts, north ... three blasts, south ... one lo-o-o-ong blast, local.

When the whistle blew, everybody ran. Arthur Wineholt worked at the post-office, and we had a call, and he came out and got in his Ford Model-T pick-up and turned around and came down and cut in back of the hole that was directly below Garner's store porch. Old man Rose was just coming down off the steps of the store, and Arthur just missed him. Mr. Rose started carrying on, and Mr. Garner said in his usual high-pitched voice, "Mr. Rose, I think that you might as well learn this as well as everyone else. When that fire whistle blows, that's a good time for old men like you and me to get up on the porch!"

[Anyhow,] after a proper interval, we would go. The interval was caused by two things, the fact that practically everybody had to come a-runnin', and [the fact that] the trouble station being unheated, the [engine's] radiator was drained in winter, and the five buckets of very cold water used to fill it sometimes resulted in starting problems. But we got there ... practically every time.

One time the engine started out and right there where it makes the first sharp turn, the truck stopped [dead] ... they'd run out of gas. Frank Mahon and I and some others were standing on the back, and I looked around just in time to see that Arthur Wineholt's vehicle was approaching very rapidly from the rear. I kind of jumped up. He hit the back of the truck, and [luckily] didn't hurt it really badly.

The only person that ever got killed in the fire department was John Kane. He was employed at Rosewood as a butcher, and another man, Harry Bissell, worked in the office up there. They had a fire somewhere around the barn, and Harry came out and jumped in his car. John Kane came out of the kitchen and jumped on the running board. He had grease on his hands and was holding onto the [window frame of the car]. Some kid ran in front of the car, and Harry swung [the wheel], and John Kane went off on his head [and was killed].

We put out a lot of woods and fields with brooms and rakes before Indian tanks came along. We put out and cleaned numerous chimneys in the days of wood-burning stoves. We cooled down some foundations, and we became pretty good at saving adjoining buildings. Sometimes we had that glorious feeling of saving the building that was on fire.

There were no water mains north of Pikesville, so we spent a fair amount of time locating accessible and pumpable streams and building strategically located dams which soon silted up. A hose lay of less than half a mile was practically a gift, and [summoning nearby fire companies for mutual aid was generally a matter of locating a telephone].

With the arrival of the thirties, a whole series of things happened. Busses replaced steetcars - no power house, no steam whistle. So we bought a siren. Then the busses moved out, a distillery moved in and we were without a home. Temporarily, we took over the basement of a garage built to replace [Hoff's] wheelwright shop (which we had lost spectacularly in a fire). As our rent of one dollar a year did not include three-phase [alarm] service, we reverted to a former sausage plant whistle hooked up to the garage air compressor. It really did

312

sound something like a pig squealing, and if nobody had been pumping up tires for a while, it would last for up to fifteen seconds.

This situation encouraged us to look for a new home. Other fire companies may have other problems, but we [in Owings Mills] have always [had our steamiest arguments] over land and buildings -- where to locate the company, what kind of building, how much, etc., etc. The Pleasant Hill and the Garrison factions finally wore each other out and the Down Town group obtained the present site where a building was built and later expanded to include a [second-floor] hall.

Progress during the thirties included pneumatic tires and a windshield - the brakes forever remained lousy - inch and a half hose, fog nozzles, gas masks, a booster tank and some very much needed firemanship training under University of Maryland auspices. We even purchased another truck, a ten-year-old American La France Cities Service Truck with eleven ladders, featuring a fifty-foot wooden monster that was undoubtedly the heaviest ladder ever built. Six good men could raise it if eight were not available, but they knew they had been working. It was the biggest ladder in Baltimore County for a long time. [It proved quite useful, but mainly for] putting ropes on flag poles and - since cats invariably picked trees seventy feet high to climb and could never climb down, only up - [it came in handy for] rescuing [errant felines] out of trees.

World War II came along. There were 34 stars in our service flag, one of them gold. Those left at home answered air raid alarms and learned how to fight fires with a two- or three-man crew. With the end of the war, a surprising number of our returnees took up with the company again, not exactly where they left off, but some distance ahead. [The building and equipment were up-dated as was training for our volunteers.]

An increasing number of our members have held positions in the Baltimore County Fire Department, including a Chief, a Chief Deputy, Battalion Chiefs, Captains, Lieutenants and fire-fighters. The company also furnished a number of officers of the Baltimore County Volunteer Firemen's Association. -*George B. P. Ward*

I used to go to all the fires. Whenever that whistle'd blow, I'd be out and down there and go with them. When Reese's barn burned, I went down there and helped pull the hose. -*Henry Clay Hipsley*

Ed Allen was a wonderful mechanic - kept that Owings Mills fire engine running like a clock. I remember when they put balloon tires on the old La France - that was a big deal.

Sometimes they'd go out and Phil Knatz would be driving that truck and - they used to call it - "snatching the gravel" with his mouth ... it was a nervous habit. They'd go down the road looking like the Keystone Kops. -*John Kellar*

[Two long-time members of the Owings Mills Volunteer Fire Company] secured appointments in the Baltimore County Fire Department. They were Donald and Horace Warren, sons of William H. and Helen Bowen Warren. Donald rose to be Deputy Fire Chief of Baltimore Co. and Horace became a battalion chief. Both brothers have now retired, but Gary Warren, the son of Horace and Betty Knatz Warren, is a lieutenant in the Baltimore County Fire Department. He is a trained paramedic and an instructor. His brother, Dennis, is in charge of the fire equipment at the Maryland Cup Company. -E. Bennett Bowen

When I was a little kid, if you went down to the fire station, night or day, there were always four feet sticking out from under the fire engine. Two of them belonged to George Ward and the other two were Arthur Wineholt's. -*William D. Groff, Jr.*

No, two of those feet were Ed Allen's. I wasn't much under the engine - I wanted to be on top of it. -*George B. P. Ward*

### Nights When the Fire Hoses Froze

They had a big fire [at Reese's farm] and it burned the barn down, burned up all their horses, the mules, everything. I was in my teens and I remember going down there to look around after the fire. I remember seeing the mules lying there, completely burnt up. -*Grace Bowen Pape*

The barn on the John Reese farm was large enough - along with several hay barracks - to house the harvest from the entire area that is now the Tollgate development. In January of 1914 the barn burned. It was before daylight on a cold winter's morning that neighbors smelled the smoke before either the Reeses or their tenant farmers, the Morans, were aware of it.

Everyone ran to the stable which was already filled with smoke. When the stable doors were opened a few animals made it to the yard, but only one or two survived the fire. Horses, cows, mules, pigs and chickens perished. Hay, straw and farm implements were destroyed.

The barn on Therapia Farm, stood where the Morningside Apartments clubhouse now stands. It was well-constructed with brick ends and was a landmark travelers on the turnpike always admired. It burned one summer day during the hay harvest.

The Groff Hall - later converted to apartments - stood on the corner of Ritter's Lane. The entire building was destroyed by fire one Sunday night in 1909. Miss Viola Paul who was seven at the time, remembers her parents taking her to safety from the flames. Mr. Oliver H. Disney, Sr., and his family watched the fire from the side porch of their home on the north side of Ritters Lane. -*E. Bennett Bowen*

The old St. Thomas rectory burnt in the summer of 1937. [The fire started between 11:30 and midnight. At the time I was a great volunteer fireman. The whistle blew, and I said, "Ruth, I got to go."

As I got out of the bed, I saw the reflection. I said, "Oh, no! Either the St. Thomas Church is on fire or the St. Thomas rectory." I jumped in the car and found out it was the rectory.

All the fire companies were called. They had to pump the water from Reisterstown Road near Painters Lane. I can't remember how many feet of hose it took.

## O. M. Fire Station

By the 1930s this fire station on Reisterstown Road was in service and the volunteer company owned three vehicles, one of which carried a fifty-foot wooden ladder dubbed "The Monster" because it was so difficult to raise. Photo courtesy of Gary Kadoff.

Mrs. Hoff was secretary to Dr. Jensen, and they all came up and carried out the records of the church. *-Elmer Hobart Schaefer*

Mr. Tase had no more than bought the Lowe property when one fine, bright Saturday morning, the barn caught fire. So the Volunteer Fire Company went back there.

Bill King and Arthur Wineholt were two of the people I remember being on the fire truck. Arthur was driving the engine, and we started to go down the hill right by the barn to get to the stream. I was up on top, throwing boots and helmets off so the men would get them. When we came back a little later, I found that where I had thrown one good, heavy pair of boots - where they had landed - was right up against a box of dynamite caps and the dynamite was there, too.

After her brother was killed by a railroad train, Miss Margaret Painter lived [at Ulm] by herself. Her house caught fire [one night], and how in the name of God we ever put it out, I don't know. It was one of the coldest nights I've ever seen in my life. We pumped continuously out of the stream and kept the hoses running. As soon as we shut down to pick up the hoses, they all froze, and we had to carry them home on a stake-body truck. We put an extension ladder on [the truck] and laid these fifty-foot lengths of hose on it and carried it back to the engine house. *-George P. B. Ward*

That's what put us to the road - the burning of the [Hoff] garage up there. Because they had thirty-five years of hard work in it. The way the fire happened was], Henry and his father took pity on this young fellow one time. He came in there and wanted to work - he had two little children and he couldn't get any work. Well, Grandfather Hoff was always ready to help somebody, he always gave the shirt off his back. So he took him on, and he had the privilege of doing what he wanted to more or less.

This one night, he got in there to fill his tank with gasoline, which he didn't have any business doing. He could have done it in the daytime. And then the lunatic struck a match to see if he had his tank filled!

In thirty-five minutes, the place was down to the ground - everything was gone! All their records and everything burned. There were twenty-five used cars burned and two tow-trucks and a couple of new cars in the show-room. It was all dead loss. About a hundred thousand dollars in those days, which would have been more today.

The insurance? - there was nothing left and records and everything burned and half the places wouldn't listen to it. So it just left them paupers. Grandfather Hoff just about cracked up. He never was himself ... he didn't know half the time where he was. *-Margaret Clark Hoff*

Elmer K--- was the biggest liar anyone wanted to talk to. You never could believe him. We were all playing cards one Saturday night, and here come Elmer and said, "Call the fire department 'cause Rosewood barn is on fire!" Sure enough it was. He did tell the truth that one time. *-Elmer Hobart Schaefer*

So many times barns burned. Sometimes lightning struck, like at Elmer Shoemakers. Or, if hay was put in green, it would get hot [and set the barn on fire.] -*Lee Fox*

My husband belonged to the [Owings Mills Fire Company] from the time they started until he was a 25-year member. But he drove so slow that when he got to the fire, the engines would be gone. -*Belle S. Zepp*

## Wheels of Chance and a Dunking Table

My father was the fire company's first treasurer. [In the early days], in order to raise money, they held entertainments, minstrel shows, movies and [all kinds of] fund-raisers. I don't remember when the carnivals started, although I do remember that they used to be held at Rosewood. -*George B. P. Ward*

When they held the carnivals where Owings Mills school is now, [they used to have trap-shoots.] I loaded the clay pigeons. Oh, man! Raymond [Moser] was a hot shot ... he was a good shot! And they had a mid-way. Bingo. They had a dance platform. And a supper. They also used to have jousting tournaments - with horses. They would be on horseback and the rings would be hanging down.

And they'd have Boob Langhorne sitting on the dunking table. [They threw baseballs to dunk him.] I always felt sorry for that guy sitting there. They used to give him two dollars a night for doing it. -*James Carpenter*

My uncle, Bill King, was the fire captain. When they had carnivals, we went to Uncle Will's house, which was over top of Garner's store, and made candy until we were sick and tired of looking at candy. [Later on] it got too much to make at one place and we had to make it at two or three places.

At that time, the carnival was held where the present Owings Mills [elementary] school is. That was an empty field and all mucky, so evidently the drainage was bad. No matter whether it rained or not, you'd find mud-puddles or soft spots.

The carnival was a big affair around here - everybody came. It started in the afternoon and they'd have the jousting tournaments. I remember Raymond Moser, Phil Knatz and a Yox. They always crowned a queen. Almost every year Phil Knatz's wife, Mary Knatz, was crowned queen. They'd put this little thing around her head. I guess whoever won got to pick the queen.

[The carnival] went on through the night. They had like a little platform set up. You could dance on there. They had different chance wheels, cake table, candy table, Bingo - all that kind of stuff. -*Genevieve Berryman Kelley*

I belonged to the auxiliary for years and years. They had the annual carnival supper. We went around and begged for what we would get. I started at Pleasant Hill and went to Mt. Wilson Lane. I took in Ritters

317

Lane, all the way back. I went to the Ten Mile House and usually got money. *-Belle S. Zepp*

Up until about fifteen years ago, the carnivals were more a home-grown affair than they are now. They started getting [commercial] rides and then more than rides. Then they got to the point that [the commercial vendors] wouldn't come unless they had the whole thing. I haven't been to the carnival in years. *-George B. P. Ward*

## The Terrible Toll of Agnes

I started the Baltimore Adhesive Company in 1949. I rented a small area in the old post-office building [former Hoff's Garage.] In 1972, [Hurricane] Agnes came through and demolished everything in its path. At least along the Gwynns Falls area. Our office, which was one of the oldest buildings in Owings Mills was gone.

The reason it happened, we believe, was [because] the embankment of the railroad was thirty-two feet higher than the grade level of [Reisterstown] road. [Only] a small culvert under the railroad [embankment] let the water into the Gwynns Falls. That got all clogged up with limbs and trees and held the water back [until the embankment finally burst and swept everything downstream.] [Then, too, there were piles of lumber all strapped together over there and when the water began to rise beyond the railroad [embankment] the lumber piles rose up and floated [so that it jammed] the culvert. When the [embankment gave way] and the lumber broke apart - flew everyplace - it took everything in its way. The railroad, the only thing that was left, was just rails hanging in mid-air.

My family and I were coming back from St. Louis that day [but by the time] we landed in Baltimore [the storm] was all over. [Driving north on Reisterstown Road] toward home, we could see water every place. We got to the top of the hill beyond Maryland Cup Company [at Painters Lane and Reisterstown Road] and we began to see water. But down under the [railroad] bridge there wasn't a drop of water on the road or anyplace.

So we went home and went to bed. I woke up next morning and went to the race track [where I was keeping the horses I trained for racing]. As I started to go in the gate, the watchman came out and said, "I'm awfully sorry to hear about your disaster." Only thing I could think about was that something had happened to my horses. "What do you mean?" [I asked him.] He showed me the paper and I saw that the whole thing, the whole Owings Mills area down here, [had been washed away.] It had all happened about half an hour after we had passed through there.

All the houses [along the west side of Reisterstown Road north of Dolfield Road, except for the middle house where the Bowerses lived] had been washed off their foundations. Benny Barr's house was completely washed off the foundation and turned around ... turned all the way around and holes in the ground like a bomb had hit it. It took Jim Wisner's store right off its foundation. The front part of our building [the old Hoff's buggy shop and, later, garage and car agency] was

318

washed completely away. The bridge [over Gwynns Falls on Reisterstown Road] was washed out.

There just happened to be about sixteen automobiles going north and south at the time the [water crashed through the] railroad [embankment] and [the cars] were all in our back yard. Mrs. Bowers [who lived in one of the houses] saved any number of people. She pitched a rope to them as they were coming out of their cars and they got in her house. One woman she throwed a rope to didn't catch it. We found her [drowned] out here the next morning.

The next morning people came to get their cars and there was lumber all over everything and everybody was looting our building.

All the empty barrels that we kept outside were washed miles downstream. Years later I got some of them back. Some had labels on them and someone would find them two or three miles downstream.

[Fortunately], the month's supply of adhesive that we keep manufactured ahead was closed up tightly in steel containers. We washed the mud off [the containers], and it was all right. We were lucky enough to have a new steam generator upstairs where the water didn't hurt it. But it took about a year and a half, maybe two years to get everything built back like it is today. Our cost of moving the houses and having the houses burned and the re-building, was in excess of about $75,000.

For a long time, there was a road block on Reisterstown Road where the four lanes of traffic [narrowed into] two lanes as they were rebuilding the bridge [over the Gwynns Falls]. That took a couple of years.

The Western Maryland Railroad re-built that trestle like it is now ... so that it could never happen again. They dredged the Gwynns Falls base out and made it a little deeper and they put rock walls around it so it would hold the water. We've never been bothered [by a flood] since. *-Harry L. Shay*

Campbell Family, about 1912

The family of Dr. William H. H. Campbell posed on the steps of their home at "Windswept": (rear) Mrs. Campbell, Dr. Campbell, Aunt Mary Warfield; (front) John, Alan, Doug, Elizabeth, Francina; (woman left middle not identified). Photo courtesy of Minna Campbell

# CHAPTER 15

## Staying Healthy

*In the early years of this century, illnesses and accidents were a far more serious matter than they are today: little was known about the means by which diseases were spread, medical technology was still in its infancy, and in such a rural community as Owings Mills, hospital care was all but unknown. Little wonder then, that practitioners of the healing arts were regarded with something akin to reverence and that folk remedies were relied upon to cure all manner of ills.*

*In the late 1800s, Owings Mills was chosen as the site of a residential training facility for retarded children. The institution, incorporated in 1888 as "The Maryland Asylum and Training School for the Feebleminded", was later changed to "Rosewood State Training School" and is now known as "The Rosewood Center." Its charter stated that "Children between the ages of 7 and 17 years, who are so deficient in intelligence as to be incapable of being educated in ordinary school, and who are not insane or greatly afflicted or deformed physically, will be admitted ... free of charge for board and tuition, upon evidence being furnished of their inability to pay." Later, older patients and those with severe defects were admitted; by mid-century, the institution housed some 2,000 retarded children and adults. Today, the trend toward institutionalization has been reversed and many of Rosewood's patients are being re-located into community homes.*

*-/-/-/-*

## A Typical Country Doctor

Doctor William H. H. Campbell was trained on Civil War battlefields - did his internship there. He remained a good family physician until even after he was an elderly man. Doctor Campbell drove [his horse and buggy] to the Chestnut Ridge and almost all the way to the Liberty Road. I was teaching at Dover Road school on Chestnut Ridge when he was an old man. He came over there in a Model-T sedan with his daughter, Elizabeth, driving him. He went to see Mr. Isaac Baublitz -- they were about the same age. [Doctor Campbell] died in about 1920. *-E. Bennett Bowen*

Doctor Campbell was in the Confederate Army. He was not a doctor in the army although I grew up thinking he was. He took medical training afterwards.

Before my time, the Campbells lived in the house that was almost directly opposite the south end of the fire house -- where the [Kimmel] tire company is now. That burned down and my father and mother took in several of the children till they got another place. The Campbells bought Spayde's place [adjacent to our farm] and lived there all the time I knew them ... until all the children grew up.

Doctor Campbell used to visit his patients in a buggy. I guess I must have been about ten years old - in summertime he would take me along, and I would drive the buggy.

The most striking experience I ever had with him was once I got an infection in my big toe, and it got all puffed up. I went limping barefooted across the field to Dr. Campbell to look at it. He said, "Let me see your foot, George." I said all right. Then he reached his hand in his pocket and got out a pocket knife as if he was going to do something to his fingernail. "What's that bird out there?" he asked me. I looked and he came across my toe with the knife. Blood flew and I flew! -George B. P. Ward

[Doctor Campbell] set my arm. Five dollars. No x-rays or anything. I carried it around in a sling, and when it was time, he took it down and did whatever was necessary and five dollars! Nowadays you've got to go through a regular procession! - in the hospital and x-rays and more x-rays when they take it out. Costs you a fortune! -Grace Bowen Pape

Doctor Campbell was wonderful ... a typical country doctor. If I'd go in Garner's store, he'd be in there, and he'd come shake hands with you. He'd come in the house when the kids were sick, and Mom would be making - you call them cookies now, but they were sugar cakes - and he'd take some in his overcoat pocket.

Doctor Campbell lived at the top of Pleasant Hill in the house Henry Lewis owns, but not in my time. When he lived there, he had children who passed away [even though] they'd be all bundled up in the winter, long underwear and stockings and all. Then, when [his] other children came along, those girls and boys went barefoot ... they went barefoot to school!

[At the time I remember, the house where Mrs. Spayde later lived] was old Doctor Campbell's house. There was a boardwalk all the way up. I'd go there with some of my younger brothers to get them vaccinated or something. Or they'd have a ring they couldn't get off - the ring came on candy - and Doctor Campbell would take the ring off. [Later,] when my brother, Harry, had diphtheria, the doctor was living back at Lycett's [Berry Hill].

I had the flu in 1916 or '17. I was unconscious. So many people died. Doctor Campbell said, "Leave the windows open." He didn't have a stethoscope - he'd put his cold ear on your chest. I still remember that. That would be his way. -Dorothy King

[Doctor Campbell] was our doctor when I was a child. He lived down at Owings Mills about two and a half miles from where we lived. My mother took me down there to be vaccinated. We walked down ... in those days, we walked everywhere. He vaccinated me then, and he scratched my arm so much I had about the biggest vaccination you've ever seen.

He had two sons that used to travel on the streetcars when my mother did. In the winter they went barefooted. So one day my mother was on the streetcar sitting with a lady and the [Campbell] boys were on the streetcar, and the lady said to my mother, "They must be very poor children because they're barefooted in the wintertime." My mother told her they were doctor's children and they should have plenty of money to buy shoes. But I guess that it was just their tradition that they go barefoot in the winter. *-Helen Kendig Bowers*

All the Campbell sons went barefoot in summer and winter. Rumor had it that because Dr. and Mrs. Campbell lost some of their first-born, they decided to let the others rough it. One day in winter with snow on the ground, Mrs. Campbell was in Baltimore and someone complained to the police about cruelty to children. When Mrs. Campbell explained, it was soon settled.

I asked [my husband], Doug, if the rumor was true that [his parents] did this to make their children healthy. He said, "Why don't you ask Father?" I never did. We did, however, start my son out barefooted until he was about six years old. *-Minna Campbell*

### The Old Country Doctors Did Everything!

When [my sister], Gladys [Fox Knatz], was about three years old she broke her arm, and old Doc Slade came down and he put it in a couple of splints. There weren't any such things as x-rays. They'd just pull it together, push it together, put some pieces of board around it and some cloth. *-Lee Fox*

When Doctor Campbell passed on, [we had] Doctor Slade. [There was also] Doctor Nichols, Doctor Royce, Doctor Palmer Williams. And Doctor Gore used to make his rounds around here on the electric car [streetcar].

Doctors [often made] their own prescriptions. They would take a piece of paper like a cigarette paper, and they had their little medicine knife, and they would sit there, and they'd take a half of this pill and a half of that, and they'd crush them and make you powders. That's how you got your medicine.

In those days, you didn't have to go to a different doctor for your eye, your foot, your head, your hands, your heart, your liver and some more. The old country doctors did everything. I swear I think they knew more than they do today! I really do! And didn't charge you no twenty dollars neither to look at you and say, "I don't know what's wrong with you." *-Virginia Clark Hoff*

[Besides Doctor Campbell, other doctors around here were] Doctor Slade in Reisterstown, Doctor Price up in Glyndon and Doctor Miller in Reisterstown. *-Helen Carpenter*

One time I had Doctor Rider. I was having a lot of trouble around my heart, and he came and said I had a rapid heart. *-Lillian Demmitt Moser*

Doctor William E. Martin was an old country doctor. He used to come back to the house many a time at night on horseback. Carried his own pills. He'd say, "Well, I guess you'll live till I get back." [He charged] maybe 75 cents. I'd like to have the money old Doc had owing him. And I'd like to have what he left. 'Cause he started [in practice] when he was out of medical school and he was about 90 when he died.

He treated anybody that was sick. During the flu epidemic, he wasn't in bed sometimes for two weeks at a time. Somebody drove for him. Dick Crooks and Josh Crooks and different ones, they hauled him and he'd sleep. Day and night. Some I knew died from the flu. But old Doc told me right there in our house, he says, "A man that don't drink whiskey ... isn't saturated with it ... I can cure him." He said the ones that drank was hard to do. He said that because of the alcohol the medicine wouldn't work. *-Frank Parker*

Dr. William E. Martin was born in 1881 to William and Mary Fitch Martin of Reisterstown. He attended public school at Eldersburg near Freedom. When Springfield State Hospital was built near his home, Martin became storekeeper for the purchasing agent, dispensing the hospital supplies. In his off-hours he sat in on a class for nurses and attendants at the hospital. Noticing his interest, the superintendent of the hospital urged him to study medicine.

Although he had no high-school degree, Dr. Martin took the entrance exam for Baltimore Medical College. In his third year, he transferred to the University of Maryland Medical School in Baltimore.

After he graduated in 1909, he moved to Harrisonville on Liberty Road. He began his practice with one horse and buggy, and, as the practice grew, added another horse. In winter, a sleigh replaced the buggy. Eventually, he purchased a Ford roadster, but roads in the area had not been paved, and he often had to reach his patients on horseback or by walking.

General practice in those days meant literally treating everything: setting fractures, treating diseases, delivering babies – 4,000 of them in his 60 years of practice. Hospital treatment was practically unheard of, except in extreme cases.

Over the years, Doctor Martin's unusual accuracy in diagnosis was recognized, and he was invited to join the staff of a hospital. But he was devoted to his practice as a family physician and decided to continue in this role.

In his early years, Dr. Martin charged 50 cents for office calls, a dollar for home visits, ten dollars for delivering a baby. Even at the time of his retirement in 1969, office visits were only two dollars.

Patients were never harrassed for money, and even the worst weather never prevented him from making emergency calls.

Doctor Martin's busy life left little time for hobbies, yet he found time for reading and had a lifelong interest in gardening. He proposed the building of a health center for the Second District, and he served on its board of trustees. He aso served as health officer for the district and was an assistant State Medical Examiner. He died in 1974 at age 92 and is buried in Druid Ridge Cemetery. *-Wilson Herera*

Mom had Doctor Campbell then, but Doctor Martin delivered babies. I think he charged five or ten dollars. I remember he came on horseback to Mary Mack's. *-Bessie Moser vonGunten*

[Doctor Martin] had a hard time getting patients – the whites didn't want to go to him because he treated blacks. [Doctor Martin] was telling me once about this one colored man who must have lived up around Sykesville. He was getting a venereal disease and he came to Doc to cure it. Came to him once, and a few years later, dang if he didn't come back again. The man [told Doctor Martin that] he didn't care once he got the sulfa – take that big old white pill and knock it out.

[Doctor Martin] was doctoring before World War I. When the flu [epidemic] came he had a big business then ... he could hardly keep up. [He charged] fifty cents at the office. For a house call it was either one dollar or two dollars. *-Carl A. vonGunten*

He never said "No", Doctor Martin didn't. When my husband was sick he'd come to the house and see him and when I tried to pay him, he'd say, "I hate to take your money, Mrs. Shipe, because I can't do him any good." But I would always say to him, "You take it, Doc ... you earned it by coming." He could truly be called "the poor man's friend" and I miss him something terrible. *-Valley R. Shipe*

Doctor Slade was a wonderful doctor and person. Three dollars was his visit price. No matter what time of night, it always stayed three dollars. Take today, just calling the doctor is twenty-five dollars. It might be more and the hair on your head will stand.

Doctor Slade used to make his own medicine. I remember one time my father-in-law had a cough. He coughed all the time. He came to me and asked if I knew any good doctors. I told him I would take him up to Doctor Slade. Doctor Slade had something there and he gave it to my father-in-law. Take so many spoonfuls every so often and don't overdo it. The cough went away and my father-in-law went off for sometime, but in the meantime, Doctor Slade died.

We went from Doctor Slade to Doctor Nichols. Another wonderful doctor. He was in Pikesville. If you couldn't come to his office, he would come to you. We had Doctor Nichols until he died and then Ruth and I got Doctor David Miller. He's the kind of "Do as I say, or don't do anything or talk." If I call my friend, Doctor Miller, he will say, "Well, what's the matter?" If I have a cold he tells me what to do. "Just do what I tell you and you'll get rid of it." He's a wonderful doctor, too. *-Elmer Hobart Schaefer*

325

And there was Doctor Warner and his wife had that high place there up on the right side [of Reisterstown Road]. He was an eye doctor. His father was before him, too. -*Minnie Clark Hebron*

Along about 1907, Doctor Ward from Liberty Road went back in [Soldiers Delight] to see a patient. It got dark because it was along about December or January and he fell in one of the mines. He was exposed there all night and contracted pneumonia and died.

Doctor Slade lived in Reisterstown and Doctor Gore lived right beside Chatsworth Avenue and Doctor Price lived in Glyndon. Some people had Doctor Naylor from Pikesville.

Doctor Rider [who lived on Church Road near Pleasant Hill Road] practiced more in the city. But he sometimes saw patients here. -*E. Bennett Bowen*

My father's [Doctor Rider] practice was in Baltimore. His medical instruments are in the medical museum at Davidge Hall of the University of Maryland Medical School in Baltimore. -*Ethel Rider*

### Cutting the Cord

I delivered babies in Virginia before I moved up here, but I never got a Maryland license. But often I'd go with Doctor Martin to help with delivering babies nearby. I figure I've helped deliver at least twenty babies in this neighborhood.

One time I went with Doctor Martin to a home where a young mother was about to give birth. "I don't think she'll deliver for a couple of hours at least," Doctor Martin said after he examined her. "I'm going back to my office and I'll be back later. Why don't you go home, too, and get some rest?" But something told me I'd better stay. Sure enough - I doubt if Doctor Martin had even gotten to his house yet when here came the baby. I delivered it all right, because I had to, but I didn't cut the cord. I sent someone to fetch the doctor to do that, because I wasn't licensed and I didn't want to be at fault if anything had gone wrong, even though I had cut many cords back in Virginia.

I recall one neighboring family where there was a new baby every year until they finally had eighteen children altogether. Folks around claimed John ---- was poorly, but I don't rightly see how the man could be too sick when he was producing all those young ones! -*Valley R. Shipe*

Mrs. Kate Moore was Elsie Marshall's grandmother, and she was a mid-wife. She delivered most of our children. "Nannie Moore", they used to call her. She would stay ten days when she came to our house. She'd get up and get our breakfast in the morning ... take care of the kids. Mama and our new baby - she took care of all that, every bit of it. -*Grace Bowen Pape*

There was a Stephens who was a great-aunt of ours who used to live around here and she was a midwife. She lived in the old house where

the Blacks lived on Reisterstown Road ... later that was the
Carpenter's house. She stayed with my mother when Roland was born.
-*Lee Fox*

My Grandma brought all the Pape children into the world. Her name
was Diana Lucas ... she was called Dinah. And all those Cole children
- my Grandmother was there when those children were born. She was
a good midwife around through the country. Where she got the experience I don't know. -*Minnie Clark Hebron*

Ma Stevens [Mrs. May Stevens (or Stephens)] was old Tom Steven's
wife. She delivered I don't know how many babies around here. And
Mrs. West was another practical nurse who came out from Baltimore.
She delivered the last of Mrs. Bosley's children that lived on Reese's
place. She delivered Mrs. Doc Slade's last boy, the little Doc Slade,
she delivered him. And Eddie Graef ... professor Graef - she
delivered every one of his children.
Another one who picked up that kind of work was Mrs. Jake Keller
who lived over here on Garrison Road. This Mrs. Keller delivered
Elmer's first baby. At that time, there were two cases ran together.
She was staying here with me at the time, and she was working with
Doctor Nichols. So Doctor Nichols and I went up and delivered Elmer's
last baby and she only came and seen us through till we got the baby
and then she went on, because she had two cases ran together.
-*Virginia Clark Hoff*

Mrs. May Stevens lived in Lillian Shoemaker's house and in the
"Breathorne" house when the Shipleys and Margaret Dorsey lived
there. She was related to Bessie Cook by marriage. Mrs. Stevens
would be as old as my grandmother - 130 years. -*E. Bennett Bowen*

There was a Miss Bailey who would come take care of Mom. She
lived back through Soldiers Delight. She'd come horseback ... tie the
horse out there [in the front yard]. She was a very nice person. I had
black hair and she'd bring me red ribbons. And I never cared for red.
Isn't that funny! When she'd go home with her suitcase, there'd be
valentines or little things in there. -*Dorothy King*

Nannie Branson was a midwife and she used to go around and take
care of all the ladies when their children were born. She was with
Mama when I was born. Very nice little colored lady ... they were
lovely people! -*Helen Kendig Bowers*

## Care For the Sick and Dying

Mrs. Susie Disney walked miles and miles over muddy roads in all
kinds of weather to tend to the sick. In the days when there was not a
trained nurse outside of the city, it was most helpful to have someone
who could take a patient's temperature and count the pulse beat.
Mrs. Disney's talent for nursing surfaced when she was still in her
teens. Dr. Campbell often praised her skill. She attended both black

327

and white and often sat by a sick bed for a week at a time. Sometimes she was the last person recognized by the dying.

Remarkably, she made no charge for her services, and many of those she helped were among the poorest of the community. Her vitality seemed endless, and with all her duties with the sick, it is said she seldom missed a church service.

Mrs. Alice Black, who was a relative of the DeMuth and the Tase families, was the friend and nurse of all the Owings Mills children who became ill at school. After she became a widow, Mrs. Black moved away from the community and her house was then occupied by the James Carpenter family. *-E. Bennett Bowen*

In those days, there were no nursing homes. Every household had two or three great-aunts who helped with care of the sick. *-George B. P. Ward*

## Painting A House for Two Gold Teeth

Doc Stumpf [was our dentist]. He lived up above where Doctor Caples used to be as you go [north] out of Reisterstown. Big yellow house on the right-hand side. I painted his house one time for him to put me two false teeth in the front. He made two teeth for me with gold crowns on them, and I had to paint the whole house to get them done. A lot of work for two teeth! *-James L. Bowers*

[Our dentist was] Doctor Stumpf in Reisterstown. Up opposite where Doctor Caples used to be. He was a rough one!

Another thing Pop did - one Sunday morning he went to town on the streetcar and came back with all his teeth pulled out. *-Helen Carpenter*

When I was about twelve years old, I had a toothache and it abcessed. Old Dr. Benson came up from Cockeysville and he put some chloroform on my nose and knocked me out then cut this thing. *-Mary Robinson Sprinkle*

It was a man at the top of [Tollgate] hill by the name of Doctor Gorgas who lived by himself. That was the oldest place, you know. We were afraid to go by this big house because he kept it so dark and everything. *-Minnie Clark Hebron*

[Doctor George Morrow] lived back as you made the turn on Kingsley Road - only they used to call it Bitzer's lane. He was the only dentist until Doctor Koerner came there afterwards. *-Grace Pape*

The only dentist I ever knew of was down here in Owings Mills - Doctor Koerner. *-Mary Kendig Gettierre*

Our dentist was Doctor Koerner. He and my father were very close friends ... they used to ride their motorcycles together. If I had to go to the dentist after school, I would walk down [to Dr. Koerner's house] and then get on the streetcar and come home. They had quite an entrance down there where you waited for the streetcar. Almost like a semi-circle. There were also ledges where you could sit. The Morningside Heights Apartments are there now. -*Genevieve B. Kelley*

[A school dentist] would come around. He set up in the upstairs [schoolroom] that wasn't being used. He had a machine that worked like a sewing-machine ... with a pedal. He'd pedal while he was grinding the teeth. Dr. Katz. He's still practicing in Pikesville. It was a very reasonable price he charged. He was also so nice with the kids and they liked him. [Some] parents came in, too. When [Dr. Katz] opened [an office] in Pikesville, he had one of the biggest and best trades of any dentist around. -*William C. Hull*

## Healing Ourselves

When I have a cut, I put salt on it. And it doesn't sting. My grandfather Nelson said when they did that to the slaves, they weren't doing it so it would hurt, they did it for healing.

Then there'd be onion plasters. You would heat the onions - in goose grease, it was supposed to be - and then put it on layers of flannel that they put on the chest.

Honey was a great thing to have. People would use it for a cough -- equal parts of honey and lemon.

Another thing -- you know those madonna lilies? ... Easter lilies? - that was good for a cut or a bruise. You put the petals in whiskey ... I guess the alcohol kept them indefinitely.

Flax-seed meal [was also good] for a stone bruise. You would put hot water with it and put it on a cloth and wrap it.

You would heat mullen leaves with lard and put that on sores and the like. And we had to have sassafras tea, you know. To clear the blood.

What berries are those that if you have clothes on the line the birds leave their calling cards? - poke berries! This person would come here and they'd gather them and eat them. He said it was good for rheumatism or arthritis. I read that they're not fit to eat - we used them for ink - but he said it helped. -*Dorothy King*

If anyone got burned, my mother knew the words you say -- a little verse. When you say those words and blow on the place that was burned, it won't burn any more and it won't blister. A man can't tell a man the words and a woman can't tell a woman. My cousin told them to me, so now, if anyone gets burned, I can take the fire out. One time my nephew's little boy got hold of the cord to the coffee pot and pulled it over on him. He was burned under his chin and all the way down his little chest. They called me, and I went down immediately and took the fire out. It stopped burning, and he stopped crying. When the doctor came, he couldn't understand why [the boy] wasn't crying since he was burned so badly. But we didn't let the doctor know what I had done. Because it could be they wouldn't believe in those things. But it works. -*Helen Kendig Bowers*

329

It seems as though my younger sister knows how to do it. If we got burned, she used to take the fire out, so I guess it worked. Or maybe it was just the modern thing that we thought it helped. I know people can take warts off. And people can stop blood. There's probably something to it. *-Mary Kendig Gettierre*

[My mother used] mullen, vinegar and salt for sprains and bruises. And you'd use mullen and brown sugar and horehound and lemon and something else for cough syrup. I tell a lot of people about mullen for sprains and they laugh at me, but it's one of the best remedies. You take the mullen and boil it with salt and drain it off and then you use it to bathe your foot or arm or whatever. Or you could wrap the leaves around it when they were hot.

During the flu epidemic, we would chew plenty of Brown's Mule. That was Doctor Martin's orders. He said that tobacco chewing would catch [the flu germs], and you'd get rid of it. Then, too, he told me that if you chew plenty of tobacco when you're feeding the threshing machine, that dust won't hurt you - [the tobacco] will catch it. *-A. Franklin Parker*

As a child, I do not remember going to the doctor's very much. For a cold we had Vicks on our nose, up our nose, on our chest. [When] you went to sleep, [you weren't] sure if you'd gotten relief or if the odor had gassed you.

Castoria was very popular [as a cure for constipation]. For congestion or an aching back [you got] a mustard poultice. This was dry mustard mixed with water, made into a paste and put on a cloth which was then slapped onto your skin.

If you had a boil, Gordshell's Salve [was applied], then you would hold a heated small-necked bottle over the boil. This would draw out the core.

If something got in your eye, you were supposed to rub it three times one way then once the other. This was supposed to move [the foreign object] out of your eye. For a nosebleed, you held a cold key at the back of the neck. *-Genevieve Berryman Kelley*

They never had the doctor a lot. People weren't taking babies to the doctor all the time or having the doctor come. A baby might never see a doctor until it was old enough to go to school and had to be vaccinated.

Lots of times, people gave children cod-liver oil in the winter to prevent colds. And some took that white stuff -- Scott's Emulsion. I don't believe it did any good! *-Bessie Moser vonGunten*

They used to get this wild camomile and make a tea with that, and that would stop whooping cough. One of my brothers, they thought he was going to die because he'd had diarrhea for so long. This tramp came along and told them to get camomile and boil it and give the kid that. They did and he got all right. *-Carl A. vonGunten*

My mother had diphtheria. That was very serious, diphtheria! I'll never forget my father. They say you disinfect with tar, you see. My father set this bucket of tar afire every morning and went all through the house with it. It must have helped because nobody ever got nothing.

If you had a bad cold, we had something they called mutton tallow ... it came from the lamb. You take this mutton tallow and put a few drops of turpentine [with it], and you put it on to heat then rub it all on your back and chest, take a piece of flannel and lay on it. It was like Vicks salve, you know. -*Minnie Clark Hebron*

There was quite a drug period after the Civil War - a lot of times it was people who had gotten started on it when they were operated on in the war and the drug had been used to put them to sleep or out of pain. They were the lucky ones. [At that time and even later], patent medicines were loaded with narcotics. Mothers were encouraged to use laudanum, which was an opium derivative, to keep children from crying. At the Harker store at Wards Chapel, they sold laudanum to customers who specifically ordered it. -*Wilson Herera*

[For colds, we used warm camphorated oil and put it on your chest and put a piece of flannel on it. For earaches, they believed if you blew smoke into the ear it helped. -*Mary Robinson Sprinkle*

Did you ever hear of a corn cut on your foot? You tied a piece of worsted around it tight and it would cure it. -Wilson Herera

Tea made from the dried stalks of yarrow was used to cut phlegm. Chestnut leaves made a "slippery tea" that also helped bring up phlegm during whooping cough.

For mumps, a hog jowl was prescribed, although I've forgotten how it was used.

Burns of all sizes were treated by soaking them with a thick, foul-smelling ointment of grease blended with lime water and linseed oil. It did good work, but it smelled - it was called "Carrion Oil."

Onions were roasted in the oven and eaten just before going to bed to prevent colds. During the flu epidemic of 1918, the only deterrent known was roast onions and whiskey.

They had a special treatment for sick babies. They measured the baby with a string and said some words out of the Bible. Then they tied the string around the doorknob. When the string wore off the doorknob, the baby was supposed to be cured. I heard that over on the [Chestnut] Ridge.

Mr. Charles Cornelius Hopkins of Ritters Lane was the most respected authority for folk medicines. He gathered herbs, secured fats and oils and made salves. He was highly esteemed by men who had problems as they aged and many declared he saved their lives by applying his remedies to relieve their internal sufferings. He used Indian turnips and other hot-tasting roots to make a linament. One of his grandsons patented the formula and put the linament on the market. -*E. Bennett Bowen*

Skunk oil was for rheumatism and arthritis. People laughed at my father because he used to skin those skunks and get the fat out of them. But there was a policeman who worked in Druid Hill Park when my father worked out of Park Terminal carbarn, and he told my father that he couldn't get his arm up to get his gun out of his holster. "I'll give $25 to any guy that can cure it," he said. My father says, "I got something for that." So my father took him a Vicks jar of this skunk oil, and about a month later he gave my father $25. That was a lot of money then.

I've been looking for a skunk, but I can't find one. If I found one, I'd skin him out and get his oil. -*James L. Bowers*

## Accidents Happen

Well, look what happened to Raymond Moser! He was gored by the bull and it went through the thick part of his leg and out through the rear. -*Lee Fox*

[My brother] Bob had a dynamite cap in his hand and it went off and shot a couple of fingers off. Dr. Campbell treated him and then sent him to another doctor. Another time, my brother Myerl was going to ride the bull, and the bull ran right through the barbed-wire fence. Dr. Campbell said that if the wire had cut a fraction an inch deeper, it would have cut his artery. -*Elsie Moser Bates*

Mr. E. G. Knatz got hit by a streetcar. Hurt quite seriously. I remember waiting for the Pikesville ambulance that was coming to get him. He was saying to his wife, Becky - "Goodbye, Beck! Won't see you any more!" But he recuperated. -*Helen Carpenter*

Accidents occurred in Owings Mills long before the day of "fender benders." A mother was making soap and her child put lye in its mouth. A carpenter's helper fell from the roof of a house and never recovered from his injuries. A man lost control of his horse on Betty Clark's hill and his neck was broken when the vehicle hit a tree and he was thrown from it. A coal-oil stove that was being filled exploded and a young woman was burned to death. A boy felt a bare electric wire on a pole at Pleasant Hill, and his fingers were seriously burned.

Two boys from the Robert L. Talbert family of "The Caves" rode their bicycles onto an ice-pond where some children were skating. The ice snapped and both boys lost their lives.

Soon after the pylon that supports the weight of the railroad overpass was installed, a car hit it and the driver was killed. After that, coal oil lanterns were posted on each side of the pylon each evening. Cars often overturned because of the open ditch that ran down the side of Reisterstown Road. A Mr. Edward Tracy was killed in 1920 when his truck plunged through the guard fence and went into the stream just north of Bonita Avenue. In 1930 two young ladies driving home from Western Maryland College plunged into the open stream near Old Tollgate Road. -*E. Bennett Bowen*

332

## Typhoid Fever and the Flu Epidemic

In 1904 or 1905, Mrs. Rachel Moran and her three sons came to work the Reese farm. Fate seemed to be ill-starred for this family, even though their crops were good and they worked hard. Shortly after Mr. Reese built a very comfortable home for the family, the mother died of pneumonia as did one brother. *-E. Bennett Bowen*

In 1904, my uncle died of typhoid. I went down to Reese's icehouse with my father to get a piece of ice to put on his head. *-Lee Fox*

When I was eleven or twelve, all the children except me got pneumonia. Lewis was the last to succumb. He was the biggest and the sturdiest of the lot, and at the advice of our hired man he carried an onion in his pocket to ward it off. But he finally came down with the worst case of all. When Lewis recovered, Doctor Campbell told him that he should be careful or he might develop tuberculosis. For a year or more after that, Lewis rushed into the backyard every morning when he got up and poured a bucket of cold water over himself [even though] the thermometer was sometimes near zero. That was his own idea. Why it didn't kill him, I don't know.

[My brother] Clement got the diptheria when quite small, and Dr. Campbell came and gave him and all of us a shot in the rear of a new serum just out. We all lived and none of us got diptheria. *-from* "Lone Hickory Farm Notes" October 16, 1955 by *Francis Sydney Reese*

[In the flu epidemic of 1916], when you went on the street-car, they had all the windows open and it was cold weather. Too many people pass the germ along. *-Dorothy King*

I think my oldest brother, Charles Franklin Clark, died of the flu. In the flu epidemic. The people that he was employed by then lived in Westminster. The lady died in the morning, he died in the middle of the day and the gentleman died at night ... all in the same day. Up in Westminster. 1918. *-Minnie Clark Hebron*

In August of 1918, the *Sunpapers* had a short article about three cases of Spanish influenza among a ship's crew of an ocean liner that had docked at Norfolk, Virginia. Then, in early September, the paper announced that a young woman had died in Baltimore from "the flu."

By the first of October, there were announcements of scores of deaths. Although the schools had opened on schedule in September, the rumor circulated that if the flu continued its rapid spread they would be closed, along with all other places where people congregated.

Cases of the flu increased to the hundreds, then to the thousands. Soon schools, movies, theaters, even churches were closed.

Emergency measures were required to care for the sick and the dying. Undertakers were hard-pressed to supply enough caskets. Local carpenters helped by making substantial plain caskets to meet the demands that increased daily. Volunteer crews dug graves and funeral services were held right in the cemeteries.

In Owings Mills, there were hardly any homes where there was not at least one case of the flu. Marshall Cockey and his wife both died in the house where Laura Redifer now lives. Two Angelier brothers living on Dolfield Road died. Albert Berryman who married Nellie Disney died and Arthur Berryman and Cecelia Berryman whose father was the undertaker. Other deaths I recall were Margaret and George Warren, the children of Mr. and Mrs. William Warren, a Mrs. Shriver. Of course, there were many others that I did not hear of or do not recall. *-E. Bennett Bowen*

During the flu outbreak, you could see the hearses going up and down [Reisterstown] road every day. Taking the dead. *-Genevieve Berryman Kelley*

## Last Rites

Preparation and care of the dead has completely changed during the 20th century. As late as 1899, the undertaker's first step was to measure the body of the deceased in order to make a coffin to fit.

[When summoned to the home of the deceased,] the undertaker brought with him a box which looked very much like a casket. Ice was placed in large metal pans under the corpse. The water drained down into lower pans which had to be emptied by hand. The interior of the box was lined and there was a sliding glass panel to cover the face of the corpse. Black drapes hung to the floor and concealed the refrigeration apparatus.

By the day of the funeral, the casket was ready, and the body was transferred to it. Until embalming became a general practice, the body was usually viewed from behind a glass covering.

Several friends usually sat up with the dead during each night before the funeral. Occasionally one of the watchers became a prankster. At one home, one of the men went to sleep, and his partner, realizing that the sleeper was very superstitious, crept to the coffin in the adjoining room and propped the corpse into an upright position. Then he sat down and pretended to be asleep also. After a while, the first sleeper awakened and decided to check on the deceased. Still drowsy, he stumbled into the room and saw the corpse sitting up staring directly at him. It is reported that his screams not only awakened his partner, but the entire household.

Relatives came from great distances to attend the funerals. Often the overflow crowd was housed and fed by neighbors.

Neighbors always brought a variety of food to the home of the deceased for the dinner on the day of the funeral. Such meals were lavish; the appetites were reported to show few signs of bereavement.

During the time of mourning, black was worn by both men, women and children. Even pocket handkerchiefs were edged in black. A supply of black-edged paper was secured for correspondence and letters were addressed in black ink.

334

Hearses were horse-drawn and hacks and carriages transported the mourners to the cemetery. In poorer families, farm wagons were often the means of transportation.

During the funeral service, young widows and fiancés were expected to faint. On one occasion, a young man died, and two young ladies attended the last rites in deep mourning, each claiming to be his fiancé with all expectations for her future life shattered.

Some enterprising "crayon artists" read the daily death notices in order to canvas the homes of the newly-bereaved for work. Such an entrepreneur would first speak to his client about the recent loss, then show samples of his work. He would promise a life-like portrait of the deceased "set in a massive gilded frame twenty by twenty-four inches in size and well-protected by clear glass." Some of the artists were never heard of again after they collected a deposit. However, many of the portraits were delivered as promised and for many years hung in prominent places in local parlors. -*E. Bennett Bowen*

## Rosewood

My father was friendly with a doctor and the doctor one time asked my father if there was any farm for sale in the neighborhood. [My father] said, "Why, yes ... right next door [to our place].

The owner of the farm was somebody named "Wood" and his wife was "Rose Wood". That's where the [Rosewood State Institution For Retarded Children] got its name. Around 1915 or 1916, we sold the hill that is in front of the administration buildings to Rosewood. It wasn't too good as a field and didn't get much working. -*George B. P. Ward*

My parents moved to Rosewood I would say in 1900, because my brother Wilbur was born the next year. At that time, a Doctor Woods lived at [what was called] Gundry Cottage [on the grounds of Rosewood]. He had given the property to the state for the feeble-minded in honor of his daughter who was feeble-minded.

My father was the electrical engineer, and he built up the power plant at Rosewood. When my father came there, all they had was a gasoline motor to generate the lights and individual furnaces in the buildings.

Everything that was bought for the power-plant my Dad bought. Any machinery that was needed, he would test it and turn a report in and if he liked it they bought it. Automobiles, everything. He tested all the oil. Any company that wanted to see oil to Rosewood had to bring a sample and he tested it and if it was good, when their turn came up, he bought the oil.

A boy who graduated from Franklin with me came to see Dad about buying oil from the company he worked for. Dad said, "You bring [a sample of] the oil out and if it's good, we'll put your name in as a supplier."

Later, the fellow came back and he said, "Well, Mr. Simmons, I'm sure the oil was fine."

Dad said, "It's no good. We can't use it."

The fellow said, "Oh, I'm sorry for that. I have a check in my pocket for $500. If you take the oil, it's yours."

My father very seldom got angry, but I can see him yet. He looked at the door and he said, "You see that door? Get out of that door as fast as you can get. And you take that damned $500 and tell them to put it where it belongs!"

At first there were only two or three children there. At that time Rosewood was wasn't under the Department of Mental Health, but was ruled by a board of governors. They had a very active ladies' auxiliary who would provide all the entertainment for the children and things like that. Later they turned [the institution] over to the state.

They kept adding more buildings to the institution. They put the administration building in the center. The girls' school, Lane, was on one side of it and the boys' school on the other. They never allowed the boys and girls to associate unless they had a dance. Then it was strictly supervised. The girls were never allowed to go anyplace without being escorted, although the boys were allowed to go outside [their cottages.]

Before they brought children into Rosewood, they would give them I.Q. tests. If they tested 90 and below, they came to Rosewood. If they tested 91 and above, the boys went to Maryland Training School [now the Charles Hickey School], and the girls went to Montrose.

The first superintendent was Doctor Frank W. Keating. He was a bachelor, very straight-laced, very mannerly. He lived in one part of the Administration Building, upstairs. His offices were downstairs.

When the female teachers [who also lived in the second floor of the administration building] went out, they had to leave the keys to their rooms. At ten Dr. Keating locked the door. If they came in after that, they had to knock and he'd come down and lay the law down before he handed them their keys.

Doctor Keating would run around, and if he saw [one of the staff] doing something a little risque, he'd say to them, "Go pack your suitcases and bring them right down here!" Then, at five-thirty in the morning, he'd come and bang on our door.

Mother would say to Dad, "Doctor Keating's down there ... something's gone wrong."

[Dad would go to the door] and Doctor Keating would say, "I want you to take so-and so's suitcases to such-and-such a place."

He was the limit!

But he was good to the kids. And he was a fine doctor. He was grand to my father and to my brother Wilbur. It was just women [he couldn't deal with].

In 1942, I came back to Rosewood as a teacher. My sister-in-law, Louise Simmons, was principal of the school at the time, and she said, "I need a teacher for the older boys [from twelve to sixteen]. Help me out for a little while until I get somebody." So I went, and they never did get anybody else."

When I went there, it just made me sick. Even though I'd lived there all those years I'd never gotten mixed up with the schools. I met the teacher whose place I was taking and she said, "Now this boy likes birds ... just give him lots of birds to look at. This boy likes to do this ... this boy likes to do that."

Boys' Woodshop At Rosewood, 1915
Boys at Rosewood received manual training as part of their curriculum. Photo
courtesy of Mary Simmons Marshall.

I said, "I don't want to know that. I want to know where is he reading? What is he doing in arithmetic?"

We didn't have books at first. There were books there, but they
were not their type [because they were designed for much younger
children. The story of the three bears. Kindergarten stuff. So we
used some stories out of books, and I wrote my own stories. I'd get
books and try them and if the stories were too easy, I'd get something
a little harder. Finally, we had a book salesman who came, and by
that time they were beginning to look into helping retarded children,
and later that became "Special Education." The salesman had some
very good seatwork books, and each child could have his own books.

We also wrote a lot of stories ourselves and illustrated them.

We got a school-bus while I was there, and then we could take the children out. Charlie Good was our chauffeur and we took them to a number of places. We took them to the *Sun* newspaper office, because some of them had been former newsboys. We took them to the telephone company so they could see the switchboard. When they started to put dial phones in, one of the men from C&P brought me a phone so we could teach the children to dial.

We took them to a bank down in Pikesville so they could see money being put in and drawn out. Mr. William Foley was in charge and he was very cooperative. They gave each of the boys a bankbook. Afterwards, we set up a bank in the classroom. If their parents gave them a nickel or a penny, they could save it. We had a sheet there and one boy was the cashier, another had to count the money, another wrote it in the book.

[Frank Velnosky, the boys' shop teacher] and I planned to take the boys out to a restaurant. I told this to one of the Jewish women who came to Rosewood as a volunteer ... that I wanted to take the boys out to lunch so they could learn to read a menu, learn to talk to the waitress, and so forth. She said, "How much [money] do you think you'll need to do this?"

I said, "At least fifty dollars. But they're saving their money."

She said, "Let them keep their own money to spend ... I'll give you the fifty dollars."

So we went to the restaurant. The boys were given their money that morning. They could pick out what they wanted [from the menu]. I would say, "Now do you know how much that costs?" They would show me the price. I would say, "That's right. Now if you buy that, maybe you won't be able to buy anything else." You see, we wanted them to see the amount they were spending.

Everything went along fine until we came to the tip. "What's a tip?" the children wanted to know.

I said, "Well, we had such good service, the young girls waited on us, they brought us our food and everything, and this is our way of saying 'thank you' to them. Each one put a nickel in," I told them.

Next day in school we took all the new words they had learned and that was our reading lesson. "Tip" was a new word in their life. We also listed everything we'd learned about going out to eat -- that we take a bath, that we wear our new clothes, that we thank the waitresses, that we thank our chauffeur who drove the bus and tell him how nice it was. All this. Manners. Everything.

Rosewood had its own band even in the early years. Professor Feldman, who was head of the Baltimore City Municipal Band came out every two weeks to conduct the institution's band. Later, one of his students, Bob Landsinger, came out and took over the band full time. *-Mary Simmons Marshall*

It gives [The Board of Visitors of the Rosewood State Training School] pleasure to state that the high standing which this institution enjoys ... has been carefully maintained. Its continued prosperity, its rapid growth in accomodations for its pupils, the increased number of its inmates, its efficient and economical administration and the great benefits conferred upon the people of the state in having removed from their midst the helpless, dependent, mentally afflicted, who, unless controlled and restrained become a charge upon the public and a menace to society, will commend it to your most favorable consideration.

The Ladies' Aid Society continues its interest in the comfort and pleasure of the children, and is highly appreciated. Their kindness and motherly sympathy for these isolated unfortunates fills their hearts with joy and happiness and helps to make their new home bright and cheerful.

The board wishes to express to your Excellency the high esteem in which Dr. Frank W. Keating is held. He has filled the position of Superintendent for 19 years with marked ability and efficiency. *—Herman Stump*, President of the Board from 14th Annual Report of the Board of Visitors of Rosewood State Training School September 30, 1915

# CHAPTER 16

## Black Cats and Shoes on the Stove

*Considering that many of our narrators lived in an era when science could do little to cure deadly diseases and was equally helpless to explain many of the natural phenonema, it is small wonder magic was often employed as a precaution and that omens were carefully heeded.*

-/-/-/-

Uncle Buck [Ritter] would come in and Mom would have the little kid's shoes up to dry [by the stove]. He's say, "Mary, that child will never rest while those shoes are there! They belong down!"

They used to say that down here where the old school house was, that was haunted. And then, in the hollow up where Carpet Fair [on Reisterstown Road, south of Franklin Boulevard] is, they say [it's haunted] there. One time when we had to go to the store, I said, "John, there's a chair there!" [He told me] there'd be ghosts there. I told Mr. Will at the fast food place [Twin Kiss Drive-in], "This place here is haunted, Mr. Will!"

And [there was] this man, Bell, who lived in the old Nelson house, the third house [north of here]. He proposed to my grandfather's sister and she did not accept him and he killed himself. Shot himself. My great-aunt Kate used to [show me the blood stain] and tell me that if anyone takes their [own] life, that blood doesn't [come off]. But you know, the boards could have been pine and it [might have] soaked in.
*-Dorothy King*

Grandmother Kendig put cats out of the house before a storm because she believed they attracted lightning.

If someone borrows salt, don't let them bring it back because that's bad luck.

Plant beans and potatoes with the eye up, or they will grow down to China.

If you make sauerkraut on a waning moon the brine will go to the bottom of the crock and the kraut will be spoiled.

My mother was very superstitious. *-Helen Kendig Bowers*

If it didn't rain on [St. Swithin's] day, it wouldn't rain for forty days.
*-Bessie Moser vonGunten*

Never take the last piece of cake, candy, etc., or you will be an old maid.

You must give a penny if you hand anyone a knife, or it will cut your love in two.

If you sew on Sunday, you will have to pick stitches out with your nose after you die.

Giving an empty pocketbook brings bad luck. Put a penny in it.

If a black cat crosses your path that's bad luck, but it's okay if you spit into your hat.

Tickling a baby's feet will cause him to stammer.

Dreaming of fresh fish meant someone in the house was pregnant.

Signs of death: Birds flying into the house; a tea-towel hanging on a door knob; a picture falling [from the wall].

Don't count the cars in a funeral procession or someone else will die soon.

If you put your clothes on inside out, it's bad luck to change them.
*-Genevieve Berryman Kelley*

If you heard a knock on the door and there was nobody there when you went, that was an omen somebody was going to die. *-Mary Kendig Gettierre*

There were a number of superstitions about lightning: On Ascension Day you must eat with spoons - to use anything sharp would cause lightning to strike you. Do not use a needle or fork when it is storming - all points draw lightning.

A person who burns brush on Sunday will have his face on the moon.

If moonlight shines in a baby's eyes the child will be color-blind.

Sleepy chickens hatch from eggs laid during dog days.

If hogs are killed during the days of the waning moon, the meat will shrivel.

A woman must never trim a man's hair, or he will lose his strength.

Snakes cause cows to give bloody milk.

"He who sings before seven will cry before eleven."

If you forget something and must turn back, sit down and count to eleven before leaving again.

To insure light bread, pinch off a bit of dough while kneading the batch, toss the broken bit over your left shoulder and say a silent prayer.

Don't let a boy with mumps cross running water.

If your shoes make your feet itch, the leather was made from an animal that had died.

The first thunder after Easter wakens the snakes.

When moving to a new home, carry the Bible in first for good luck.

"A whistling woman and a crowing hen is fit for neither God nor men."

Don't cut your hair when the moon is waning or you will have headaches.

Several places in the neighborhood were thought to be haunted. The cupolo on Phil Knatz's house [at Therapia Farm] was said to be frequented by the ghost of one of the Frangmeyers. A house on Pleasant

Hill Road was said to be haunted by a deceased wife who returned to haunt her husband. Ghosts were also thought to frequent a spot on East Pleasant Hill Road near the Pleasant Hill Church graveyard. Horses were said to shy at an unseen object along Caves Road. And, of course, the ghost of John Berry was said to haunt Deer Park Road at Berry's Hill. *-E. Bennett Bowen*

They say that if a colored person came [to your house] on New Year's Day, that would bring you good luck. But never a woman -- that would bring you bad luck ... don't let a woman in your house on New Year's Day. Ike Ghee used to come to our house and Mama'd give him wine.

Another thing they firmly believed was that you never make a change when you come and go. [Visitors always had to go out the same door they came in.] We were born and raised to it - never let a person "cross your house" as they called it.

The old-time people did [believe in] those things - the younger generation laugh themselves to death! I was in the nursing home after I had an operation and I was supposed to go home on Saturday. They say that "Saturday flitting is short sitting" - that means that if you move on Saturday you won't stay long. I said, "I'm not going home on Saturday!" I didn't. I waited until Monday morning. That's foolish, I know, but a lifetime habit's hard to break. *-Grace Bowen Pape*

Edward G. Knatz
Photo courtesy of Frances Knatz Price

# CHAPTER 17

## Some People We Remember

*While Owings Mills has produced no figures of national importance, there are a number of local residents who were remembered by many of our narrators as being exceptional and worthy of comment. There seems no common thread that would explain why memories of these particular persons have been so long retained, and their lives, their personalities and their occupations are as disparate as they are intriguing.*

-/-/-/-

### "E.G." -- Edward Gerhart Knatz

Edward Gerhart Knatz was a German immigrant who settled in West Baltimore near Hollins Market. His father operated a grocery store where he specialized in sugar, coffee, tea and goods not easily obtainable in the nearby market. E.G., as he was generally known, entered his father's business and was popular as a clerk in the store. Later, he opened his own store, specializing in sugar, molasses and a few imported products.

E. G. Knatz married Sarah Rebecca Hoffman and they became the parents of seven boys and one girl. The two oldest children were twin boys, one of whom died in infancy. The other, P. Hoffman, became an artist of considerable talent. Edward Gerhart, known as "Hartzie", entered his father's business and made his home in the city. John, the third son, was jovial and well-liked; he married and moved to Westminster where he entered the chicken business. Bolton E. Knatz served in World War I; he lived most of his adult life outside of Maryland. [Philip, Stuart and a daughter, Frances, remained in the Owings Mills area.]

In the late 1800s, the Knatz family moved to the former Grupy/Fangmeyer farm which is the area occupied by Morningside and a large field beyond the railroad tracks now occupied by the Colts football complex.

Philip became proprietor of "Therapia", the Knatz farm in Owings Mills [now site of the Morningside Apartments]. He married Miss Mary Turnbaugh and their children were Philip, Jr., Betty, Becky and Phyllis.

345

R. Stuart, who was in the automobile and insurance business, lived in his father's home. He married Gladys Fox and they had one son, Robert S. Knatz, a realtor who now lives in Reisterstown. A daughter, Frances Knatz Price, who resides on the Garrison Forest Road, became a teacher. -*E. Bennett Bowen*

My grandfather moved out here in the late 1800s. [At first], they used to come out only in the summer time, but early in 1903 they moved here permanently. My father was born here.

At that time [my grandfather] owned a house as well as Therapia Farm. The house and the farm were originally owned by my grandfather's sister who married a Fangmeyer and my grandfather [later] bought it, I understand. Another house that was identical with my grandfather's house was the one that was at the entrance to what is now Morningside Heights -- the house where Miss Minnie Koerner lived. -*Robert S. Knatz*

[Mr. Knatz] was a tiny little dark-complected man with whiskers. Very tiny. [He had something to do with [a sugar company in Baltimore]. Then he sold it. To King Syrup ... Mangels-Herold. -*Virginia Clark Hoff*

Me and all the Knatz boys were great friends. Even the old man -- Mr. Knatz. I'd go over to [Carp's] barber shop and he'd be in there and he'd always have something he wanted me to come over to the house for. He had the prettiest dahlias all the way up through that bottom. I don't know how many times I had to go over and see his dahlias. He used to ride the streetcar, and he always used to sit on the back seat alongside of me. -*Henry Hipsley*

In 1905 a section of railroad was re-located. They straightened it and made a double-track road. Mr. Knatz opposed greatly their putting the pylon in the middle across Reisterstown Road. He wanted a single span. Nobody supported him so we got the pylon - it's still there - and it has caused a number of accidents as he forecast. -*E. B. Bowen*

Mr. Knatz was a constant visitor [at the old Owings Mills Elementary School.] He was very small and a little unique with his little goatee and his mustache and he was always twirling the ends. He had a cane. He would come in and talk to Mr. Shaver up front ... take his cane and point all around. He was on the school board you know.

They always had refreshments at PTA meetings and different parents would fix them. This once, my mother was on the committee and cup-cake papers had just come out. She said, "I'm going to put mine in the papers because it's easier [to serve]."

They noticed Mr. Knatz was a long time eating his cake. He said, "Bertha, you've always been such a good cook, but the crust on these cupcakes is really tough!" He was eating the paper! -*Genevieve Berryman Kelley*

I'll tell you somebody else who walked with a cane - that was Edward Knatz, the sugar king. He must have been a trustee ... because he had the habit of coming and stomping around with that cane during school. I let him know. I said, "Look, you may be a trustee, but you're not going to do that here!" "Who's talking to me like that?" he said. But he was all right after I talked to him. He just liked to come up there and let people know who he was. *-William C. Hull*

Well, many times at eight, nine o'clock I'd be sweeping the floor ready to close and old Mr. Knatz would come in. Of course, no one could out-talk Mr. Knatz! *-Frank Burkholder*

## Wesley and Mary Mack

You see, Wesley [Mack] was pretty religious. He used to like to talk about King Solomon. He'd talk about how Solomon was richer than any of these rich guys ... how they couldn't hold a candle to him with all these horses and things he had. [Wesley] was pretty good - he knew his Bible. *-Carl A. vonGunten*

I can see him going along now [in his long overcoat]. His mother was a thoroughbred Indian. She had long hair down to here in big plaits. They lived back in Soldiers Delight. *-Minnie Clark Hebron*

The Mack family lived first on the Lehnert property. There was Si, Wes, Norris, Oscar and their mother and some daughters. [Later] they lived in the house down over the hill on the Dolfield place. The most memorable one of the Macks was Mary. She was Wes's wife. For years, she'd go to Mr. Garner's store on Saturday after she had collected her week's money for washing. She bought her supplies and put them in a gunny sack and tied it shut. When she got two sacks full - she took care not to put too much in the second one - she'd place the first sack on her head and she'd hike on back Dolfield Road. She told me once that the trip back there was hard, but the peace and quiet when she got home was worth it. *-E. Bennett Bowen*

[The Macks] worked hard and did their best to bring their children up. Wes Mack had the original old handlebar mustache. It really did come out and go down. He would be talking and you couldn't take your eyes off that mustache because he could make it turn so.

He was a good gardener. He did a lot of work for Mother. He used to stand down there in that flower garden and he had that darned long coat on - hot as the devil! I'd ask him, "Wes, what in the world you got that overcoat on for?" "Well..." he'd twist his mustache and say, "you know this overcoat keeps the cold out in winter and keeps me warm. Likewise, I wear this coat in summer to keep the heat out and keep me cool." And he'd be sweating! *-William D. Groff, Jr.*

I remember him coming to the church and always interested in the church. He made a loan when they first started building the church. He gave $67 and I've got records of where his money was paid back.

He was quite a character. He always used to say to me, "Watch and pray! Watch and pray!" We used to laugh when he said that, but that is more true now ... that's about what you can do – watch and pray.  *–Viola Clark Nesbitt*

Miss Katie Cradock, about 1950
Photo courtesy of Mary Simmons Marshall

## Miss Katie Cradock

[Miss Katie Cradock] was just like something on a wire! – wiry as she could be up until she was pretty near a hundred years old. She'd get up a bunch of children that needed attention, needed glasses or something, and she'd take them to Hopkins, and she'd spend the day, and she'd bring them home, and she'd dump them off out here, and she'd say, "Margaret, will you take these children home for me?" Well, Margaret got the job of delivering all the kids home!

[Miss Katie] was very funny – she'd get on the streetcar and she'd say, "I'm sorry, but I haven't got any change." And she got in the car, and I don't think she ever paid any carfare.

Miss Katie got what she wanted, believe me! She'd stomp that little foot of hers and shake her fist and she'd get what she wanted. She had that [Confederate] Soldier's Home [now Maryland State Police Headquarters] down there [in Pikesville] restored.

That was ready to be bumped down, but no sir! – it didn't get bumped down! And that's there today just due to her.

And the Health Center [in Pikesville] likewise. She did an awful lot around this neighborhood, I'm telling you. If anybody needed anything, they'd get it, and she'd see to it that *somebody* would pay for it. It never seemed she had the money to go ahead, but she'd demand what she wanted and she got it. Nobody was ever too big for her to stand up to. *–Virginia Clark Hoff*

She taught me in Sunday School and she didn't take any foolishness! There were about five of us in the class – the Knellers, Elizabeth Perkins and one of the "valley girls". One time I said something and she said, "Hush! Don't be so fresh!" *–Ruth King*

It didn't matter what denomination ... mattered not at all. At Christmas when they gave things out, if there were people in need of something, she'd ask the class to find out. Some kids would say, "They don't come here to Sunday School." She'd say, "That doesn't matter!" She'd give to anyone if they'd need this or that. ... [go] to their door summer or winter – there'd be something to eat or drink.

This is what Miss Katie would say [to the streetcar conductor]: "Stop at the black walnut!" As if everybody knew what kind of walnut tree it was! And if Miss Katie saw something she wanted, she'd just bring it out on the streetcar just like that ... not wrapped or anything. See, that was all right for Miss Katie to do that way. Now someone like me would be too proud, but here she was with her wealth and a blue blood and everything setting up front on the streetcar! *–Dorothy King*

I used to ride the streetcar with [Miss Katie Cradock] when we were going to school. She was very small but very lively. Just always talking. And she always used to have some little boys or girls riding with her on the streetcar that she was taking care of. Took children down there [to Trentham], I don't know whether to raise but to care for ... had them there so many weeks. Like, you know, they could bring in the wood or the kindling and do this or that and they got fed well.

I understand that when [Miss Katie] passed they were supposed to build that Kernan's Hospital there [at Trentham]. But there was some sort of misunderstanding between she and her brother ... that's a long story, you know ... that's what you call backwoods talk or backstairs, or whatever. *-Viola Clark Nesbitt*

Girl Scout Troop 83 met here at the school. They were sponsored by Miss Katie [Cradock]. She was really a community worker. We'd borrow everything down at St. Thomas church when we had a Christmas program. And she gave us I don't know how many pictures to put in the halls. She'd come up here with those long skirts! And the way she died! *-William C. Hull*

Miss Katie Cradock was very much involved in all kinds of church activities. They had a junior choir while I was of an age to be in a junior choir, and she was the supervisor of it. She sat about five pews back from the front and she used to shake her head, shake her head – well, she had a tic, but she also had plenty of reason to [shake her head]. I once got into a semi-fistfight sitting up in the chancel – that was when she really shook her head! *-George Ward*

Once a year, she sent us boys up to a camp in Canada for a week ... we'd stay in those cabins up there. *-John Kellar*

Agnes [Cradock] used to get so mad with Katie Cradock. She said that Katie ran around all the time and didn't do anything. Those times ... [the Cradocks] had help. Mr. Thomas Cradock would go to Baltimore and bring out the help to work on the farms. My husband could never understand that. He said, "Why with those old big-behinded horses, it would be better to sell the farm ... he's not making anything ... feeding those horses all winter." Of course that cheap labor was what caused [Miss Katie's] death. One night they thought this fellow that had been [working] during the day had gone home, but he didn't. He had bought a lot of beer and went in the barn ... and got drunk. Then he ... robbed and beat Miss Katie to death. *-Laura W. Redifer*

I was a little boy when the last generation of Cradocks were in their prime. They were very good friends of my family and we used to go down there [to Trentham] on Sunday afternoons, driving in the buggy or the runabout. There was Mrs. Cradock who was a very old lady whom I hardly remember. Her children were Mr. Tom, Mr. Arthur, Miss Katie, Miss Agnes – Agnes was a very good-looking redhead – and Miss Lilly, whose actual name was "Julia."

By 1953, Tom Cradock had died, Agnes Cradock had died, and Miss Katie and Arthur were left. Some colored man broke in the house and chopped Miss Katie up with an axe and attacked Mr. Arthur. I was in the fire department at that time and [my son] George, Junior, had just joined the fire department. In the middle of a very, very cold night, we were wakened by the fire siren. When we reported down to the fire house to see where the fire was, we found out we were wanted to form a posse. We were to attempt to track down the person who had attacked Miss Katie and Mr. Arthur.

We went down to the Cradock house in cars, must have been about fifty people there - police, firemen, other. Some of them had brought guns - thank God I didn't have any guns! That was a little scary.

The idea was that the man [who committed the crime] had apparently rushed out of the house and was not too far away. There was right heavy snow on the ground. It had been trampled up, though, by all these people arriving; there wasn't much chance of tracking him.

It was extremely cold and the part our group from Owings Mills was assigned to was to go right to the top of Tobins Hill, the woods there that came down to Greenspring Valley Road [and Reisterstown Road]. We spread out in a line about fifteen feet apart and beat our way through that woods over to Cradock's Lane. They had just timbered out that woods, and there were tree tops and limbs and God only knows what all over the place. You practically had to go on your hands and knees. We were trying to stay about twenty feet apart and there were plenty of times you didn't know where the nearest person was.

I was a little bit scared. Anyhow, we all eventually got back to the house [without finding the man]. By that time, Miss Katie had died. We were very much upset about it, but nothing could be done.

The next morning, I was a little bit late going to work after being up at night. Going down Reisterstown Road, right at the center of Pikesville where the Odd Fellows Hall [Red Man's Hall] was, they had a road-block set up. They were stopping every car that came down the road to look and see if this colored person was in the vehicle.

Actually, that's the way they caught him. He had apparently hidden overnight in the barn over at the Blaustein property. In the morning, when he thought everything had calmed down, he came out and hitched a ride. When they got down to the road-block, before they were anywhere near where the police were, he jumped out and started to run. They caught him. -*George B. P. Ward*

In the midst of dealing with some person who had strayed far from the moral and social code, she would speak in no uncertain terms of what she considered the wrong action and then, with great tenderness and wise counseling, would bring to bear on the situation constructive thought and action necessary to help restore a broken life, oft-times from the midst of degradation and shame. Fearlessly, she would interview judges, police, physicians and business men ... ever ready to break a lance in what she considered a worthy cause. Her shocking death cast a shadow over many lives. -*The Reverend Philip J. Jensen*, in a memorial to Miss Katherine Cradock. In reprint edition of Eleanor Stewart Heiser's book, *Days Gone By* June 22, 1953

Old Katie, oh, yeah! If I'd got a-hold of that bird that used the axe on her, they wouldn't have had to try him. I'd of hung him sure! -*Frank Nelson Schaefer*

## Albert Eiser, A Genuine Handyman

Albert Eiser - he was also known as Albert Sellman - was a handyman, a genuine handyman. He could do anything! He lived in a little

house on Academy Avenue, but he was born over near Foster's farm –
back in the woods in a log cabin right beside a stream.

He used to come for threshing or if something needed repairing. He
was always handy with a hammer and a saw. He could lay bricks, he
could pour concrete, he helped to build chicken houses. Signs of his
work are all over our place.

He had a green thumb and he raised rabbits and pigeons and chickens and guinea pigs and white mice. He was a great collector – he
had a donkey and a cart and he'd collect all sorts of things as he made
his rounds. *-Waiva Dean Reese*

### "Doctor" Demmitt

My grandfather had this medicine he used to make. It was called
Demmitt's Catarrh Medicine and Liver Pills. Actually, it was a patent
medicine, but he would never patent it. He was a little hard-headed.
He said if he patented it, everyone would know how he made it.

He used local herbs and all in it. He made it down the cellar. It
was stinking stuff sometimes when he was brewing it.

At one time there, he was doing pretty good ... had a couple of
wagons and salesmen and all. The Vicks people wanted to buy his
formula, and he was almost ready to sell it to them. Then they said
that if they bought it, they'd have to change its name ... it could no
longer go under the name of "Dr. Demmitt's Catarrh Medicine." When
they said that, the deal was off. *-John Kellar*

The Demmitt Family, about 1915
"Doctor" Demmitt surrounded by his six duaghters and several of their friends.
Photo courtesy of Lillian Demmitt Moser.

[Doctor Demmitt] made pills. They were for constipation. I don't remember what he said was in them. It was something that looked like soft coal ... real black. Everyone bought them. Grandfather Hoff always had those pills in his pocket. Now they recommend Milk of Magnesia. -*Virginia Clark Hoff*

My father would make his catarrh medicine in a big kettle, he'd have a big iron kettle he made it in. We used to have to fill all these bottles. [The medicine] had menthol in it ... it'd clear your head right up. -*Louise Demmitt Fox*

He used to walk like over to Oakland and he'd be gone a week or so at a time when he was on the road. He had catarrh medicine and liver pills. He told the story on himself about the liver pills: Somebody had this dog that was constipated and he said, 'Give the dog a couple of liver pills.' And he said he never did see the damn dog after that! -*Lee Fox*

### Frank Price and "Morgan"

[Frank Price] had a farm out on Gwynnbrook Avenue. In earlier years he was a motorman on the streetcars. Then he started farming and he used to bring his milk down to the Gwynnbrook station where they sent it to Baltimore. Each morning he would come in the store, and he would get two cakes of yeast and a bottle of Coke and he had a special candy he bought – a coconut ball covered with chocolate. If you didn't have that kind, he didn't want any. He would sit in the store and eat his yeast and drink half of the bottle of coke and then he'd take the other half out and give it to his horse, Morgan. That horse would drink the Coke same as a person.
Frank Price lived alone. Part of his house was burned and then he just lived in a couple of rooms.
After they stopped shipping milk from the Gwynnbrook Station, he had to haul it down to Owings Mills and send it into Baltimore. He had a horse and a cart. One time he was driving out on Reisterstown Road and a car hit him.
He was hurt very badly that time. He was in the hospital for quite a while but they got him mended and he came back and went back to work. He was a very strong, husky man. -*Helen Kendig Bowers*

Frank Price's father and my mother were brother and sister. I used to ride down there on Saturday night and he loved to play checkers. We'd set there and play checkers all night. -*Henry Hipsley*

When we first moved down from Westminster we lived at Frank Price's farm. He was never married. I don't think he ever owned a car. He must have saved all his money and invested it. He always had a mouthful of gold teeth, you know. -*Bessie Moser vonGunten*

Mr. Price used to come out in the field here and spread manure. Oh, he was a strange one! Everybody said he was well fixed as far as money goes, but he was just an old hermit. He lived in the worst poverty. He had cut a hole in the door so the dogs could go in and out and he'd buy a great big bag of dog food and just set it there for them to eat when they wanted. *-Elsie Durham*

Frank Price came from Burnside Farm to become a conductor on the streetcars. That's where he got the seven or eight thousand dollars to buy that farm back there [at the intersection of Garrison Forest and Gwynnbrook Roads].

We had a little pot-bellied stove in the mill office. Mr. Price would come in and he'd be soaked ... have that cow-manure - you know how that smells! - and he'd come up and hang around that stove. I'd usually find something else to do away from there ... down in the mill. He wore the worst clothes you ever saw. He was just as apt to stay wet for four or five days ... sleep in the barn ... did everything he could to kill himself and lived to be 83 or 84.

His horse's name was Morgan ... a great, big gray. There was a kind of rut on the side of [Bonita Avenue], and his cart's wheel would cut down in that rut and Frank would sort of sleep and old Morgan would just walk along ... go right along down the road. Morgan knew *exactly* where to go ... he'd cross the railroad track by himself, looking both ways, go down Reisterstown Road, look up, look down, and then the horse decided when to go across the road.

That darn horse was addicted to Coke. Mr. Price would go down there to Wisner's store, buy that Coke, a chocolate bar, cigars and a dozen old saltines. When he'd come out of the store that horse would start to whinny. Frank would hook the bottle right in the corner of the horse's mouth, and he'd take the whole thing - Glub! ... Glub! - the whole thing!

That was the horse that got hit in front of Wisner's store. He'd been knocked about as far as from here to the other side of that kitchen. He ended up in front of Warren's house, next to where the glue factory is now - Hoff's old garage. Morgan was all wrapped up in the electric wires, and he had sense enough to stand there until somebody came.

[They took Frank Price to Maryland General hospital] and Daddy said to me, "You're a great friend of his. You better call down there and tell them this man [only] *looks* like a rag-picker."

I got hold of someone at Maryland General and told them a man was coming in unconscious, and he would look like the worst bum you've ever seen, but he's from out here at Owings Mills and he owns a beautiful farm and he's worth a lot of money. "You take care of him, give him the very best of attention and I'll guarantee you'll be paid." They worked on him and I talked to the doctor later and he said, "I'll guarantee that your description was right!" *-William D. Groff, Jr.*

### Captain John R. Sherwood and Watson Sherwood

[The Sherwoods] lived on Park Heights Avenue in the winter. Captain John R. was captain of the Old Bay line. Oh, he was a nice man.

I've hunted rabbits with Captain John R. and he used an old black-powder musket. He could hit them with it.

Henry Yox was the farm overseer [on the Sherwood place]. "Daddy" Yox. The Sherwoods would come out on the streetcar to Owings Mills and have Henry meet them. Two horses and a surrey ... surrey with a fringe on top. Then they got an automobile ... old Chalmers ... only had one door. Two doors in the back but only one in front. It was a right-hand drive. The gear-shift was up in the door. Oh, that was old!

That family, all of them were real nice - Watson and John and [the] three girls. I've hunted rabbits with them all. -*Frank Parker*

Old Mr. Sherwood was a rather tall man and Mrs. Sherwood was a small woman - right perky. They came here in the summer and went down to Sarasota [Florida] in the winter.

John and Watty [started the (Sherwood Oil) Company]. They had Betholine and Richfield. Richfield was the straight gas and Betholine was the good [higher octane] gas. At one time that was the big thing around here. Their signs were these elephants ... big cement elephants. That was their emblem. -*Bessie Moser vonGunten*

Watson Sherwood was a lawyer and he handled [a legal matter] for my grandmother, the little affair when us kids were all minors when my father died. He lived down on Rosewood Lane. In fact, Mr. Marshall who built this house [also] built that house ior him. -*Lee Fox*

When I was a little kid, Fred Dolfield owned the property on the opposite side of Rosewood Lane from us. [Fred's father], A. Y. Dolfield, had bought it along with other property around Owings Mills. Watson Sherwood bought it and built a house there. I helped him build it. I was about sixteen [at the time].

We were reasonably friendly with the Sherwoods. When it got to be my third year of law school, I decided I had better be hunting a job. This was 1931, and I finally got a job with Mullikin, Stockbridge and Waters. What I didn't know was that at the same time I was negotiating with them for a job, they were negotiating with Watson Sherwood to join the firm. He and I practically walked in there the same day. We both had a falling out with the firm eventually, and, again, this was the same day. We both left and eventually had an office together downstairs in the same building.

Watson Sherwood represented Sherwood Brothers [Petroleum Company]. [His father], Captain John R. Sherwood, eventually became president of the Old Bay Line, [a steamship company out of Baltimore]; he was the one who bought [the farm on Sherwood Road]. John W. Sherwood, who was Watson's brother, was the organizer and president of Sherwood Brothers, Inc. [Petroleum Company].

Watson built what he called Persimmon Lodge - a log cabin [on the Sherwood farm]. He and Fred Dolfield and a couple of other guys had the Red Dog Lodge. Watson and Fred used to go up there on Sunday mornings and just sit around on the porch and look out across Soldier's Delight.

Watson used to get Huey Zeigler to work for him. He would be sitting out on his stone terrace and he would say, "You know this is just the same thing as having a mortgage on this place. What I have to pay Huey to get the weeds out is just about the interest on a mortgage. I can never pay it off." *-George Ward*

Mr. Watson Sherwood had his first law office in the house where the post office was before he spread out and went into town.
We used to visit him ... used to sit over there in the pines at his cabin in the woods. Of a night where them whipporwills would be screaming. Henry would be bound to go over and see Mr. Sherwood and I would be scared to death of those things a–screaming! *-Virginia Clark Hoff*

### "Bumblebee": Raymond Thuma

Do you know what Bumblebee could do? He could take a piece of paper and hold it up over his head and cut out the most wonderful things. He always had a shopping bag. *-Helen Carpenter*

He used to walk the car–tracks! Never fall off. He'd go by our house, and even if it was two or three o'clock in the morning, he'd yell out: "Toddy Carpenter! ... Toddy Carpenter!" He hollered out at every house he passed. *-James Carpenter, Jr.*

[You'd see him] along the road and at carnivals and back at Angelier's. Cutting out things and making music. I think he played the mouth-organ. He went to a lot of people's houses. He had a sister up in Taneytown he stayed with a while. People couldn't call him by his right name because they didn't know it. But that noise, he always made ... like a bumblebee humming. *-Bessie Moser vonGunten*

He was always at the carnivals. I think he got his paper from a paper mill up in Hampstead. Of course, you had to pay for these things, but they were absolutely perfect. He came from Rosewood. He wasn't [retarded] enough to stay there. Ilf you gave him a sandwich and a cup of coffee, he would eat it and be on his way.
In World War II when sugar and candy was unavailable, a person could go up to Bumblebee and ask for a Hershey bar and he would reach inside his shirt and pull one out and sell it for 25 cents. (The going price was 5 cents ... and Hershey bars were much bigger.)
Bumblebee could clack his feet on the railroad tracks, sing and cut out at the same time. One time when I was a newspaper man, I had a free afternoon and decided to go to the old Gayety Theater on Baltimore Street. As I was watching the show I felt someone tap my shoulder and a voice said, "You think I'm crazy, but I got in here for nothing." It was Bumblebee.
Another time Gordon White and I were in an ice-cream parlor, and Bumblebee asked us for a ride down the road. We pointed out a car and told him to go sit in it. He did so, not realizing it wasn't our car at all, but someone else's. When he found out the joke we'd pulled on him, Bumblebee cussed a blue streak. Wouldn't talk to either of us for about two years. *-Roland Fox*

# CHAPTER 18

## All-Togethering It Over Politics

*Political ties in Owings Mills - as in all of Baltimore County - were overwhelmingly Democratic. For those with an active interest in government, political affiliation fulfilled both a civic and a social function.*

$-/-/-/-$

Way back -- I remember them talking about it more than anything - Mr. Roy Lowe was killed coming down from Goodwin's [Livery Stable] in Reisterstown. You know, all the fun they had then was when it was politic-ing. That was something! They'd gang there at Reisterstown and chew it over and then when they got to the blacksmith shop or something like that [they'd start fighting about it.]

[Anyhow, a group of fellows] were coming down the road from Goodwin's, and colored boys - they'd all-together it sometimes - they threw stones. Roy didn't die that night, but he died the next day after the stone struck him back of the ear. Roy was a law student at the time, only about twenty-one, twenty-two years old. -*Dorothy King*

Until about 1910, it was necessary to go to Reisterstown to vote. Until 1920, only men could vote.

Dishonest polling practices were often discussed. One man recalled: "Drinks and money flowed near the polls. When I left home on election day, I determined to get as much as possible of both. I sold my vote to each man who asked, pocketed the money, drank the whiskey and went on to find another sucker. After I had as much money as seemed reasonable, I went into the polls and voted for whoever I chose." -*E. Bennett Bowen*

In November 1928, the Fourth District Democratic Club was started by William D. Brown, Lester W. Brown, Charles S. Brown and Charles L. Hammond, who later became Treasurer of Baltimore County.

We started this club during the Al Smith campaign, when they started to mix religion with politics. We all felt that this would be the wrong policy.

We started to get precinct workers in each of the five precincts -- Reisterstown, Glyndon, Owings Mills, Delight and Boring. Chestnut Ridge was added later, making six precincts.

The Fourth District Democratic Club, about 1955

The 4th District Democratic Club took an active role in local and state politics. Shown left to right: Fred Cooper, Louis Susemihl, Charles Forbes, Jr., Daisy Linker, Baltimore County Commissioner Dale Anderson, Robert S. Knatz, Jr., Adelaide Huffman, Philip Knatz, William D. Brown, Dan Allewalt. Photo courtesy of William D. Brown.

In later years, the wives of the members were invited to join also. Mrs. Daisy Linker was the only woman committeeman to be elected by the Fourth District. Christian H. Kahl was elected County Commissioner and then Chief Executive of Baltimore County. Daniel Brewster was elected to the U. S. Senate.

I can't remember the Club ever endorsing anyone in any primary, but in the general election the Club worked for the Democratic nominee. Neither can I remember ever losing a general election for the nominee in Baltimore County.

Before the Franklin D. Roosevelt election, we had a Torch Light Parade which started in Reisterstown, through Glyndon, down Reisterstown Road to Pikesville, circled in Pikesville and returned to the Firemen's Grove in Reisterstown. At least fifty or more cars participated, each car having two flares on it.

If the Club wanted something done in the district, two members would go to the Commissioner or Chief Executive and they were always recognized. Most of the policemen, firemen and Fourth District road workers were endorsed by at least two or more club members.

Every year we held some affair at the Firemen's Grove and had corn, hot dogs, potato chips, pretzels, soft drinks, etc., all mostly donated. We also had a raffle of a ham or something of the sort. We charged one dollar per person, and the profit [usually] amounted to $100 or a little more.

I remember going to a political affair at Timonium Fair Grounds when Governor Lane first requested a sales tax of one cent on each dollar. A man threw a handful of pennies in [the governor's] face. Governor Lane said, "Good! That's the way the pennies will start flying in to the state of Maryland!" That is only one of the old but good memories that I have. -*William D. Brown*

# CHAPTER 19

## Our Place in World Events

*While, in many respects, Owings Mills has been, and remains, a backwater where world affairs are concerned, our lives nevertheless reflect and are shaped by the events that move nations.*

-/-/-/-

### Hard Memories of Slave Days

My grandmother was a slave. She was what was called a "bound" person, she was inherited, one to the other. [She was owned by] the Worthington family up in Worthington Valley. She had a sister that was with her and somehow there was a disagreement – her sister didn't want to do [what they wanted her to] – and they sold her down to Georgia. And when you would be sold to Georgia, that would be the last you'd ever hear of each other.

This is a story Grandma told me one time. This is a horrible story, but I remember her telling it. She said that one of those Worthington women was an invalid, and she couldn't get out of her wheel chair. She had this little slave boy to tend to her. He would attend to everything – chamber pots and everything.

Now this chamber pot was a very fine piece of porcelain, big and heavy. One day the boy had emptied the pot, and when he came to open the door it took a piece out of the pot. And this was awful! The woman had this old whip that she whipped slaves with across her lap and she said to him, "I'm going to beat you to death today, or I'm going to Hell trying to do so!"

As she said that, she took this whip in her hand and came down with it toward the boy. She didn't get him, although she hit so hard she left a mark on the door. And with that, she fell out of her chair dead on her face.

All those things, my Grandmother used to tell me. She'd tell about times way back and the tears would roll down her face. She'd cry and I'd get to crying and we'd all have a crying time. But that was the way those people lived – they had those great big farms with lots and lots of people that they kept around. All up that [Worthington Valley] way's haunted. *–Minnie Clark Hebron*

361

My father told me some about old Dick Worthington for whom Worthington Valley and "Dick's Hill" [on Greenspring Avenue] are named. He heard this from an itinerant shoemaker who traveled through the country and would stay several days at each house while making and repairing shoes. According to the shoemaker, one Sunday morning while he was fixing shoes for Dick Worthington and his slaves, he was sitting on a stonepile with Dick, watching the slaves file by to church. Several times, when a light-colored child went by, old Dick said, "That's one of mine."

It is said that Dick Worthington never married, that he was very vigorous, and that every morning he would run to the spring, about two hundred feet from his house, jump in and run back to the house cursing and yelling. [The Worthington] farm now belongs to young [Alfred] Vanderbilt, and I saw Native Dancer, the top horse of 1954, there in the barn. -from "Lone Hickory Farm Notes", October 16, 1955 by *Francis Sydney Reese*

[At Greenspring] they had slave quarters in the back yard and others spotted around - one up on the hill where the Slagles live. Some of the slaves lived in the back of the main house, which was unusual.

When Grandmother was in boarding school, her mother wrote her a letter which I still have. [The letter said] she was trying to get somebody to take one [of the slave women] because there just wasn't enough for her to do.

My grandmother told me that she wouldn't go back [to slave days] for anything in the world. She said, "Nobody knows how much responsibility it was! We had to feed them and make all of their clothes ... every single solitary bit of their clothes."

There was one slave over there who wouldn't wear any shoes. Winter or summer, nothing on her feet. My uncle said, "You ought to [have seen] her slide on the ice!" She would go up to Cradock's with an empty mug and say that nobody would give her anything, would they please give her some molasses. They'd fill her mug up with molasses and she'd come on home with it. I guess she was hungry for something sweet.

Every Christmas, everybody on the place would be put on the wagons and taken into town [Baltimore] for one day. They'd be given a fun time ... a little bit of money to spend.

When slavery was over - after the Civil War - those old slaves did not leave that place until the Old Missus died. -*Frances Benthall Marshall*

I remember Essex. That was the only name I ever knew for him. He was a big fellow, a teamster. Essex was a mystery man to everyone. Only on rare occasions would he have anything to do with anybody, black or white. When he became ill, he asked for a Catholic priest. He told the priest that he grew up on a Catholic plantation and that he had killed a white man and fled north.

Aunt Hanna Robinson, an old colored lady who had been a slave, lived behind Mr. Garner's store in a little log house before the railroad came. She had many of the characteristics of slave days -- she smoked a pipe and as she worked she chewed snuff.

Jess Cook and his family lived in a shanty beside a stream in Soldiers Delight. Jess said that when he got his freedom it took him thirty years to find out that if he was going to eat next week, he had to earn the money to buy the food. Because he was so used to having the handout from the master.

There were several others in the community who had been slaves: two I recall are the Reverend Henry Bell and Charles Coll. -E. Bennett Bowen

## Echoes of The War Between the States

My grandfather, [John Brown] was in the Civil War. "I don't like to talk about it," he says, "but I'll tell you boys so you know what you might have to put up with."

[He said] most of [the fighting] was hand-to-hand. They had a bayonet on their rifle. The rifle shot only once, and then you had to re-load it. So when you shot that once, you'd better be ready with that bayonet. Besides the rifle and bayonet they had a sword or stabbing knife or something they carried on the side of them.

He was sixteen when he enlisted, and he told them he was eighteen. He was in there four years and I think he got wounded twice. He came through Harper's Ferry, and he was commander when they took Harper's Ferry.

And he wound up at Gettysburg. He said that was awful, hand-to-hand fighting. There was a place called Devil's Den, and he said right there it was kind of a basin, [bodies] were laying seven and eight thick on top of one another. He said that when you stepped off [the bodies], blood would come to the top of your shoes.

He said it was tough. Couldn't get nothing to eat and no place to get it. Went that way for three or four days, and finally they killed a bulldog and roasted this bulldog. John and I laughed and said, "You helped to eat a dog!?" He says, "Listen, boys - when you're hungry you'll eat anything." That's what he told us and I guess he was right. -Joseph Brown

My grandfather King was in the Civil War. He was fourteen years old. The Antietam Battle - that was supposed to be the bloodiest battle of the war - he talked about that. He'd tell us that he stoked the fire for the engines on the trains. The train had been bombarded, and most of the soldiers were either hurt, laying in the gutter, or laying someplace. And he was laying in the gutter in the blood. He'd say, "I recollect that the blood was running down the ditch beside the train, it was so bloody."

The men were coming along to gather up the wounded, and they said, "Here's King. He doesn't drink and he doesn't smoke - let's see if we can save him." They picked him up and took him for help. And he was only fourteen.

After we got cars, we would take Grandfather up to Antietam, and he would tell us more about it than the guides. I was a kid then, and I'd think, "Oh, I get so tired of hearing this story!" Now I would just love to be able to talk to him ... ask him about it. -Genevieve B. Kelley

My Grandfather Clark was a Captain in the Civil War. He and his middle son were both killed in the battle of Antietam and left my grandmother with three little boys [to raise]. That's when she married Henry S. Fitch.  *-Margaret Clark Hoff*

[My father, Frank Reese, told me that] during the Civil War, Grandpa Reese hid his horses in a deep woods back of his farm (now the site of the Pikesville Sportsman's Club), so that the Rebs retreating from Cettysburg would not get them. He kept on the place [only] an old blind mare to haul the milk to the railroad station. The Rebs took her and started to ride her off, but when she ran into a tree they turned her loose, and she came home. Dad said also that the Rebs raided Painter's ice cream factory at Owings Mills and filled their hats with ice cream, which they called "frozen mush." -from "Lone Hickory Farm Notes" October 16, 1955 by *Francis Sydney Reese*

My mother, [Rachel Clark], was born in 1864. She didn't know much about the Civil War. But she said that when she was a girl and was working around, they had this song going:
"Hang Jeff Davis on a sour apple tree,
Hang Jeff Davis on a sour apple tree,
Hang Jeff Davis on a sour apple tree,
His soul goes marching on!"
She was singing this, and a man said to her, "What did Jeff Davis ever do to you?" She said, "He didn't do anything to me!" and she went right on whistling and singing this piece - "Hang Jeff Davis on a sour apple tree!" *-Minnie Clark Hebron*

On July 1st, 1913, many Owings Mills citizens turned out to see the veterans of The Grand Army of the Republic pass through on their way to a reunion in Gettysburg. The tollgate was thrown open, and people stopped work and lined up along the Turnpike to see the veterans pass.
Many of the veterans rode in horse-drawn vehicles. The cavalrymen had fine saddles; a few of the veterans were riding horseback as they had years before. It took almost an hour for the parade to pass.
Veterans who came from great distances and the more aged, used the Western Maryland Railroad. Some even rode the Emory Grove streetcars to Glyndon, then boarded the train at Glyndon Station.
In a little less than a year after this grand reunion, World War I started in Europe. Many young men who admired the beautiful horses and splendid equipment of 1863 joined the armed forces three years later. But theirs was a somber Army without the brass trimmings and glitter of the Civil War uniforms. *-E. Bennett Bowen*


## Halley's Comet of 1910

In 1910, there were people living who had viewed Halley's Comet in the 1830s. My great-grandfather, who was born in the 1820s, described the comet to me long before it became visible in 1910.

When the comet did become visible, it was more beautiful than I had ever imagined. It was first glimpsed after midnight, but the appearance became earlier each night. It looked like a rapidly moving star followed by a shimmering gauze-like tail filled with small stars. The entire comet seemed to reach a quarter of the distance around the horizon.

After a number of sightings early in the year, it disappeared. We were told it would appear again in October, and it did. It was in reverse, so it seemed, for the incandescent veil looked as if it were pulling the comet. -*E. Bennett Bowen*

### From Argonne Forest to Verdun

It was cold, I'm not kidding you, up in those trenches during Wolrd War I. We couldn't make a fire because it'd make smoke. There was a canal running from the Meuse River where I used to pump water out to take to the front. That canal was about [four feet] deep, but it was dry, so Henry Simmons and I, to keep warm, we dug a place up in the canal bank. We used to sit crawled up in there.

Henry was a cook in the supply company. When we were at Fort Meade, I hauled all the goods from the warehouse to the kitchen. When I went down to Camp Meade to Company F they wanted all experienced horsemen to step one pace to the front. The captain of the supply company picked me out. It was six of us, and he grabbed me. I guess he could tell I was a countryman.

Over on the other side, I never had no trouble with the French horses, stallions or anything. I'd pet them horses and get on the good side of them and hook them up to haul water. I could do anything with them. I hauled water right up Hill 360 at Death Valley. Fellows came crawling right out of the trench and gave me the devil [for being so reckless], but I sat right up there and held the lines. They came out, and the spigots were all around [the cart], you know.

In the Army - eating that hardtack - I had bridgework all the way across here, and I busted it all to pieces. It was so hard you'd have to suck on it for a while and then chew on it. Army biscuits, like.

I been in the heaviest battles on the Western Front. With the 313th and the 379th. I was in Death Valley drive ... I was in Argonne Forest ... the Battle of Verdun. Three battles. Three of the heaviest battles on the Western Front. I got gassed in the last drive and got bronchial pneumonia on top of it. I lay in a hospital in France from the 11th of November to the following June. -*Henry Clay Hipsley*

My husband [Jim Hooper] was in the Spanish-American War. During World War I, he trained in Austin, Texas, to be a pilot. He only got as far as New York when the war ended. -*Elsie Marshall Hooper*

Mr. Stewart came around and said, "Joe, ain't you in the draft?" I said, "Yes, I am ... I'm looking to be called any time." He said, "Well, look - I can't get help on the farm and I'm on the exemption board. If you stay here and work, I'll try to keep you out of the Army as long as I can." I said, "Well, Mr. Stewart, all the other boys are going."

My mother and father said, "Well, go on and take it. You might not have to go in the Army. If you go, you'll get killed, and we won't know where you're at or nothing."

I went down there and told him I'd take the job. So Mr. Stewart said, "Now soon as you get a call from the draft board, you let me know right away." I says, "Okay." Then he says, "I don't pay much." I says, "What do you pay?" He says, "Nine dollars a week."

So I stayed there, and finally I got a call, and he went down and got me off for thirty days. Thirty days were up, and I got another call and went, and he got me off for thirty more days. Next time, he got me off for three months. Then I got another call to appear immediately, and Mr. Stewart had to go to Washington and Annapolis and I don't know where all. He told them, "He's my farm manager. I can't do without him." So he got me in 3-C.

So I was working down at Mr. Stewart's, and we were up in the field husking corn and these whistles got to blowing. My cousin, George Curtis, says, "You hear that? The war's over!" He took off the strings around his waist that we were tying fodder with, throwed his corn-chopper down and says, "I'm going to find out." So he went down to Shawan store – I think Ed Wheeler kept store there at that time – and they said the war was over. *–Joseph Brown*

All during the war when they were putting up those big warehouses, [I was hauling building supplies at various Army camps.] Mr. Clarence Veach and I went up to Camp Meade with our mules and wagons and worked there until it got so cold the ground froze. The following Spring, I went down to Holabird and worked down there. The mud was so bad that you put two bags of cement on a wagon and it was all a mule could do to get through with it.

Mr. Veach had five teams of horses and I had two. He went up to Magnolia, which was part of Aberdeen Proving Ground, and got a job as team foreman. I took the seven teams up there.

Then, in August, I come twenty-one and I got my notice to be drafted. So we closed up and came home, and I got ready to go in the service. That fall they called me, because flu was so bad, and they wanted five or six to fill up a company.

They took us all over to Catonsville and then downtown. When we got down there, they only wanted four of the six of us who had showed up, and I was one of the two who got sent home. This was in October and I came home and the flu kept getting so bad that they didn't call any more [recruits].

Then the Armistice was signed. I was back helping Andrew Disney pick up potatoes at the old Disney farm. I remember that plainly, because I was tickled to hear that the war was over and I wouldn't have to go. *–Lee Fox*

In late 1917, the first U. S. troops went into battle. Owings Mills people were thrilled by news of the 313th and delighted when it was confirmed that the flag was first carried into battle by an Owings Mills man, John Kellar. Upon his return from the war, Kellar married Miss

Thelma Demmitt. Their two sons now live on Pleasant Hill Road. -*E. Bennett Bowen*

I remember convoys going past [on Reisterstown Road]. [The soldiers] wore puttees ... they wrapped their legs [in them]. The boys would take grapes to them. -*Dorothy King*

Women formed knitting groups. We had meatless days and wheat-less days and heat-less days. We aimed not to burn any coal, and my father would gather up chips, and we'd burn cinders to keep us warm. For meat, we'd use fish or eggs.
The wheatless days my mother would use graham flour. We were also urged to save more wheat flour by eating corn bread for at least several meals each week.
People were encouraged to can vegetables. The Food Administration sent out pamphlets which contained detailed directions for successful canning of lima beans, string beans, beets and other vegetables. -*E. Bennett Bowen*

[During World War I,] you had to buy so much cornmeal to get a pound of flour. [My brother] Arch [Arthur Moser] was in World War I, but he wasn't overseas. And of course Jim Hooper and some of the Reeses and Henry Hipsley. -*Bessie Moser vonGunten*

During World War I, I knitted little squares about five inches wide. My aunt next door taught me how to knit, and she would crochet [the squares] together and make them into blankets. She belonged to the Red Cross. I had a little certificate showing that I was one of the youngest knitters during World War I.
[At that time], we lived on Reisterstown Road at the Berryman place [now 11112], across from Doctor Claude Warner, an optician. Claude Warner was in the Army and when he'd come home on leave, he'd bring soldiers with him for the weekend. It wouldn't be too long [after he got home] before he came over [to our house]. My mother would say, "Here comes Claude to get you." He'd say, "Get her all dressed up."
I was four or five years old at the time. My mother would dress me up with a simple-looking rosette thing across my forehead, and I was to go over and dance and sing for the soldiers.
The church did the same thing - they didn't have anyone sing or dance, but they'd invite soldiers from Fort Meade up for Sunday Service, and then the congregation would invite them home for dinner. I can remember the soldiers coming to our house for Sunday dinner and that was just wonderful! Of course, they'd tell stories. -*Genevieve Berryman Kelley*

During World War I, an Army caravan camped for the night at Rosewood Lane, and every damned girl in the community under the age of twenty-one made it her business to take a walk that evening. -*George B. P. Ward*

## Peter Zouck Post #521, Veterans of Foreign Wars

I'm one of the charter members [of the V.F.W.] I joined when it was up here on Kingsley Road - they rented a room up there. [About fifty years ago,] I'd just built my house, and I wanted an edger to sand the edges of the floors. Henry Simmons says, "I'll tell you what I'll do - if you join the Veterans, I'll come up there at night and edge." And he did. And I joined the Veterans. That's when they first started in Owings Mills.

There were only five or six [members] when it started. Henry Simmons and I and a boy down there at Garrison, I forget his name. [Later], we moved down to the powerhouse, a room at the front. Then, when the Owings Mills [Volunteer Fire Company] built this engine house, they came down there. *-Henry Clay Hipsley*

VFW Post 521 was chartered May 31, 1939 with fourteen members. John E. T. Kellar who served overseas with the U. S. Marines in World War I [and who had] the privilege of carrying the first American flag into the trenches [was elected commander].

According to an account [preserved in the post's memorial case], Lieutenant Zouck, [for whom the post was named] was killed in action while charging two machine guns at St. Michael, France, during the battle of Meuse-Argonne in World War I. A graduate of Franklin High School, [he is] buried in Romine Cemetery near St. Juniern, France. *-Carol Pollack* - Excerpted from an article in *Community Times*, June 21, 1984

## The Most Unpopular Law

Prohibition proved very definitely that you can't make laws to control people's behavior. It was proven around here in dozens of sad instances. [Stills] started at Delight and went on back [toward Soldiers Delight]. They also started on Berryman's Lane and the product was brought out. They also operated on Chestnut Ridge.

I had [students] in school who told me about the government men raiding the still. In at least one instance, a school child used as an excuse for not finishing his homework assignment the explanation that "the government men came and we had to put the still together again, so I didn't have time for my homework."

There were many jokes about bootlegging that went around the community. One of them was about a lady bootlegger who stood weeping beside the coffin of a deceased customer. Someone said to her, "Well, you should cry! After all, it might have been your "hootch" that killed him." Oh, she replied, "I'm not crying because he's dead, but because I've just lost a damn good customer!"

There were no taverns in Owings Mills at that time. They closed Hitshue's Tavern, Hobbs's in Reisterstown, the Ten Mile House and the Eight-and-a Half Mile House in Pikesville. They were all closed.

Naturally the customers [who formerly patronized those taverns] were going to get their alcohol [elsewhere] and they did. It was not a

popular law anywhere. You can't legislate people to be good.  -E.
Bennett Bowen

Watson Sherwood and Fred Dolfield used to go up to Red Dog Lodge
on Sunday mornings and just sit around on the porch and look out over
Soldiers Delight. One of their favorite stories was about a guy named
McNeill. He was the one that had the still back there. They used to
buy liquor from him. He came up one Sunday morning, and he stood
and shifted from one foot to the other. Finally, he said, "Could I interest you-all in buying a still?" -George B. P. Ward

I've set on the front porch many a night and could have shot the
jugs out of [the bootleggers'] hands with a high-powered rifle. Up that
bottom. You know when you went out that old lane from our house
toward Zeigler's ... that creek that comes down through there?
Straight up there at the edge of the woods is where they were.
One time one of those guys told my mother there was a lot of
blackberries up there and she could come up and get them. She told
them she didn't feel like it, she said she didn't feel like going up in
the hot sun. So long in the afternoon sometime a tap come on the
door. Here this man stood with a big bucket full of berries. One of
the guys who was bootlegging! He says, "Will you bake us a pie?
There'll be a bag of sugar down directly."
I never seen the still up close. I stayed away from them. But I
know [where the remains are of] the boiler in the other one they blowed
up. That was a big operation. That was where those holes are in the
bank as you go toward Deer Park Road. I was cultivating in the garden
with Old Nell, and I heard somebody hollering something, but I
couldn't make out what it was. I looked up and the next thing I seen
this boiler coming up above the trees. Revenue people. It was about
a 60-horsepower boiler ... a regular big steam boiler.
I think [the men who were operating the still] had an inkling, you
know, so they scattered out. One of them went to a farm and went to
setting up barley without even being asked. -A. Franklin Parker

I went [near one still] with [my brother,] John, once and I said,
"John, what are all those sugar sacks?" And he said, "Wouldn't you
like to know!" -Dorothy King

I never heard anything about Prohibition. Never had any of it around
me. Outside of homemade wine and a good bottle of whiskey, my
father always used to see to it that we had that in the cupboard.
-Margaret Clark Hoff

## The Great Depression

In the early 1930s - soon after I started school - things started getting rough. My father lost his job. Then the family had to start helping one another out. If you had someone in your family that had a
good job, they helped the others make it through. If you didn't have

that – or have some other kind of income – you were very close to being in real serious problems.

Mr [William D.] Groff's father had lent my father the money to buy the house Mr. Dolfield had built behind Owings Mills school. [At that time] my father had a good job as draftsman for Baltimore Gas and Electric, and he made the unheard of salary of sixty dollars a week. He arranged to pay Mr. Groff back sixty dollars a month. [After he lost his job], my father's World War I pension of sixty dollars went to Mr. Groff every month.

I had some very nice aunts and uncles who used to help out ... give me things I'd never have gotten if it hadn't been for them. In the afternoons, I'd go out and cut lawns, work in gardens and make my money. My father was doing everything he could –– for a while he was driving a cab in Baltimore. Probably came out some weeks making about three dollars. One time he threatened to take my lawns away from me, because I was making more than he was.

On Saturday night, if I'd been cutting lawns and had a few dollars, my mother, my father and my brother and I would go to the movies. It would cost one dollar [for the entire family's] night out. The movie cost ten cents each for my brother and I and 25 cents each for my mother and father. When we came out afterwards, we would each get a hot dog. That was an evening out – off of my dollar. A lot of fun.

When I finished school, I wanted to take up the carpenter's trade. My father went to see Mr. [Robert] Turner, [a local contractor]. but Mr. Turner couldn't take me on because there were a lot of skilled carpenters out of work. So that was why I went in the Navy in 1940 ... July 3, 1940. *–John Kellar*

[The Depression] didn't affect us so much for this reason: we had the ground and we had the chickens and we didn't buy much. *–Sarah Cox Hewitt*

During the Great Depression of the 1930s, some persons found their savings gone and their homes only worth trifling prices. Houses on large lots that would sell for sixty or eighty thousand dollars today, were sold for two thousand dollars. *–E. Bennett Bowen*

[When I was working in Baltimore] during the Depression, the street corners filled with people selling apples at five cents each. Those of us that had jobs bought one each day, even though my salary was $12 per week. *–Genevieve Berryman Kelley*

We lost the shirt on our backs! The banks closed. My mother lost every penny she had. We had just sold our farm to Rosewood [State Institution for Retarded Children] and deposited the money in the Title Guarantee Company and that was that. *–Margaret Clark Hoff*

I'm telling you, things were tight! People just didn't have anything ... they were hungry and everything else. I remember one family walked from Hannah More Academy down to Owings Mills to get a loaf of bread. But I must say, I've been the most blessed person in the world – I went to work for the American Ice Company in '28 and even in '32 I made about $32 a week, and I lived like a lord on that. A dozen eggs was only twelve cents and such as that. *-Lee Fox*

One family lived back across a field and we had a hard time keeping those children in school. So Mildred Jones, the attendance officer, said to me, "Bill, can't you go back there with me?"

I'm telling you! - I never saw such a bare house in my life! They didn't have anything to eat! [Mildred] said, "Bill, why don't we get a basket of groceries and some meat and take it back there - they're liable to starve to death." I said, "Sure, I don't mind ... I didn't know it was that bad." *-William C. Hull*

During the Depression, my father received nine dollars a week in WPA wages. He had to sell our house because of the taxes. In addition to the WPA wages, we got government food. The canned meat tasted and looked like horse meat ... it was so bad we couldn't eat it. Sometimes we lived on potato soup. My first job was at Hill's Grocery on Main Street in Reisterstown. I made three dollars a week. *-Irma Crunkleton*

I don't think living was as hard then as it is now. Everyone more or less had their own garden. You would get ice from the ice-man or from a neighbor [who had an ice-house]. You didn't have your income tax. Besides, you didn't live like today. When you look back on [real-estate] tax bills that were eight and twelve dollars! And if [those] were paid, you would sort of be at ease. *-Dorothy King*

### World War II: The Fighting Front

I served this country for about three years [during World War II]. I was in fire-fighting outfit 2018, Aviation Fire-fighting Platoon. Half the time we were on air bases; we were with the Air Force mostly.

I went over to England and then into Switzerland and Holland. Then I was in Germany until the war was over. That's when I came back home. *-Elmer Hobart Schaeier*

World War II was a terrible time for me. My husband was drafted at age 32, and I had a 10-day-old son when he left.

The newspapers played up all the battles, which kept you very uneasy all the time, not knowing if your loved ones were safe or not until you received a letter. The mail was slow and letters from my husband were censored for quite some time because he was in the Philippines. They could not write where they were or about any battles. Until he got accustomed to that, my letters were full of holes. They cut whole paragraphs out with a razor blade. Sometimes I would get ten letters in one delivery, then no more for three weeks.

We could use V-Mail, which was a 8-1/2- by 11-inch sheet of paper that you wrote your letter on, folded it over and put the address on the outside. It was then condensed to 4- by 5-1/2-inch size. The armed forces could use this free, but sometimes you needed a magnifying glass to read it. *-Genevieve Berryman Kelley*

I had a cousin, Wilbur Williams, who was in World War II. His brother was his commanding officer, and they were both in the Air Force. His brother issued him [the orders] to go on the [mission] where he was shot down. He was a prisoner for a long time. He's a fellow who weighs two hundred pounds now, but he only weighed ninety-six pounds when he was liberated. -*Elsie Durham*

Little Nelson Bolton who lived two or three houses farther back Dolfield Road [than the Campbells] had been killed in the service. When I got home [on leave], I went to see Mrs. Bolton [to pay my condolences]. After I'd paid my visit to the Boltons I decided to stop at the Campbells on the way home to say hello to them.

[Minnie and Douglas Campbell, Sr.] were delighted to see me. We were sitting there talking - I've never forgotten this - and there was a rap at the door. Mrs. Campbell said to her husband, "Who in the world could that be? Doug, go answer the door."

It was a state trooper. He was bringing the news that their son had just been killed. To see the two of them ... I didn't know what to say. If ever there was a hole I could have crawled into! I've never forgotten trying to console them ... there's nothing much you can say.

I was in all five of the invasions. Africa, Sicily, Angio, the big invasion in Europe and then southern France. I saw a lot of people killed in the war. Usually there'd be boats brought from these landings, and the doctors would all do down on the nets, and you'd see them look at a person, and then you'd see them take a blanket and cover that one over and move on to the next. It often struck me when that doctor was there and pulled up that blanket that I knew whoever it was was dead and the doctor knew it. But what grief that was going to mean a week or two weeks later at some poor devil's door! -*William D. Groff, Jr.*

When [my son], Doug, Jr. left [to go in the service], he and Gordon Harden, Jr. tore a dollar bill apart to be joined after the war. The half came back in Doug's belongings, and Gordon still has his half.

Mary Bolton was at our house early in the morning after hearing about my son's death. She seemed to know just what to say to ease the sorrow. Her son, Nelson, was killed just about a week before. Her son, Bobby, wrote a beautiful poem about the men who gave their lives to "make the world safe for democracy." Rather ironic after all that has happened since. -*Minna Campbell*

My Dear Mrs. Campbell - There's so much we've wanted to write and tell you about our platoon leader, Lieutenant Campbell. We can't just say that he was a good and natural soldier. No. There's more to it than that. I guess the best way of explaining it was the reactions of his men when we heard the news that night of November 20th in a crude little home in Alsace-Lorraine.

Lieutenant Campbell was missing all day. As we impatiently waited for any news that night on the straw-covered floors of that miserable house, we spoke of how he didn't have to go where he had gone. He could have sent one of us. Instead, he took it upon himself, knowing how dangerous it might have been. He never wanted to give us anything too difficult or dangerous to do. He'd much rather do it himself. The packages he received from you, his "Sally", he'd share with us. He was a "regular guy," and even though we'd never say it aloud, we loved him.

The doors opened, the news was received. The reactions sent chills through your body. Tears streamed down our faces. A sob could be heard here and there in the room. The "regular guy" was dead.

Maybe this [letter] isn't too much encouragement now. It may only bring a tear to your eye. We sincerely hope it brings a little satisfaction to you to find out what we thought of your "Doug." We were his boys, men from every corner of America who trusted and were thankful for having a soldier like him to lead us. Respectfully – From a letter to Mrs. Douglas Campbell, Jr. from the *men of the 101st Engineering Combat Battallion* [fourteen signatures are attached]


## World War II: The Home Front

During the war, we were rationed for gasoline, sugar and shoes. We were issued books of stamps and had to present a stamp to make a purchase. The gasoline didn't bother me, but it was rough on people that had to drive to work. The shoe stamp was my problem because children outgrew shoes so quickly.

A lot of us did knitting for the Red Cross. They would give you wool and instructions and a date to be finished. I knitted sleeveless Navy sweaters. *-Genevieve Berryman Kelley*

During World War II, we had German prisoners here [at Lone Hickory Farm] to cut the corn. They always had one man who didn't work – he was the boss. He lined them up and gave them the word to go and take their corn choppers and chop corn. He'd tell them when to stop and they'd stop right on the dot and wait for the next command.

They did a very good job. They were available through the Farm Bureau and we signed up to get them. We picked them up at Pikesville Armory and took them back there [at the end of the day]. *-Waiva Dean Reese*

They got after people on the farms to black out their windows so there wouldn't be any lights. I know when I went over to Uncle Andrew [Disney's], my aunt had put up curtains to all her basement windows so there wouldn't be any lights showing if they had to go down there to fix the fire or anything.

[Rationing] was severe that time. It affected people in the city more, because in the country they had pigs. I know my uncle in New York City – I was going up there for a few days – he said, "Bring your ration book because we don't have enough meat." Uncle Andrew sent him a ham, and that was a big saving for them. *-E. Bennett Bowen*

[In the schools] we had air-raid shelters. At Garrison, we used to take the kids and line them up against the wall. At Owings Mills, we took them down the cellar. They couldn't talk ... you had to be very quiet. But the children didn't mind ... they weren't frightened. I suppose I was more scared than they were.

Then we had to do the [registration for the distribution of ration stamps] at the school.

At Garrison School, we had to go down there at night and register [all the men] according to their age and occupation. I remember one time I was down there and Mr. Jensen came in [Philip Jensen, rector of Saint Thomas Church]. He was talking to Mr. John Nelson who was a member of the church. After they filled out all their forms, I read them over and [found that] Mr. Jensen had signed Mr. Nelson's name! I had to go to his house and get him to do it all over again. *-Helen Carpenter*

I remember Jim Payne came down to register for the draft. Tony Lehman registered him and - [as a joke] - he said, "All right, Jim, go and pack. We've got you a uniform, you're leaving tonight." That was the last we saw of Jim Payne - he shot across Reisterstown Road and down to Dolfield. Scared to death! *-William D. Groff, Jr.*

During World War II, the water tower [at Pleasant Hill] had a guard on it all the time. Because they were afraid of water contamination [by saboteurs]. It was highly fenced and guarded very carefully.

After war was declared, Civil Defense was started. I was made head Civil Defense nurse. Hannah More School [in Reisterstown] was supposed to be the hospital if we ever had any trouble, which, luckily, we didn't. But we used to have meetings and mock air-raids and mock casualties and that sort of thing. We'd have runners -- my daughter [Jane Morris Penny] was old enough at the time to be a runner. *-Catherine Dimmling Morris*

Gas rationing [during World War II] went on from '42 to August of '45. The gasoline ration board was down at Red-Men's Hall in Pikesville, [on Reisterstown Road between Walker Avenue and Old Court Roads]. You were asked how many cars you had and what your car was used for - that was the important thing. Then you were issued ration stamps accordingly. You only got so many stamps and they had to last a certain period of time. You also received a ration sticker which you put on your windshield.

Most of my customers [at Burkholder's Service Station] had "A" stamps - they lived in the neighborhood and just drove around the neighborhood. They would get three gallons.

[Rationing] created a line at my station the day before it went into effect. You'd better believe it! I had customers I'd never seen before! The place was out-of-date, but on the last day before you had to use ration stamps, it looked good to a hell of a lot of people!

Sometimes [I had difficulty] getting enough gas. When the delivery trucks stopped with gas, you took it. The gas went into whichever tank was low, so that "Shell" gas might come off a "Texaco" truck and vice versa. You could get as much gas as the ration stamps you had on hand. It was the same way with tires. I gave a Goodyear salesman stamps for twelve tires I never got - he was transferred to Pittsburgh with my stamps.

Of course, it was a pain in the neck, those stamps. In cold weather, we had to stand there and tear them out of the books.

Inevitably, [there was cheating]. Someone who didn't use all their stamps would give them or sell them to a friend or neighbor. Trucks were allotted more gas, naturally, and maybe a man didn't use his truck much that week or that month, but he had these stamps and they represented a valuable commodity, you know. And of course the farmers were issued all the stamps they'd reasonably want. I daresay all their tractor gas didn't always wind up in a tractor.

During gas rationing, occasionally a soldier or a sailor returning to his post - perhaps Fort Meade or Bainbridge - would stop by the station low on gas and with no ration stamps. Since it was illegal to sell gas without proper ration stamps, I would pump a couple of gallons into their vehicle's tank, refuse payment, and send them on their way.

And when I put my "No Gas" sign up, I always had fifty gallons in reserve for the Owings Mills fire truck.

Personally, I was area Precinct [Air Raid] Warden. My area was bounded by St. Thomas lane on the south, Gwynnbrook and Featherbed Lanes on the north, east to Church Road. When the alerts were announced, I was contacted by phone from headquarters in Towson. Of course, the siren would also go off.

I would tend to many things. We had our organization of air-raid wardens, assistants, messengers, fire-watchers. About twenty people. [In case of an actual bombing], the messengers would notify the precinct, and the precinct would notify the District Warden, up to Towson. Equipment would be dispatched to the scene - fire-trucks and ambulances. Wardens vehicles had flags on the bumpers along with very dim lights. But of course gasoline was not too plentiful, and you didn't do any more driving than necessary.

I answered every alert personally. I was tied down here at the store [Burkholder's Store and Service Station], so I was the ideal person for it.

[People had to black out their lights when there was an alert.] The air-raid wardens would check on them to remind them that maybe a shade wasn't quite proper. I even got called down for my key-hole in my own house. Clara McCubbin caught me on that.

The wardens would also stop other motorists and tell them to pull off the road and get shelter. During one alert, we were blacked out and a Greyhound bus stops in front of my place. I had a roomful of passengers until the all-clear signal came.

During World War II, Owings Mills school did not have a telephone. When I received an alert, I would go over to Mr. Hull, and the school would practice their air-raid drill.

I guess a lot of us thought [we'd never be bombed], but who knew? We went under the assumption when me made our plans and practices that we'll be ready *if* we are bombed and we'll be ready *when* we are bombed. Of course, we never were, but I feel that Owings Mills had good air-raid protection. -*Frank Burkholder*

Northwest Expressway, 1986
The Northwest Expressway (Interstate 795) carries thousands of commuters each day through once fertile fields and quiet neighborhoods. Photo courtesy of the Maryland Department of Transportation, State Highway Administration.

# CHAPTER 20

## When Progress Strikes

*Having lived most their lives in a quiet, rural community, our narrators have been forced in recent years to adjust to overwhelming and often baffling changes. A new expressway to replace the crowded Reisterstown Road, a subway terminus, the targeting of Owings Mills as Baltimore County's newest "town center", the conversion of agricultural land to residential and commercial use have all irrevocably altered the quality of life in our community.*

*Perhaps it is their responses to the changes they are experiencing that best reflect the basic character of not only our narrators but of our community as well.*

-/-/-/-

### Soaring Population Figures

When I was appointed postmaster in 1950, the receipts were just a little over $8,000. At that time, $8,000 was the benchmark for being a 2nd-class post office and [Owings Mills post office] had just gone 2nd-class. When I left there in '66, receipts were up to almost $500,000. That was in a span of sixteen years.

In the meantime, a lot of industry came in. Maryland Cup came in and made Owings Mills go from second-class to first-class in one year. The change was so rapid that I got several calls from headquarters in Washington wanting to know what I'd done to inflate the receipts to get [upgraded] in class. Because the postmaster got a raise when you got more business - that reflected in your salary.

And it's just gone on and on. I think now [1985], the receipts for Owings Mills are well over a couple of million dollars. *-Morris G. Richardson*

The first summer after we moved to Walnut Avenue, we'd sit out on the lawn and it would be twenty minutes before a car went by. Today, of course, it's all built up. Now the farm has been sold and will be developed shortly. Everything around there is nothing but houses, houses, houses. The place where we lived previously on Reisterstown Road is apartment houses. I understand that in one day ninety children enrolled in Owings Mills School from those apartments.

377

I am now in the Queen Anne Apartments on the old Cradock property. When I first moved out here, this was all one big, beautiful farm. *-Catherine Dimmling Morris*

So many houses and apartments! More stores. More schools. It's more like a city than the country now.

At Christmas we used to go around to the neighbors and they'd come to us ... get some cake and cider. Now, you know, I don't go to any of their houses and they don't come to see me. Not like in the olden times. *-Lillian Demmitt Moser*

### The New Super-Highway

Reistertown Road...at the present time is unsafe as a modern traffic facility. Heavy peak-hour volumes consistently overload the existing road, causing unsatisfactory operating conditions.

If [a] rapid transit facility is not built, public transportation in the northwest corridor would...be a continuation of the present inadequate bus service...totally unable to meet future transportation needs because of...traffic-clogged streets.

...three proposals: Northwest Expressway, Rapid Transit Facility, and some improvement to existing Reistertown Road are needed to meet current and future transportation requirements. -from Final Section 4 (f Statement, Relocated U. S. Route 140) and Phase I Rapid Transit, Baltimore City Line to Owings Mills, *U. S. Dept. of Transportation and Maryland Dept. of Transportation*

I've walked every foot of [the right-of-way for the Northwest Expressway. I thought it would have been built before this, but they got to politicking it down the other side of Baltimore County. Well, they're building some of it now.

Why they selected [to take it through part of the Painter property near the old mill] I don't know. It looked to me like the world's worst spot to build it. I've seen that meadow and the other meadow where the dinner theater is [Painter's Mill Music Fair], I've seen them level full of water. *-Joseph Simonds*

We have fears about what the Northwest expressway may do to our McDonogh School springs. We may have to go on county water. *-Paul Carre*

### Mass Transit

Metro commuters can expect to make the 14-mile trip from Owings Mills to Charles Center [in downtown Baltimore] in twenty-five minutes. During rush hours...trains [will] arrive...at Owings Mills station every twelve minutes.

The Owings Mills station is located in the median of the Northwest Expressway, just north of Painters Mill Road. The [parking] lots...can accomodate 3,500 cars. -from brochure for Metro opening, *Mass Transit Administration*, July, 1987

## Ever-Escalating Land Values

A proposed 5,500-home "urban village" in Owings Mills would be Baltimore County's first planned community and its largest residential project.

The developer filed Friday for county approval of the project on the shore of Red Run Lake...a reservoir to be created by damming Red Run...stream. -Sheridon Lyons, *The Baltimore Sun*, June 8, 1986

Saks Fifth Avenue, the high-fashion, high-price New York department store, is...completing negotiations for a site in...Owings Mills. -*The Evening Sun*, January 26, 1984

"Warehouses, Traffic will Replace Fields, Cows in Owings Mills." "Mammoth Development Planned in Owings Mills." -headlines in *Community Times*, January 23, 1986

People say to me, "What are you going to do? Suppose they take the [Mount Pleasant A. M. E.] church away and take the cemetery and everything?" I say, "Well, we have to just go ahead. All those people out there are in heaven safely. And what they're going to do will be done because progress can't be stopped." Can't do anything about that. They offer you a certain amount of money, and after a while they condemn it, so what are you going to do? It all belongs to the state in the end. -*Minnie Clark Hebron*

Since World War II, the greatest change has been with the development of the land. Mr. Reese's farm is Tollgate; Mr. Knatz's farm is Morningside; other farms have gone the same way. The holding companies have the land back behind Tollgate. All that land has gone out of production - we've gotten rid of some very productive land. -*E. Bennett Bowen*

I can't really afford another farm. Even way out they're going for $1,500 an acre. There's no way in the world a farmer like me can afford to buy that and ever hope to get out of debt. -*Carl Reter* quoted in article *The Evening Sun*, April, 19, 1976

We [at McDonogh School] have been told by a prominent realtor that this eight hundred acres is one of the outstanding chunks of land left in the whole metropolitan area. John McDonogh was buried here around World War II, and we hope he's here for good. But eight hundred acres times X number of dollars is a nice little nest egg. -*Paul Carre*

My father wouldn't let a tractor on the place ... it would mash the ground down. Everything was done by horses. And they come in here now, the fertilizer trucks and that has weed-killer in it. The weed-killer goes in the streams and that's what's killing the Chesapeake Bay. -*Sarah Cox Hewitt*

[The most dramatic change in Owings Mills in the time I've been here] has been the expansion of homes and industries. We've got the industrial park back [Dolfield Road] ... we got the Colts out here now.

But the biggest thing is the homes. All the garden apartments and the stores, the schools. These things spring up and you don't even notice it. I can't even find my way around.

When I eat down here at Samuel Owings Restaurant, or what used to be the Samuel Owings - Country Fare now - I tell them [the site of Maryland Cup Company] used to be a cow pasture and they can't believe that. [Or] they begin to tell me about the history of the [restaurant] building and I say, "Let me tell you something! This house wasn't even good enough for people to live in. Cows herded in it. -*Harry L. Shay*

They tore everything down except Reese's old house on Tollgate Road. That's where all of Tollgate is now - built up in houses. Same with the Painter place down there that Saffell bought. He sold it off in pieces. Cup factory [Maryland Cup] bought a part of it, Lyon Brothers another part of it and back on the other side of the railroad they tore it all down. Now they got all them shops and all them buildings.

I tell you, they sort of developed the thing, but what they did to the area ruined the beauty of it. There's no beauty to it anymore. It isn't like country. -*Elmer Schaefer*

George Horvath made my day not long ago. He told me he just wrote a check to the people who owned what used to be a farm ... the one the Northwest Expressway right-of-way is going through. He told me it was for something like three and a half million dollars. We sold that farm in '41 for $9,000 ... about $100 dollars an acre. I figured out the state paid $28,000 an acre. That's odd ... that in my lifetime that would happen. -*Morris G. Richardson*

## Better Trained Teachers, Better Informed Children

In my thirty-seven years of teaching in Baltimore County, I saw many changes in education - from stoves to central heating, from walking to school to bus transportation, from soup and sandwiches supplied by patrons to cafeterias equipped with all modern facilities for preparing hot meals. Other changes I have seen are school nurses, eye and ear testing, visual aids, prayer not allowed, Christmas plays not allowed, field trips, school teachers, teachers' aides, libraries, television in the schools, courses of study, integration, instrumental music and art instruction. -*Helen Carpenter*

The main difference we've got between people today and years ago is the drug traffic. That is the number one enemy of our young people today. We've got the laws, but the trouble is to enforce them. A girl was talking to one of the teachers and she said, "You can't tell me!" [Forty years ago,] they didn't have that attitude.

But we had so many [other problems] forty, fifty, sixty years ago. We had the problem of taking care of the slow learner and nothing was done for them. Nothing was done, [either], to take care of the child who learned rapidly. And no provision was made for children to go on [with their education], those who didn't have the means to pay for their board or transportation.

When I was in school and when I first taught, we had one text-book and maybe one reference book for each grade. Today they have an abundance of books that are written on a level they can read.

Even the slowest child -- who wouldn't have been in school at all until about 25 years ago -- is learning something. I can remember some who just sat in the primary room until they got to be teen-agers and were out of school. When I first started teaching, I had a boy who was twelve or thirteen and he was still in first grade.

And [students] today have teachers who are trained. My first teacher was an 8th grade girl; she had no training beyond 8th grade.

Today we fit the work to the child [whereas] years ago, nobody bothered about fitting anything. You had to sink or swim.

Years ago, very few people went to high school. [Those who did go] were among the few. Things have improved tremendously, and the whole state is much more informed than it was in older times. -*E. Bennett Bowen*

I still think I had a better time when I was a kid than kids do now, and they have everything under the sun. I think television is the ruination of the lot of them! -*Sarah Cox Hewitt*


### Things that Hang in Our Minds

My grandfather got to talking one time, telling us what was going to happen and all. He says, "You're going to see buggies running without horses." Now there was nothing said [at that time] about automobiles, and we laughed at him. He said, "Don't laugh! I can't see it, but you boys will see it!"

He says, "I'll tell you something else - over the course of time, a man's going to fly up in the sky same as buzzards! Now don't laugh, 'cause I mean it! After they get it so's one man goes [up in the sky], they're going to have it so they can haul them up there same as trains on a track." We'd keep thinking about that and we'd giggle to ourselves and think it was funny, you know.

He said these things hung in his mind. He said it's going to be a war every other generation. And it's happened. He said the colored people are going to have as much rights as the whites. He said the colored race is going to rule the world and when that happens, the world's coming to an end. So everything he said is coming fast ... everything's coming true. -*Joseph Brown*

We didn't get electricity in the house until 1967 because Dad didn't approve of modern conveniences. Then we got the washing machine and the electric iron and television and electric radio and clocks and things like that. Up till then we just had the old-time things. *-Helen Kendig Bowers*

This place was nothing like this. This used to be practically a private lane to [St. Thomas] church. But the way you see them go by there now, I'm not safe to go to the mail-box. They go out here, and you wonder how they'll ever stop when they get to Reisterstown Road. Travel faster and get smashed up quicker!

I declare, it seems like people have less time. The more push-buttons they get, the less time they have and the more stewed-up they are, just running around like they're ready to fly!

And it's a shame they've knocked so many of these old houses down. They don't realize the material that's in them. The material they're putting in today, if you leaned against the wall, I think you'd go right through! It's terrible!

And so much plastic! You buy an expensive chest of drawers today – five or six hundred dollars – and the bottom is made out of cardboard. Half of this beautiful [furniture] you think is mahogany is plastic. If you sit on it, you don't know if it's going to crack or what's going to happen.

Even your food doesn't taste the same. They've got that chopped up and mixed up so it doesn't taste right. The flour is cut ... they're using artificial sugar. Sugar's poison. So what isn't poison? Everything. All the medicine has got after-effects ... side-effects.

These youngsters coming up, I think they've lost a lot, I really do. They call it progress, but I don't know whether it's progress or not. *-Margaret Clark Hoff*

We have all the conveniences, but I sometimes think we were better off without them. We took life easier, our money went farther, we didn't know what crime was – that was something unheard of. We never thought about not going out at night, we never even locked our doors. *-Catherine Dimmling Morris*

Everybody's crazy and they only have one thing in mind – money! They don't care what they do to get it or who they do it to. [Used to be,] everybody stopped to talk with everybody and just exchange little things, and nobody thought anything about it. But now it's so different – nobody trusts people, you know. *-Minnie Clark Hebron*

I think nowadays you've got a lot of different things on your mind to what you did then. You get ready, and you got to work, and you come back and then have to prepare for the next day already. Everything's in such a hustle and bustle ... you don't even have time to remember anything. *-Mary Kendig Gettierre*

I don't know, there's something about that old style of living, there's a certain amount of grace goes with it. *-Viola Clark Nesbitt*

# BIBLIOGRAPHY

Note: the following abbreviations are used:
 BCHS = Baltimore County Historical Society
 BCPL = Baltimore County Public Library
 CCHS = Carroll County Historical Society
 Md. Rm. = Maryland Room of Enoch Pratt Free Library, Baltimore
 MHS = Maryland Historical Society

Abbott, Collamer M.; "Isaac Tyson, Jr, Pioneer Mining Engineer and Metalurgist"; *MHS Magazine*; vol. 60; 1965

Allen, The Rev. Ethan, D.D.; *The Garrison Church: Sketches of the History of St. Thomas Parish, Garrison Forest, Baltimore County, Maryland 1742-1852*; Edited by The Rev. Hobart Smith, M.A., Rector, St. Thomas Parish, 1898; with additional sketches, appendices and indexes; James Pott & Co.; New York; 1898

Baker, Gordon Pratt, ed.; *Those Incredible Methodists: A History of the Baltimore Conference of the United Methodist Church*; Baltimore Commission on Archives and History, The Baltimore Conference; 1972

Carothers, Bettie Stirling; *Maryland Slave Owners and Superintendents - 1798, Vol. I*; Lutherville, Md; 1974

Carothers, Bettie S. & Barnes, Robert W.; *Index of Baltimore County Wills 1659-1850*, MHS

Cordell, Eugene Fauntleroy; *The Medical Annals of Maryland, 1799-1899*

Cox, Mrs. T. Newell; *History of Pikesville*; unpublished scrapbooks; Randallstown Branch, BCPL [microfilm]

County Council of Baltimore County; *Master Plan for Owings Mills New Development Area*; Towson, Md.; 1984

Davidson, Isobel; *Real Stories from Baltimore County History*; Tradition Press; revised and adapted, 1917; re-issued, 1967;

Dickson, Isaac N.; "The Early Days of Reisterstown and Vicinity"; from booklet issued by Reisterstown Kiwanis Club; 1947; BCPL, Reisterstown Branch

Farrell, Michael R.; *Who Made All Our Streetcars Go?: The Story of Mail Transit in Baltimore*; National Railroad Historical Society Publications; Baltimore; 1973

Fielding, Geoffrey; "Gilmor's Field Report of His Raid in Baltimore County"; *MHS Magazine*; vol 47, 1952

Focke, F. B.; "Winchester, Owens, Owings, and Related Families"; *MHS Magazine*; 1930

Gittings, D. Sterett; *Maryland and the Thoroughbred*; The Hoffman Bros. Co.; Baltimore; 1932; [Md. Rm.]

Gontrum, Edwin K.; *Sidelights in the History of Baltimore County*; privately published; 1966 [Md. Rm.]

Gould, Clarence P.; *Money and Transportation in Maryland, 1720-1765*; Johns Hopkins University Press; 1915

Hartzler, Daniel D.; *Medical Doctors of Maryland in the C.S.A.*; Tri-State Printing; Funkstown, Md; 1979

Hollifield, William; *Difficulties Made Easy: History of the Turnpikes of Baltimore City and County*; Baltimore County Historical Society; Cockeysville, Md.; 1978

Hopkins, G. M.; *Atlas of Baltimore County, Maryland*; Philadelphia, 1877

Kavanaugh, Maureen, with appendix by Jacobson, Robert; *File Report Number 181: Phase 11 Archeological Investigations at the Painters Mill Site (18 BA 106) and the Gwynns Falls Site (18 BA 112). Northwest Expressway, Baltimore County, Maryland*; Maryland State Highway Administration; 1983

Killough, Edward M.; *History of the Western Maryland Railroad*; rev. ed; Baltimore, 1940

Manakee, Harold R.; *Indians of Early Maryland*; pamphlet; MHS; 1959

Manakee, Harold R.; *Maryland in the Civil War*; MHS; 1961

Marks, Lillian Bayly; *Reister's Desire: The Origin of Reisterstown, Maryland, founded 1758, with a Genealogical History of the Reister Family and Sketches of Allied Families*; Pridemark Press, Inc.; Baltimore; 1975

Marye, William B.; "The Old Indian Road"; *MHS Magazine*; vol. 15; June, September and December, 1920

Maryland Department of Forests and Parks; "Indians on the Patapsco"; Oak Leaflets #15; December, 1968

McGrain, John W., *Grist Mills in Baltimore County*; Baltimore County Public Library; Towson, Md.; 1980

Owings, Addison D. & Owings, Elizabeth S.; *Owings and Allied Families: A Genealogy of Some of the Descendants of Richard Owings I of Maryland 1685-1975*; Polyanthos; New Orleans; 1976

Painter, Orrin Chalfont; *William Painter and his father, Dr. Edward Painter: Sketches and Reminiscences*; Arundel Press; Baltimore; John S. Bridges and Co.; 1914

Phillips, J. C.; *Choate Family of Baltimore County, Maryland*; privately printed; 1979

...............; *Polk's Directory of Maryland Farmers, 1894-1895*; [Md. Rm.]

...............; "Park and Tilford Distillery"; Power Pictorial; vol. 28; June, 1934 [Md. Rm.]

Ridgely, Helen West; *Historic Graves of Maryland and D.C.*; BCHS

Ridgely, Helen West; *Old Brick Churches of Maryland*; Anson Randolph, NY; 1894

Rouse, Parke, Jr.; *The Great Wagon Road*; McGraw, Hill; NY; 1973

Shipley, Charles L.; *The Old Confederate Soldiers' Home*; 1944

Siousset, Annie Leakin; *Old Baltimore*; Macmillan; 1931

Spencer, Edward; "Soldiers Delight Hundred in Baltimore County"; *MHS Magazine*; vol. 1; 1906

Thomas, Dawn F.; *The Greenspring Valley: Its History and Heritage, Vols. I and II*; Maryland Historical Society; Baltimore; 1978

United States Department of Agriculture; *Soil Survey of Baltimore County, Maryland*; March, 1976

U. S. Dept. of Transportation, et al; *Final Section 4(f) Statement; Relocated U.S. Route 140 (Northwest Expressway), Baltimore City Line to Reisterstown and Phase 1 Rapid Transit, Baltimore City Line to Owings Mills in Baltimore County, Maryland; Volume II of II*; U.S.D.A. et al; undated (circa 1975)

Williams, Harold A.; *The Western Maryland Railway Story*; photos by A. Aubrey Bodine; The Western Maryland Railway Company; Baltimore; 1952)


Material from the following publications was included in the research for this book:

*American Sentinel and General Advertiser*; Westminster, Maryland [CCHS]

*The Baltimore County Advocate*

*The Baltimore Gazette and Daily Advertiser*

*The Baltimore News-American*

*The Democrat and Carroll County Republican*, Westminster, Maryland [CCHS]

*The Dial*; yearbook of Franklin High School, Reisterstown, Md.

*The Evening Sun*; Baltimore, Md.

*Federation PTA News*; Baltimore County, Md.

*History Trails*; BCHS

*Maryland Journal*

*Maryland Monthly Magazine*; Reisterstown, Md.; [Reisterstown Room, Reisterstown Branch, BCPL]

*The Reisterstown Voice*; Reisterstown, Md.; [Reisterstown Room, Reisterstown Branch, BCPL]

*The Sunpapers*; Baltimore, Md.

*Union News*; Towson, Md. [Md. Rm.]


Extensive use was also made of resources contained in the following locations:

The Library and Vertical Files of the Baltimore County Historical Society

The Library and Files of the Maryland Historical Society, Baltimore, Md.

Methodist Museum, Lovely Lane Methodist Church, Baltimore, Md.

Vertical Files of the Maryland Room, Enoch Pratt Free Library, Baltimore, Md.

Vertical Files of the Carroll County Historical Society

Records archived at the Maryland Hall of Records, Annapolis, Md.

The following maps proved helpful in locating landmarks in the Owings Mills area:

*Atlas of the County of Baltimore, Maryland*; Bromley, 1898, Plate #29

*Baltimore & Baltimore Co., Md. Street Map*; ADC; General Green Way, Alexandria, Va., 22312; 1985

*Map of the City and County of Baltimore, Maryland from Actual Surveys, 1857*; Robert Taylor

*U. S. Geological Survey #9, Reisterstown, Md., 1953, photo-revised in 1966 and 1974*; AMS 5662; IV, NW Series, V833

# APPENDIX I

## Oral History Narrators

Unless otherwise noted, all narrations are from Oral History Tapes in files of Owings Mills History Council

1. Barnhart, Helen French ****
1A. Bates, Elsie Moser
2. Bowen, E. Bennett
3. Bowers, Helen Kendig
4. Bowers, James L.
4A. Bowers, Margaret
5. Boyd, Eva Triplett **
6. Brown, Joseph
7. Brown, William D.
7A. Burkholder, Frank
8. Campbell, Minna
9. Carpenter, Helen
10. Carpenter, James, Jr.[1]
10A. Carpenter, James M.
11. Carre, Paul
12. Crunkleton, Irma Williams
13. Durham, Elsie
14. Englar, Paul
15. Fox, Lee
16. Fox, Louise[2]
17. Fox, Roland ***
18. Frank, Nettie Clements
19. Gamber, Ethel M. ***
20. Gettierre, Mary Kendig[3]
21. Grimes, Gladys
22. Groff, William D., Jr. **
23. Hebron, Minnie Clark
24. Herera, Wilson **
25. Hewitt, Sarah Cox
25A. Hipsley, Henry Clay
26. Hoff, Margaret Clark
26A. Hoff, Virginia Clark
27. Hooper, Elsie Marshall
28. Hull, William C.
28A. Hunt, Mabel Triplett

29. Jensen, The Rev. Philip[4]
30. Kellar, John **
31. Kelley, Genevieve Berryman
32. King, Dorothy
33. King, John **[8]
33A. King, Ruth
34. Knatz, Robert S.[5]
35. Lyon, Robert **
36. Marshall, Frances Benthall
37. Marshall, Mary Simmons
38. McGrain, John ****
39. Morris, Catherine Dimmling
40. Moser, Albert G.
41. Moser, Catherine B.[6]
42. Moser, Lillian Demmitt
43. Nesbitt, Viola Clark
43A. Nixon, George **
44. Offutt, Nancy
45. Pape, Grace Bowen
46. Parker, A. Franklin
47. Redifer, Laura Wimsett
48. Reese, Waiva Dean
49. Reese, Francis David[7]
50. Reese, Francis Sydney
51. Richardson, Morris G. **
52. Rider, Ethel ***
53. Schaefer, Elmer Hobart
54. Schaefer, Frank Nelson
55. Shay, Harry L.
56. Shipe, Valley R.
56. Simonds, Borden ***
58. Simonds, Joseph
59. Smullen, Dorothy ***
60. Sprinkle, Mary Robinson
61. Stone, William F.

389

62. Swann, S. Donovan
63. Swem, Anna King ***
64. vonGunten, Bessie Moser
65. vonGunten, Carl A.
66. vonGunten, Samuel
67. Ward, George B. P.
68. Waters, Somereset ****
69. Whitman, Susan White ****
70. Woolford, Mike ***
71. Worthley, Jean Reese **
72. Zepp, Belle S.

** Denotes narration taken from tape of Owings Mills History Council meeting
*** Denotes narration taken from telephone conversation with the author
**** Denotes information taken from letter to the author

1. Helen Carpenter Tape
2. Lee Fox Tape
3. Helen Carpenter Tape
4. from reprint edition of *Days Gone By* by Eleanor Stewart Heiser, 1953
5. Lee Fox Tape
6. Elsie Durham Tape
7. from "Lone Hickory Farm Notes", October 16, 1955
8. from Dorothy King tape